THE HOODED EAGLE / Modern German Drama on the New York Stage

PETER BAULAND

SYRACUSE UNIVERSITY PRESS

For My Mother and Father

—he who sits obscure
In the exceeding lustre and the pure
Intense irradiation of a mind,
Which, with its own internal lightning blind,
Flags wearily through darkness and despair—
A cloud-encircled meteor of the air,
A hooded eagle among blinking owls.

—PERCY BYSSHE SHELLEY
"Letter to Maria Gisborne"

Preface

The prospect of seeing the drama of foreign lands on the American stage once held little appeal not only for the chauvinists in the expensive orchestra seats, but also for the critics, born of the genteel tradition, who dictated the tastes of nineteenth-century theatrical fare in this country. The American stage was a provincial enterprise long after Europe's playbills had become international. Yet, for years there had been direct imports and most American plays were imitative at best, while many of them were merely the refleshing of a European skeleton which was then dressed in buckskin or homespun. For a play from foreign sources to succeed on the commercially oriented stage of New York, it was necessary to Americanize its characters, settings, and details. Such concessions are common to this day, for the American drama is an art that must struggle to retain its integrity in the middle of an industry. We have countless examples of what happens when artistic creativity is placed under the dicta of shopkeepers.

The xenophobia manifested on the New York stage before the 1920's reflected the cultural insecurity of a young country trying to establish for itself the one thing that it lacked: a tradition of its own. But the foreign play, sometimes in favor, sometimes in disrepute, has always been a part of the American theatre. Since the end of World War II, imported drama on the New York stage has increased both in volume and in importance. It is, today, a respectable even if sometimes misused, abused, or misinterpreted aspect of our theatre. Americans lost their fear of the European drama at the same time that their own came of age.

This study is a critical history of the modern German drama in translation and adaptation on the New York stage from 1894 to 1965, from the first imported play of German naturalism to the first important plays written in German since the end of the Hitler era. It discusses the major movements of modern German drama; compares significant plays produced in English in New York with their German texts; records and evaluates the critical, scholarly, and commercial reception of these plays; and considers their relationship to native American drama.

The very nature of the German drama invites the inquisitive scholar and critic, for there is little doubt that it is the most variegated, possibly the most chaotic, and probably the most daringly experimental of all modern European dramatic writing. Its technical innovations, its philosophical themes, its stylistic originality, and even its unbridled excesses challenge and demand critical analysis. But to consider German drama in its relationship to the American stage presents a most peculiar problem. Schiller once said that the theatre is a moral institution, an intellectual arena where a people's ideas, ideologies, and ethics are debated and given living, dramatic form. This notion has been the central driving force of the serious German drama and the principal attitude of the German playgoer. The primary American view of the theatre has been that it is the most prestigious segment of the entertainment industry. This is, of course, not to say that there are neither serious dramatists nor intelligent audiences in the United States, and certainly Germans have no objection to being amused. There is also little doubt that for as long as memory exists, the stages of Germany have exhibited more than their share of banal, commercial trash. However, the overriding attitudes of the two cultures toward what the theatre is all about are emphatically different, and this has had a profound effect on the German drama's history on the New York stage. It is also not surprising that the dramatic writing of Germany, always experimental, flourishes in the United States when the American theatre also tends to experiment. Thus, it was most influential in the twenties, and is again a moving force in recent years.

The terms "American theatre" and "New York stage" often appear to be interchangeable in this book. That is not an oversight but an unfortunate fact. At the present time in America, the fact is slowly losing its unchallengeable status, for there seems to be a very real and long overdue movement away from centralization. However, in the years under study here the professional American theatre is virtually the sole property of New York City.

My inclusion of the Austrian and Swiss drama as part of the German will hopefully offend no one. It reflects no political or territorial ambitions, only a definition of German drama as that body of dramatic work written in German.

If the spelling "theatre" used by an American seems a pretentious affectation (and it usually does, to me), I regret the offense. I use it in the interest of clarity, because "theater" is also the German word, and it appears frequently in the text. I use the spelling "theater" in direct quotations, or in reference to names of playhouses preferring it.

Most of the major plays considered were available in one or both languages. (Biological, political, and genealogical circumstances have conspired to make me bilingual.) However, certain sources, some statistics, and a number of plays and/or their German precursors themselves are lost to us. These omissions are sometimes the result of inadequate records, sometimes the product of adaptations so free that they make recognition of the original text impossible. These situations occur almost exclusively in the areas of pre-1920 drama and of largely insignificant plays. The statistical information in this investigation is more reliable for Broadway than for off-Broadway, which cannot allow itself the luxury (and the scholar the convenience) of accurate and exhaustive records.

Comment contemporaneous with each production shows the responses of both critics and reviewers. It is intended to display the policies and views of a variety of periodicals as well as of major critics. The choice of newspapers, magazines, and journals reflects the scope of criticism from the commercial to the scholarly. It is representative and cross-sectional, not total.

The excerpt from Shelley that suggested the title for this investigation is really an outrageous expropriation, but an irresistible one. The passage refers to Coleridge, but it epitomizes the German drama: intense, cerebral, metaphysical, cynical, gloomy, ethereal, impassioned, haughty, solitary, brilliant, didactic, and often obscure. A hooded creature cannot easily be seen; it, in turn, has great difficulty in establishing contact with the confused observers who encircle it. And by happy accident, the national symbol of Germany is an eagle. So is that of the United States, but the makers of the American theatre are a distinctly lesser breed of bird.

The University of Michigan   PETER BAULAND
January, 1968

Acknowledgments

For their kind encouragement and insightfully constructive advice, I express my sincere gratitude to Robert E. Spiller, André von Gronicka, and Warner G. Rice.

I should also like to thank the Office of Research Administration of the University of Michigan for generously supporting the preparation of the manuscript.

To my wife, Abby, go my deepest thanks—for reasons too familiar to be recorded, for virtues too personal to be paraded, and for labors too important to be left without praise.

P.B.

Contents

THE HOODED EAGLE

1

Naturalism, Neoromanticism, and *Kitsch*:
1894-1918

I

German drama has been performed on the American stage since this country's first great theatrical manager, William Dunlap, adapted August von Kotzebue's *Menschenhass und Reue* and presented it on December 10, 1798, as *The Stranger*. For years the romantic melodramas of Germany, Americanized though they may have been, were among the most popular offerings in the theatres of the United States. Despite occasional performances of plays by Lessing and Schiller, it was the work of Kotzebue, a professional statesman as well as the author of more than two hundred now almost forgotten plays, that achieved the greatest success until the year 1819, when the German diplomat-playwright was assassinated, we are assured, "for political rather than artistic reasons."[1] As Dunlap had been the moving force behind the first important phase of German drama in the United States, so Augustin Daly, the outstanding theatrical manager of the latter decades of the nineteenth century, was responsible for the second. His countless adaptations, based on translations that he had commissioned, were from playwrights who have faded even from German dramatic history, but they were played to responsive houses in New York for many years.

Most historians begin discussion of the modern drama with the "free theatres" of Europe and the new movement they presented, naturalism. The theatre of Germany was one of the main centers for the development of this drama, revolutionary in both theme and form, but most American managers were less than eager to undertake the importation of German naturalism, a genre without bloody romance or broad farce to please the patrons. The second-rate German drama had always been a valuable commodity on Broadway, but the introduction of serious naturalistic plays caused legal, critical, and commercial trouble in New York.

The structure of the German theatre system, the attitudes of its audiences, and the function of its dramatists in society, which are far removed from the world of the American entertainment industry, must be examined in order to understand the plays that Germany yielded in the 1890's. "The proportion of serious plays, both old and new, presented on the German stage is considerably larger than in almost any other country."[2] The number of theatres showing first-rate repertory is also far greater, and the amount of space devoted to the drama in the German daily press dwarfs that of other nations. This may be so because of the German theatre's decentralization, an outstanding feature that differentiates the professional German theatre from that of other countries. Subsidized by city or state as a necessary and desirable cultural institution for a population whose love of the theatre borders on the fanatical, the German theatre has never been compelled by commercial interests to limit itself to a Broadway or a West End. Consequently, the drama in Germany has never become the slave of a single city's tastes or of a single audience's demands.

After the death of Hebbel, in 1863, German drama declined sharply in quality. Life was dominated by the problem of national unification; the quest for money and power motivated the actions of the bourgeoisie; utilitarianism pervaded the German spirit. The only significant dramatic figure during the seventies and eighties was Richard Wagner, but his romantic ideals and aggressive nationalism were channeled in directions far removed from the sordid chaos of a commercial society overwhelmed by its own shabby middle-class values. The temper of the time of unification and of the tyranny of the middle-class morality has been present in Germany ever since. The theatres were packed with audiences enjoying their new affluence while laughing at feeble farces or crying over sentimental domestic melodramas. It was the German play of this era that was imported in large quantities for American consumption during the Daly years and that was then revived almost until the time of World War I by the entrepreneurs of Broadway.

The only German man of the theatre who did anything to combat the sterility of the national stage during the third quarter of the nineteenth century was Duke George II of Saxe-Meiningen. It was largely through the Duke's efforts that Germany in those years became the source of a new theatre technique the mechanical fruits of which are seen on the world's stages to this day. He began what Brahm, Reinhardt, Lautenschläger, Craig, Appia, Jessner, and others were to perfect. It was the company of the Duke of Saxe-Meiningen that first devised new ways to handle crowd scenes realistically and excitingly, that first insisted on ensemble and repertory playing, that first performed Ibsen in Germany (1875), and that first took its repertory abroad. In the 1880's the Duke's company played to great acclaim in

London, in St. Petersburg, and even in New York. If the Duke's penchant for realistic staging occasionally compelled him to behave excessively (he once actually used a dead horse on a set), he can be forgiven, for he was the first force behind the movement of improved stagecraft that was to be one of Germany's major contributions to the entire world theatre.

Every young German writer of the closing years of the century hoped to write his own rules, to create his own world. This spirit of artistic anarchy has been present in German dramatic writing ever since, for the chaos that is Germany has been renewed every twenty years or so since its unification. Sometimes the upheaval has been purely economic or political; once it defied human description. The drama of modern Germany is the drama of rebellion and chaos. Unrestricted by conventions, it fluctuates between high quality and absurd banality, between disciplined form and artistic anarchy. Experiment has been "the very motive power of the German drama,"[3] unshackled as it was unrooted, in the years since the rise of naturalism. Experiment, in and of itself, is certainly not tantamount to quality, but the very tradition of German drama is experimentation.

In 1883 in Berlin, Adolf L'Arronge, a playwright of the romantic tradition, founded the *Deutsches Theater*, one of Europe's greatest houses. Ibsen's fame originated in Germany, the land where he spent much of his voluntary exile, the land where his plays were being widely performed at a time when he was being shunned in most other countries. But the strongest impetus to naturalism was the "free theatre" movement, begun in 1887 by André Antoine's *Théâtre Libre* in Paris. In 1889, Otto Brahm founded the *Freie Bühne* in Berlin; this theatre became the home of European documentary realism in the closing decade of the nineteenth century. Brahm finally took over the *Deutsches Theater* in 1894 and controlled the German naturalistic stage until his own protégé, Max Reinhardt, led the neoromantic reaction against the narrowness of the theatre of social verisimilitude. When we consider that Stanislavsky did not establish the Moscow Art Theatre until 1898, that it was 1899 before Yeats and Lady Gregory started the organization that was to be the Abbey Theatre in 1904, and that it was not until 1907 that Strindberg founded his little theatre in Stockholm, we see the extent of the pioneering work done by the German naturalistic theatre.

In their writing as in their actions, Brahm and his followers felt that truth was inseparably bound with nature, and that the human condition was the product of forces beyond the control of man, but that the social order in which man lived was capable of being improved. It was the responsibility of the artist to fill the stage with the

faithful reproduction of reality and thereby point the way to reform.
From the beginning, it was the sordid aspect of reality upon which
the movement concentrated, and a limited view of life was established
by the insistent examination of slices of life almost always taken from
the bottom. Brahm's *Freie Bühne* developed a drama, dated though it
may be today, that attracted world-wide interest for its delineation of
human suffering.

The materialistic interpretation of history begun by Taine and the
spreading of the philosophy of Social Darwinism were at this time
influencing literary creativity both in Europe and in the United
States. But in America, the drama seemed to be the only literary form
unaffected. The American theatre public of the eighties and nineties
refused any part of this unmannerly intrusion upon its complacent
gentility. In 1883, Modjeska starred in *Thora*, actually Ibsen's *A Doll's
House* reworked to suit the New York audience by giving the drama a
happy ending in the form of a puritanical sermon asserting that a
woman's place is in the home. Such emasculation of serious theatre
was the rule, not the exception, in New York. William Winter was the
most influential American drama critic at the end of the century, and
the attack that he led against Ibsen was merciless. The Norwegian
playwright had no Shaw or Archer to champion him here, and he was
either defamed or ignored. But Winter was far from alone. Naturalistic drama, even of the mildest sort, was not considered suitable subject matter for a theatre the express purpose of which was to serve the
well-to-do with gentle forms of diversion. The New York theatre of
the nineties, except for its halls of vaudeville and brassy musical and
comic entertainment, was the domain of the affluent. The scholars and
critics of this tradition were disdainful even long after the end of
World War I. As late as 1937, in a supposedly revised work, we read,
". . . it must be recognized that great as the power of Ibsen and
Strindberg may be, they present those facts of life which men must
forget if life is to be noble or even endurable."[4] No one, certainly not
the New York playgoer of the 1890's, ever enjoyed being reminded of
the things he wanted to forget.

The first important work of German naturalism performed in the
United States was Charles Henry Meltzer's translation of Gerhart
Hauptmann's *Hanneles Himmelfahrt*. Given as *The Assumption of
Hannele* on May 1, 1894, it was closed after one performance, banned
by the New York authorities as blasphemous. Although the play had
been hailed on the continent, it had been refused a hearing in England (except for one private performance in 1904) and was not seen
there until 1908. After that one evening in the spring of 1894, it was
not seen again on the New York stage until 1910.

Hauptmann was in New York at the time of the 1894 premiere at Miner's Fifth Avenue Theatre. He had come here in an effort to gain a reconciliation with his estranged wife, who was residing in the United States. After the performance, the playwright was arrested along with the producers of the play and taken down to New York's City Hall to hear a lecture on morality and to have his play officially closed by the municipal authorities. When the reviews of *Hannele* came out the following morning, even the *New York Times,* the only paper to praise the play, added that it was "horribly sacrilegious." Gerhart Hauptmann returned to Germany, unsuccessful as both husband and dramatist, with a sad impression of the United States, an impression he was not to revise until 1932, when he was received here with a tumultuous welcome on the occasion of the Goethe celebration.[5]

Hanneles Himmelfahrt, written and produced in Germany in 1893, was a partial abandonment of naturalism. Its dream sequences and metrical passages were hardly social verisimilitude, but its theme is undiluted naturalism. Brief and intensely moving, Hannele's story is that of a delirious girl who has visions of a heaven that is totally unorthodox by any theological standards, but is founded on perfectly logical premises: her desire for a paradise beyond this life which gives her all the things that a cruel earth has denied her. It is a heaven where she may eat meat instead of bread crusts, wear Cinderella garb instead of rags, and receive a mother's love instead of her scorn.

The play opens with a conventionally naturalistic scene depicting a group of the wretched poor, the type of mass hero that Hauptmann, in such plays as *The Weavers,* was to substitute for the standard central figure. The dialogue of these people makes the cant phrases of everyday religiosity sound totally hypocritical, even meaningless in the face of the horrors of reality. The characters are the victims of all that Social Darwinism said they were heir to. With remarkable sensitivity, Hauptmann creates the dream world of the feverish young girl. In a series of hallucinations, all of Hannele's childish and romantic fancies come true in glaring contrast to reality. The world of her dreams, full of the imagery of the Grimms' fairy tales, is not only that of the abundance of things of which she has been deprived but also that of angels and music, as the hymns and Sunday school lessons to which she was exposed would have them—and these seem particularly silly. This vision of heaven, not the horror of Hannele's life, shocked the sanctimonious. The dominant social feeling of the 1894 audience was still that the poor had no one but themselves to blame for their poverty. The portions of the play considered most abhorrent were Hannele's equation of her death with a wedding (the beginning of a new and beautiful life), and her projection of her teacher, Gottwald, on whom she has a schoolgirl's crush, into a Christ figure who is both lover and bringer of death. There is an inexorable logic to these hallucinations; a girl like Hannele would imagine such things to enable her to escape from the squalor of her life. But Hauptmann does not dare leave a final impression of the poetic or fantastic in his play. After building to a fervently lyrical climax, he switches back to reality without benefit of transition, and thereby redoubles the image of the harshness of life. All the trappings of the heavenly vision disappear from the stage. There are three short lines of brutally terse dialogue and we are back in the poorhouse. The girl is dead.

That this play met with such loathing in New York is understandable. The production came at a bad time, for the general climate among the theatregoing public was optimistic, and those accustomed to a prosperous economy could neither sympathize nor empathize with Hannele. She was a girl from a strange milieu, the product of a cultural heritage totally foreign to the American audience.

A constant obstacle in the translation of any German play into another language is the nature of German dialects. One of the first things that the naturalistic movement had done away with in the German drama was *Bühnendeutsch:* a classical form of the language that was spoken as it should be written, with the formality of the court, the pulpit, or the lectern. In Germany, even educated usage in the different parts of the country reflects a clearly distinguishable dialect. Although this situation prevails in most modern societies to some degree, the difference between formal and colloquial language is far more pronounced in German than in most other major modern languages. Consequently, Hauptmann employed dialect, painstakingly reproduced, in his plays, many of whose published versions even Germans were not always able to comprehend. Second editions in formal German with only a note to explain the difference from the acting version were not uncommon. When Hauptmann's plays were rendered into English, the adapters had a limited choice of alternatives, all tried and all inadequate. The play could be translated into conventional English with no regard for dialect, resulting in an attendant loss of texture. The dialogue could be written in an American dialect of a geographical area and social class closely parallel to the German, yielding a distracting incongruity. A synthetic dialect could be created by the adapter, but this produced the most disastrous, and often ludicrous, results.

Charles Henry Meltzer's translation of *Hanneles Himmelfahrt* was a total failure. One wonders how the play would have been received had his version been faithful rather than a conscious effort to use diction which catered to American taste.[6] The dialect in Meltzer's text

is so unreal that it destroys the intent of the naturalistic passages of
the play. His scenes in which the child's longings are discussed are so
excessively sentimentalized that the entire flavor of brutality is lost.
His rendition of the verse passages is almost pure jingle.

Meltzer took a straightforward descriptive word such as "*Maigrün*"
and translated it as "rich robed in the mosses of May"; the directness
of "*Hochzeitsgeläut*" became "the chiming of joybells"; even the simple "*Blumen*" was transposed into "lilly and rose." In the naturalistic
prose passages, Meltzer constantly expanded such concrete images by
Hauptmann into pseudopoetic diction which invariably mollified the
harshness of the original. The resultant English text frequently obscured clear lines by resorting to inflated rhetoric. In the verse sections Meltzer often employed rhyme where Hauptmann had
consciously avoided it. Compare the terse German:

> Das goldene Brot auf den Äckern,
> Dir wollt es den Hunger nicht stillen;
> Die Milch der weidende Rinder,
> Dir schäumte sie nicht in den Krug.

with Meltzer's greeting-card doggerel:

> Thy hunger cried out to the reaper
> In vain, as he garnered the grain.
> For milk thy poor lips went a-thirsting—
> They thirsted again and again.

Meltzer revised this passage for a later version, but not with significant improvement, as:

> The life-giving grain as it ripened
> Thy craving for bread did not heed.
> The kine as they grazed in the meadows
> Denied thee their milk in thy need.

The hymnlike quality does not appear in Hauptmann. "Thee," "thy"
and "kine," in their pseudobiblical diction, destroy the tone of the
familiar "*dir*" and the peasant-like "*Rinder*." How much more successful is the 1951 rendition by Horst Frenz and Miles Waggoner:

> The golden grain in the fields
> Would not still your hunger.
> The milk of the grazing cows
> Foamed not in the pail for you.

A few decades after the production of this play, the difficulties that
Hauptmann had created for Americans in both theme and form faded,

but by that time his early works of great power had unfortunately become dated.[7] Gerhart Hauptmann never attained any significant literary stature in the United States, and his influence on our drama was far less than that of American letters upon him.[8] The fate of the 1894 production of *Hanneles Himmelfahrt* set the pattern for the reception of all of Hauptmann's naturalistic plays on the New York stage. This was the age of the great stars. The audience was drawn to the theatre by a personality more than by a play, but the dramas of the naturalistic movement were relatively untouched by star performers and prudent managers alike. Although naturalistic fiction was already finding wider acceptance in the United States in the last few years of the century, the new drama had yet to establish itself in New York.

Five months after the Broadway fiasco of *The Assumption of Hannele,* naturalism suffered another defeat, for economic and political reasons as well as artistic. Hauptmann's *Die Weber* had censorship problems all over Europe because of its potential, frequently fulfilled, as a piece of labor agitation long before "agitprop" was a fashionable technique. On October 8, 1894, a production of the play was given in German at the Thalia Theater by a group of amateur performers. The production had been instigated by an organization of anarchists who wanted it shown in New York and then in Newark, which was at that time torn with labor problems. The German-language press of the New York area became immediately apprehensive, fearing that the production had been organized only to foment trouble.[9] When it was then performed, these fears were corroborated. The moving story of the abused Silesian weavers, displaced by mechanization, was totally corrupted. The part of Baumert, the most vocal character, was played by the well-known German-American agitator, John Most, and there were many passages added to the text which clearly revealed the intent of the production. Even the *New Yorker Volkszeitung* commented that an injustice had been done to Hauptmann, that the performance was by incompetent zealots, and that the entire production with its unforgivable interpolations was merely another instance of the exploitation of naturalistic plays with labor themes (a practice not uncommon on both sides of the Atlantic which was damaging the reputation of a serious art form). The Newark performance was forbidden by municipal edict because of the strike threat already brewing there. If there had been any hope of giving Hauptmann a second hearing on the English-speaking stage of New York after the performance of *The Assumption of Hannele,* it was now dead. It was more than five years later when one of his plays again appeared on Broadway, and that was one of his nonnaturalistic dramas, *The Sunken Bell.*

The name of Hermann Sudermann was usually linked with that of Gerhart Hauptmann during the early years of the naturalistic movement, but it did not take long for the differences between their works to become apparent. Despite the fact that Sudermann's fame declined rapidly, so that he was passé by 1910, his plays were more successful outside of Germany than those of his Nobel Prize-winning countryman. Sudermann's dramas have all the trappings of naturalism without any of its real technique or substance. Yet for a few years his thematic material qualified him for inclusion in the new group of dramatists. Actually, his plays relied altogether too heavily on the old theatrical trickery of "Sardoodledom" while taking advantage of the new wave of popular material. By 1910, public and critics considered him a purveyor of trite melodrama and cheap theatrical tricks. His first play, *Die Ehre* (*Honour* in its American version of 1895), was produced in Berlin in 1889, and it brought its author instantaneous fame. Its contrast of rich and poor living side by side in the Berlin of its day gave it a sense of social import and immediacy that labeled it naturalistic despite its traditional form and diction. The New York production aroused little interest and closed after eight performances.

While Hauptmann could find no American audience, Sudermann held the stage in New York and Chicago in both English and German for years. His greatest success, *Heimat,* first seen in Germany in 1893, was first produced in New York on January 28, 1894, as *Magda* and starred Madame Modjeska and Otis Skinner. The play was revived by Modjeska the following year and by many others with distressing regularity until 1926. From the beginning, emotional actresses grabbed ravenously at the part of Magda, and not one could lay claim to the title of "prima donna" without having played it. The Magdas of the stage are a hall-of-fame catalog: Modjeska, Bernhardt, Duse (who played it in Italian in New York in 1896), Campbell (who used it for her New York debut), Fiske, Nethersole, and Kalich. International controversy raged to decide who was the world's greatest Magda. The two strongest critical camps were the supporters of Bernhardt and their enemies, the devotées of Duse. In the midst of the fight were Sudermann himself and George Bernard Shaw, both favoring the Italian actress,[10] as did James G. Huneker. But this was no mere battle of stage personalities. The Duse-Bernhardt conflict over the proper interpretation of Magda lay at the root of an entire upheaval in acting technique at the turn of the century. Bernhardt represented the stylized histrionics of a day gone by; Duse disapproved of the cult of exhibitionism by the grand ladies of the theatre and sought instead to portray a character faithfully, with an eye toward detail and credibility rather than glamor and grandeur. Almost all the reviews of *Magda*

devote most of their comment to the interpretation and realization of
the title role; it was soon a vehicle and no longer considered a serious
play worthwhile on its own merits.

Sudermann's play seems ludicrously melodramatic today. Its neat
climax and tidy denouement come at the end of a standard series of
devices carefully arranged to arouse suspense. Beneath it all is the
struggle between the bourgeois conventions and the libertinism incarnated in the figure of the "new woman." The stock figure of the
coarse but honest father, a retired officer who prefers his daughter's
death to her dishonor, is particularly difficult to accept. His convenient
heart failure just before he is about to shoot his adamant and errant
daughter is one coincidence too many in a play already full of contrivance. *Magda* held the American stage as long as there was an
audience eager to see a star display her full range of melodramatic
pyrotechnics. When the play was revived on January 26, 1926, starring Bertha Kalich, in a revision of the standard translation by C. E.
A. Winslow, it managed a run of twenty-four performances. At that
time, Joseph Wood Krutch's comment was kinder than most: Miss
Kalich was "vigorous and effective if not particularly subtle" in a play
with "sledge hammer blows with which it drives home its now fairly
obvious thesis."[11]

The popularity of Sudermann on the New York stage at the turn of
the century can be more clearly understood when we note that this
was also a time for the great popularity of the surface realism of
Clyde Fitch, Augustus Thomas, and David Belasco, who were also
hiding preposterous contrivances beneath the patina of verisimilitude.

American translations of Sudermann's plays are quite poor; the
originals are much more convincing. The Winslow text of *Magda* was
full of ludicrous attempts at literal translations of idioms. Any colloquial statement of disgust in English would be a better rendition of
"Pfui Deiwel" (dialect for *"Teufel"*) than the awkward and meaningless "Phew! The devil!" The translation also avoided all harsh language in deference to the genteel. In the climactic confrontation between Magda and her father, the officer looks at his daughter with
loathing and simultaneous hurt disappointment. Just before his fatal
seizure, he shouts at her, *"Du Dirne!"* In the Winslow version, the old
soldier works himself into a frenzy only to say nothing stronger than
"You jade!"—hardly a convincing portrayal of the anguish of an honor-
able officer and gentleman who cannot, yet must, believe that by his
standards, his beloved daughter is a whore.

Whole meanings are sometimes reversed or at least distorted in
most of the translations of both Hauptmann and Sudermann, and even
where they are faithful to the text they are bereft of all style.[12] A case

in point is Edith Wharton's translation of Sudermann's *Es Lebe das Leben* as *The Joy of Living*. Miss Wharton, a notable stylist in her own prose, lost all texture in her rendition of the German play. Unable to recast the idiom or reproduce the mood, she wrote a version that sounds childishly trite in most of its dialogue.[13] Miss Wharton has the heroine, Beata, speak these lines to Norbert, a rigid young law student:

> I've no sympathy with unnecessary martyrdom. Keep a cool head, dear boy, and don't be drawn into controversy just yet. Haven't I often told you that this college duelling you rail against is only a preparation for the real battle of life—the battle of ideas and beliefs?

Sudermann's text is:

> Nur liebe ich das unnütze Märthyrertum nicht, mein Freund. Du sollst klaren Kopf behalten und dich nicht vorzeitig verbittern . . . Diese Duelldinge, die dir heute wunder wie wichtig erscheinen, weil du Corpsband und Schläger noch immer über deinem Bett hängen hast, die sind nur ein harmloses Vorpostenspiel gegenüber den grossen Fragen, den grossen Gedankenkämpfen, die erst noch kommen.

Not only is the sarcastic *"mein Freund"* rendered as the warm epithet "dear boy," where a literal "my friend" would better have conveyed the meaning, but the gist of the passage is totally reversed. Norbert does not "rail against" duelling; he thinks it *"wunder wie wichtig,"* as seen by the swords and emblems hanging over his bed. Beata does not consider fencing to be the proper "preparation for the real battle of life"; she calls it silly child's play when compared with the real problems of existence. Miss Wharton's translation exchanges the attitudes of the two characters in a crucial scene of the play.

The Joy of Living, first given in Berlin in 1901, was produced by Charles Frohman on October 23, 1902, and starred Mrs. Patrick Campbell, who also directed the play. It is one of Sudermann's stronger plays, for it deals with the world he knew best and was able to reproduce on the stage with a minimum of hokum: the Berlin of his day. The fairly standard tale of adultery and political intrigue is a plot device through which Sudermann examines clashing moralities both personal and political, and his play was, in 1901, a strong commentary upon the unsavory public and private life of the Berlin upper-middle class. Today, *The Joy of Living* seems inordinately mild in everything but its overwrought melodramatics, but when Miss Wharton's adaptation appeared, it became one of the most controversial plays of its decade. There was no middle ground; the New York critics either damned or lauded it. There was no difference of opinion concerning craftsmanship, for it was only later examination that showed how inadequate the Wharton translation was. The entire controversy centered around the thematic material of the play.

Theatre Magazine, a periodical usually concerned only with the "show business" aspect of drama, brushed Sudermann's play aside in December, 1902, as a conglomeration of verbose talk about psychological problems in the light of socialistic tendencies. The *New York World*'s reviewer said that it was "within the limits of the frank discussions of social corruption which have no right in the interests of public decency to be exploited on the stage and no claim on the ground of moral deductions to be drawn from them, to be performed before the mixed audiences in places that are essentially of public entertainment. It is a disheartening clinic of morbid emotions, in which there is not one gleam of light, not one ray of pleasure, and not one moment of relaxation."[14] Comments such as this give clear indication of the criteria used in 1902 for the evaluation of a serious play. This was no longer the darling Sudermann who had provided the genteel with their various Magdas. When *The Joy of Living* closed after nineteen performances, it was taken on the road in hope of more enlightened reception outside the social circles of New York. The result was equally disastrous. On April 7, 1903, the *San Francisco Examiner* said that Sudermann "has taken the slop hopper and dumped it on the front lawn."

Praise for the New York production had come from the *Herald,* which called the play truthful and powerful, and above all from the *Times,* which called *The Joy of Living* "the high water mark of the intellectual drama."[15] This overstated the case somewhat, but the *Times* was more interested in defending what the play stood for than it was bent on praising the script itself. On the Sunday after the opening, the *Times* flatly declared that those who had condemned the play on moral grounds obviously did not understand it.

In retrospect, *The Joy of Living* seems an unlikely candidate for such controversy, for it is really a formulaic play full of the artificiality and absurd pathos that usually insured commercial success at the turn of the century. But the play did come to grips with some serious problems, no matter how romantically it may have solved them. Sudermann strongly attacked society's insistence on valuing conventions that have lost their meaning, and he dared to say that love and idealism can defeat their own purposes if they are not firmly based on facts rather than self-deception. Illusion smashers were not appreciated on the New York stage in 1902.

Only three weeks after the opening of *The Joy of Living,* a new German play appeared on Broadway which was a substantial critical and commercial success. *Maria von Magdala (Mary of Magdala)* was the work of Paul Heyse, better known as a novelist of the *Goldschnitt* tradition. The American production was presented and staged by Harrison Grey Fiske and starred his wife, Minnie Maddern Fiske, and the elder Tyrone Power, a combination of names unquestionably responsible at least in part for the acceptance of the play. But it was the adaptation that made the real difference, for it was a remarkable example of a most unusual kind of change in the transition from German to English.

Heyse's play was forbidden by the censors in Germany—hardly a good prognosis for American production in 1902. The adaptation was by the very drama critic who led the opposition to Ibsen, William Winter. The English rendition of the play was a tour de force: Heyse's drama was in mildly naturalistic prose; Winter's version was in verse. It was this basic change which altered the texture of the entire play. The story revolves around Jesus, although he never appears, who is presented as his contemporaries in the story would see him—as a man, not a sacred character. Judas is presented as a Hebrew patriot who defects because of his loss of faith in a leader who had failed to free the Jews from the bondage of Rome, and who had talked when he should have acted. The betrayal results from rage. Mary of Magdala and Judas were lovers; when she turns to a belief in redemption of the soul from sin through divine love and goodness, Judas feels that he and his cause have been betrayed by Maria and Jesus alike.

In his preface to the printing of his adaptation in 1903, Winter stated that the German original, though human and compassionate, lacked "poetry" and spiritual quality, that it had no refinement, that it was too specific, too brutal, too frank in its discussion of the heroine's shame. These things that Winter found inadequate in the play were, of course, Heyse's very intention in writing a realistic play about a historical situation that had never been used before as the basis for a drama about human passions. Winter was assuredly correct in believing that the New York audience would have found *Maria of Magdala* offensive and sacrilegious in its original form, but for him to state that he was doing what he did in order to compensate for Heyse's inadequacies is typical of his lack of perception and understanding of the new drama of Europe. Winter translated the prose original, then rendered it into verse, but in the course of the second stage of adaptation, he also made numerous changes in structure, in character, and most importantly, in the tone and focus of the play. Winter's *Maria of Magdala,* totally desexed, was a puritanical, senti-

mental play in uninspired verse which paid tribute to the best known
of redeemed sinners. What had in its original form been a study of
human passion, divided loyalties, and persecution became a morality
play. In Heyse's work there were sympathetic Roman statesmen and
soldiers; Winter's version presented stereotyped "baddies" not far removed from the stock villains of Hollywood's biblical spectacles. The
hero of Heyse's play was Judas; no American, least of all Winter,
would have allowed that on Broadway. Not even the Germans had
permitted it.

A look through the magazines of the first decade of the twentieth
century reveals numerous articles devoted to discussions of the immorality of the stage and the specific deleterious effect of the new
European drama on the American, but it is almost axiomatic that
yesterday's naturalism is today's romance. On September 17, 1904,
Sam Shubert, one of the most conservative, dollar-conscious producers
in New York, presented Charles Swickard's translation of Franz
Beyerlein's *Zapfenstreich,* once considered a searching study of the
horrors of the military caste system in Europe. However, *Taps,* as it
was called here, was even in the year 1904 considered a romantic
melodrama. Sudermann's *Magda* was already assuming the stature of
a perennial classic, and his *The Fires of St. John* caused little stir
when presented at Daly's Theatre in November of that year, despite
the fact that its subject matter was the conflict between the Christian
morality man had devised for himself, and the pagan instincts within
man that rebelled against that morality. The English title was ill
chosen and misleading in its religious connotation, but the production
closed after eight performances, not nearly enough time to give any
but the most outrageous plays notoriety. Sudermann's *Johannisfeuer*
actually refers to the Scandinavian midsummer-eve celebration which
plays such an important role in Strindberg's *Miss Julie.* When *Johannisfeuer* was given in England, it was more correctly entitled *Midsummer Madness.* In 1906-1907, the E. H. Sothern-Julia Marlowe
repertory company included among its selections Sudermann's
Johannes (John the Baptist). Unlike Heyse's *Maria von Magdala,* with
its shock effects on a religious theme, *John the Baptist* is merely an
attempt to present a biblical story realistically. It is little more than
an adventure story.

At this point the incidence of German naturalism on the New York
stage, never really high, dwindled to almost nothing. Audiences and
critics had made fairly clear that there was no demand for it and that
it was unpalatable even in the watered-down versions offered here.
But by 1909-10, the season of the success of Edward Sheldon's *The
Nigger,* the audiences gave at least a slight indication of being ready

for something beyond romance and farce, and Mrs. Fiske again turned to the German drama for her latest vehicle. In the spring of that season she appeared in *Hannele,* a new translation of the Hauptmann play by Mary J. Safford with the metrical passages rendered by Percy MacKaye. The new English text was still far from satisfactory in its duplication of mood and in the texture of its dialect, but it was a distinct improvement upon the Meltzer version. Apparently *Hanneles Himmelfahrt* defies translation, for even the best English texts lose the particular, earthy flavor of Hauptmann's dialogue. Or maybe it is that today's reader or viewer cannot accept the incongruous combination of the slice of lowly life with the poetic, despite the fact that the modern drama is noted for its frequent use of various styles within the same text, albeit these are usually complementary rather than contrasting.

Mrs. Fiske's *Hannele* was not met by the indignation that had closed the production of 1894. The accusations of blasphemy and immorality were minimal in 1910, but still the production survived for only sixteen performances. This time, feeling was strong against it not so much for its thematic material but for its stylistic departures from acceptable well-made plays. The conservative *Bookman* said that "this curious composition is certainly not a play, and we need consider it, therefore, only as a poem. So considered, its very substance appears basically unimportant. What passes through the delirious mind of a German peasant, aged fourteen, who has been educated only in the symbolism of a very primitive religion, can hardly enfold any meanings of profound philosophic and poetic import."[16] Apparently the spokesmen of the genteel tradition felt that the play had nothing serious to say, for its conflict was seen from the point of view of a person without the proper breeding to comment upon such matters. *Theatre Magazine,* presenting the purely theatrical standard of evaluation, said that it was "staged with beautiful effects, but the intent of it all is pathos . . . [the play is] not for the pleasure seeker or the minds content with the merely theatrical."[17] There were reviews, however, which took the play seriously, notably that in the *New York Dramatic Mirror,* which discussed the play with insight and intelligence, approved of it in both conception and realization, and called it a "powerfully moving picture."[18] This production of *Hannele* was the closest that the play ever came to having a hearing on Broadway in English that was either artistically or commercially successful.

The last important play of German naturalism that was performed on the New York stage before the outbreak of World War I in Europe was the work of a minor dramatist, Max Halbe, whose early plays about free love and socialism received little international attention.

The play which brought Halbe fame in Germany was *Jugend,* appearing in 1893 immediately after the first big wave of naturalistic plays. Herman Bernstein's translation, *Youth,* opened on June 11, 1911, in New York. It was withdrawn after seven performances, the same number of showings that it lasted when it was revived in a little Greenwich Village theatre in 1920.

Youth is a simple love story of two youngsters in East Prussia who are thwarted by German-Polish friction, by the fanaticism of a young priest with frustrations of his own, by a narrow-minded provincial society, and by that overworked device of the drama of the nineties, heredity. The situations in which the young lovers are enmeshed, indeed their very act of falling in love, all seem to result from forces outside their control. The trappings of the story are naturalistic even though the relationship between the young boy and girl is lyrically romantic. Today, the play seems to be pure romance, for it is contrived beyond all reasonable bounds.

The excesses of *Youth* become doubly apparent in its English version which destroyed the best thing in the play, the natural flavor of the dialogue which in German had resulted from Halbe's keen ear for the colloquial. The Bernstein translation, like a later one by Sara Tracy Barrows which was never produced, has the clumsy, involuted style of a literal school exercise; it emphasizes the sentimentality in the boy-girl relationship rather than the criticism of human life that Halbe had proposed in a play that is essentially without hero or heroine or even villain, for that matter. In Halbe's drama there are only the forces of law, nature, economics, and biology at play. Bernstein's play avoids this naturalistic tone by making the zealous priest more a conscious villain than a victim of his own passions. Consequently, the very aspects of *Youth* that would differentiate it from a hundred plays like it were removed in the course of adaptation for the American stage. Furthermore, in its characterization of the young man, the German original deals seriously with his inner conflict resulting from the clash between his personal and the social standard of morality. The American version glosses over this aspect of Halbe's play. The drama which was produced at the Bijou Theatre in 1911 was no longer naturalistic; it was a sentimental melodrama about the hard luck of a rural Romeo and Juliet. It is because of the romantic tone of the adaptation that the final killing of the young man by his beloved's half-witted brother seems preposterously melodramatic; and the girl's passionate behavior, rather than being the legacy of her mother (ever since *Ghosts,* the European drama had been full of genetic fallacies), becomes a silly, unmotivated recklessness. Rather than deal with the conflicting emotions within the young priest, the

American version turns him into a one-dimensional ogre. Instead of dealing with the conflict of the generations within the play as the struggle between enlightenment and outworn tradition, it passes this off as the romantic rebellion of the young. *Jugend* is hardly a great play; Halbe's script actually invites the excesses that Bernstein interpolated, but it deserved better treatment than it received in *Youth*.

When the play was printed in translation, Ludwig Lewisohn wrote a glowing introduction not all of which can be taken seriously, for Lewisohn was an overly enthusiastic Germanophile in those years and one of the few champions of naturalism on the American stage; but his charge that Halbe's play was destroyed by both American translation and Broadway production was justified. The *New York Dramatic Mirror* reported that the audience on opening night took the performance very lightly. In fact, no one seemed sure whether it was meant to be serious or comic. Critical opinion in the *Dramatic Mirror* was usually insightful and enlightened, and the reviewer found *Youth* "intellectually interesting, but emotionally . . . dead."[19] He went on to say that it was contrived, illogical, and poorly acted. It is strange that he should find the play noteworthy for intellectual rather than emotional values, for it is the latter for which the adaptation strives. The most significant comment in the review is that "the translation was frequently stodgy and even foolish." Very few of the commentators in the periodicals took note of the translator's craft in these years. They tacitly assumed that they were seeing the same play that had been performed in Europe.

Of course, there were also the usual critical absurdities and irrelevancies. *Theatre Magazine*'s reviewing staff kept its record of banal evaluations unblemished by stating, "The intent of the play is good enough, but the lesson is not half brought home. The young man goes scot free. . . . Death should be his portion also . . . [the play] is not edifying."[20] It was possible, so it seems, to interpret Max Halbe's *Youth* as a play about the evils of premarital sexual relations and to say that the drama fails in its moral obligation because not all of the sinners are punished equally.

Youth might well have been more pertinent in the United States were it not a portrait of characters and a way of life totally foreign to our audiences. The drama of German naturalism leaned heavily on details of local color and cultural idiosyncrasies to lend mood and credibility to situations that were, essentially, not far removed from the romantic melodrama of twenty years before. The very elements within it that made it an interesting departure in dramatic form had to be removed when the plays were translated. Details, usually about the seamier aspects of life, were deleted, and the tone that gave credence to German productions was lost. In creating American versions that would have immediacy for our audiences, adapters turned German naturalistic plays into American melodramas. Of course, many of the best plays of this genre were so involved with matters concerning German life at the turn of the century that they were meaningless outside that country and were never exported.

Not all critics were insensitive to the changes that were being effected in plays as they crossed the Atlantic. In the spring of 1912, Warren B. Blake noted in the *Independent* that excessive liberties were being taken with foreign scripts in order to please American audiences. There was often no proof that the changes gave the New Yorker what he really wanted, only what the managers thought he wanted, and the lengthy annual list of failures on Broadway ever since its earliest days shows that producers are hardly infallible in their evaluation of public taste. Blake further pointed out that the process of adaptation does more than relocate places and rename characters. It changes action, distorts character, romanticizes endings, and often falsifies the original thematic material. It is at this time that serious critics were beginning to note the subtle distinction between translation and adaptation. Translation all too often was uninspired; it sterilized the original and deprived it of its idiom, one of the significant changes brought about by naturalistic drama. Adaptation implied commercially motivated compromise. When the author of an American version was listed as adapter rather than translator, critics and scholars took this to connote, not without frequent justification, that the play had been seriously tampered with. The translator and adapter are neglected artists in their own right. To render a play into a different language and not to destroy its mood and intent, while giving it the same import that it had for its native audience, takes no small amount of both linguistic and theatrical sensitivity.

Because of the impending conflict in Europe, far fewer German plays were being presented in New York by the 1913-14 season. Only the farces and operettas, which were from a world far apart from the immediacy of geopolitics, held the stage.

The first play of German naturalism to appear on Broadway after the outbreak of the war was *The Song of Songs*, adapted not from a play, but from Sudermann's novel, *Das Hohe Lied*. Sudermann had decided against dramatizing the piece of fiction, for he felt it to be too episodic to make a good play. He was right. Nevertheless, Edward Sheldon's American adaptation ran for 191 performances after its opening on December 22, 1914. In its attempt to turn novel into play, the drama became a lengthy series of detached sequences, very crudely strung together without benefit of effective transitions. Sudermann's novel is the sordid story of the degradation of a woman who cannot cope with the forces of the society about her and who gradually sinks to the point of total submission, the loss of all will to struggle against what she feels is inevitable. Taken out of its German milieu by Sheldon and set in the United States, *The Song of Songs* chose to concentrate on the romantic involvements of the heroine rather than on the study of instinct at war with morality and the individual in conflict with the standards of the group. *The New Republic* decried the theatricalism of a script that could have treated a serious issue.[21] *The Nation* called it a "crude melodrama [with] brave pretensions to realism," and further blamed Sheldon for making it so, and for missing all but the externals of the story in general and of the sex relationships in particular.[22] The play was still too dangerous a topic for Broadway in anything other than the most superficial treatments. A fairly perceptive article in *Current Opinion* attempted to analyze the essential differences between European and American drama, and refers to *The Song of Songs*, noting its "lightness of touch quite alien to the methods of the German [Sudermann], who is solid and heavily intellectual."[23] The anonymous author of the article sees this "lightness of touch" as the main difference between the European and American theatres. The insistence on the heavy intellectuality of Sudermann is silly, but it indicates that even those sensitive to the problems of the imported drama were overwhelmed by it. Apparently anything other than the lightest froth or tale of surface excitement was construed as intellectual drama.

On December 14, 1915, Mary Morrison's translation of Gerhart Hauptmann's *Die Weber* opened at the Garden Theatre. Sponsored by Augustin Duncan and directed by the great German-born champion of Hauptmann, Emanuel Reicher, who also acted in the play *The Weavers*, became the first highly praised work of German naturalism to appear on the New York stage.

The Weavers had been Hauptmann's first resounding success in Germany. Written in the Silesian dialect, though later rewritten in *Hochdeutsch* for publication purposes, the play was produced in Berlin at the *Freie Bühne* after the Prussian government had first tried to stop it. The feeling was strong that Hauptmann's piece smacked of socialism. The play was forbidden in the provinces of Germany and in much of Austro-Hungary for years. It is the story of the weavers of Silesia, driven by despair to rebel against their employers in the 1840's when machinery had relegated the workers of the entire industry to the slag heap of progress. Their uprising is quickly smashed by the army. The emphasis in characterization here is not on individuals, although a few have distinguishing traits, but on the multitude of small characters. Hauptmann presents the mass as hero (one hears echoes in the cry of "*das Volk*" in the 1930's and notes the sad evolution of the concept). The mass is also the absolute victim of its own world. The mass has no insight; it only has dreams. It is for these dreams that Hauptmann shows great compassion. He was sensitive to the suffering that simple people are capable of enduring, and he tried to represent it on the stage with a minimum of sentimentality.

Each of the five acts of *The Weavers* is almost self-sufficient. It is thematic material rather than plot which gives transition to the entire drama, and the song, first of the soldiers and then of the weavers themselves, "Bloody Justice," serves as a leitmotif throughout. In its structure *The Weavers* presages the *Massendrama* of Toller, and to some extent the epic theatre of Brecht.[24] The play is powerful not only because of its naturalistic techniques, but for the very aspects of it which departed from the strictures of German social verisimilitude of the nineties. Despite the great amount of violence and the use of mob scenes and the historical background of one of the most disastrous aspects of the industrial revolution, it is the unifying tone of the play rather than its details which give it its greatest force. Its stage directions, clearly reflecting as do most of Hauptmann's early plays his background as a writer of narrative, give clear indication of the totality of effect that he had conceived in *The Weavers* and the remarkable facility with which he realized that concept. Eric Bentley maintains that Hauptmann's plays, including *The Weavers*, are "unhealthy, not as their early critics felt, because they mention sex, poverty, and disease, but because they dwell upon sex, poverty, and disease without interpreting them."[25] Hauptmann did not concern himself with nuances in his naturalistic dramas, but to deny him even the smallest amount of sensitivity and insight seems too strong an indictment. That the work of Hauptmann has paled woefully over the years is an undeniable fact. Today his plays seem dated, awkward, didactic, and provincial; but the slice of life that he took was a significant one, and his technique was a new departure. Ironically, Hauptmann's later plays, conspicuously without rough edges and crudeness of style, were also bereft of any power.

The amateur German production of *The Weavers* in 1894, corrupt exploitation that it was, apparently made producers wary of presenting the play on the English-speaking stage. At that time, the papers had called the play brutal, ferocious, commonplace, something vulgar, not even a play. Only the finest German-language playhouse in New York, the Irving Place Theatre under the direction of Heinrich Conried, produced *Die Weber* on April 1, 1896. The press lauded it. *The Weavers* had its first hearing in English in its 1915 translation.

The milieu of the play was still a strange one to Americans, and its run of eighty-seven performances was hardly spectacular, though in that year quite respectable, but critical acclaim was almost unanimous—the first time for a German naturalistic play.

Theatre Magazine called it "one of the most stirring of realistic dramas dealing with modern social conditions,"[26] an unusual remark from a periodical seldom concerned with any aspect of a play save its box-office potential. The *New York Dramatic Mirror* of December 25, 1915, said it was "probably the most graphic picture of human misery ever written." *The Nation* heaped abundant praise on Emanuel Reicher for his acting and for his direction and stated that "opinion may differ as to the permanent value of such a play as *The Weavers;* there is no doubt as to the strength of this first American performance in English."[27] *The New Republic* concurred,[28] and the *New York Times'* review of the morning after the opening said that *The Weavers* was an "elaborate and deeply impressive production . . . one of modern Germany's great plays." It was the only one that ever made a positive impression on American critics and audiences.

The great flaw in German naturalistic drama was its insistence on the need for the *Lebensbild* on the stage, thus devoting the bulk of its attention to photographic detail of the misery of human life. It was only a matter of course that such plays, with few exceptions, would focus on surface reality. Dramatists soon wrote conventional plays full of a realism so limited in both time and space that they would be meaningless even in Germany not too many years hence and, as in their American importations, meaningless even to their contemporaries in another land. If naturalism in the German drama was a literary form as well as a philosophy, it had already lost its distinguishing characteristics by the first decade of the twentieth century. By the time that it came to New York, it was already a passé form in its native land. Germans had tired of naturalism's constant depiction of human suffering as the product of external circumstances without regard for inner conflict or character traits.

It is customary today to brush aside the achievements of naturalism from Germany and other countries and to dwell on its excesses. In the light of the plays of social realism of the 1930's and the achievements of the realistic motion picture, the scenes of life presented in naturalistic drama at the turn of the century seem anything but a believable slice of life. Yet these plays were the work of men who dared to speak of tragic subjects in language other than poetic, men who had great power and often great imagination. At their best they wrote plays with dignity and an awareness of the suffering of man in the past century. With a keen eye for their society, they dared to write of the horrors of contemporary life rather than to evade it or glorify a long dead past. They were a part of that emerging drama at the end of the nineteenth century which gave us Ibsen, Strindberg, Chekhov, and Shaw, and which has influenced playwriting in men as recent as O'Casey, Odets, and Miller. Naturalistic drama at its best always transcended verisimilitude; only when the photographic presentation of reality was an end unto itself, in either writing or production, did the play become a superficial exercise in depicting the sordid.

German naturalism in particular was very narrow in its scope. It was too firmly rooted in the details of everyday German life of particular locales to be suitable for production in a totally foreign land. This provincial quality, coupled with the linguistic problems inherent in the texts, made translation or adaptation a most difficult challenge. Even when the task was well done, there was the problem of the New York audience. If these plays were a revolution in Germany, a country conducive to theatrical experiments, what kind of reception could be expected in the United States?

The time lapse between the era of naturalism in Germany and its acceptance in the United States is significant. By the time it was discovered here, the "new" drama was no longer new, and Americans were developing a naturalistic drama of their own. Even a play such as Hauptmann's *The Weavers* was not given on Broadway until twenty-three years after its Berlin premiere. It seems reasonable that work of such deep social consciousness should have found an audience in the days of muckraking. Even the reader of fiction was more receptive to foreign naturalism than was the theatregoer who sought escapist entertainment or an edifying play with a puritanical moral to bring down the curtain. What theatrical demand there was for realism, not only in the opening years of this century but ever since, was for plays about local problems, the social strife of our own municipalities, not Germany's. The cult of the documentary play persists on the stage, in the motion pictures, and on television in the 1960's. American audiences, basically a breed of fundamentalists in drama, still find it difficult to accept a truth that is not literal. Either it is reality as captured by the camera eye or it is fiction at its most fanciful. That which is not historically true is therefore without meaning in real life. John Gassner feels, and there is much to corroborate his beliefs, that in the days before our own drama gained world stature, the New York audience was not really interested in humanity's problems at large, only in its own problems in particular. And when the public said that it wanted realism, it really sought pseudorealistic melodrama.[29] The changes made in the German plays which were adapted for American consumption bear this out in almost every instance.

II

The drama of neoromanticism, a convenient but vague tag, rose as a quick and vigorous reaction to naturalism in the German-speaking theatre. It encompasses all but the most trivial theatrical fare and the province of naturalism in the modern German drama before World War I. Neoromanticism has come to mean that upper-middle-class comedy which was the peculiar romance of Vienna (seen at its height in the plays of Arthur Schnitzler), the baroque spectacle that was the dramaturgy of Max Reinhardt and his disciples, and the verse-drama revival led by Hugo von Hofmannsthal and some lesser practitioners. The charm of *Alt Wien* was imitated and exploited for years after its usefulness had expired. Its sensibility was replaced by sentimental nonsense and nostalgia, sometimes with music, sometimes without. The spectacles of Salzburg and Berlin that were the genius of Reinhardt were never to be duplicated without benefit of the motion picture.

In retrospect, there was also a fourth element of the neoromantic movement: those plays by realists and naturalists which today lack any relationship to the real world and some of those that were never intended to. The great pitfall of verisimilitude is that yesterday's world of actuality is today's never-never land, a world long gone which assumes charm and warm memory in the recalling.

If naturalism sprang from the world of northern German industrialism in the late nineteenth century, neoromanticism was born of the way of life that was, and to many still is, Vienna. The world-weariness of the city dweller, his warm and compassionate humor, and his love of leisurely enjoyment became the source of many plays written in a nostalgic style, the stamp of which has been unmistakable.

Continental neoromanticism won more supporters among the public and the critics than did naturalism in New York in the years at the turn of the century. However, the greatest successes were from the French, particularly plays in the vein of the poetic romance of Maeterlinck and the bravura of Rostand. The best-received German neoromanticism was the spectacle play, but Reinhardt did not really bring it to New York until some years after its European vogue. The exception was *Sumurun,* imported in 1911-12.

During the last decade of the nineteenth century, the popularity of

Victorien Sardou was still pronounced on the American stage. Little wonder then that Hermann Sudermann's work found acceptance here that was never afforded the drama of Gerhart Hauptmann. The architectural design of Sudermann's plays shows the ever-present touch of the puppeteer of melodrama, whose histrionics are much less the product of a deterministic concept of causality than they are of an adherence to the principles of the well-made play. The scene in which Magda confronts her father lies a good deal closer to Sardou than to Hauptmann, and the praise of the "joy of life" enunciated by Sudermann's Countess Beata is that of a world which antedates Ibsen's Osvald Alving. Beata believes it can be attained while Osvald has been stripped of such illusions. *Ghosts* (1881) is twenty years older than *Es Lebe das Leben,* but it is the Sudermann piece that is the nineteenth-century play. Sudermann, reconsidered today, can be more clearly understood in much of his work as a latter-day romantic rather than a naturalist, and maybe American audiences were more drawn to his work for that reason. He offended the arch-puritans, but he did not have the revolutionary tone of the true determinist.

The romanticism that held the New York stage most tenaciously at the turn of the century was not the poetic style of the new European movement, but the stormy histrionics left over from pre-Darwin days. Each season saw some new dramatization of *The Three Musketeers,* and James O'Neill's *Count of Monte Cristo,* first done in 1883, was still popular in New York in the 1900-1901 season, the same year that Bernhardt played *Hamlet.*

On March 26, 1900, Charles Henry Meltzer's translation of Hauptmann's *Die Versunkene Glocke* opened at the Knickerbocker Theatre for a run of forty performances as *The Sunken Bell.* It was Hauptmann's first complete departure from naturalism and had proved highly successful in its German premiere in 1896. The praise which it received in New York was both for its merits as a play and for the performances of its stars, E. H. Sothern and Edith Taliaferro, both of whom assuredly helped to make the production a popular success. *Die Versunkene Glocke,* dealing as it does with the popular German theme of the problem of the artist who is torn between the pagan world that is his art and the middle-class Christian world that is his community, and who finally finds both worlds closed to him, could easily have been a clumsy allegory had its characters and language not given it a tone that, in the German, is poetic in its feeling despite its excessive sentimentality and lack of restraint. Meltzer's translation is a distinct improvement over his 1894 *Hannele,* for he finds himself more at home with the language of the unreal world. Hauptmann's diction is even further sentimentalized and overinflated by Meltzer, but it seems reasonable to assume that he did this not from lack of sensitivity but from a desire to conform to American dramatic taste of 1900.[30] The folklore of the German woodlands permeates the text of both the original and the translation, but too often the folklore becomes the mystique of a fairyland. Still there is an artificial pretentiousness in the Meltzer version not to be found in the texture of the original. At the same time that *The Sunken Bell* was playing at the Knickerbocker, a German production of it was on display at the Irving Place Theatre. For those critics who saw both, there was no question that much was lost in the American version, and that the German-language theatre's staging of the piece was also superior.[31] While interest in the poetic fantasy lasted in the American theatre, *The Sunken Bell* was clearly Hauptmann's best-received play except by the hearty few who championed naturalism. There were also those who commended the Hauptmann of both *Hannele* and *The Sunken Bell*. In 1909, critic Charles C. Ayer said that "both of these plays are for the more serious minded . . . their mysticism is not calculated to appeal to the frivolous amusement seeker."[32]

Whereas the continental neoromantic movement was an attempt to create a poetic drama that transcended everyday life, the style of translation given these plays on our stage indicates that to the American audience they were not a new phase of the modern drama but a return to the accepted style of the nineteenth century. It is therefore not surprising that many older romances were being revived by the Broadway producers. German plays among these were Solomon Mosenthal's *Deborah* and Friedrich Halm's *Der Sohn Der Wildnis*, both produced during the 1897-98 season. *Deborah*, known as *Leah the Forsaken* in Augustin Daly's adaptation, was first seen in Germany in 1849. The story of the Jewess who in a world of Christian scorn sacrifices herself for the Christian she loves was one of those perennially popular "four-hanky" melodramas that allowed the affluent ladies of New York to have a good cry without ever exposing them to the misery of real life. Three months after the opening of the Daly revival, another translation of Mosenthal's drama by Isaac C. Pray opened at the Fifth Avenue Theatre under the play's original title.

Halm, who wrote under the name Münch-Bellinghausen, had written *Der Sohn Der Wildnis* in 1842, and it was first produced in New York in English as *Ingomar* in 1851. This translation by Maria Lovell became an oft-repeated favorite of the devotées of sentimental melodrama. The revivals in November, 1897, and May, 1904, were the last for this play, fondly remembered by 1909 as "stilted and old fashioned."[33] The play is forgotten today except for James Joyce's refer-

ence to it in *A Portrait of the Artist as a Young Man* and Miss Lovell's
famous line, "Two souls with but a single thought / Two hearts that
beat as one," typical of the tone of the entire piece. That Halm's
romance of a latter-day noble savage was still considered a salable
commodity in 1904 is indicated by the fact that the revival of that
year was produced by Charles Frohman, a shrewd businessman, and
starred Julia Marlowe, Tyrone Power, and Frank Reicher. Apparently
the distinction between German romantic and neoromantic drama
was not perceived by the Broadway moguls or by their audiences.

In February, 1905, the Progressive Stage Society presented *Flirtation,* the first New York performance of a play by Arthur Schnitzler.
It received more attention when it appeared on Broadway in 1907 as
The Reckoning, although the usual published translation of *Liebelei* is
Light-o'-Love. Arthur Schnitzler (1862-1931), a doctor of medicine
who wrote his thesis on hypnosis as a treatment for neurotics, had a
lifelong interest in the development of psychiatry, but it was as the
dramatist of upper-middle-class life in Vienna that he earned fame.

Schnitzler's most comfortable form was the one-act play. Even his
full-length dramas are so episodic as to be a series of autonomous
scenes, as in *Anatol* and *Reigen.* Schnitzler's sphere was the erotic,
the game between male and female that some call war, but he never
wrote for sensation or without good taste. Ever the clinical doctor, he
wrote plays that accepted human folly, particularly that which is the
vanity of the world of self-deception. There is a tone of longing and of
indefinable sadness in Schnitzler's comedies. He describes human experiences that are joyful yet simultaneously sad because they re-
emphasize the transient nature of pleasure. Life is charming for the
Schnitzlerian *bon vivant,* but at his back he always hears what Mar-
vell heard, and he is reminded that day-to-day existence is an empty
affair. That all this charm and joy can exist in a world that his skepti-
cal eye sees as tired and decaying saddens the doctor as well as the
humanist.

Schnitzler laments a lost tradition. This may be one of the reasons
that his plays found little favor in the United States, a land seeking to
find rather than to revitalize its roots. Abused all his life by the
nationalist, anti-Freud, anti-Semitic press and finally banned by the
Nazis, Schnitzler never recaptured his pre-World War I popularity on
his native stage or on foreign ones, for Schnitzler's world had died
with that war. The ghost of *Alt Wien* still lingers in the Austrian
capital to this day, but for those who have never lived in Vienna, be it
Schnitzler's or today's pale shadow, the realm of this drama is romantic, even sentimental. Only to the initiate of that city and to the
serious critic elsewhere is Schnitzler the social realist, the psychologist

as playwright that his countrymen consider him. In the popular audience, only those who share his sense of loss and sadness for a time that is no more are attuned to his drama. The Viennese salon comedy has never appealed to the American taste for cruel laughter. American comic characters laugh at others, not themselves; American comedies deal not in warmth or charm but in insult and wisecrack.

The *Reckoning* ran for seventy-three performances beginning February 12, 1907, and was revived for twenty-four more on January 13, 1908. *Liebelei,* first produced in Vienna in 1895, shows a stronger naturalistic influence than the comedies for which Schnitzler is famous. It exhibits his medical, dispassionate view of life but is suffused with the compassion and sentiment of the comedies. Neither reformer nor philosopher, Schnitzler studied the amusing sophisticates who tenuously tread the comic-tragic line, as well as those people who seek escape from the harsh circumstances of their lives. *Liebelei* considers both of these social groups. Schnitzler carefully analyzes the societal structure, the psychological involvements, and the interpersonal relationships that make up the area which gives the title to one of his plays, which might well stand as the name of the major concern of all of his drama: *Einsame Leben—Lonely Lives.* The middle-European *Weltschmerz* is a symptom of a tired but civilized people. It is not the impetuous rebellion of younger societies. Schnitzler's characters consider their past with both longing and regret in a world that is as disillusioned as it is urbane.

Liebelei neatly contrasts the idle upper class and the simple folk in the opposing forces of two young men and the ingenuous girl and her father with whom they become involved. But where Schnitzler's famous Anatol is a charming bounder, Fritz and Theodor, the unheroic heroes of this piece, are shallow men-about-town. There is nothing really funny about this play, and after its promising first act, it turns out to be quite heavy-handed in the original as well as in translation. The fragile Viennese comedy was better suited to Schnitzler's style and temperament. Neither genre was acceptable to American tastes. The New York audience likes its naturalism without regret and its humor without compassion.

Translations of *Liebelei,* like most American renditions of Schnitzler, are literal and schoolish. The idiom that resulted from Schnitzler's sensitive ear is probably beyond the power of translation. His natural, witty recording of the speech of Vienna somehow sounds foppish in English. What is charming in German becomes pompous in translation.

The 1908 production of *The Reckoning* was preceded by a curtain-raiser, Schnitzler's one-act comedy, *Literatur,* known in this transla-

tion by Charles Harvey Genung as *The Literary Sense*. The characters
of this popular piece are the ne'er-do-well high comedy types which
Schnitzler handles best. Amoral, irresponsible, and thoroughly charming, the Schwabing[34] bohemian, her baronial fiancé, and her former
lover convey the constant feeling that life was fun even if decadent in
those days, and that those days (even in 1901, the year of the play's
premiere) are gone. *Literatur*, one of Schnitzler's most delightful one-
acters, appealed to only a limited audience in America; but those who
praised it usually did because the play's charming situation stood up
quite well despite the unfamiliarity of the society Schnitzler wrote
about. The one-act comedies of Schnitzler given in New York failed or
succeeded as farce at face value. Their social criticism was never an
interesting issue to American audiences.

When a revival of *Literatur* was included in the fifteen one-act
play repertory which the Washington Square Players presented in the
1915-16 season at the Bandbox Theatre, the Players rejected the inadequate Genung translation and substituted a new one by Elsie Plaut.
The *New York Dramatic Mirror* thought it an entertaining comedy
whose wit and "mastery of phrase and situation" could be enjoyed
without demanding credibility.[35] The *New York Times* praised the
"shrewd observation" of Schnitzler in "his usual cynical vein," but
although the reviewer conceded that *Literature* was the best of the
four brief plays on the Washington Square bill, he attacked the amateurish production and the surface acting.[36] The organization that was
soon to become the Theatre Guild had not yet found acceptance as a
part of the professional theatre, and for good reason, but there was no
uptown producer who even dared to exhibit a Schnitzler comedy in
1915. When the Washington Square Players moved to the larger
Comedy Theatre in the fall of 1916, they again included the
Schnitzler one-acter in their season, but the reception was no different.

During the years preceding and including World War I, Arthur
Schnitzler's one-act comedies were periodically to be seen both on
Broadway and in the budding little theatres. One of the most popular
was *The Green Cockatoo*, subtitled "a grotesquerie in one act" (translation by Philip Littel and George Rublee), produced by Harrison
Grey Fiske on April 11, 1910, as the curtain-raiser for the production
of *Hannele* that starred his wife.

As late as 1931 *The Green Cockatoo* could be seen in Eva Le
Gallienne's Civic Repertory Company, and it has been given by numerous universities in both English and German. Set in Paris on the
eve before the revolution, it is a picture of the impending downfall of
the old aristocracy everywhere. Finally forced to separate reality from

their illusions, the characters are all unmasked and left with only their vanities. Half the characters are improvisational actors in the café, The Green Cockatoo, and by the end of the play it is hard to tell which people in the story are play-acting and which ones are not, for there is sham in all of their lives. The boundaries of reality and illusion are indefinable, and the one real criminal in the pack is taken for the most unconvincing actor. Written in 1898, *Der Grüne Kakadu* foreshadows the work of Pirandello. Set in Robespierre's Paris, but about the end of Franz Josef's Vienna, the play had to stand without social connotations and without the comic ease of Schnitzler's dialogue when it was presented in New York. The *New York Dramatic Mirror* was almost alone in commending Fiske's production, saying it was a good play well done.[37] Far more typical was the *Bookman's* reaction that it was "merely a theatric *tour de force*," a play which confused and mystified its audience, which the reviewer said was unforgivable.[38] *Theatre Magazine* displayed its customary lack of perception: the play has "no significance, but it is something of a novelty . . . entertaining."[39]

Arthur Schnitzler had begun writing the series of sketches that was to become *Anatol* as far back as 1891, and single scenes were performed on the Continent to great popular and critical appreciation. It was not until 1910, however, that these scenes were joined to form a complete play. The resulting play was produced in both Vienna and Berlin. Anatol, the "light hearted melancholic [who is the central figure of the piece is the] prototype of . . . the Viennese *fin de siècle*."[40] The play conveys a wistful sense of the search for love which should be something shared, yet always seems to end as a game with a winner and a loser. Schnitzler himself had written some early works under the pseudonym of Anatol, but the character in the episodic play is not to be mistakenly construed as autobiographical. He is, as the *Dramatic Mirror* said, "the polygamous animal in which Herbert Spencer once summed up all mankind. But the lovely thing about him is his geniality and utter detestation of hypocrisy. He runs the whole gamut of possible 'affairs' without once besmirching his honor. . . . He sins as a perfect gentleman should, if he should sin at all."[41] Amid all the amorality proposed by the *raissoneur* of the sketches, Max, we have Anatol himself, really a moral individual but incurably romantic. If the sage comment of Max is Schnitzler speaking, Anatol is old Vienna unburdening itself. *Anatol* is a simultaneously sad and joyous farewell to a world now dead, yet the epitome of relatively trouble-free times for the prosperous and the bourgeois. In the most delightful sequence, "*Abschiedssouper*" ("The Farewell Supper"), Anatol is trying to end an affair graciously. Before he has the opportunity, the girl dismisses him. And so it was with the modern Viennese and their nineteenth-century way of life. They wanted to say goodbye to an age that had long beaten them to departure. *Anatol*, in part or as a whole, was Schnitzler's most popular play in Europe.

Winthrop Ames produced the play in New York on October 14, 1912, at the Little Theatre, where it ran for seventy-two performances with John Barrymore in the leading role. The production gave five of the original seven sequences[42] in a translation by Harley Granville Barker, whose introduction to the published version of his rendition, *The Affairs of Anatol*, is revealing. He maintains quite correctly that in a faithful translation the peculiar charm of Schnitzler's dialogue would be lost. To recreate it in English would require another Schnitzler. Barker insists his version be called a paraphrase, and it is, in the recreation of the particular mood of Schnitzler, a most commendable job. The trouble with the Barker text is that it was cast in the British idiom, which was almost as foreign to New Yorkers of 1912 as that of Vienna. The flavor of the German comes largely from the ease and the lightly facile diction of Schnitzler. The Viennese theatregoer heard the dialogue in the leisurely cadences of his sophisticated townsfolk; the New York viewer heard it in the somewhat stilted parlance of Mayfair. Someone should have done for New York what Barker had done so admirably for London.

The reviewer for *Life* immediately saw what was wrong: the loss of language and the concessions that were made to the genteel tradition, unable to stand Dr. Schnitzler's medical frankness. "Something must have evanesced in transit," the review stated. "[The] original brilliancy . . . may have been lessened . . . by deference to . . . Puritanism."[43] Moreover, most critics were quick to notice that Barrymore's performance was all on the surface and played with one eye on the audience. He tried so hard to be charming that he came off as an unctuous fraud. This is not Anatol. *Life* said that the result of the changes from the original was "champagne without bubbles." *Theatre* evaded the issue by dealing with the morality of the play.

> To the question whether these episodes are moral, one is tempted to equivocate by saying that they are artistic. Schnitzler's writing is always refined; there is nothing ugly or coarse or vulgar, nothing repellent here. One must be grateful to him for what he does not say. He has the gift of silence and says the unsayable without asteriks [*sic*] and without offending.[44]

Apparently the question of offense became more important than the actual merit of either the play or the adaptation. When it went on the road, the *Chicago Record Herald* said that "the intention of the thing is deplorable; its effect is tedious and insipid."[45] Years later, revivals of *Anatol* no longer had to face excessively puritanical houses, but a play that had become palatable was then no longer playable. The generation that mourned the old Vienna was itself a thing of the past after World War I.

The season of 1910-11, which saw the first United States performance of Maeterlinck's *The Bluebird*, was also the year of the neoromantic Viennese comedy that became a commercial success in New York. Leo Ditrichstein's adaptation of Hermann Bahr's *Das Konzert* opened on October 4, 1910, and ran for 264 performances. Bahr was the most notable of Schnitzler's followers. He wrote about eighty plays, most of them undistinguished, but this one comedy (produced in Berlin in 1909) captured a mood of wit and nostalgia the balance of which he never achieved again. Actually, Bahr is much better known today as a critic than as a playwright; it was Bahr who wrote the first really important book on expressionism and who edited the influential *Freie Bühne* in Berlin.

The Concert is the flimsy tale of an urbane and egomaniacal musician who cannot refrain from becoming infatuated with the young ladies who study with him. Only his wife can extricate him from his involvements, and she does so with a constant *élan* that always unnerves the artist before restabilizing him (and, of course, putting him at the mercy of the woman from whom he must then again stray, only to be reclaimed again in a never-ending cycle, more amoral than immoral). The characters, the dialogue, and the farcical situations, however, were not enough to insure popular success for this play, as they were not enough for Schnitzler's comedies, or later for Molnár's, on the New York stage. The success of *The Concert* was not Bahr's; it was Ditrichstein's. Leo Ditrichstein was a German-born actor who starred in and adapted many of the farces and musicals of his native land on the American stage after he had spent some years in New York's German-language theatres while learning to master English. Ditrichstein's instincts and talents were as commercial as they were considerable, and he knew his audience. His adaptation of the Bahr comedy, produced and directed by David Belasco and starring Ditrichstein himself, was Americanized in setting and character and made every possible adjustment to remove the last trace of the Viennese from the original. *The Independent* echoed the appraisal of all the reviewers on March 7, 1912: "delightful." Ditrichstein had followed the formula that had proved successful in the transplanting of so many lightweight pieces of foreign origin; he removed from them the trappings that branded them foreign, and thus distasteful, to the audiences that came to see purely commercial dramatic fare. In June, 1916, *Das Konzert* was given in German at the Band Box Theatre. No faithful version of Bahr's comedy ever came to Broadway, but Ditrichstein was unquestionably justified in believing that the original was not a sacred text.

In 1916-17 two more of Bahr's comedies were staged but without the success of *The Concert. The Poor Fool* was Mrs. F. E. Washburn-Freund's version of *Der Arme Narr* which found its way into the Washington Square repertory on March 21, 1917. The *New York Times*, kinder to the Players' aspirations than most papers, thought it a foggy piece and said that audiences that would see the one-acter would be "bewildered and a little bit bored."[46] *The Master*, a translation of Bahr's *Der Meister* by Benjamin F. Glazer, opened at the Fulton Theatre on December 15, 1916, and survived for forty-seven performances on the strength of a few reviews that liked it despite the fact that it was excessively talky. The play, an attack on quack doctors and gossips, suffers from a lack of both brevity and subtlety. The central character, a fake doctor, complicates his precarious situation by dabbling in polygamy. The trouble with the script is that Bahr presented his denunciation of a fanatic who thinks that man can guide his actions by reason alone in the form of situations so laden with garrulousness and buffoonery that the central issues were totally lost. *Theatre*'s comments that the play was an unsuccessful mixture of realism and caricature and that there was too much talk was representative of the reactions of commercial reviewers.[47] The *Times* praised *The Master* for its dissection of the "too-articulate radical . . . [and the] would-be superman," but saw that "for all its ostensible transfer to an American locale, [it is] as Teutonic in manner and matter as a pretzel."[48] Arnold Daly revived *The Master* for thirty-nine performances beginning February 19, 1918, only one month after he had produced and starred in Bahr's *Josephine*, a play which made him the object of public attack. *Josephine* is a satirical comedy which in 1918 was construed as German propaganda, and although Daly denied and refuted the propaganda charge in the *Times* on February 10, the play closed after twenty-four performances.

A translation by André Tridon, presented by the Washington Square Players on January 10, 1916, marked the first English-language production in New York of a play by Frank Wedekind.[49] *The Tenor*, as *Der Kammersänger* is usually known in English, deals with the private unmasking of a public idol who is the slave of his art rather than master of it. The singer, a Philistine, is so concerned with his fame that he has no time for his work or for the people in his life. Wedekind, iconoclastic as always, smashed all the popular misconceptions about art and artists in dealing with a heartless poseur who is merely a commercial hack. A man without feeling or sensitivity can never be an artist, only an exhibitionist. The play is one of the popular comedies of Wedekind's canon of social criticism. It is far removed from the protoexpressionism for which he is best remembered today. The production at the Band Box was mildly praised by the *Dramatic Mirror*[50] and the *Times*.[51] Shortly after this premiere of *The Tenor*, the Irving Place Theatre produced Wedekind's *Erdgeist* in German. *The New Republic* commented that a Forty-second Street audience would have extinguished that in one night.[52]

The mildly cynical, neoromantic comedies of Germany and Austria apparently appealed to the Washington Square Players. Furthermore, many of them were in one act, and the repertory of the players for 1916-17 consisted of twenty-two works in this form. On November 13, 1916, a program opened at the Comedy Theatre which the *Times* called the Washington Square's best yet when the reviews appeared.[53] One of the entries was *Altruism*, Benjamin F. Glazer's rendition of a broad farce by Karl Ettlinger, a German writer far better known for his humorous verse and sketches in the Rheinland dialect than for his plays. *Altruism*'s first American production, ten months earlier at the Little Theatre in Philadelphia by amateurs under Glazer's direction, was so well received that the translator offered the piece to the Greenwich Village company, and it met with immediate approval. The play is a bitter, cruel, and grotesque charade concerning human greed, for which reason it may well have had greater appeal to New York audiences than the sentimental and kind comedies of Vienna.

On February 11, 1908, Arthur Symons' translation of *Elektra* by Hugo von Hofmannsthal had opened at the Garden Theatre with Mrs. Patrick Campbell in the title role. It lasted for nine performances. Hofmannsthal was the chief German exponent of a real challenge to naturalism, the return to a poetic drama. His plays, impassioned in their verse, made no reference to contemporary social problems. Theirs was the world of the myths and legends of ancient Greece or medieval and renaissance Europe. Hofmannsthal's talents, like those of his followers, were more lyrical than dramatic, and it is as poets rather than as playwrights that they are remembered today. His verse plays never commanded an audience in the United States, and his prose comedies have never been produced here.

Hugo von Hofmannsthal's verse is called "luxurious" by his admirers[54] and "neobaroque" by those less enamored of his style. He is best known to American audiences today as the librettist for Richard Strauss' *Arabella, Die Frau Ohne Schatten, Der Rosenkavalier*, and the *Elektra* based on the play. The verse of *Elektra*, like all of Hofmannsthal's, defies translation, and the poetry is the best element of his dramas. *Elektra* was produced in Berlin in 1903 by Reinhardt, who was responsible for the staging of most of Hofmannsthal's plays, and who together with him founded the Salzburg Festival in 1913. It was Hofmannsthal's *Jedermann*, his spectacular version of *Everyman*, that opened the first festival.

Almost every line of the German text of *Elektra* is of high-voltage intensity. It is passionate and romantic and bears as little stylistic similarity to its Greek source as it does to the many modern French reworkings of the classics. Poetry and character are the elements that determine the success or failure of the retelling of an oft-told tale, and the most interesting elements of Hofmannsthal's play lie in his language and characterization. The image of the huge purselike fishing net which traps the House of Atreus is central in Aeschylus' trilogy, and the German poet retains this unifying symbol, but here the resemblance to the *Oresteia* ends. The plot of *Elektra* is patterned after Sophocles, but the calm and dignified Greek heroine who seeks justice becomes a wild and passionate woman consumed by fury in the German version. Such unrelieved dramatic development was too operatic even for American theatrical taste in the first decade of the twentieth century. Arthur Symons' translation, faithful in mood and intensity to the original, was an admirable attempt at an impossible task. Hofmannsthal's verse dramas have justifiably survived as operas and as poetry to be read rather than performed.

In addition to the development of the free theatres in the late nineteenth-century drama, there was another growing movement; the central principle of it was that all aspects of a play's production should emanate from the creative vision of a single artistic intelligence responsible for synthesizing all elements of the play from its interpretation to its mounting. The primary proponents of this theory were Adolphe Appia and Gordon Craig, who maintained that the imitation of the school of verisimilitude should be replaced by a suggestive simplicity wherein music, scene, lighting, character, language, and dramatic action strive for a single and harmonious unity of effect. The desired product was the *Gesamtkunstwerk*. The procedure by which it was achieved was *Inszenierung*, and this central design was the responsibility of the superdirector who envisioned, executed, and gave focus to the whole, the *Regisseur*. The modern drama's most inspired and energetic *Regisseur* was the man who put the theories of Appia and Craig into practice, Max Reinhardt.[55]

Reinhardt and his company did not enter New York in full force until the 1920's, but Winthrop Ames, an American producer with enthusiasm and imagination, convinced the German impresario that he should bring a play here in 1912. On January 16 of that year, *Sumurun* opened at the Casino Theatre. Reinhardt had previously taken the play to England, where it had failed because of the inadequate stage facilities provided in London. Ames promised him that in America *Sumurun* would have the benefit of all of the devices that had made the play so successful at the *Deutsches Theater* in Berlin. Reinhardt arrived with his full company, but their reputation had preceded them. The New York audience, primed by many newspaper and magazine articles lauding the master,[56] was prepared to see magic, and the ballyhoo that greeted Reinhardt was never again equaled until he returned some years later with his spectacle, *The Miracle*. The man who had already become a myth did not disappoint his public in 1912.

Sumurun is a wordless play which Reinhardt arranged in nine tableaux based on a story from Friedrich Freksa's book, *Tales of the Arabian Nights*. It had been in the Berlin repertory for three years, and it was an exhibition of all of the visual and technical stage wizardry that the *Gesamtkunstwerk* employed to evoke from its audience a feeling of emotion coupled with awe. *Sumurun* was "one of the seeds of the new movement in scene design soon to manifest itself on our stage."[57] Its use of moving panoramas, advanced lighting techniques, and the *Kuppelhorizont*, a curved cyclorama that increased tenfold the possibilities of depth perspective, were among the innovations of German stagecraft that so strongly influenced Robert Edmond Jones and Norman Bel Geddes. The production was, according to the *New York Dramatic Mirror*, a tribute to the seemingly impractical theories of Gordon Craig, for Reinhardt had turned them into a reality.[58] The visual splendor of *Sumurun* was actually achieved with economy. The physical structure of the settings was simple; Reinhardt was a master illusionist who had taken lessons from the oriental theatre as well as from Craig and Appia. His use of the runway as a means of breaking through the fourth wall to the audience was derived from the Kabuki theatre, and it served as the basis for his later circus staging, the first step in the modern theatre's revival of arena stagecraft. *Sumurun* was also one of Reinhardt's ventures into drama with a massive cast. His handling of crowds was as carefully planned as a choreographic pattern. Victor Holländer had composed a score to accompany the pantomime tale of Sumurun and Nur-al-din, and the total effect of the production was a visual and musical spectacle that left few viewers unmoved and no critics unenthusiastic.

The technique of the production and the artistry of its mounting completely obscured the fact that the play was without much substance. Several reviews said of *Sumurun* that its action was so swift and engrossing that the audience forgets that there is no dialogue. The play was praised by the *New York Evening Post*, the *Boston*

Transcript, the *New York Tribune,* and *Literary Digest* for its sensu-
ous mood and its depiction of primitive emotions with masterful
stagecraft. The influential critic, Arthur Ruhl, said in comparing Reinhardt's work to the compulsive clutter of detail of Belasco that "he
hits the imagination instead of merely filling the eye."[59] The production of *Sumurun* in 1912 showed American producers an entirely new
conception of dramatic spectacle, but it was not until the 1922 production of *Johannes Kreisler* and Reinhardt's return in 1924 with *The
Miracle* that Broadway saw another such extravaganza.

By 1918, Broadway was no longer hospitable to plays admittedly
German no matter how far removed they were from the international
conflict. Even the little theatres abstained from their production with
the exception of the Greenwich Village Theatre whose performance of
The Big Scene, Charles Henry Meltzer's translation of Schnitzler's
Grosse Szene, was, on April 18, 1918, the last German play to be
presented in New York until March, 1920, when the Provincetown
Players gave the same playwright's *Last Masks (Die Letzten Masken).*
As always, only the off-Broadway theatre was prepared to risk anything. An era of importation had ended with the rise of violent anti-
German feelings in New York, and the neoromantic drama, never
warmly accepted by our audiences nor adequately rendered by our
adapters was forgotten in New York after the impetus of World War I
sentiment had spent itself.

III

By far the largest number of German plays produced on the New
York stage between the years 1894 and 1918 were those which in their
native land are known as *Kitsch.* The term encompasses all of the
horrors usually ascribed to the eighth-rate products which make up
the major share of playbills both in Germany and in the United
States. It is the commercially inspired junk that affords escapist entertainment for the great number of customers who keep the moguls of
the theatrical industry solvent. Often it is a delightful diversion.
Kitsch is not to be mistaken for serious dramatic or musical efforts
which fail to realize their intent; *Kitsch* aims low and hits. The work
of the slicks and the hacks, it has always been the bread and butter of
Broadway and Hollywood. It tends to thrive in an environment of
commercial theatre. That the word describing this genre is German is
no accident, for the farces, operettas, and melodramas which flooded
the popular German theatre of the late nineteenth century established
an audience eager for this fare. It might actually be more accurate to
believe that the bourgeoisie that comprised much of the audience in

the Germany of that era created the demand. The monster has been self-sustaining ever since.

Not only Augustin Daly but many of his contemporaries imported the German farces of von Schönthan, Blumenthal, Kadelburg, Fulda, Stobitzer, Kraatz, Stein, Willner, and many others who were less prolific. The adaptations were usually very free, the characters and scenes were Americanized, and the dialogue was given local humorous allusions. In addition to these slight comedies and trite romances, there was the operetta, probably the most popular Germanic importation of all until the American musical comedy developed a style of its own in the 1930's. Broadway managers thrived on the operettas of various Strausses, von Suppé, Lehár, Kalman, Fall, and Eysler. The Viennese operetta outlived its nonmusical compatriots by many years, and though its books and lyrics are today a charming atavism at best, its scores are still performed for and enjoyed by those who no longer associate them with nor ever knew the plays that introduced them. It is almost impossible to distinguish many American operettas from their Germanic models. The perennially popular *Student Prince*, presented for the first time in 1924 with Sigmund Romberg's music, had for many years been enjoyed as *Old Heidelberg*, Wilhelm Meyer-Förster's sentimental comedy. Romberg also reworked a number of German operettas. Many American musicals, while not based on plays from Germany, were set there or in Austria or in Switzerland. In the years 1907, 1908, and 1909 Broadway offered such titles as *Lola from Berlin, The Toymaker of Nuremberg*, and *The Girls of Gottenburg*, all by Americans. October, 1907, saw the first of many performances of Lehár's *The Merry Widow* which immediately inspired many American imitations. There was even a parody of it, and fads such as Merry Widow hats, drinks, hairdos, and dresses had a brief flurry. In September, 1909, F. C. Whitney produced the first American performance of *The Chocolate Soldier*, Rudolf Bernauer and Leopold Jacobson's very free adaptation of Shaw's *Arms and the Man*, which had been set to music by Oskar Straus. It was revived with various degrees of success until the days following World War II. The everpopular *Fledermaus* has been seen on Broadway as *Night Birds*, *A Wonderful Night*, *The Merry Countess*, and *Rosalinda* as well as under its original title. This most famous of all operettas eventually found its way into the repertories of the finest opera companies. Not even World War I, which aroused such violent anti-German feelings in this country, diminished the popularity of the operetta form. All that was required was a change of setting; the production of Kalman's *Das Schwarzwaldmädl* in 1917 as *The Riviera Girl* is typical of such transplantings. There were also many musicals which, although obvi-

ous in their origins, listed no program credits to a German source
during the war years. These are only a few instances of the multitude
of operettas which were a Broadway staple for so long. There seems
also to be little doubt that the line between the German and the
American operetta is very thin. The transition between the two was
effected by many composers, librettists, lyricists, producers, and performers who were themselves immigrants or children of immigrants
from Germany, Austria, Hungary, and Czechoslovakia (Bohemia):
Otto Harbach, Karl Hoschna, Sydney Rosenfeld, Sigmund Romberg,
Jerome Kern, Oscar Hammerstein, Leo Ditrichstein, the Shuberts,
Klaw and Erlanger, Charles and Daniel Frohman, Florenz Ziegfeld,
Arthur Voegtlin, Edward Knoblauch, Gustav Kerker, Rudolf Friml,
Gustav Luders, Ludwig Englander, and Albert von Tilzer (a most
unlikely name for the man who wrote "Take Me Out to the Ball
Game"). Furthermore many of the most frequent adapters, such as
Glen MacDonough and the brothers Robert B. and Harry B. Smith,
were also the librettists for a number of original American musicals.
Their styles and themes were unquestionably affected by their ac-
quaintance with German operettas.

In December, 1909, Charles C. Ayer said, "that there has been
much plagiarism from Germany, there can be no doubt. Many a German farce with an unpronounceable title is made over into an American play with American scenes or names. Sometimes a vague
acknowledgement by the American adapter is made."[60] It seems impossible to ascertain exactly how many and which works of American
Kitsch owe their existence to a German source. The catalog of only
those admittedly adapted is numerically overwhelming. Operettas enjoyed the longest runs of any German plays ever produced on the
New York stage, and their influence on the American musical comedy
is obvious. It also seems feasible to believe that the German farce, so
often imported, exerted some influence on the American. American
comedy in its cruelty owes more to these banal pieces than to the
high comedy of Paris, London, Vienna, and Budapest.

The incidence of German farce in New York tapered off sharply
after World War I; the operetta survived the conflict and was rein-
forced by the work of Americans whose family roots lay near Vienna.

IV

In addition to the development of the drama in the years between
1894 and 1918, there are a few significant technical and organiza-
tional aspects of the theatre in Germany and in the United States

which are germane to this study: the innovations in the mechanics of
stagecraft, the nature of the German-language theatre in New York,
the advent of the American Syndicate, and the rise of the little theatres off Broadway.

Many of the technical devices which are today taken for granted
in the theatre were developed by the Germans in the years around the
turn of the century. In 1896, in Munich, Karl Lautenschläger designed
and installed the Western world's first revolving stage, based on a
primitive device of the Japanese theatre. The houses of Munich, Berlin, and Dresden were, in those years, the seat of almost all of the
significant experiments in stagecraft. In addition to the revolver,
there were many other advances: total redesigning of lighting equipment and patterns in order to do away with the shadows, the artificial effects of footlights, and the necessity for excessive makeup; the
construction of wagon stages on casters which could be quickly and
quietly rolled in from the wings so that massive settings could be
changed with a facility unknown before;[61] the designing of rising and
sinking stages so that by the use of lifts and winches, the playing
levels could be altered; the invention of the *Kuppelhorizont,* a con-
cave shell at the back of the stage which with proper lighting gave a
new perspective to outdoor settings previously unattainable with the
straight canvas cyclorama; the use of the Linnebach projector, a lighting device which could cast images from behind the stage onto a
screen so that settings could be changed by merely casting a new
image—a device particularly useful in dream or hallucination scenes
and of which the later expressionists made frequent use (the Linnebach was often criticized for the distracting shadows that it cast, but
it was not obsolete until very recent developments in stage lighting);
the return to permanent and unit stages for the production of classical
and renaissance plays, a design recently revived again for many of our
festival theatres; the abolition of the proscenium and the use of a
circus theatre by Reinhardt, the purpose of which was to destroy
picture-frame theatre and push the play right into the audience, a
device which greatly influenced the proponents of epic theatre in the
thirties and also marked the first step in the events that led to the
revival of arena theatre after World War II; the development by
Leopold Jessner of stage settings which were made of stairs and plat-
forms only so that the fluidity of dramatic action envisioned by Gordon Craig could be facilitated by using lights, costumes, and props
judiciously, and never moving one major piece of scenery throughout
the play.

Kenneth Macgowan, Robert Edmond Jones, Norman Bel Geddes,

Mordecai Gorelik, Lee Simonson, and many other American designers of the years when our own theatre matured studied their craft in Germany.

All of these innovations were astronomical in cost. Despite the fact that Americans made much use of the new German stagecraft, its technical wonders never appealed anywhere else in such profusion as in their homeland. The investment was too great a risk for our commercially sponsored theatre. Furthermore, this sort of lavishness soon became the province of the films.[62]

The German-language theatre of New York thrived for many years. It perished after World War I, unable to withstand the violent anti-German feeling in the city and unable to find an audience once the generations of nineteenth-century German immigrants had died out. Their children were culturally assimilated, and many of them had only feeble control of the language. While it prospered, the German theatre of New York was as accomplished a professional drama as the United States had known. The Irving Place Theatre was the most famous of these playhouses. Norman Hapgood, the noted critic, called it New York's finest house of the classics, better even than Daly's Theatre during his lifetime.[63] The Irving Place had a repertory company with no stars other than on the occasion of a guest appearance of a player from Germany. It taught a lesson in the value of ensemble playing that Broadway never learned, but which gave instruction to the little theatres in Greenwich Village from which the first really important American drama was to grow. Plays that no Broadway producer dared to present were regularly to be seen on the stage of the Irving Place, and many works by Ibsen, Hauptmann, Wedekind, and Schnitzler were performed there years before they were ever given in English. A number of German-born actors were trained at the Irving Place while they learned English so that they could appear on the American stage, and though some of the actors later deserted for the wider fame and fatter paychecks of Broadway, many stayed with the German-language theatre throughout their careers. Of the latter, Rudolf Christians was probably the most famous.

The German-language theatre was autonomous. It existed outside the jurisdiction as well as the atmosphere of Broadway and was not subject to its commercialism, its censorship, or its audience. It was this isolation that finally helped to destroy it, but in its playbills one could see how different the German theatre was from the American in the years before World War I.

Much of that difference can probably be traced to the founding in 1896 of the infamous Syndicate by a half-dozen men, the most influential of whom were Charles Frohman, Marc Klaw, and A. L. Erlanger.

In their attempt to create a national clearing house for theatrical bookings, they established a monopoly which eventually controlled not only the important theatres all over the country but also what was played in them. They would not allow managers of the theatres they owned to book presentations that were not under Syndicate control, and they destroyed the "road" by flooding it with shows the purpose of which was to recoup losses sustained in New York. In an era known for its rampant abuses in the name of free enterprise, the Syndicate brought about the final metamorphosis of the theatre into a business known to this day as "the entertainment industry." By 1906, the Syndicate chiefs controlled more than seven hundred theatres. Their hold was finally broken, not by political pressure or by legislation, but by competition. Independent producers began to play the same game, and it was the Shubert Brothers (Lee, J. J., and Sam) who finally beat them at it. The Shuberts never exerted the same power as Klaw and Erlanger, but they did control the major portion of the nation's legitimate houses as late as the 1950's when a federal antitrust suit forced them to relinquish some of their holdings. The business atmosphere created by the sixty-year hegemony of men who saw the drama merely as a means of making money has left a permanent mark on the American stage. It can be seen in the quality and scope of the world that is Broadway to this day.

The German drama in New York before the armistice was not well received in its naturalistic or its neoromantic manifestations. It had little effect on what was considered the first-rate drama in our country, although it did impress the little theatres and the serious critics. The most common role of the German drama in New York was that of providing the *Kitsch* that our native hacks could not turn out in sufficient quantities to meet the public demand. The reasons for the failure here of important German plays between 1894 and 1918 are clear: an audience that wanted entertainment instead of drama, the genteel tradition of criticism, the commercialism of our theatre system, the inadequacy of translations and adaptations, and censorship. Other factors were the lack of immediacy in thematic material for American audiences, the incompatibility of New York's grand style of acting and naturalism, the difference between the New York and Viennese ideas of comedy, the desire for glitter and spectacle, the avoidance of the sordid, and simple jingoism. While technical innovations from Germany were praised, dramatic ones were not. But the serious modern German drama from before World War I, unwelcome on Broadway except for its gadgetry, found a showplace at the Provincetown and at Washington Square, and thus became part of the tradition in the American theatre which, after the war, brought it of age.

2

Spectacle and Experiment:
1918-28

I

Subjectivity in thematic material and experiment in form were the chief characteristics of the outstanding German plays brought to the New York stage in the decade following World War I. The experimental drama from Germany which was performed in this country in the 1920's aroused critical interest never previously here afforded a German play, nor ever extended again until the 1960's.

As all other forms of European drama were not imported by the New York managers until quite a while after they had spent their impetus in their homelands, so the German ones were not given an American hearing until long after their native premieres. Rather than risk the failure so frequently insured by an artistic innovation, the commercial producers chose to wait until they felt that audience demand or curiosity had made the time right for production. From a business point of view, the cautious waiters were as unsuccessful as the early adventurers, for the experimental German drama never received the public acclaim that insured a long run. However, it came to the New York stage at a time when serious criticism was far more receptive to foreign ventures than back in the days of imported naturalism.

The last serious German play to be given in New York, before the Broadway theatres succumbed to the wartime spirit and excluded Teutonic drama, was the work of the first and possibly the most controversial modern German experimental dramatist, Frank Wedekind. His *Frühlings Erwachen* had been produced in German at the Irving Place Theatre under the management of Gustav Amberg on March 22, 1912, and was very well received by both the German- and English-language press. The *Dramatic Mirror* said that "its adaptation into English is hardly probable, for its fate would be problematical."[1] The play was not seen in English until March 30, 1917, when an obscure organization that listed itself as the Medical Review of Reviews presented *The Awakening of Spring* as a "membership produc-

tion" at the 39th Street Theatre. Apparently, the sponsors of the play
had anticipated trouble. Wedekind's play had been written in 1891
but was not produced even in Germany until 1905 when Reinhardt
staged it brilliantly and it ran for 325 performances. The first American performance, twenty-six years later, encountered even greater difficulties than had the 1894 *Hannele.*

On the day that *The Awakening of Spring* was to open, New York
License Commissioner Bell saw a noontime rehearsal, called it "contrary to the public welfare,"[2] and forbade the performance. Only a
hastily obtained court injunction enabled the matinée to begin at four
o'clock. The reviews ranged from ecstatic artistic praise to absolute
moral condemnation. The play was closed after that one performance,
and on May 2, all productions of *The Awakening of Spring* were
forbidden in a decision by State Supreme Court Justice Erlanger.
Little is known of the performance save its legal troubles. Burns Mantle, who did not even mention the existence of the play in his 1916-17
yearbook, led the opposition in the morning papers in a tirade that
was more antiforeign in general, and anti-German in particular, than
it was anti-Wedekind. It was the typical response of the self-righteous
puritan who was then chief spokesman for the genteel tradition. He
said:

> We resent it . . . when we note that practically every vice report
> that is published, and every degenerate tendency or crime that is
> traced to its source, is found rooted in the minds and muck that
> are not native to this country . . . as propaganda they like it in
> Berlin. Its creation there would indicate that they need it in
> Berlin. We are quite content that they should keep it in Berlin.[3]

The Broadway audience and reviewers felt that immorality was foreign to American life, and drama concerning it was undesirable.
Those who preferred illusion to reality in their lives also expected it
on the stage. There was not another professional production of *The
Awakening of Spring* in New York until it was done off-Broadway in
1955, by which time it had become a pale museum piece.

Considering the nature of the New York theatrical scene of 1917,
the hostility toward Wedekind's play is understandable. *The Awakening of Spring* is a play with no semblance of unity in either theme or
form. Its treatment of the adolescent love relationship of Melchior and
Wendla, based on the ignorance imposed on them by a strait-laced
parental world, is naturalistic. Its attack on the school system, the
official bureaucracy, and the middle-class morality is one of the first
instances of the modern German drama of social satire whose chief
exponents were Frank Wedekind and Carl Sternheim. The scene in
which the school board, ostensibly reviewing the case of Moritz's

failed examinations, falls into a furious argument about whether a
window should be open or shut in the committee room is, for all its
effective albeit heavy-handed burlesque, out of phase with the rest of
the play. The final scene in the graveyard, wherein the shade of
Moritz, with his head under his arm, and a character known only as
The Man with the Mask contend with each other as the death force
and the life force for the spirit of Melchior, is usually regarded as the
major link between Strindberg and the German expressionists. The
joining hands of naturalism, social satire, and early expressionism in
The Awakening of Spring marks it as one of the early manifestations
of the mixture of styles within the same play that was to become such
an outstanding characteristic of modern world drama. Its chaotic
form, however, was jarring to Americans, who also found its naturalistic themes offensive, its satire inapplicable, and its protoexpressionism
confusing.

Even if *The Awakening of Spring* had not offended, anti-German
feeling began running so high in 1917 that acceptance would have
been almost impossible for any play. At this time, public schools were
under constant pressure to discontinue the teaching of German, and
both civic and religious organizations protested strenuously against
the performance of German music, operas, and plays. On April 15,
1917, only two weeks after the production of Wedekind's piece, the
New York Times ran an editorial condemning this attitude for its
naïve nationalism, but public opinion was already beyond recall. During the seasons of 1918-19 and 1919-20 there was not a single play
performed on Broadway which was admittedly of German origin,
though the music, setting, plot, and characters of quite a few of the
operettas given during those years had the suspicious ring of *Alt
Wien*. The little theatres had to curtail their schedules appreciably,
for they were hard hit by loss of manpower to the armed forces.
During those two seasons even the little theatres produced only one
play known to be from the German, Schnitzler's one-acter, *Last
Masks*, and this performance by the Provincetown players was not
until March 26, 1920.

Most of the violent anti-German demonstrations were against the
German-language theatres and operas. Two veterans' organizations,
the Navy Club and the Christian Corps, were reported by the *Times*
on March 16 and 17, 1919, to have been ready to use machine guns to
stop a performance at the Irving Place. On May 22, 1919, threats were
again received that soldiers' and sailors' groups would raid a negligible play, *Der Himmel Auf Erden,* but nothing came of it. When the
Star Opera Company wanted to sing in German at the Lexington
Theatre on October 15, 1919, the American Legion voiced strong

opposition and coerced Mayor Hylan to agree to a ban. The Star maintained that this action was outside the mayor's jurisdiction, asked for police protection, and opened. The veterans' groups charged the theatre, threw eggs, and smashed windows. A number of people were injured, and Hylan again pressed for a closing. The theatre's attorney, M. D. Steuer, filed for a temporary injunction against Hylan and obtained it on October 22. Two days later, the Star Company gave *Die Fledermaus,* always sure to fill the house, but attendance was poor and financial peril superseded political. When Justice Gingerich ruled that all performances must be stopped until peace was re-established, the Star, already beaten at the box office, acquiesced. In 1921, Wagnerian opera was still being sung in English even at the Metropolitan, while it was already being sung in its native language without incident in traditionally Germanophobic Paris.

After the war, the foreign-language houses of New York began to disappear. The German repertory houses in particular crumbled in the 1920's. The pressure exerted by anti-German organizations was not the chief factor in their fall, but it contributed significantly. More important was the erosion of the audience. The generation of '48-ers, that massive wave of German immigrants who had arrived in New York in the mid-nineteenth century, was dying. Their children became assimilated by American culture, and their grandchildren frequently knew no German.

When hostile feelings declined in the early twenties, German plays were again imported. In that decade New York audiences saw representative drama from a number of German theatrical movements: social satire, spectacle, warmed over naturalism and neoromanticism, and expressionism.

The modern German drama of social satire began in the 1890's, but its stage was not that of the theatre. It is only in recent years that Americans have been able to understand the milieu in which it was performed, for the spiritual child of Munich's Schwabing in 1900 lives today in the unwashed world of the Greenwich Village coffeehouse. Skits, songs, monologues, and improvisations were performed in the dingy cafés scattered throughout the neighborhood of the University of Munich. Truly creative humorists did not leave them until their commercial potential was realized and they became a tourist attraction. The *Überbrettl,* as it was called, was essentially a cabaret devoted to social and political criticism; it was here that men such as Frank Wedekind first sang and recited, accompanying their harsh voices by strumming amateurishly on a guitar. After World War I, Bertolt Brecht began in the same fashion, and the technique of the improvised song later became a central part of his dramaturgy and poetry. The *Überbrettl* remained on the Munich scene until Hitler squashed it. When its writers and performers emigrated, many to the United States, and tried to establish a political cabaret here, they found no audience for this peculiar form of satire.[4] Today it flourishes in London, New York, and Chicago, as it does on the Continent. Angry young comics, improvisers, and songsters have become a heavy industry, and commercialism is again in the process of turning their intelligent satire into popular burlesque. It was on the tiny stages of the cabarets and in the satiric review, *Simplizissimus*, first published in 1896 in Munich, that the playwrights of German social satire were first heard. They were developing their craft at the same time that the naturalists and neoromantics held the stage, but their influence and power were not felt until years later in the major playhouses.

Frank Wedekind (full name: Benjamin Franklin Wedekind) was born in 1864, the son of a '48-er who, though he had returned to Germany and later settled in Switzerland, remained a naturalized American.[5] Although the younger Wedekind was never in the United States, he liked to fancy himself an American citizen, and this country always represented for him a symbol of artistic as well as political freedom. His illusions were never smashed, despite the fact that at the time of his death in 1918, that one notorious performance of *The Awakening of Spring* and an earlier production of the noncontroversial *The Tenor* were his only plays ever performed in New York.

Wedekind's dramas, in their own chaotic way, attacked the hypocrisy and the moral cowardice of the last years of imperial Germany. His assault on the middle-class morality was, in fact, so excessive at times that he offended even his sympathizers. He often shocked for the sake of shock, and today many of his strident scenes seem woefully overwrought, even ludicrous. His dramatic episodes of a world out of focus presaged many of the techniques of expressionism, as did his impassioned diction. Also, it was Wedekind who began the genre of the tragedy of adolescence, which fascinated German playwrights compelled to study the psychopathology of youth's rebellion against the parental world. Even the Nazi propagandists, years later, leaned heavily on this theme, and though it was from the beginning usually presented in naturalistic terms, Wedekind's *Frühlings Erwachen* opened both realistic and fantastic possibilities.

Between the closing of *The Awakening of Spring* in 1917 and the off-Broadway performance of *Erdgeist* as *Earth Spirit* in 1950, the only professional production in New York of a play by Frank Wedekind came on May 11, 1925. This was Samuel A. Eliot, Jr.'s translation of *Erdgeist* known as *The Loves of Lulu*. The German play, written in 1894, was first produced in Leipzig in 1898; its first successful staging was Max Reinhardt's 1902 presentation in Berlin. It was *Erdgeist* and its sequel, *Die Büchse der Pandora (Pandora's Box)*, not granted a permit to be performed in Germany until 1919, that earned for Wedekind his notorious reputation: that of being nothing more than the prophet of a cult which maintained that all human action was the product of tyrannical sex drives, and that in the face of this pressure, man cannot have both happiness and dignity. The reputation was undeserved, for despite Wedekind's insistence on the power of glandular forces, this is certainly an oversimplification of his motives, and he seldom dealt with sex naturalistically.

Erdgeist is Wedekind's symbolic portrayal of human society, not as a rational organization but as a circus of wild beasts. The play's chief character, Lulu, is not a character at all. Wedekind said she was the personification of evil without volition—the natural evil of man. The dramatic action is introduced by a circus manager, training animals with a bullwhip while he recites his fervent verse-prologue to the play, which is Wedekind's personal view of the world, the theatre, and the human beast. The playwright frequently acted in his own plays; the prologue to *Erdgeist* was his favorite role.

Erdgeist, like most of Wedekind's plays, is tense and frenetic. Its characters all seem to border on chronic hysteria, and its scenes and dialogue are usually fragmentary. The total effect of the piece is chaos, anger, nervousness, rebellion, and unrest. Wedekind's study of an evil force, personified by Lulu, which through sexual compulsion attracts all men only to destroy them in a series of grotesque and violent scenes, is an overwrought dramatic frenzy. The continuity of the play is very hard to follow even in German, but the Eliot translation, which ran for sixteen performances, is incoherent and incomprehensible.

Edmund Wilson, in *The New Republic*, said that the performance was shoddy and slow. Everyone on the stage seemed to be in a stupor; it was apparent that neither the director nor the actors knew what it was all about, and the result was a bizarre charade that struck the audience as some sort of disjointed nightmare the result of which was humorous.[6] Stark Young reported in the *Times* that the audience guffawed throughout.[7] If *Erdgeist* had anything to say to even an intelligent American audience, this production failed on all counts. *Pandora's Box* is even more chaotic than *Erdgeist* and adds nothing to it. It has never been performed professionally in New York. This brace of plays is also the basis for Alban Berg's controversial opera, *Lulu*.

Despite the fact that much of Wedekind's work was intended only to shock and startle, his dramaturgy exerted definite influence on early expressionism, and "his experimentation in epic structure and the grotesque . . . looks forward to Brecht, Dürrenmatt, and the theatre of cruelty."[8] His function as one of the turn-of-the-century social satirists of Germany was significant only in that country itself, for the methods and the themes of the *Überbrettl* and *Simplizissimus* were long dead before their kindred forms were born in the cafés of the angry young rebels of the 1950's and 60's.

The other two major playwrights of the German movement of social satire were hardly represented on the New York stage. Not a single play by Carl Sternheim ever had a professional production on or off Broadway before the 1960's, and the few by Ludwig Thoma which were done were negligible. Sternheim's satire avoided the ponderous moralizing of Wedekind, although he also attacked the bourgeois morality. His characters were types, not people, and his diction was crisp and nonrealistic. His "hectic, staccato"[9] dialogue, which became known as the "telegram style," was a major contribution to the technique of expressionism. His subject matter, the banal society of unimaginative, callous materialists which he felt was doomed to extinction, became a favorite topic of the revolutionary German leftist playwrights of the twenties, even though Sternheim himself did not "credit the lower classes with superior moral standards; their one and only ambition [was] to obtain middle-class respectability."[10] Sternheim's *Die Hose* (1909) and *Der Snob* (1913) have been translated into English and published as *The Underpants* and *The Snob*, but long after his plays would have been pertinent on the American stage.

Ludwig Thoma was younger than Sternheim, and before he joined the staff of *Simplizissimus* had written many popular humorous essays under the pseudonym of Peter Schlemihl. Charles Recht translated Thoma's *Morale* and with the help of Sidney Howard prepared an acting version which the Actors' Theatre produced on November 30, 1925, four years after Thoma's death, as *Morals*. Probably the only reason it was finally given was because of the commercial success in New York of bordello farce; here was a ready-made success. Thoma's play was an attack on hypocrisy; the president of an antivice society is caught consorting with the enemy. It arrived in New York too late for anything other than commercial exploitation. George Jean Nathan said he used to like the play in German and still thought that there was fun and satire in the script that the present production missed, but that on the whole the piece had become stale. It should have been done years ago, before it was dated.[11] Joseph Wood Krutch agreed, but thought it was still funny despite the fact that it preached to the converted.[12] The *Times* also thought that the play was dated and said that what had once been a satire was now, particularly in the present playing, a farce.[13]

The plays of German social satire never came to the New York stage full force. While the Weimar Republic was in upheaval and Germany was threatened with numerous social revolutions, the United States was drenched with prosperity, optimism, and an illusory security. The stage of each country reflected the temper of its viewers. There was no time for cranks and rebels in the popular theatre of New York. The social problems of Germany were not pertinent here, and the plays were far too topical to sustain the interest of an American audience.

II

It would be misleading to indicate that the German experimental drama which appeared on the New York stage between 1918 and 1928 far outweighed the plays of other styles which were also imported. Foreign operettas and *Kitsch*, though far less frequent than before the war, were still played in abundance. The incidence of naturalism and neoromanticism declined but had a marked afterglow, particularly in the tragedies of adolescence. At the end of the decade New York audiences got their first look at the new German realism which flourished in the late twenties and early thirties, the *Zeitstück* and the *Neue Sachlichkeit*. And second in importance only to the representatives of the movement of expressionism were the spectacle plays of Reinhardt between 1923 and 1928.

The German operetta had never really disappeared from Broadway even during the war years; it was too salable a commodity. However, it was successfully hidden by producers who chose not to reveal the sources of the greatly Americanized musicals. By 1920 it was safe to admit to adaptation again, but habit had dictated that the books of these operettas should be more American than before the war. In May of 1921, the Shubert Brothers presented Oskar Straus's *Der Letzte Walzer* as *The Last Waltz* with a text that was suffused with all the Balkan intrigue and Franz Josef splendor that the cliché-prone adapters, Harold Atteridge and E. D. Dunn, could muster. The Viennese hero, however, was turned into an American adventurer abroad.

The Last Waltz was anything but that. During the 1921-22 season, Henry W. Savage (who was also responsible for the first production of Wagner's *Parsifal* in English) revived the version of *The Merry Widow* that he had produced in 1907-1908. The Shuberts resuscitated the 1909-10 adaptation of *The Chocolate Soldier,* and they also presented Willner and Reichert's *Das Dreimäderlhaus* with Franz Schubert's music, which became the hit of that and numerous later seasons as *Blossom Time*. It was also the Shubert Brothers who, in 1923, successfully produced *Caroline*, a musical based on an operetta by Hermann Haller and Eduard Rideamus. The settings and characters of *Caroline* were transplanted to the American Civil War, but the stamp of *Alt Wien* was unmistakable. The German operetta, albeit not *echt*, was finally made completely at home on Broadway when, in 1924, Sigmund Romberg set Wilhelm Meyer-Förster's romantic comedy, *Alt Heidelberg*, to music as *The Student Prince*, popular to this day. By 1926, adapted operettas were playing all along the New York theatre district. *Countess Maritza* had the same adapter, producer, and even director as *Naughty Riquette*, which had opened only five days before it. Here was clear indication of the mass-production techniques with which these commodities were turned out. During those seasons of the inflated play schedules, which were brought about by postwar prosperity and the construction of new theatres, producers turned once more to the romantic *Kitsch* farce in order to fill empty stages. A few ran, but in the main, they disappeared quickly from the playbill. The operetta had survived the war with ease; the farce had succumbed. The difference was the music. Without it, the triviality and absurdity of the texts were too painfully on display.

Some plays from the German naturalistic movement were given in New York in the 1920's, but it was already difficult to distinguish most of them from the melodrama associated with romanticism. What had seemed brutally real only twenty years before now appeared overwrought. Actually there was some interest in slice-of-life theatre during the decade despite the fact that it was already looked upon as slightly archaic. Yet the serious plays of European naturalism were even less successful in the 1920's than they had been before the war. Maxim Gorky's *The Lower Depths*, first given in Russia in 1902, was finally produced in English in New York by Arthur Hopkins in 1919. The play had been presented in the German-language theatre back in 1903. The dramas of German naturalism in particular were poorly received. This may be due in large part to the fact that those chosen for performance during the 1920's were particularly melodramatic, although melodrama is what commercial producers thought the audience wanted.

On November 15, 1920, William A. Brady produced Benjamin F. Glazer's translation of Karl Schönherr's *Der Weibsteufel* as *Thy Name Is Woman*. Schönherr, a minor dramatist at best, was given to romantic excesses even more than Sudermann, and Glazer's translation capitalized on every one of them. The play managed to run for 120 performances because it was exciting, but Alexander Woollcott's evaluation of it as a melodrama played with "the blacksmith touch"[14] was the critical consensus.

The farce about the teenager has been a popular Broadway staple for many years, but the serious treatment of the problems of the adolescent was a dramatic vein relatively unmined before the years following World War II. Consequently New York managers never imported many of the significant German plays on this theme which were written by the playwrights of the school of social satire, nor did they do justice to the tragedies of adolescence which came from the "new realism" movement of Germany in the late twenties and early thirties. Americans were then involved with their own social problems. It is indeed unfortunate that the dramas of the struggles of youth which were adapted for New York consumption were the weakest of the lot, the melodramas which were superficially naturalistic. Conroy and Meltzer revived Max Halbe's *Youth* on October 26, 1920, and presented it at the little Greenwich Village Theatre under the direction of Emanuel Reicher. Its run equaled that of the 1910-11 season's Broadway production: seven performances. Ludwig Lewisohn, writing in *The Nation,* found it hard to believe that Reicher was responsible for the performance. Everything was wrong but the sets and the lights. The acting was sentimental; the characters were presented in black and white only; the histrionics were excessive. Lewisohn, still fond of the play, said the fault was not Halbe's but the production's. He maintained that the boy and girl had been turned into a "flapper and a halfback."[15] The play invites the kind of butchery that it received, but Lewisohn's anger is quite justifiable. The *Times* passed *Youth* off as an "awkward translation [with an] incompetent performance."[16]

What brief might be held for the performance of the German naturalistic tragedy of adolescence in New York was destroyed on October 10, 1921, when Arnold Daly presented *The Children's Tragedy* at the Greenwich Village Theatre. Karl Schönherr's German play was a faintly naturalistic melodrama. The English version, again by Benjamin F. Glazer, was befogged by an inept search for an idiom comparable to Schönherr's untranslatable Tyrolean dialect for which he had an uncanny ear.[17] The plot concerns the interaction of two brothers and a sister who discover that their mother has a lover. The situation makes the three teenagers turn on each other in their misery. The dialogue is sharp, and the simplicity of the play heightens the plight of the children. The drama is, however, melodramatically resolved by violence and death. The younger brother shoots the lover, then dies of a fever; the sister is assaulted and hardly seems to mind, so resigned has she become to the horror of life; the older brother runs off in despair. What might have been a substantial play in more disciplined hands became an unrelieved fright in Schönherr's. What value there was in *Kindertragödie* was destroyed by Glazer's transla- tion and the production. Alexander Woollcott reported in the *Times* that "a simple, moving and genuinely dramatic play submitted in Greenwich Village to the most destructive . . . the most ill-advised and calamitous performance . . . in many and many a day."[18] The following Sunday, Woollcott amplified. Apparently the management had cast three adults in the major roles. Cramming them into knicker- bockers and forcing them to behave like children yielded results that were ludicrous rather than tragic. It was perfectly obvious to the entire house that even the twelve-year-old boy was being played by an actor well into his thirties. The fiasco ended after eight perform- ances.

If it was too late for Hauptmann before the war even to a respon- sive audience, it was certainly a great risk for Arthur Hopkins to produce *Rose Bernd* on September 26, 1922. The translation was by Ludwig Lewisohn, who had damned so many inept renditions of Ger- man plays by others. He received the same treatment from his fellow critics. *Theatre* called the play dull, heavy, and dated, and it demol- ished the actors, particularly Ethel Barrymore in the title role.[19] Woollcott, albeit he was a man given to easy superlatives, called it "the finest performance she has ever given,"[20] but attacked the trans- lation for the false ring of the homemade dialect that Lewisohn em- ployed to give the illusion of Silesian.[21] Stark Young reviewed it for *The New Republic* at the same time that he gave his comments on the opening of *R.U.R.* It was clear that serious critics were far more interested in the new experiments than in the warmed-over plays of the 1890's. Young felt that the self-conscious production defeated Hauptmann's naturalistic intentions.[22] There were even reviews such as Gilbert Seldes' in *The Dial* which not only disapproved of the acting and the translation but even questioned the importance of Hauptmann.[23] The question was valid if Hauptmann was being re- garded as a contemporary rather than as a writer of what had already become museum pieces. *Rose Bernd,* the story of a poor but noble girl exploited by her social superiors must, in 1922, have seemed woefully sentimental. In an article by Lewisohn himself in the *Times,* he ascribed the failure of *Rose Bernd* to miscasting, bad direction, and vile acting.[24] He was unquestionably right, for such mishandling hap- pened all too often on Broadway and still does. Art and commerce come together to present a serious play. Both sides must give in at least in part to the other, and the result is compromise, the failure to satisfy the requirements of either camp. But Lewisohn's translation was most assuredly another contribution to the inadequacies of *Rose Bernd*. The very flaws against which he used to declaim were painfully apparent in his text. For example, Lewisohn lost idiom, dialect, and rustic character by translating *"Mir hoan a Hihnla zu pflicka!"* as "We've got a little private quarrel," when a more satisfying rendition of "We got a chicken to pluck" would have been "We got a bone to pick."

Apparently the lesson of *Rose Bernd* made little impression, for a number of other tired German plays of naturalism found producers in the twenties. The performances were invariably romantic interpretations, and the plays were mounted for their sentimental values. On February 15, 1924, Eva Le Gallienne revived *The Assumption of Hannele* in Meltzer's inadequate translation. George Jean Nathan's comment summed up the problem: "Miss Le Gallienne's idea of the play, unfortunately, seems to be somewhat at variance with the author's."[25] It was a sentimentalized Sunday school production. John Corbin observed that the translation, in its clumsy switching back and forth between stilted diction and artificial colloquialism, played right into the trap of Miss Le Gallienne's "high tragedy" style.[26] *The Assumption of Hannele* closed after three performances. The only good that came of it was the vindication of the notorious 1894 production. An article in the *Times* revealed that all those who called the play blasphemous and were responsible for its closing, including Mayor Gilroy, had never read or seen the play. The whole anti-Hauptmann crusade of 1894, it turned out later, was based on hearsay.[27]

The Shuberts revived Beyerlein's *Taps*, which had already been archaic in 1904, on April 14, 1925. The reviews were kind to the production because it was so well played, but they damned the piece itself. Nathan said that *Taps* seemed good years ago only because most military plays are so bad, and that it was a skilfully constructed melodrama which, on second look, had little substance.[28] Stark Young felt that the play was meaningless here because the military caste system was a peculiarly German phenomenon. He added that the play was "unconvincing . . . old-fashioned," but well-acted and directed for what it was.[29] *Taps* lasted for thirty-two performances, eight more than the following season's revival, the last, of Sudermann's *Magda* which could not hide its age despite a revised translation. It had become clear by the mid-twenties that German naturalism, dated even in its native country, was now not only outmoded but undistinguishable from the neoromantic drama.

Interest in the plays of the neoromantic movement was minimal in the 1920's. The only works in this vein that achieved any degree of acceptance were by the Hungarian Ferenc Molnár. It was often their sentiment rather than their wit which appealed, and their sometimes lengthy runs could usually be ascribed to sophisticated staging and to the drawing power of Alfred Lunt and Lynn Fontanne who starred in most of them. By 1929, there was even a market for imitation Molnár, and the Theatre Guild produced *Caprice*, translated by Philip Moeller from a comedy of Sil-Vara (pseudonym of a middle-European playwright, Geza Silberer, who wrote in German). It was financially successful; of course, the Lunts starred. However, the desire for the charm of Vienna which some audiences cultivated came not from any real rapport with its tradition but from an appreciation of its more genteel superficialities. Consequently, there was still no demand for Schnitzler on the New York stage, but pale imitations, conspicuously bereft of sex, by Americans who set their plays in a fictitious Vienna, were acceptable. Such comedies as Channing Pollock's *The Enemy*, which played over two hundred performances in 1925-26, were typical of this *Ersatz-Wien*.

By the mid-twenties repertories of classics were also fading. The old stars who played them were aging, and their style of acting was outmoded. By 1922, even Sothern and Marlowe had lost much of their drawing power. The Guild, interested in the new German staging techniques, wanted to combine new craft with a classic, and to begin their 1928-29 season, they imported Friedrich Holl from the *Volksbühne* in Berlin to direct a production of *Faust*. With good German intellectual techniques of the twenties, Holl, aiming for the meaning rather than the lyric pathos of the piece, pruned all the operatic elements from the play in his interpretation.[30] It ran for forty-eight performances, kept alive by Guild members who had season subscriptions, but audiences were unhappy with the cerebral *Faust*. They did not want Goethe; they wanted musicless Gounod.

Even the little theatres which had stuck doggedly to mounting the one-acters of Schnitzler in their early years gave up, and there were only a few pieces of neoromanticism that found their way to Broadway in the twenties. The best of them was probably Rudolph Lothar's urbane comedy, *Der Werwolf*, in Gladys Unger's adaptation, *The Werewolf*, as misleading a title as was ever given a play. Most reviewers loathed it, and only the titillation-prone segment of New York's playgoers kept it running for 112 performances in the fall of 1924. George Jean Nathan berated the reviewers for hating *The Werewolf*, saying that they merely reflected the attitudes of a puritanical audience toward a play which dealt both humorously and frankly with adultery, a theme which met with the approval of the genteel

only when presented in a moral tone. "To get by the American reviewer," Nathan said, "a sex farce or comedy must be merely a
teaser."[31] He felt that the translation was honest and adroit but that
the direction was awkward and that *The Werewolf* was played with
"all the finish and smooth movement of a brewery wagon." Stark
Young agreed in the *Times*[32] except that he also thought that Miss
Unger's translation suffered from the same rigidity as the Archer versions of Ibsen.[33]

On December 15, 1924, *The Mongrel* opened at the Longacre
Theatre and limped on for thirty-two performances. The adaptation
was by Elmer Rice from Frances C. Fay's translation of a play by
Hermann Bahr. The German text vacillates between naturalistic
melodrama and *Volksstück* comedy, and in this mismarriage lies the
flaw of the original play in which Bahr wanted to try his hand at
naturalism but could not refrain from injecting the humor of Austria.
The adaptation understandably missed the comedy because its particularly rural and provincial qualities prohibited transplanting. Thus
concentrating on the melodramatic plot, it emphasized the basic shallowness of the play. Bahr's play first appeared in Europe in 1914. By
1924, it seemed "frankly insignificant" to Joseph Wood Krutch, who
added that "although the play . . . has been badly mangled [in adap-
tation], it is hardly worth while to protest."[34] Stark Young also found
it dated and given life only by the performance of Rudolph Schildkraut. Young maintained that the play needed rapport among the
actors and an intimate, realistic comic touch, all of which were
absent. It "needed a German company, perhaps," he said, lamenting
that the actors were not all Schildkrauts.[35]

The last significant play from the neoromantic movement which
was given during the decade was Arthur Schnitzler's *Der Ruf des
Lebens* in Dorothy Donnelly's adaptation, *The Call of Life*. It was
produced by the Actors' Theatre on October 9, 1925, and starring Eva
Le Gallienne, who apparently languished over every slightest possibility the script offered for sentimentalism. Actually, *Der Ruf des Lebens*
was one of Schnitzler's early plays and is full of youthful romantic
excesses fused with the discussion of social problems that in their
technique show a marked kinship with the plays of Ibsen. Doctors of
medicine who write plays, such as Chekhov and Schnitzler, seem
unable to refrain from injecting the character of the physician-
raissoneur into their pieces, and *The Call of Life* suffers from the
ponderous preaching of such a doctor. Schnitzler's play seemed to be
inspired by his dissatisfaction with the structure of Austrian society
and his fascination and personal involvement with the new developments in the fields of psychology and psychiatry. The play concerns

people so deeply involved with themselves that they become incapable of communicating with each other. Each of the characters is trapped between his own frustrated desires and the outworn traditions of his society that surround and bind him. Life requires the ability of the individual to cope with reality, but conflicting loyalties and uncontrollable feelings lead us to the escape found in illusion. Consequently, when we hear the "call of life," we are able to answer only in self-destructive ways. The play is about the human being's right to get something out of life in the face of all the public mores and private compulsions that hinder him. The trouble with *The Call of Life* is that although its first act is a superb piece of craftsmanship in its characterization and realistic dialogue, it then falls apart into disjointed pieces of sentimental melodrama which are both "trite and obvious."[36] Public opposition to Schnitzler was aroused, but only briefly and mildly, by the mercy-killing of the tyrannical old father who uses his illness as a weapon. That this act is both condoned and unpunished within the play offended an audience which did not see that Schnitzler was contrasting this death with numerous silly and useless ones in *The Call of Life*.

Joseph Wood Krutch said that "the Schnitzler who wrote *The Call of Life* has not yet arrived at the conviction, so plainly expressed in later plays, that existence is a game played against an antagonist who always wins and whose name is Boredom."[37] Krutch felt that the play betrayed the author's youth. There is no doubt that the play is atypical of the main body of Schnitzler's work. Both *The New Republic* and the *Times* agreed that the play went to pieces after the first act,[38] with Stark Young further asserting that the production emphasized the mawkishness of the last act. The script itself has this weakness, but playing it for its late pathos rather than its early realism unquestionably added to the unsuccessful performance.

The critics and playgoers of the 1920's found little sympathy for the comedy of the neoromantic movement and even less for its sentimental plays, which were admittedly inferior. Few of them were done in New York and none was successful.

III

The most profound impression made on American viewers and critics by any German neoromantic was that of Max Reinhardt, whose spectacle plays were the end product of a revolution in European stagecraft. Strindberg, in his introduction to *Miss Julie*, had attacked the outmoded methods of scenic design and stage lighting which the fourth-wall cult of the nineteenth-century realists had imposed upon the theatre. It was in the years between 1895 and 1905 that the drawings and essays of Adolphe Appia of Switzerland and Gordon Craig of England began to break the strictures of the older conventions. Their theories were first put into successful practice in Berlin by Reinhardt. Appia, whose interests at first lay in the field of opera, particularly Wagner, set forth the notion that the mounting of a play was a pictorial as well as a dramatic event; to conform to the needs of the play, the stage picture must be dynamic rather than static. The scene and light must move with the progression of the play. This he felt was to be achieved by a totality of effect in which music, motion, word, costume, and light were coordinated into a fusion that left a single dramatic impression. Appia maintained that such a unified work of art would strengthen the action of the drama, but all that was not actual play had to be integrated, for no single aspect of the production could draw attention to itself. Appia's chief inadequacy stemmed from the fact that he was not of the theatre and could not envision the technical problems that his theories presented. For Appia to succeed, he would have needed the motion picture. Gordon Craig, from a theatrical family, knew the limitations of the stage and added a simplicity of design to Appia's theories, although most of his sketches called for settings larger than any stage could hold. Nevertheless, the simplicity that he proposed but could not execute, based on the belief that suggestion could create physical reality in the imagination of the audience, became the groundwork for a practical realization of stagecraft that freed the drama from the physical chains of Sardoodledom, just as Ibsen, Strindberg, Chekhov, and Shaw had freed it from the literary chains. The mechanical advances of the German theatres made them the logical stages for the presentation of the play that was to be a *Gesamtkunstwerk*, a total work of art. To achieve it, there had to be a central intelligence and sensibility that coordinated all the elements of production, the *Regisseur*.

Max Reinhardt was the most energetic and unquestionably the most gifted of the *Regisseurs*. Reinhardt turned theatres into cathedrals and cathedrals into theatres. He staged the Hofmannsthal version of *Everyman* in the main church of Salzburg, *Faust* in the Imperial Riding School of Austria, *The Merchant of Venice* across a Venetian canal, *A Midsummer Night's Dream* outdoors in Berkeley, California, and in the Hollywood Bowl, and Mozart operas in the *Redoutensaal*, the baroque ballroom of Maria Theresa's palace in Vienna where they are occasionally performed to this day. He also managed theatres in Berlin and Vienna which were devoted to light comedy. Reinhardt varied his theatres and his staging techniques according to the particular needs of the play he was directing. It is incorrect to think of him as the creator of only spectacles, the plays for which he was best known in the United States, for Reinhardt's repertory which toured the world also included work by Schiller, Shaw, Grillparzer, O'Neill, Kleist, Euripides, Goldoni, and Tolstoy. "Between 1905 and 1930, Reinhardt personally directed 136 plays for a total of 8,393 performances. Of this total, 2,531, or almost a third, were of plays by Shakespeare."[39]

The reception that Reinhardt's production of *Sumurun* had received in New York in 1912 was uninhibitedly enthusiastic. In 1924 he returned to Broadway with his most famous spectacle, *The Miracle*. Even the jingoistic Mantle begrudgingly admitted that "for some weeks thereafter there was not much else talked about in theatre circles."[40] It is unfortunate that Reinhardt's reputation in this country rests principally on *The Miracle* which, for all its *Gesamtkunstwerk* splendor, is a naïve romance which obscured from many Americans the fact that Max Reinhardt had also directed some of the greatest dramas in the history of literature.

The advance publicity received by *The Miracle* insured its commercial popularity, but whether or not the run could recoup the astronomical cost of production in New York was questionable.[41] Reinhardt brought all of his intricate mechanical equipment, scenery, and costumes from Germany along with most of the incredibly long cast. His New York producers, Ray Comstock and Morris Gest, engaged one of the city's biggest theatres, the Century, and its interior was almost completely rebuilt to accommodate the Reinhardt apparatus and settings. When the work was completed, the Century had been transformed into a Gothic cathedral. The opening performance of *The Miracle* in January of 1924 was attended as if it were the social event of the New York season. Even the *Times* felt called upon in its review of the following day to list numerous members of visiting nobility and New York "society" who had been there along with many noted artists of the theatre, among them Luigi Pirandello.[42]

Like *Sumurun*, *The Miracle* had no dialogue. It was billed as a "legend in eight scenes" which Reinhardt had conceived from a book by Karl Vollmöller, *Das Mirakel*. The story is of a young novice who doubts her suitability for holy orders and flees from her obligations to the church. During her absence, a statue of the Madonna comes to life and performs the girl's duties. After a series of experiences in the outside world, the novice returns to the church, contrite and prepared to ask for forgiveness. She finds that her absence has gone unnoticed, and the miracle of the Madonna is revealed to her as she returns to the cloth, strengthened in her faith and in the knowledge that her calling is a true one. It took genius to transform this silly little medieval *exemplum* into a moving play. Reinhardt did it with his beautiful integration of setting, lighting, movement of both groups and individuals, costumes, music, and pacing. His sense of mood and scene and emotion expressed without words, and his drawing of the audience into the aura of the cathedral by playing much of the pageantry in the aisles and compelling the viewers to feel more like communicants than customers, yielded that balance of visual, tonal, and dramatic elements which comprised the *Gesamtkunstwerk*. The critical acclaim accorded *The Miracle* was almost embarrassingly lavish; the play was such an eyeful that most, though not all, reviewers chose to dismiss the inherent hokum of the drama and concentrate upon the wizardry of Reinhardt.

George Jean Nathan said of the play that "the theatre that we have known becomes lilliputian before such a phenomenon. The church itself becomes puny."[43] In the same review he expressed self-hatred for sounding like a publicity agent by his use of seemingly indiscriminate superlatives, but although he disliked raving about any play he found himself unable to avoid it. Arthur Hornblow gave the most unqualified praise of all: "The finest thing ever seen in this country,"[44] and Mark Van Doren was almost as enthusiastic.[45] The only objections, and those qualified, were by Stark Young and Ludwig Lewisohn, neither of them ever fond of romantic drama. Young thought *The Miracle* a great spectacle that, in its overwhelming visual effects, makes one forget for the moment that there is really not much behind this "long exercise of skill, energy and money."[46] Lewisohn saw it as "the most astonishing and astonishingly beautiful thing in the entire art of the theater [despite the fact that it is pure romanticism and pure] flight from reality into an easier world of accident and wonder."[47] He praised the craft of Reinhardt as both artist and theatrical manager in a later article, but still felt that the play itself was a "trivial fairy tale [about] the moment of profoundest ignorance and superstition in the history of the West."[48] He added, "I turn from such fables . . . to things that matter."

That *The Miracle* is a philosophical triviality is undeniable, but in this particular *Inszenierung*, Reinhardt was seeking an emotional, not an intellectual response. Articles about *The Miracle* appeared in almost every major magazine throughout the United States for the remainder of the season. Even *Scientific American* and *Architectural Record,* in their April, 1924, issues had extensive pictures, diagrams, and discussion of the complicated technical aspects of the production. *The Miracle* ran through the remainder of the 1923-24 season and well into the next one. For all of its expenses, it was the most lucrative show ever housed at the Century until that time. It probably could have played for much longer had the engagement not been curtailed so that the company could meet previous commitments, among them a long booking in Chicago. After the success of *The Miracle,* Reinhardt resolved to return to the United States with a complete repertory.[49]

Reinhardt arrived in New York in the fall of 1927 "with a shipload of actors and tons of scenery direct from four or five of the principal German theatres."[50] The ballyhoo that greeted him in the press, the popular magazines, and the theatrical trade journals was indescribable. Although Burns Mantle's anti-European jibes were seldom to be taken seriously, he was not exaggerating when he said that "from the billing you gained the impression that whenever Mr. Reinhardt leaves Germany and takes his actors with him the theatre either goes completely into mourning or dolefully pegs along pending his return."[51] Reinhardt again took over the Century Theatre, and he outfitted the stage with all of his own equipment, including his own patented circular platform stage, an improvement on the old revolvers, which through clever scenic design compensated for the amount of floor space usually lost by the use of a turntable.

The Reinhardt repertory was international and carefully selected to show off every one of the master's staging effects. It was further a playbill consisting mostly of plays familiar enough or so emphatically spectacular that there was no problem created by language barriers in this day before the installation of earphones and simultaneous translation. The Reinhardt company played in German, but this did not deter New York audiences from filling the Century. The opening selection, given for twenty-three performances beginning November 17, 1927, was the famous mounting of *A Midsummer Night's Dream,* complete with the Mendelssohn score. There followed productions of Tolstoy's *Redemption* (more picturesquely titled *Der Lebende Leichnam—The Living Corpse—*in German), Goldoni's *Servant of Two Masters* (as *Diener Zweier Herren*), and Büchner's *Dantons Tod,* the last in an enormous *Inszenierung* which accepted all the invitations for excessive pageantry tendered by the script. There were also some lesser plays to round out the bill.

But the most spectacular of the Reinhardt importations was Hugo von Hofmannsthal's version of *Everyman,* which opened on December 7, 1927, as *Jedermann.* The resemblance to the medieval play is minimal, for the Hofmannsthal-Reinhardt *Everyman* is not every man. He is a wealthy burgher trying, at the last, to cajole his way into heaven. Many members of the cast were internationally known actors,[52] and some of them were later to emigrate to the United States after the rise of Hitler and become involved in the early forties with an organiza-

tion known as Theatre Friendship House, which revived this version
of *Jedermann* in May, 1941. At that time Brooks Atkinson, reviewing
for the *Times* and reminiscing about the 1927 production, pinpointed
the excesses of the play. "Taken out of its period, *Everyman* seems to
modern ears uncomfortably like an immorality play. . . . Everyman
manages to have a lot of cake and eat it too. He is rich and sinful; he
. . . holds iniquitous wassail with his mistress and revellers. Although
an eleventh hour conversion gets him into heaven with enviable alacrity, it takes a keener eye than this theatregoer has to detect any
improvement in his moral character."[53] But Mr. Atkinson did recall
that the Reinhardt production of 1927 was "miraculous," particularly
the elaborate opening banquet scene and the cannonading Voice of
the Lord that disrupts it. *Jedermann*, which Hofmannsthal had written to be the first production of Reinhardt's Salzburg Festival, was
originally presented in the cathedral plaza and on the church steps in
the Alpine city. With the mountains nearby and the ornate splendor
of baroque architecture surrounding the spectacle, it was unquestionably a magic ritual to behold, but when seen within the confines of a
theatre, it exhibited that excess and empty theatricality which more
and more began to swamp the play itself in Reinhardt's work. *Jedermann*, as play, is untenable as a modern work and is a corruption
when passed off as a medieval one. Yet its visual and tonal magic
were undeniable, and it tempted the imagination of a number of
Reinhardt's imitators. An English translation was made of the Hofmannsthal text by Sir John Martin Harvey which was played in Strat-
ford-on-Avon, in London, and in Hollywood (1936) as *Via Crucis*.

It was in Hollywood that Reinhardt hoped to establish a theatre.
He dreamed of a new cultural center in the newest area of American
expansion. Max Reinhardt never achieved his dream of an American
Salzburg, for neither financial backers nor audiences were enthusiastic in their support. California, even more than New York, was hostile
to any art form that was not primarily executed for profit. Despite
many spectacles that he staged in the vicinity of Hollywood, both
outdoors and in, Reinhardt found no acceptance. Even in San Francisco, by all standards the most enticing city in the West for a cultural venture, he was only mildly received. Reinhardt's greatest
success in California came from a venture, the feasibility of which he
doubted strenuously. He made a motion-picture version of *A Midsummer Night's Dream* with the most improbable Shakespearean cast ever
assembled (e.g., James Cagney as Bottom; Dick Powell as Lysander;
Mickey Rooney as Puck; Joe E. Brown as Flute). The purists cringed,
but this had never bothered Max Reinhardt before, and the film was
a huge success commercially, and many responsible critics added that

the achievement was also an artistic one. Reinhardt elicited an easy naturalness from his essentially non-Shakespearean performers that he felt he could not get from stage actors of Shakespeare whose style was too broad for the close-up camera.

The motion picture as an art form held little appeal for Reinhardt. He disliked its lack of contact with a live audience, its blatant commercial orientation, and its overweaning emphasis on "prettiness." Reinhardt generally disliked handsome performers. He felt that they tended to exhibit rather than act. Fritz Kortner, the eminent German actor, director, and writer, began his career by seeking a position with Reinhardt. All of his associates had thought that Kortner had considerable talent for acting, but that he was far too ugly to get an engagement. So well known was Reinhardt's predilection for homely actors that it gave Kortner his well-founded hopes.

Most important of all, Reinhardt found it impossible to work under the pressures of New York or Hollywood. He wanted time, for he worked with exacting attention to detail, and the rehearsal rules of Broadway and the financial pressure of the movies both denied him this.

The spiraling costs of stage production ever since the 1930's have all but prohibited managers from mounting plays in the tradition of Max Reinhardt even if there were a demand for them. Lavish musical comedies today must run for well over a year in order to recover their original investment. The expense of huge spectacle can be incurred only by those with the prospect of a mass audience. And so, the theatre that Reinhardt envisioned is today the province of the very motion pictures he held suspect. The cast of thousands that thunders across the cinemascopic wilderness is creating a spectacle that for all its grossness and tastelessness is the latter-day Reinhardt. Even his son, Wolfgang, is now involved in the production of these films. Were Max Reinhardt alive and his aesthetics still the same, he would probably now be working in the movies himself. The technique of Reinhardt on the stage was curtailed and supplanted by the film.

It is unfortunate that Max Reinhardt fell victim to Germanic excessive behavior even as did the expressionists, for whom he had little regard. As the years of his creativity progressed, he became more enamored of stage as stage than as a home for the drama. Bentley referred to Reinhardt's productions, particularly his Shakespeare, as suffering from elephantiasis. Furthermore, the *Inszenierung* became better and better than the plays for which it was employed. It was this progression toward empty theatricalism and the passing of the spectacle drama into the films that so harmed the reputation of the man who was a myth in his own lifetime. Yet it is too easy to forget that there was a Reinhardt who had nothing at all to do with spectacles, but who was almost unknown in the United States.

IV

In the twenty-five years after the emergence of naturalism there was what for Germany can be considered a period of comparative social and political stability. However, the years immediately preceding and during World War I led to the complete dissolution of the fabric of the country in almost every way. The Weimar Republic which rose from the revolution of 1918 was ideologically opposed to the imperial Germany of the past. Yet the public was so deeply rooted in its old notions of national destiny that it was unable to accept even the incipient stages of democracy, and the Republic, externally democratic but in essence still substantially authoritarian, was ripe for inroads from both the extreme right and left. It was the social panacea of the left that commanded an early following after the war, particularly in southern Germany; but before the twenties had spent themselves, the philosophy of destiny and force had again captivated the *Kleinbürger* with its dream of Wagnerian grandeur, and the portals were held uncomfortably wide for fascism. It was during those years of impending and actual war, revolution, futile political reform, and social instability that the movement known as expressionism flourished. Its life span is usually placed between 1910 and 1925. The revolutionary theatre of Germany lost its impetus after the democratic parliamentary government was established. It was then that the conservatives took over the nation, but only with the help of the ultra-right. In this coalition lay the germ of the destruction of the Weimar Republic and the rise of Hitler.

Typical and symbolic of the mood of the entire movement of expressionism is Munch's painting, "The Cry," a grotesque picture of a terror-stricken man who seems to be screaming from his very depths as he almost charges face-front right out of the painting and into the arms of the viewer. A few years after the execution of the picture, Hermann Bahr was to say that the chief characteristic of expressionism was the shriek.[54]

Expressionism has always posed a problem of definition, for the term is a single-bed blanket trying to cover a double bed. Description is far easier and more sound, for to state that expressionism is a highly emotional and subjective presentation of the inner man in objective art form is a dangerous oversimplification, vague because the limits of the form are themselves nebulously defined. Expressionism is not nearly so impossible a concept to deal with concretely if we do not expect rigid rules and limitations within the genre and if we avoid the fallacy that it is an isolated manifestation of Germany in the years between 1910 and 1925. All the intensity and passion of expressing what goes on inside one man's heart and head by viewing the external world through his subjectively distorted vision rather than that of the detached observer goes back as far as the roots of the interior monologue in fiction. Expressionism can be traced to works in the field of drama alone which are as old and as varied as the frantically visionary speeches of Cassandra in *Agamemnon*, the Elizabethan soliloquy, the hallucinations of Macbeth and Richard III, the passionate speeches of *Sturm und Drang* heroes, the *Walpurgisnacht* sequence of *Faust*, and the episodic violence of Büchner's *Woyzeck*, all attempts to give objective reality on the stage, not to what the disinterested onlooker sees but to what the involved protagonist experiences internally. The expressionists of the theatre attempted to do for drama largely what Joyce and Kafka did for fiction.

The direct forerunner of expressionism in modern drama was August Strindberg, particularly in *A Dream Play*, *To Damascus*, and *The Ghost Sonata*. In these plays, Strindberg sought to reproduce the inexorable logic of a dream to the dreamer. Further transitional styles can be seen in the frenzied scenes as well as in the use of nameless symbolic characters in the work of Frank Wedekind and in the "telegram style" of dialogue used by Carl Sternheim. It is clear that although the German expressionistic technique in drama reflected the chaos and upheaval of the war and the revolution, and that it underwent enormous changes during those years, it was not a completely new departure in dramatic portrayal of the subjective, by whatever name we call it.

The harsh use of colors, non-representational forms, and distorted perspectives of expressionist painting (Kokoschka, Klee, Kandinsky), the jagged lines and pain-wracked figures of expressionist sculpting (Barlach), and the impassioned, apocalyptic, and Whitmanesque texture of early expressionist lyric poetry (Heym, Stadler, Werfel) were all carried over into the theatrical form that sprang from the movement. The object of the young revolutionaries in dramatic structure was to depart from the play that sought truth in a return to the observation of nature. The expressionists hoped to free themselves from nature and return to a concept of art that concentrated on the artist's vision rather than on objective reality.[55] The action of an expressionist play usually unfolds through a series of scenes denoting stages of "development of the central character toward a spiritual goal,"[56] known as *Stationen*, a term clearly alluding to the Stations of the Cross. This central figure can usually, but not always, be identi-

fied with the author, and all the secondary figures can be viewed as
projections of the protagonist's inner struggle. The audience sees the
distorted world through the eyes of the distraught central character,
and it shares his nightmares, his hallucinations, and his awareness of
reality in terms of symbol rather than fact. In general, the expressionistic playwright considers inner experience more revealing than external life. He chooses for himself the difficult task of giving that
experience objective representation.

The expressionistic movement emphasized the importance of spirit
over matter. It saw man himself as a driving force in human destiny
and not merely as the victim of an imposed environment. Feeling that
man makes his own world, the expressionists consequently reacted
violently against naturalism and its view of causality. Nor could they
accept neoromanticism and its refusal to face the chaos of contemporary life while it dwelled on a day gone by. Consequently the expressionists usually attacked the bourgeois morality and the society that
fed it. They are, however, not to be confused with the politically
oriented playwrights of the 1930's, for whatever leftist tendencies may
be discerned in expressionistic drama sprang from the rebellious ethic
of middle-class intellectuals and visionaries, themselves an object of
attack by the proletarian leftists of the thirties. Politics itself was
always secondary to the quest for an ethic in the work of the expressionists.

Expressionism was a strikingly new technique; the expressionist,
however, had nothing strikingly new to say. It is consequently the
form more than the content of this genre which is distinctive. The
expressionists were not the first dramatists to realize the limitations of
the stage (particularly that of the theatre of verisimilitude) in showing
an audience the enormous difference between what people say and do
and what they think and feel. Since the expressionists believed that
the internal point of view reflected the real man, any playwright who
strikes beneath the surface of action and word and probes the un-
spoken point of view may be construed as an expressionist, whether
he employs the interior monologue technique of O'Neill in *Strange
Interlude* or the "certain private conversations," often with the self,
both past and present, of Miller's *Death of a Salesman*. Clearly,
neither of these plays has much in common with the episodic, shrieking dramas of post-World War I Germany. They serve to indicate that
later playwrights found some of the techniques of expressionism useful, and that after the German movement expired, single aspects of it
became dramatic devices used within the framework of less radical
forms. Expressionism as a self-contained form was dead after 1925, but

its influence is felt to this day in its methods which have spilled over onto the common ground of the modern drama.

During the years that expressionism flourished in Germany, each of the plays falling into the category had most or all of the following characteristics: (1) allusive, suggestive, and symbolic settings that indicate the *response* of the protagonist to reality rather than the *stimuli* that evoke it; (2) the rapid succession of highly emotional scenes, or *Stationen,* and the rejection of conventional causal developments, transitions, and details of plot, thus yielding an unrelieved, episodic, and fragmentary structure which the expressionist believes is a more accurate depiction of human experience than a logically constructed pattern; (3) action that suggests rather than depicts, and which imposes on the viewer a more universal frame of reference than would a limited realistic situation; (4) reduction of characters to types and the subordination of all minor figures in order to enhance the focus on the internal struggle of the protagonist which is given objectivity only insofar as it is an externalization of his state of mind; (5) attack on the middle-class morality, mechanization, materialism, and militarism which in no way tries to hide its didacticism; (6) use of ecstatic, high-voltage, elevated, and poetic staccato diction which contributes largely to the mood, pace, and harsh rhythm of the play, and which also serves to point up the essential meaninglessness of human conversation (a theme later to be vital in the Theatre of the Absurd, in many ways an inheritor of expressionism) and the general automatic responses of the external man to experience; and (7) emphasis on problems of the spirit (which supersede those of matter) and insistence on man as a driving force capable of revolution, positive action, and redemption on earth (rather than as a victim of an environmental tyranny which is doomed to the process of disintegration that modern man and contemporary society accept as inevitable and refuse to challenge).[57]

Walter Hasenclever's *Der Sohn* (1914) became the watchword of the young generation despite the fact that much of it was realistic and even *Sturm-und-Drang*-ish (although it should be noted that expressionism was a more romantic movement than expressionists cared to admit). The theme of the play, the struggle between the generations in the middle-class home, is a common one today, but the total condemnation of the father in Hasenclever's play gave the young German intellectuals who were tired of the old *Kleinbürgerlichkeit* a cause with which they could identify. When the war began, the importance of the theme of *Der Sohn* faded. Father became unimportant when placed next to the world he had made. Militarism, the omnipotent

state, capital, exploitation of the common man, and the depersonaliz-
ing machine became the new enemies. Furthermore, the advent of the
war had refocused the efforts of the German stage on typical wartime
fare: patriotic plays, historical plays (most of them about the glories of
Frederick the Great), and escapist *Kitsch*. Most of them were traditional and realistic. This trend declined after the first two years of
combat, and after 1916 the outspoken antiwar play dominated serious
drama. Many of these ventures were expressionistic in sum or in part.

The three most important German dramatists of expressionism
were associated with the antiwar spirit, but their chief work is part of
the revolutionary aspect of the movement. The New York theatre
produced some of the work, albeit not the best, of Georg Kaiser, Ernst
Toller, and Franz Werfel during the 1920's. Kaiser's *Von Morgens bis
Mitternachts (From Morn to Midnight), Die Bürger von Calais (The
Citizens of Calais)*, and *Die Koralle (The Coral)* (the first part of his
Gas trilogy), were all staged in Germany during the war, but the
plays of Toller and Werfel were not seen there until after 1918.

In 1922, Burns Mantle said that the American "play-going public
. . . refuses to have its feelings harrowed in the theater, whatever the
benefit to its soul."[58] There was, however, a segment of the New York
audience that would not subscribe to Mantle's dictum. It was on the
hope that they were in sufficient numbers that the Theatre Guild
planned its season, as did the only other organization with the courage to experiment, the Provincetown Players. While native drama was
emerging from the small house in Greenwich Village, the Guild continued its campaign to bring the best of the European writers to
American audiences.

The frequency with which the word "expressionism" was being
heard in New York theatrical circles at this time was noteworthy.
Critical comment among the less informed tended to use the term
interchangeably with "impressionism," but interest had most assuredly
arisen in this mysterious and abstract form of German drama. Although the expressionist movement had already spent the greater part
of its impetus on the German stage by 1922, it was during the closing
weeks of the spring of that year that New York audiences had their
first opportunity to see an adaptation of such a German play. The
Theatre Guild presented two special performances of Kaiser's *From
Morn to Midnight* in May, 1922, for its subscription holders, and
added the play to its regular repertory on June 5.

The critical furor aroused by the presentation of this play seems
somewhat strange, for the Kaiser piece was not the first expressionistic play to be seen in New York; it was only the first *German* one.
Eugene O'Neill's *The Emperor Jones* had enjoyed a run of 204 per-

formances during the previous season at the Provincetown, the theatre that was, even at the time of the opening of the Kaiser play, in its third month of performing *The Hairy Ape*. Expressionism had come to the attention of American dramatists long before it had reached the commercial New York stage. The new experiments had already taken root in the little theatres in the Village, but *From Morn to Midnight* was the first play of its kind seen by the Broadway audience, and it was the first German play that the Guild had ever produced.

Its author, Georg Kaiser (1878-1945), is today remembered as the chief exponent of the expressionistic drama in Germany and the only one whose work has had a significant revival in that country after World War II. Certainly the most disciplined craftsman of the form, his art lacked the emotional excesses and the youthful quest for vague panaceas that so often marked and marred the work of his compatriots. Kaiser, unlike almost all of the other German expressionists, wrote his best-known plays not in the heat of youth but in the sage, albeit impassioned, years of his maturity. His justifiably best-known play in Europe, *Die Bürger von Calais*, was written when Kaiser was thirty-nine years old; indeed, his first published work did not appear until he was thirty-three. By his own admission, his dominant theme in all of his work was the regeneration of man, that search for the "new man" whose actions are guided by love and reason so constantly recurring in the entire expressionist movement (and most clearly found in Kaiser's *Die Bürger von Calais*, a play of surface history, loosely based on the chronicle of Froissart). The theme of the play is that of the sacrifice of the self for the common good, and it was, in 1914, the first really powerful appeal for moral regeneration in the face of the old monarchial Germany.

Kaiser's plays are plays of ideas. He never made any attempt to present real people speaking real language, and although some of his early plays were in the Wedekind-Sternheim tradition of the satire of the bourgeoisie, Kaiser seldom attempted to thrill and shock as did his two predecessors, despite the undeniable originality and pyrotechnics which can be seen in such plays as the *Gas* trilogy.

Quite early in his career, Kaiser acquired the epithet that stuck to him until the day of his death: *Der Denkspieler*. Intended as praise of his intellectuality, it acquired the connotation of bloodlessness. That his regeneration theme is presented rationally rather than emotionally when contrasted to other expressionists is no reason to assume that he had lost sight of humanity, that he was merely an unemotional machine. Kaiser was anything but that. In 1921 he moved into the home of friends at their invitation and remained there while they went on a trip. During the absence of his hosts, Kaiser, hard-pressed for funds, sold their valuable furnishings, for which he was later brought to trial and was sentenced to six-months imprisonment, despite his Cellini-like claim that the artist was outside the law. He was not trying to gain attention; he was serious in this belief. The incident gave him notoriety and was quite possibly the basis for the strikingly similar situation in the adventures of Gulley Jimson, artist-hero of Joyce Cary's novel *The Horse's Mouth*. Kaiser was not a Jimson; he was also not an electronic computer.

From Morn to Midnight is Kaiser's best-known work in English and his only major play ever done on Broadway, although it is admittedly not one of his best. On June 5, the Guild decided to add the play to its regular repertory, and on June 26 moved it from the Garrick to the Frazee Theatre where it ran for twenty-four performances. The primary responsibility for the production was in the hands of Frank Reicher, son of Emanuel Reicher who had brought *The Weavers* to the American stage. The younger Reicher directed the Guild production of the Kaiser play and also played the leading role. It was his effort and enthusiasm that caused the board of the Guild to admit *From Morn to Midnight* to its regular schedule.

Although written in 1912, the play had not been given in Germany until 1916, when Max Reinhardt staged it at his theatre in Berlin to great critical and public acclaim. It had been translated into English by Ashley Dukes, British author and critic, and *From Morn to Midnight* was the first German play to be given in London after the Armistice.

The Guild decided to use the Dukes translation of this *Stationen* drama, a play depicting the evolution of a man's set of values in a succession of stages presented in rapid sequences with a dreamlike continuity. The plot concerns a cashier (as usual, he has no name) who absconds with a large sum of money from the bank where he is employed. In the episodes that follow, the audience sees the nightmare world that forms and reforms itself in the mind of a middle-class everyman whose banal wish-fulfilment fantasies have come true. In his efforts to make up for a lifetime of frustration, the cashier learns that the money does not help, but it is only through this escapade that he could learn that the emptiness of his life has nothing to do with material things. In the moment of his greatest despair, he throws the banknotes to a crowd at a race track and is totally disgusted by the furiously bestial fight that the bettors wage for it. In each of the scenes, or stations, the cashier loses another of his illusions, then goes on to the next until nothing is left. The first loss is of the illusion of sexual adventure; he has stolen the money in a mad effort to become the lover of a coquettish woman who turns out to be a respectable, bourgeois mother. The next smashed vision is that of himself as a man who can laugh at death and disappointment. Of course, he cannot; he is human and therefore afraid. The cashier has had a lifelong belief that somewhere there is a grand scheme of things that transcends the petty life of his burgherly home, and that he has a place in that scheme. His third disillusionment is his discovery that he is really no happier anywhere else than he was in his joyless home. Finally, he loses the last bourgeois belief that the mere possession of money can free the individual from the dictates of an oppressive and moribund society. But in his reckless spending at the races and in his grotesque binge at a cabaret, he sees that wealth without purpose is also a false value. Finally, denuded of all of his dreams, he leaves the audience with its own particular little illusion: that life is worth living. Kaiser says that it is not unless it is devoted to the regeneration of man, and it is on this note that the play ends as the cashier, who has shot himself in a Salvation Army hall, dies with a gasp and a sigh that sound like "*Ecce Homo.*" The play thus closes on a note of regeneration. The dominant tone is still one of despair, but Kaiser allows for one glimmer of hope for man. Yet we dare not interpret the ending as a plea for some foggy Christian ethic; Kaiser's values approximate that classic code but reject all aspects of its institutions. Although the play is incontestably didactic, it never suffers from that peculiarly American and French form of didacticism: self-explanation within the text.

The Theatre Guild went to great pains to stage *From Morn to Midnight* effectively, even experimenting with the oft-castigated Linnebach projector and using it to gain the bizarre effects of the nightmare quality essential to expressionism. A snow-covered tree blurred, faded, and became a skeleton, and in the last scene, when the lights go off suddenly, the Linnebach turned the tangle of wires in the Salvation Army hall into yet another skeleton. In the symbolic transfiguration of tree and electrical network, Kaiser bares both nature and machine in their oppression of the individual who has rendered himself out of joint with his world.

The play has all of the major characteristics ascribed to expressionist drama as it explores the subjective world of the pitiable cashier. If it is not as effective as some other plays of the movement, the reason may well be the inherent inferiority of the cashier. From the beginning, he has no hope of being the "new man." He lacks that basic dignity that Kaiser, even more than other expressionists, insisted upon. Consequently, we are dazzled by the spectacle of the play, but

we are not emotionally involved with the plight of the protagonist as
we are in *Die Bürger von Calais*. Furthermore, Kaiser never had any
notions of a Brechtian *Verfremdungseffekt*.

The translation by Ashley Dukes is excellent. The play loses a
good deal of the shrillness that Kaiser so painstakingly wove through
his choice of words and phrases by playing with sounds, but Mr.
Dukes has reproduced the nervous staccato effect of the dialogue with
remarkable felicity. The sharp repartee is also lost in Dukes's more
formalized diction, but the frantic exchange of fragmentary conversation is really, in most cases, the responsibility of the actors and their
director. The basic problem here is that it takes the translator more
words than it did the author to create the desired mood, but even
though Dukes's tone becomes somewhat flat, he recreates Kaiser's
basic mood. The translations of some words are not quite as harsh as
their original forms; some of the guttural Teutonic brutality is gone.
Yet Dukes displays a keen ear at times. In the cabaret sequence, a
masked woman in harlequin costume dances grotesquely around the
cashier's table, answering each of his questions with a single word:
Sekt. "Champagne" would deprive the hearer of the cobra-like hiss
that was Kaiser's intention. Dukes substitutes "Fizz!" The only really
major change effected by the translator is his subdivision of the play
into clearly distinct scenes. Kaiser allowed the sequences of the nightmare to flow one into the other. However, a play which in its original
milieu has as one of its major purposes the depiction of the hollowness
of the pre-Weimar monarchy was effectively adapted for British and
American audiences by channeling this particularly German theme
into the exposition of the vacuity of middle-class values everywhere.

The Guild production aroused great interest even if not unqualified enthusiasm. "The critics were respectful, but deemed the treatment a bit difficult for American audiences."[59] The lack of sensitivity
with which it was appraised was not uncommon in the case of an
unconventional drama. One of the major difficulties that *From Morn to
Midnight* faced was the ill-chosen date of its presentation. It is
axiomatic in Broadway circles that initial production of a serious play
in hot weather marks it for failure. With its regular run not beginning
until June 26, 1922, *From Morn to Midnight* fell victim to a law that
to this day remains intransigent, even in the face of air conditioning.
In any event, the play received infinitely more attention than its brief
run would lead us to believe.

Mantle paid it hardly any notice in his yearbook, merely acknowl-
edging its existence. Yet in 1962, albeit with hindsight at its bidding,
an introduction to *From Morn to Midnight* appeared in a popular

anthology and called the Guild's production "a major event in the course of American drama."[60] Comment from critical corners in 1922 was far from unanimous. The critic from *Bookman* called it a "tremendously moving production [whose] appeal is not easy to define [but] the sensation it arouses is distinctly a novel one."[61] Ludwig Lewisohn had the greatest praise for the production in general and for Frank Reicher in particular, although the play represented a point of view with which he was basically out of sympathy.[62] Lewisohn thought the play to be nihilistic and cannot really be blamed for his interpretation, although Kaiser's intent was quite the converse. The liberal *New Republic*, always kind to ventures more intellectual than commercial, found it to be fascinating, but more for its technique than for its content, decrying the fact that "the irony is peculiarly German in its grotesque and ugly flavor," but continuing by saying that "we feel nothing—and perceive everything."[63] *The New Republic* also felt that Kaiser's play lacked anything positive to counteract the bleak core of the drama, and that it did not fulfil the real promise of expressionism. This view was echoed by Gilbert Seldes, who recognized the fact that this was not one of Kaiser's best plays. Mr. Seldes was enraged at the popular press whose glib reviewers found it "dull or mad."[64] Even trade journals such as *Theatre* approached the production with distressing superficiality and a vision so engrossed by the novelty of the stage effects that it was oblivious to the substance of the play.[65] It was not uncommon for the hack journalists of Broadway to like *From Morn to Midnight* for all the wrong reasons. In general, the popular press which even then exerted the greatest influence on the box office condemned the Guild's production, while the more literate periodicals admired it. Newspapers review a play the day after it opens; magazines often are unable to print comment until after a play has been withdrawn for lack of an audience.

More than a year before the New York production of *From Morn to Midnight,* Kenneth Macgowan had said of the play:

> [It] is a bizarre piece that breaks far too many dramaturgic idols for popularity here and now, yet it is unquestionably filled with a very intense sense of the deep emotional background against which life passes. Kaiser has succeeded in getting past the surface of reality. He has penetrated the basic stratum of man's psyche. To do this, I take it, is the purpose of expressionism . . . the problem of the future playwright is to escape from realism without turning his back on the world.[66]

Despite the brief course of Kaiser's play on Broadway, a new door had been opened. Only one season later, audiences and critics, though still not exuberant, accepted and applauded Meinhard and Bernauer's *Johannes Kreisler* and even Rice's *The Adding Machine*. Two seasons later, the Guild dared to produce Toller's *Man and the Masses*.

Some more recent criticism has felt strongly that *From Morn to Midnight* had "direct influence on Eugene O'Neill, Elmer Rice, and other American playwrights who responded to the challenge of expressionism" and that Kaiser's work was "instrumental in establishing the new shrill, abrupt, and depersonalized style on the American stage."[67] Others have maintained that the effect on American dramatists was less direct, stating that "it is probable that the style of *From Morn to Midnight* influenced playwriting, although our writers were not necessarily conscious of indebtedness to Kaiser and his expressionist colleagues."[68] On one hand, Barry Ulanov maintains that Eugene O'Neill was "much impressed by Georg Kaiser's *From Morn Till Midnight*[69] . . . and determined to express in a similar way a texture of modern life that he felt as tragic."[70] J. Wesley Thomas avows that "Obwohl O'Neill sagt, dass er nie eine hohe Meinung von Kaisers Von Morgens bis Mitternachts gehabt habe, ist doch sein eigener The Emperor Jones . . . in mancher Hinsicht dem deutschen Schauspiel merkbahr ähnlich." ("Despite the fact that O'Neill says that he has never held a high opinion of Kaiser's *From Morn to Midnight,* his own *The Emperor Jones* is in numerous respects certainly remarkably similar to the German play." [trans. mine][71]

It seems reasonable to believe that even if no single play exerted great influence on O'Neill's expressionism, the manner and the matter of the entire German movement assuredly did. Eugene O'Neill maintained that he learned more from Strindberg, usually considered the father of modern expressionism, than he did from any other dramatist, and this may well be so. He further averred that he had learned German only in order to read Wedekind in the original, and this may certainly be the case. However, the stylistic resemblances between *From Morn to Midnight* and *The Emperor Jones*, between *The Coral* and *The Great God Brown*, between Werfel's *Spiegelmensch* and *Days Without End,* and between the two last plays of *Gas* and *Dynamo* seem more than coincidental and point to at least an acute awareness on the part of O'Neill of the work of both Kaiser and Werfel.

It is fitting that the Theatre Guild's private production of *From Morn to Midnight,* the final new play of the 1921-22 season, was also, in its regular booking, the opening drama of the 1922-23 season, the season during which expressionism achieved recognition, if not respectability, on the New York stage.

The Theatre Guild's first new production of the 1922-23 season was Karel Capek's *R.U.R.* Its 184 performances reflected increased audience interest in bizarre, non-realistic, and highly symbolic drama of a stark nature (albeit *R.U.R.* is also quite sentimental) as did the 136 performances of Brock Pemberton's production of Pirandello's *Six Characters in Search of an Author* which opened in October of 1922. The length of these engagements, while hardly spectacular, was definitely more substantial than the customary duration of an experimental drama on Broadway in the years preceding. Neither Capek's play nor Pirandello's can be construed as expressionistic in over-all technique, but many of their devices and their thematic material are certainly tangential to the movement.

When the Selwyns produced *Johannes Kreisler* at the Apollo Theatre on December 20, 1922, it drew much critical attention. The play, directed by Frank Reicher, fresh from his engagement with the Kaiser play, starred Jacob Ben-Ami, rapidly establishing himself as the chief dramatic actor of European experimental plays on Broadway. *Johannes Kreisler* was billed as a "fantastic melodrama" in Louis N. Parker's adaptation from Carl Meinhard and Rudolph Bernauer's *Die Wunderlichen Geschichten des Kappelmeisters Kreisler,* based on the life and works of E. T. A. Hoffmann. Meinhard and Bernauer were not allied with the expressionist movement but were rather in the school of hacks turning out sentimental comedy, with or without accompanying waltzes, in Vienna. Incidental music for *Johannes Kreisler* was by Emil von Reznicek, composer of minor operettas. However, the technique of this play was decidedly expressionistic and was probably inspired by the fad appeal of expressionism in the German-speaking countries in the 1920's. Its commercial potential in the United States was considered by the producers to be greater than that of German hard-core expressionism, for *Johannes Kreisler* used only the surface gimmickery of the style and fused it with a totally romantic plot and protagonist.

Johannes Kreisler has forty-one scenes presented in the rapid succession of a movie scenario. Its sentimental story is told in flashbacks, not as the historical events occur but as they appear to Kreisler in his feverish recollections. At the curtain's rise, Kreisler, an old man, is about to tell his life's story to his friend, Theodor. The expressionistically viewed autobiography makes up the bulk of the piece with the realistic transitions between memories taking place in Theodor's room. In hallucinatory, imaginative, and symbolic terms, Kreisler reviews his idealistic youth and his successful but unsatisfying years of maturity. As a young man he wanted to compose an opera about the sprite Undine, and in all the objects of his frenzied love throughout his lifetime he sees this idealized figure. He first sees her in Julia, a sweet young lady whose family opposes the match because Kreisler is poor, and whose priest interferes in order to gratify his own desire to see Julia enter a convent. The second ideal woman appears when Kreisler's opera is to be produced in Potsdam. He falls in love with the Princess Euphemia, but the Lord Chamberlain will not allow the commoner to approach the noblewoman. To complicate matters further, the theatre directors ask Kreisler to insert an absurd and meaningless ballet into his score. Kreisler refuses to acquiesce to commercial interests and the producers cancel the performance. After this setback, Johannes Kreisler becomes a successful composer. One day he meets the third incarnation of his ideal, the soprano who is to sing the role of Undine. She dies in his arms during a performance of the work. Kreisler has a life of fame and glory, but the inner man always remains frustrated. After the last flashback, the scene returns to Theodor's room and Kreisler dies. The substance of *Johannes Kreisler*, despite some teasing symbolism, has nothing to do with the tenets of expressionism.

For the New York production, the stage was divided into six smaller ones, all on different levels. Scrims were used extensively, and sharp spotlighting illuminated focal stage areas while others were left in total darkness. The actors, blinded throughout the performance by the intricate and elephantine lighting system demanded by the play, had to be led from scene to scene by guides in black who were unseen by the audience. Some of the expressionistic staging techniques were startling. In one hallucination, Kreisler sees a backdrop of sharp and hideous color patterns in front of which he envisions a toppling cross. On it, he sees Julia being tortured by the priest and by a millionaire. In another scene, which begins in total darkness, these same two tormentors are joined by the Lord Chamberlain. They harass Kreisler in his sleep. All the audience sees are disembodied heads and some selected, stylized limbs belonging to the three spectres. As they dance around Kreisler he tries to fight them off, not physically but with his music from *Undine*. The pace of the music quickens and its beat becomes more savage. Kreisler strikes at the three with his baton and decapitates them. The audience sees the limbs freeze as the heads roll and Kreisler falls unconscious. In the scene wherein the composer's third beloved dies, Kreisler is wired and floats from his box in the opera house to the stage so that the singer may die in his arms, although the "arms" are really Kreisler's music, in the grip of which the girl expires. All three of the ideal women were played by the same actress.

The temptation to intellectualize the play is great. Kreisler's art can be construed as the extension of himself and the only meaningful part of his existence in the quest for his ideal. The three tormentors may be said to symbolize the tyranny of social class distinctions, the bourgeois morality of outworn social codes, and materialism against which the hero rebels. Such liberties, however are dangerous. Meinhard and Bernauer had no such dedication to expressionist ideals, and the total effect of *Johannes Kreisler* is not a call to revolution but a foray into sentimentalism. The technique of the play is unquestionably expressionistic, but that technique was exploited for its commercial and visual values both in Germany and in the United States. *Johannes Kreisler* presaged the function of expressionism in modern drama after the movement died: its use as a device to present dreams, hallucinations, and subjective flashbacks within the framework of more realistic or romantic drama, for which purposes it is used to this day on stage, screen, and television with no regard for the ethics or aesthetics of the original German expressionists.

The critical reception of *Johannes Kreisler* was mixed. The *New York World* called it "one of the most amazing experiments our theatre has seen."[72] The *Daily Mail* said that "the novelty of this fantastic melodrama is unimpeachable,"[73] and Stark Young felt that the tension created was so engrossing that the over-all effect of the fantasy was totally convincing.[74] Ludwig Lewisohn saw in *Johannes Kreisler* a world whose allusions, heritage, and mood, though fascinating for Americans, were foreign to them. He felt that to those who had rapport with the traditions indigenous to the play it was a beautiful and moving experience. To the rest it was a slick spectacle.[75] Lewisohn seemed to succumb to the nostalgia and sentimentality of the play, a rare experience for him, and it speaks for the power of *Johannes Kreisler* over even antiromantics.

Negative reaction came from the *Bookman,* whose reviewer said that "you have the feeling after seeing 'Johannes Kreisler' that a cumbersome and noisy steam shovel has been clawing away all evening in the effort to bring to light a beautiful, but rather tiny, pearl."[76] The *Times* also considered the play a "scenic novelty . . . muddled [and] slow" which suffered from excessive mechanical gadgetry for the substance involved.[77] There were many others who also wished that some of the visual magic had rubbed off on the play itself, although only *Theatre* went so far as to say that *Johannes Kreisler* was "mad in conception and half incoherent in its adaptation."[78] *Scientific American* ran a special article on Svend Gade, the Danish designer who invented the complex machinery for the play. The discussion and diagraming of the stage devices implied that even if *Johannes Kreisler* was no landmark in art, it was certainly an achievement for modern technology. Even those who berated this piece of romantic expressionism for being a cumbersome spectacle did not level that charge against Reinhardt's *The Miracle* the following season.

Johannes Kreisler ran for sixty-five performances. It made expressionistic drama no more palatable to the New York audience, for it was really outside the main stream of the movement, but it did help to condition the public to accept staging devices that were always in danger of calling too much attention to themselves. In later works, the viewers could concentrate on the play without being unduly distracted by the paraphernalia.

On December 24, 1923, the Theatre Guild tried another expressionist experiment. The date marked the beginning of a brief series of matinée performances for Guild subscribers of *The Race with the Shadow,* adapted from Wilhelm von Scholz's *Der Wettlauf mit dem Schatten.* Again, Jacob Ben-Ami starred in the production directed by Philip Moeller. The play had attracted little attention in Germany where its pseudoexpressionism was immediately apparent. It was withdrawn quickly in New York where producers were now able to see that surface expressionism was not popular. Consequently, Macgowan, O'Neill, and Jones attempted the real thing and presented Strindberg's *The Spook Sonata* during the 1923-24 season. It lasted for twenty-four performances. Finally, the Theatre Guild decided to include another piece of undiluted expressionism in its regular schedule, and on April 14, 1924, it produced Ernst Toller's *Masse-Mensch* in Louis Untermeyer's translation, *Man and the Masses.*

Ernst Toller, who was born in Germany in 1893 and committed suicide in New York in 1939, was the chief exponent of the political phase of expressionism, and as both playwright and poet is probably better known outside of Germany than any of his colleagues. Toller was a typically contented middle-class German intellectual when he volunteered for army service at the outset of World War I. The war soon changed his entire view of man and society, and he joined the extreme leftist movement in Munich after he was discharged from the military because of nervousness, instability, and newly acquired fervent pacifism, which the old monarchial guard could interpret only as an irrefutable sign of madness. His revolutionary activities in Munich during the closing years of the war landed him in jail where he wrote his first play, *Die Wandlung (Transfiguration)* in 1917 and 1918. The piece is clearly expressionistic and largely autobiographical. It is a *Stationen* drama of alternating scenes of the real experiences and of the subconscious mental flow of the protagonist who progresses in stages from a patriot to a revolutionary. *Die Wandlung* attracted immediate attention in Germany, for it is a very powerful cry for a new ethic despite the fact that the shriek is unrelieved. In

his own notebooks and letters, Toller admitted that he suffered from
excess in his writing. It was the very type of excess that denied Toller
any success on the American stage and that spelled the end of expressionism in Germany for both Toller and most of the others. All of
Ernst Toller's plays have the same theme: There must be a revolt
against the old order which brought war and exploitation to Europe;
a new age of love and brotherhood based on social and political
reorganization must be proclaimed. His theories do not really get
much more specific, and there are numerous critics who see, with
ample justification, that Toller was not so much a Marxist-Trotskyite
intellectual rebel as he was a belated Byronic romantic. His philosophical proposals in *Masse-Mensch* owe more to the early nineteenth-
century poets than to the late nineteenth-century political economists.
Byron's first speech in the House of Lords was a defense of the
Nottingham workers whose uprising is the subject matter of Toller's
Die Maschinenstürmer. Indeed, it is Byron who speaks the prologue
to the play, and the actor who portrays him then becomes the protagonist of the main body of the piece, Jimmy Cobbett. *Masse-Mensch*
(1920) and *Die Maschinenstürmer* (1922) were also written while
Toller was in jail, this time for his activity in the Munich uprising of
1919.[79] *Masse-Mensch* marks the height of Toller's expressionism, for
already in his next play a more realistic style sets in. Later, in *Hinkemann*, his impassioned diction remains, but the play is even more
realistic than *Die Maschinenstürmer*. *Hoppla, wir leben!* (1927) is in a
style which Erwin Piscator made famous. Expressionism is assuredly
there, but in the use of film, loudspeakers, simultaneous scenes, newspaper headlines, and slides, the play bears closer resemblance to
Brechtian epic theatre than to expressionism.

But Toller's verse, his early drama, and his impassioned beliefs
belong most emphatically to the expressionist movement. His whole
attitude was oriented to the 1920's. Even his later non-expressionistic
work is retrospective in theme and subject matter. Unlike most of his
fellow expressionists, Toller believed not only in the need for moral
regeneration but for actual social upheaval. He did not have that
implicit faith in man's inherent goodness that his politically more
moderate colleagues had. Toller's youthful dreams did not collapse, as
Fechter the famous German dramatic historian maintains, when
reality overtook him and made him a bitter cynic. Toller's late skepti-
cal tone stemmed from the fact that all the horror that he had seen in
the twenties came back in yet more hideous form in the thirties. He
and his friends were again on the run, chased this time by the very
men to whom the Germans had mistakenly turned when men such as
Toller had pleaded for a new order.[80] Toller believed that justice

must be pursued. Only in this endeavor can man endure his suffering, much of which can be assuaged, some of which can be abolished, but a part of which there will always be to which there is no solution. That which can be cured, according to Toller, is that which results from man's lack of reasonableness or refusal to use his reason. He must be taught. It is that which is beyond human rationale for which Toller saw no cure. After a period of acute depression, although some friends also suspected severe physical illness, Ernst Toller took his own life in 1939. This "Jewish pacifist with the soul of a St. Francis"[81] had, in the 1920's, taken the dramatic technique of expressionism to the limit that it could go, short of total subjective chaos and incomprehensibility.

The Theatre Guild's production of *Man and the Masses* was directed by Lee Simonson who also designed the settings. Simonson was one of those Americans who had studied staging in Germany. During the two summers he spent in Munich and Berlin, he had become devoted to the painstaking technique of Reinhardt in controlling, moving, and composing mob scenes on stage in a setting that contributed to the totality of effect. Simonson had also seen the original production of *Masse-Mensch* in Berlin in 1921 which was directed by Jürgen Fehling, a master of expressionist staging. He patterned his mounting of the Toller play on Fehling's.[82] Judiciously using the crowd in choreographic patterns and making maximum use of ramps in the settings, Simonson was able to create the illusion of motion, revolution, and the inexorable ascent of the masses to a position of mob rule.

Man and the Masses is constructed very much like the earlier *Transfiguration.* Its *Stationen* are also alternating scenes of real and symbolic action, albeit both are expressionistic. The characters are nameless types whose individuality is minimized even more by the omnipresent masses. The protagonist, The Woman, is a *Hausfrau* type who joins the revolutionary movement while her husband staunchly supports the old order of middle-class values. (In the Berlin production of 1921, The Woman was played by an unknown young actress named Maria Dietrich who shortly thereafter changed her first name to Marlene.) When the play begins, the war is still in progress. The capitalists, whom Toller holds responsible for the conflict, are presented in one dream scene as grotesque stockbrokers buying or selling war bonds depending on the progress of the war. They dance around the desk of the exchange in the rhythms and to the accompaniment of cacophonous jazz strains. The Woman asks the masses to go on a general strike to stop the war effort, but she is opposed by The Nameless One, spokesman for the masses, who urges not passive resistance but open revolution. A civil war ensues between the army and the rebellious masses, with The Woman, opposed to bloodshed, caught between them. She further opposes the masses' rebellion against "machinery." Machines are to be controlled, not destroyed, she avers. The revolution fails, and the triumphant reactionaries, holding The Woman as culpable as the masses, arrest her. She is offered freedom by her burgherly husband; she refuses. She is also offered her liberty by The Nameless One if she kills a prison guard; again she refuses. In the final confrontation between The Woman and The Nameless One, he states the materialism of the masses by asserting, "Our cause comes first!" She counters with Toller's idealism: "Man comes first." The Woman is executed, but two of her fellow female prisoners are seemingly converted to her way. The theme is the same as that stated by the sister of the hero in *Die Wandlung:* "Wer zu den Menschen gehen will, muss erst in sich den Menschen finden." ("Whoever wishes to speak for humanity must first discover the humanity within himself." [trans. mine]) Toller saw the monster of blind rebellion as no better than the Moloch that is the supreme state. The means, when corrupt, are not justified by the end. Despite his political protestations, Toller's cry for revolution was the usual expressionist plea for moral regeneration rather than for bloodshed. He opposed proletarian tyranny even as he opposed proletarian art. When the priest tells The Woman in her death cell that man is inherently evil from the first and will ever remain so, she replies that this is irrelevant, because man is groping for the good and if he makes a reality of the dream of universal brotherhood, his quest may find consummation. Such a philosophy is hardly the dictum of the Bolshevik bogeyman that the Nazis were later to posit as the spectre against which all good German authors should unite.

Louis Untermeyer's translation which the Guild used was almost literal. His words were well chosen, and he nearly duplicated the mood of the German, although Toller's harsh staccato was impossible to render into English. As an experiment, *Man and the Masses* commanded a great deal of critical interest. As theatre, it was simply too strident and too overwrought for even the most open-minded Americans to accept. Unqualified praise for the Guild production came from very few quarters, and the thirty-two performances that the play lasted received far more respect than admiration. The chief praise was again reserved for the mounting of the play and for the technique rather than for the substance. This seems to have been the fate of all German expressionism on the New York stage, particularly that which like Toller's play was unrelieved and undiluted.

Ludwig Lewisohn thought *Man and the Masses* "a great play

greatly produced," but predicted that it would "have only a very brief run."[83] Stark Young felt that "To see *Masse-Mensch* tried out . . . on our stage . . . is a genuine privilege, however boring, for me at least, it turned out to be."[84] It was Young's belief that "expressionism as a serious method has very little point and little that is new," and that it is best as a staging device for selective use in satire, comedy, or the delineation of the absurd. The thematic material of the movement, Young continued, is platitudinous, vague, and sophomoric, and as drama it is lifeless. Later American practitioners of expressionism agreed with Young and judiciously used expressionistic techniques for the very purposes he had suggested.

There were numerous voices which damned Toller's play completely. George Jean Nathan, forgetting for the moment that he was a Germanophile, said, "it is anything but a good play. It is in essence and execution little more than a harangue atop a soapbox . . . the method of staging is at every point more interesting than the manuscript."[85] Arthur Hornblow called the play "gloomy, depressing, dull . . . incoherent, [and] formless."[86] John Corbin said that it was just plain bad, that all the characters do is take turns rhapsodizing, and that the "effect of monotony is persistent and unrelieved."[87] Corbin noted in his review that the techniques of expressionism had been used more sparingly and to good advantage in Rice's *The Adding Machine*, Lawson's *Roger Bloomer*, and Kaufman and Connelly's *Beggar on Horseback*. When *Man and the Masses* was produced in New York, expressionism was already dying on the German stage, and it had already found its niche in American drama as a technique rather than as a way of life. The excesses of Toller's play were unpalatable, and the Guild was in peril of alienating even those friends who supported its experimental policies. Shortly after its production of *Man and the Masses*, the Theatre Guild began its slow trend to a more conservative repertory and the erasure of the epithet bestowed upon it by the Hotel Algonquin wits: "the Buda-Pesthaus."

The season of 1924-25, during which the disastrous production of Wedekind's *Erdgeist* appeared, also saw the presentation of the most puzzling piece of German expressionism to reach New York. On January 26, 1925, the Provincetown Players gave *Jenseits*, a metaphysical enigma in five acts by Walter Hasenclever (who was suffering from a case of too much undigested Strindberg), which Rita Matthias translated faithfully as *Beyond*. The play has two characters who speak to each other, to themselves, and to the audience. Their diction is a highly charged staccato, passionate, unrelieved, and often a series of nonsequiturs. The development of the plot situation is fragmentary and sparse. There is no regard for the passage of time; hours pass in seconds and seconds are frequently presented in many minutes. The concept of reality presented in *Beyond* is highly subjective. The total effect of the play is supernatural and nightmarish. In it, a woman is visited by her absent husband's friend. While they speak, word comes that the husband has died, and the woman sees the spirit of her dead mate incarnated in the body of the friend who also feels this transmigration of spirit. After a bizarre night, daylight breaks the illusion, and the man and woman see a new life for themselves. During the course of the play, the couple is haunted by the husband's ghost, numerous hallucinations, dissolving walls, trees growing into windows, and their own shadows which they are able to observe growing. The play seems to be a discussion of the belief that meaning in life is found only in death, and that only in death is there any of the regeneration that more materialistic expressionists are seeking. In his presentation of life and death as part of a continuum, Hasenclever exhibits a nebulous familiarity with some tenets of Buddhism. Indeed, the Provincetown's program notes to *Beyond* stated that the playwright was an avowed Buddhist, but the concepts are never made clear by the text of the play. The string of associations made by the characters in the dialogue of *Beyond* are usually intensely personal and frequently incomprehensible, so fragmented is the development of the piece. *Jenseits* had appeared in Germany in 1919 and was considered even there as a step outside the reasonable bounds of expressionism. Americans were still testing in 1925, but in *Beyond* they discovered that there were limits to the technique, and that the presentation of a play on the stage does not allow its viewer the time for reflection at the moment of experience that Joyce and Kafka allow their readers (and rereaders). *Beyond* was the last piece of extreme German expressionism seen in New York in the 1920's.

When the Provincetown production opened, the reviews were uniformly harsh. Joseph Wood Krutch said that *Beyond* "must hide mysteries which this reviewer, at least, was unable to penetrate . . . [it is] a wild farrago of incoherent mysticism . . . too abstract to be drama, too inconsistent to be philosophy, and too vague to be even a creed."[88] Stark Young, reviewing for the *Times*, was not at all moved by the play but found it an interesting experiment and commendable only as such. It was to the credit of the people at the Provincetown that they were not afraid to try all manner of things.[89] What praise was given the production was reserved largely for Robert Edmond Jones's imaginative setting. Again, it was technique alone that found approval.

The last of the major expressionists whose work was produced in New York in the 1920's was Franz Werfel, a mystic like his colleagues from Prague, Franz Kafka and Rainer Maria Rilke. Werfel first attracted attention as a lyric poet of expressionism striving for what he called *Lebensgefühl, Daseinsgefühl,* and *Ekstatische Wirklichkeit,* a subjective and ecstatic sense of life and reality.[90] He also sought moral regeneration but through human awareness of personal responsibility and exercise of the will which was man's in the choice between good and evil. At no time was Werfel inclined toward politics or revolution. His search was for an ethical and religious credo the basis for which he saw in Greek legend and biblical myth. In later years, Werfel, albeit one of the founders, tired of expressionism and even disavowed it somewhat. At no time was the stage simply a moral institution for him. All of his plays were more theologically and metaphysically oriented.[91] His characters were always masters of their own fate and will. Franz Werfel never exhibited the penchant for didacticism shared by other expressionists. He saw the theatre as a place for plays and for pastime *(Zeitvertreib).* Although his plays were intensely symbolic, that symbolism never got in his way nor called attention to itself. It was a bonus for those who saw it, but the first apparent level of the play was always meaningful and could be thought of as self-sufficient. Werfel's theatre was one of music, magic, myth, and mystery; he was not concerned with objective reality.[92] His interest in music and in opera was reflected in his plays and in his lifelong interest in Verdi, on whose life he based a book and the libretti of three of whose operas he reworked in German, *La Forza del Destino, Simon Boccanegra,* and *Don Carlos.*

Werfel's first important play, *Spiegelmensch (Mirror Man),* was originally conceived as a ballet but was finally realized as a three-part drama constructed on the pattern of a Greek trilogy. Written in 1920, *Spiegelmensch* was Werfel's most distinctively expressionistic play. Its lyricism is pronounced as is its ecstatic tone. The play is concerned with the struggle between a man and his mirror image, symbolically representing what Werfel saw as the dual personality of every man, the forces of good and evil struggling within him. Werfel's constant theme in all of his plays is this notion that the most dramatic combat of all goes on within man himself, the battle between the divine and the satanic forces locked inside each one of us. *Spiegelmensch* ends in the mountains of Tibet, with all their mystical overtones, where man and image are finally reunited as the good triumphs over the evil, never to destroy it but to assimilate and control it. Werfel's later plays tended to be more and more realistic in their technique, but he never lost the fervor of his ethical commitment. Although *Spiegelmensch* has never been produced professionally in this country, New York audiences saw more plays by Werfel

than by any other German expressionist, despite the fact that only
The Eternal Road (1936-37) and *Jacobowsky and the Colonel* (1943-
44) in a greatly changed American version ran for more than one
hundred performances.

Werfel's first play to be seen in New York was *Bocksgesang,* translated by Ruth Langner as *Goat Song* for the Theatre Guild production which opened on January 25, 1926, under the direction of Jacob
Ben-Ami. "*Goat Song* left nobody neutral. Some it perplexed, some it
revolted, some it filled with excited enthusiasm."[93] The Guild considered the play, which ran for fifty-eight performances, an artistic success despite its financial failure, and felt that it had widened the
foothold for serious drama on the commercial ground of Broadway.
Goat Song, which was written in 1920, inspired controversy concerning its interpretation and it received much space in both newspapers
and magazines. There were even discussion groups throughout New
York's more intellectual circles which met to puzzle out the meaning
of the play.

The title, *Goat Song,* is a literal translation of the Greek
$\tau\rho\alpha\gamma\omega\delta\iota\alpha$–tragedy. The term may well be rooted in the rituals to the
goat-god in ancient fertility practices which developed into the
springtime festivals of Dionysus. In addition there is the connotation
of the cry of the scapegoat. *Goat Song* takes place in the Balkan area
where the atmosphere is rife with the superstitious traditions of monsters, werewolves, and vampires. A farmer and his wife have for years
hidden their monstrous child, part man-part goat (an idea Werfel got
from a boyhood visit to an institute of pathology in Prague where he
saw teratological monsters). The father wants to kill it, but the local
physician wants to take it to an institution in the city. The doctor,
after a visit, neglects to lock the hut in which the pitiable monster is
held. The man-goat escapes. The monster is never seen throughout the
play, but his horrible shadow appears and his painful cry is heard
periodically. The primitive peasants of the area, victims of their wildest superstitions, are gripped by fear, only to be released when the
monster is killed in a forest fire, but not before the innocent heroine
of the play has given herself to the dreaded man-goat out of pity and
in the hope of assuaging him. The play ends as the girl, Stanja,
announces that she will bear the monster's baby.

The mood of *Goat Song* reflects the entire emotional upheaval of
the post-World War I era with its constant reference to political and
social turbulence. Again pitting the good against the evil in the individual, Werfel uses the monster as the organism both horrible and
pitiable in whose body both forces are imprisoned and whose cry, or
song, is simultaneously the sad cry of the sacrificed scapegoat and the

impassioned love cry of the fertility goat, as well as the cry of recognition of the classically tragic hero. He is also a holy, sacrificial beast who dies in the forest fire but is unsinged. In the body of the escaped monster, Werfel sees "the challenge of man's primeval instincts to the established order."[94] The monster himself finds his release in escape, but the people find their release only in destroying the monster. Although they do kill the goat, the germ of the eternal Werfelian duality is already in Stanja's body. Violence has defeated its own ends, for the cycle is ever renewed and violence breeds only more violence. Fear and oppression nurture it, and it can only recreate itself. The play further shows the effects of human superstitions. Significantly, it is the physician, the voice of humanism and scientific inquiry, whose forgetfulness releases the monster. The doctor pities the goat; its mother instinctively loves it. There are aspects of the mystery of the human personality in all its good and evil manifestations which reason cannot comprehend and which intuition cannot understand. Werfel, in Goat Song, has tried to explain the inexplicable duality in man that makes him simultaneously the object of both love and revulsion, that makes him both tragic and great—and all these themes are synthesized in the central symbol of the man-goat monster in all its connotations. On the level of Werfelian Zeitvertreib, Goat Song is an eerie horror story; on its symbolic levels it invites many interpretations. Goat Song is a play which demands much from its audience.

In its highly subjective symbolism, in its use of types in the mass scenes, in its poetic diction in the more impassioned passages, and in its thematic material, Goat Song has much in common with expressionism, but Werfel's play is decidedly different from the work of Kaiser or Toller. Modification of excesses seemed to be the only way to make expressionistic techniques a permanent contribution to modern drama, and Werfel, always the disciplined intellectual, never fell into the strident tones of some of his colleagues in his work.

Ruth Langner's translation was almost literal and therefore preserved Werfel's play while avoiding the Americanizing liberties usually taken with his work. However, that virtue was also Miss Langner's chief fault, for her Goat Song sounded too much like a schoolroom exercise. All of the texture of Werfel's dialogue was lost. Where the original showed the playwright's ear for dialect, the translation substituted an artificial quaintness. Werfel's lines had a smooth, poetic flow; Langner's lines were impossible to speak without making an actor feel awkward and self-conscious. Werfel's play had wit; Langner's dialogue was humorless. Furthermore, she translated idioms instead of finding suitable substitutes for them. Her version is full of

such insensitivity to connotation as mistaking demonstratives for definite articles, as in her rendition of even the obvious *"Der Dummkopf!"*
as "The stupid" rather than as "That fool!" Often the literal translations approach total meaninglessness, as in her Hangman's response to
being insulted, "Ow, what, what a name." In the German, *"Ah was!
Solche Namen!"* it is clear that *"Ah was!"* is not the equivalent of
"Ow, what" but something closer to "Aw, c'mon!" All of the music of
Werfel's unerring choice of words was gone in the Theatre Guild
version. Nevertheless, Miss Langner was faithful to the play even if
inept at rendering the language into English.

"Aside from a few scathing criticisms, the reaction of the critics
was favorable . . . all in all, this play . . . was a success."[95] Joseph
Wood Krutch joined in the popular game of interpreting *Goat Song's*
symbols, but maintained that the play was good even without the
metaphysics because Werfel was also a poet and a fine storyteller.
Krutch saw the monster as the sin of nature, unwanted but guarded,
who is released through the ineptness of a rationalist (the doctor) who
believes in the inherent goodness of nature. The released monster then
becomes an agent of destruction, but when the people finally think
him dead, and therefore think themselves purged of the evil within
them, we see that he is to be reborn from the body of innocence. Evil
is always with us and cannot be explained away intellectually.[96] Stark
Young showed the play to be a direct descendant of Euripides' *Bac-
chae* and an analysis of the Dionysiac nature of man. Young called it
"the most important play of the season."[97]

Among those who were not so enthusiastic was Barrett H. Clark,
who though he admired the play said, "Being rather a thinker and
poet than a playwright, Werfel was unable to express himself completely and sufficiently through the idiom of the theatre . . . he has so
much material he cannot digest it, and if a dramatist can't do that,
what does he expect of an audience."[98] Arthur Hornblow, never kind
to experiments, thought *Goat Song* "dull, noisy . . . unpleasant [and]
repellent," though excellently played.[99] Brooks Atkinson's reactions in
the *Times* were also mixed. He felt that the play had "moments of
great power [but that it] breeds confusion as it goes along,"[100] and
that the chief trouble was that *Goat Song* presents the general in
terms of itself rather than in specifics.[101] The critic of the *Bookman*
discussed Werfel's play in conjunction with another current production, O'Neill's *The Great God Brown*, and damned both as incoherent,
confusing plays without a semblance of clarity.[102] He did not, however, note that Werfel and O'Neill were concerned with a similar
theme, the duality of man's nature, in their respective plays, nor did
he observe the relationship between Werfel's human monster, the

Dionysiac goat, and O'Neill's Dion Anthony, who had within him the natures of both Dionysus and St. Anthony.

There is no question that *Goat Song* was an enigmatic play and that it came as an unpleasant shock to an audience unaccustomed to a theatre of ideas, but for once a play which was an indisputable box-office failure received the critical attention it deserved and the praise that made the Guild feel well justified in its presentation.

Ben-Ami was so convinced of the importance of Werfel that even while *Goat Song* was playing at the Guild Theatre, he accepted the offer of the Fifth Avenue Playhouse company to direct and star in yet another Werfel play, *Schweiger*. In a translation by Jack Charash and William A. Drake, *Schweiger* opened at the Mansfield Theatre on March 23, 1926, two months after the premiere of *Goat Song*. The play failed to get the attention of the earlier piece and closed after only thirty performances. *Schweiger,* which was first performed at the German Theatre in Prague in 1923, marks an even sharper break from expressionism than *Goat Song*. Although thematically closely akin to *Spiegelmensch* and *Bocksgesang* in its treatment of the dual personality of man given dramatic representation in the struggle between evil and divine forces within the hero, *Schweiger* is quite realistic in surface technique despite its melodramatics. The hero, Franz Schweiger, an honored and respected man in a small community, is loved by his fellows until he is discovered to have committed murder in his past. The memory of the event and even his real name have been repressed because of therapy received at the hands of an experimenting psychiatrist who appears in the play and revives Schweiger's memory of past events. The ensuing conflict drives Schweiger to suicide. It is only his wife who keeps him stable for a long time, but when she withdraws her support, Schweiger's baser self destroys him. The cause of all the evil in the play is the loneliness from which only love can redeem man. Schweiger recognizes the evil within him, but he feels that it is the result not of any inherent baseness but of disassociation from man and human problems.

Beneath the *Zeitvertreib* level of the play lies Werfel's concern with the entire apocalyptic mood of the twenties and his sense of foreboding of the evil forces about to be rereleased in Europe, even as he had envisioned them in *Goat Song*. The play also reflects Werfel's interest in the then flourishing Viennese school of psychiatry as well as in his always present mystical predilections, seen in his work since his university days in Prague. It is particularly interesting that the characters in *Schweiger* which reflect these Werfelian interests are not standard dramatic types. The psychiatrist is a sadistic, monarchistic, anti-Semitic, anti-Freud monomaniac, and the priest rather than the scientific rationalist is the *raissoneur* of the piece. It is the priest who presents Werfel's notion that it is not madness or the incomprehensible or the subconscious that has man in thrall but evil, and that which drove Schweiger to his demented actions was not the irrational or non-rational, but the satanic force within him. In keeping with Werfel's other plays, the conflict is based on the internal struggle of Schweiger, for there is an immense capacity for good within him; it is this force which has made him an honored man for so many years until the return of the vicious psychiatrist. The good within Schweiger finally prevails, albeit in an act of desperation. Evil, says Werfel, is part of the totality that also includes goodness, and the greater the evil, the greater is the goodness that rises to do battle with it. Even in this play, so realistic in stage technique, the ethic of the expressionist makes its presence felt.

Werfel's *Schweiger*, in addition to the development of its central problem, also contains an insightfully comic satire on provincial political saviors and hasty social panaceas. Furthermore, there is an abundance of witty dialogue and a keen sense for dialectal idiom such as one might find in the plays of Odets. All of these elements which lend texture and latitude to the play faded in the transition to English, and the play emerged as a melodrama about a man and his struggle to suppress an old homicidal mania. The play seen on Broadway was a cumbersome and morbid drama that received an almost unanimously unfavorable reaction from critics and reviewers. The brief and flippant evaluation by Robert Benchley, which stated that "it was frightful,"[103] was typical. Brooks Atkinson's comment was that Werfel was slovenly as a playwright, for despite his always fine story level and his commendable philosophical and poetic touches, Werfel's dramas lack clarity, and it is impossible to ascertain whether the author's thought or only his dramatic realization is vague.[104]

The greatest theatrical success of any of Werfel's plays in Europe was *Juarez and Maximilian,* published in 1924, first produced in Magdeburg in 1925, and most effective in the Vienna production later that year under the direction of Max Reinhardt. The play won the Grillparzer Prize. The Theatre Guild, still convinced of the importance of Werfel as a dramatist, but retreating more and more from extreme, foreign experiments, presented this essentially realistic play on October 11, 1926. Philip Moeller directed, and the cast included Alfred Lunt, Harold Clurman, Edward G. Robinson, Morris Carnovsky, Cheryl Crawford, Dudley Digges, Sanford Meisner, and Margalo Gillmore. The production received the full benefit of all the Guild's resources, but closed after forty-eight performances.

The play is based on an incident occurring at the time of the

American Civil War. Napoleon III, who had attacked Mexico, withdrew and left the Crown Prince Maximilian as governor when the
United States invoked the Monroe Doctrine. Maximilian had to bear
the consequences for Napoleon. The Mexicans revolted successfully
under the leadership of Juarez and his general, Porfirio Díaz. Maximilian, captured and shot, is presented as a man of integrity and
honor who took the blame for atrocities that were not his own doing
in this shameful series of events filled with Machiavellian incidents of
political opportunism and irresponsibility.

Werfel's play shows Maximilian's high regard for both Juarez and
Díaz and his contempt for Napoleon. Díaz, in turn, has only admiration for Maximilian, who is trapped between his ideals and his re-
sponsibilities. The Crown Prince is destroyed because he chooses to
hurt no one but himself, and he will not sacrifice his integrity for
expediency. The hero of *Juarez and Maximilian* is a tragic figure by
even the most rigorous classical standards.

The reviewers found the play intellectually stimulating, but slow,
and though elaborate, theatrically dull. Lawrence Langner said later
that the final run-through before the opening—without costumes or
scenery—was exceedingly moving, but somehow the elaborate physical
trappings buried the play, and those who had wept at the bare production were unmoved by the dressed one. Real people had become
historical figures.[105] Praise for the play came from Joseph Wood
Krutch who saw Werfel's message in the end of the play, wherein the
heroic Juarez, who has never been seen, is described as a wrinkled
little old man. The redeemer of freedom is only "the old lust in a new
form." Therefore, Krutch maintains, Werfel has presented historically
and realistically exactly what he had to say in *Goat Song*.[106] Stark
Young also praised the play and said that it was the sort of intelligent
drama needed to "dilate the scope of our theatre."[107] Young also
noticed that to which few critics were sensitive: the mechanical dullness of the translation. Again it was Ruth Langner who had rendered
the play into English, and she repeated all of the inadequacies of her
Goat Song translation.

The chief problem with the Guild production seems to have been
the acting and direction. Gilbert Seldes,[108] Arthur Hornblow,[109] and
Brooks Atkinson[110] all berated the play for its slow, cumbersome, and
muddled production. The most common charges leveled were that the
actors were unintelligible and sluggish and that the changing of
elaborate realistic scenery was interminable. Atkinson's comment
summed it up: "[The play] dissipates its theme in scenery and lifeless
acting."

How *Juarez and Maximilian* could have been so mangled by the

Guild is not understandable. They had carried off so many more difficult assignments. After this play, all producers agreed that Werfel was
simply not for American audiences. Not until Reinhardt staged the
pageant *The Eternal Road* was Werfel's work seen again on Broadway. After the failure of *Juarez and Maximilian* in New York, Warner
Brothers bought the rights to it, combined it with additional material
from Bertita Harding's novel *The Phantom Crown,* and made the
highly successful motion picture *Juarez.*

The American theatre may have been influenced directly only by
the stagecraft of the expressionist movement and its possibilities for
selective use, but the generation of American playwrights who
emerged in the 1920's saw far more in expressionism than mere stage
trickery. Foreign expressionism was imported by the New York entrepreneurs after it had already found its way into American plays.

Eugene O'Neill's *The Emperor Jones* opened at the Provincetown
in the 1920-21 season. Almost all of its action except the opening and
closing scenes is the subjective vision of Brutus Jones. The play develops along a series of *Stationen,* each one ending in Jones's discharging of another bullet to kill his hallucination. The dialogue
(much of it monologue) is impassioned, feverish, and unrelieved; its
staccato is emphasized by the insistent tom-tom beating throughout
the play. With each successive hallucinatory scene, Jones loses another item of his clothing in symbolic representation of each layer of
civilization that is stripped from him in O'Neill's gradual exposition of
the primal man, taken back in history to his roots. The theme may be
the quest for the Jungian race consciousness and for the deepest re-
cesses of the human mind that hide the mystery and the motivation of
man's innermost drives rather than the quest for the "new man"; but
The Emperor Jones is unquestionably expressionistic in dramatic
technique, and despite O'Neill's denial, resembles Kaiser's *From Morn
to Midnight* except that the cashier loses his illusions by progression
and Jones loses his by regression.

The Hairy Ape, which opened in 1921-22 before *From Morn to
Midnight,* is also a *Stationen* drama in its presentation of Yank's progress from stokehole to cage as he urgently seeks a place in which he
"belongs." The naked mannequins along Fifth Avenue, the symbolic
white dress in the black bowels of the ship, and Yank's immolation in
the cage are clearly devices of expressionism. In fact, O'Neill said,
"The whole play is expressionistic,"[111] referring to details that might
not seem so at first glance, such as the coal-shoveling scene. O'Neill
wanted a specific rhythm created by the shovelers, although no one
would really execute the job that way. He may very well have had
the scene of the coalheavers in Strindberg's *A Dream Play* in mind.

The stokehole scenes in *The Hairy Ape* also parallel the factory
scenes in Kaiser's *Gas I*, and the similarity between the dramatic
functions of the furnaces and the machines in those plays is noteworthy.
Furthermore, Yank's attitudes and even the imagery of his
speeches are much like those of the Billionaire's Son in *Gas I*. *The
Hairy Ape* resembles the plays of German expressionism not only in
technique but even in theme.

On March 19, 1923, the Theatre Guild presented the first American
play of unmistakable expressionism to be performed on Broadway.
Although Elmer Rice never employed the technique so fully in
any other of his plays and disavowed any conscious use of it in this
one, *The Adding Machine*'s stylistic origins were clear. The play had
both staunch defenders and violent attackers in critical and journalistic
circles. Over the years, it seems to have held up better than most
of American expressionism. On April 4, 1923, in *The Nation*, Ludwig
Lewisohn said that *The Adding Machine* was "without question one
of the major achievements in the entire field of the American arts."
On the other side were the traditionalists and the genteel who were
outraged by Rice's play. Burns Mantle in his yearly survey quickly
glossed over the production by referring to it as "another impressionistic study."[112] As late as 1925, Mantle still insisted on calling all
expressionistic plays "impressionistic." There is little argument for the
Teutonic compulsion to conform to rigid categories of "isms," and
many plays assuredly defy such pigeonholing, but to use "expressionism" and "impressionism" interchangeably is more than mere disre-
gard for academic distinctions. Even more distressing than Mantle's
dismissal of the play is Arthur Hobson Quinn's doggedly literal reading of *The Adding Machine*. He referred to it as "a sordid analysis of
human life and an absurd description of heaven, couched in terms of
exaggeration and so-called expressionism, which for a short time de-
ceived some critics as to its importance."[113] *The Adding Machine*, in
its *Stationen* development of the story of Mr. Zero, in its reduction of
characters to types (Zero, Shrdlu, One, Two, Three, etc.), in its settings of whirling turntables, walls decorated with numbers, and an
adding machine over which men crawl, employs every one of the
major devices of expressionism, even to the extent of artificial dialogue and choral speaking.

During the 1925-26 season, O'Neill's *The Great God Brown* ran for
171 performances. In its treatment of the two alter-ego central characters, William Brown and Dion Anthony, and in the duality of the
character of Dion himself, there are striking parallels to Werfel's
Spiegelmensch and to his Dionysiac goat. Furthermore, the diction of
The Great God Brown is Kaiserian, and the plot situation bears a

remarkable resemblance to *Die Koralle*. The Billionaire placing the
dead Secretary's coral on his own watch chain so that he can exchange roles with his exact double closely parallels Brown's taking of
Dion's mask and putting it on himself. In *Die Koralle*, *Spiegelmensch*,
and *The Great God Brown*, the hero assumes both the personality and
the physical appearance of his alter-ego through a symbolic action. At
the same time that O'Neill's play was being performed in New York,
Kaiser's *Gas* trilogy received its first professional performance in this
country at the Kenneth Sawyer Goodman Theatre in Chicago. O'Neill
used the mirror-image device once again in the split characters of
John and Loving in *Days Without End*.

It was also during the 1925-26 season that the Cherry Lane Theatre produced John Dos Passos' *The Moon Is a Gong*, a play which
included a funeral in which mourners do the Charleston around a
corpse almost as the stockbrokers dance around the bourse in Toller's
Masse-Mensch. Dos Passos' play also has a scene in which the dead of
a train wreck are brought back to life, and another in which a thief is
chased over the rooftops of grotesquely stylized houses. *The Moon Is
a Gong* resembled both the expressionistic plays of Germany and the
dramas of John Howard Lawson whose *Roger Bloomer* and *Processional* also made liberal use of the technique.

The Provincetown presented e. e. cummings' *him*, clearly a cousin
of expressionism, during the 1927-28 season, also the year of O'Neill's
Strange Interlude in which he was able to make use of the subjective
point of view without sacrificing dramatic objectivity. Expressionism
had become a useful technique for O'Neill, something to be subordinated to and integrated with the entire drama rather than an end
unto itself, although he was to return to a far less subtle exploitation
of the genre in the following year's *Dynamo*. In its attempt to show
the displacement of the God-image by an inhuman and inhumane
machine on which man immolates himself, *Dynamo* points at one of
the main themes of the *Gas* trilogy. The use of expressionism to ex-
pose the horrors of a mechanized life remained alive even through the
many plays of the Federal Theatre during the depression. Although
these dramas were more strongly influenced by the devices of Erwin
Piscator, the mark of the twenties is clearly upon such works as
Sophie Treadwell's *Machinal* and Marc Blitzstein's *The Cradle Will
Rock*.

But it was the play which had opened at the Broadhurst Theatre
on February 12, 1924, which more than any other actually presaged
the eventual function of expressionism in American drama after the
furor of the original movement had abated. Marc Connelly and
George S. Kaufman had neither read nor seen Paul Apel's expression-

istic comedy, *Hans Sonnenstossers Höllenfahrt (Johnny Sunbumper's Tour of Hell)*, but they were told about it by producer Winthrop Ames who wanted them to write an American version of the play. Connelly and Kaufman took off far from their source and adapted Apel's idea rather than his play. The result was the highly successful *Beggar on Horseback*. In it the telegram diction of expressionism, the possibilities for extravaganza, dream sequences, character reductions, and the rapid succession of scenes were all exploited for satiric and farcical purposes. The grotesquerie that *Beggar on Horseback* made of the depersonalized commercial world opened up the possibilities for expressionism which have made the technique a permanent part of fanciful American comedy on stage and screen in both dramatic and musical entertainment. In later years, no one was even to think of it as expressionism any more; it was part of the common ground of imaginative humor used by artists and hacks alike. Only two years after *Beggar on Horseback*, Kaufman was writing bizarre comedy sketches for the Marx Brothers in such works as *The Cocoanuts*, full of expressionistic devices undreamed of by the humorless practitioners of the form in Germany.

Expressionism had revolutionized German stagecraft and put the quietus on verisimilitude except for the short-lived "new realism" plays of depression-wracked Germany. Expressionism as a self-sufficient German movement died in 1924, shortly after it had established its tenuous foothold in the United States. Although the movement faded, its dramaturgy, sensibly ameliorated, became a major part of the craft of the modern drama. There was some attempt on the part of desperate post-World War II Germans to resuscitate strident expressionism, as in Wolfgang Borchert's *Draussen vor der Tür*, but in the main the manifestations of the technique are more restrained and selective, as in the work of Dürrenmatt, Frisch, Rutenborn, Gressieker, and Wittlinger.

The American Theatre actually presented very few of the plays of German expressionism. There were no New York productions of any of the plays, expressionistic or not, by Barlach, Kokoschka, Bronnen, Goering, Jahnn, Kornfeld, Sorge, Sternheim, Unruh, or Johst (the least talented of them all who fittingly became the German stage's chief spokesman for Adolf Hitler). More important, there were no productions of some of the finest plays by Kaiser. The highly metaphysical aspect of expressionism never found a stage in the United States. The plays seen here were the ones of protest, those of the "shriek." The Germans always admired the intensely personal and the philosophically abstract on their stage, and these phases of expressionism were never too well received outside German-speaking areas. Philosophical drama in New York in the 1920's was chiefly the province of the little theatres and of the Guild, and it was in these houses that the German dramas were played.

Between 1925 and 1928, both domestic and imported serious drama found a new acceptance on the New York stage. Interest in European plays by both critics and audiences rose simultaneously with the quality of native drama. The American theatre lost much of its jingoism when America itself produced important plays and playwrights. The American audience could accept the foreign theatre, at least in part, after its own had matured. The American drama, secure in its new stature, had no further need of defense mechanisms. In December of 1924, Barrett H. Clark was inspired by the many good native plays of the past two seasons, particularly *Desire Under the Elms*, to say, "What American play written between the landing of the Puritans and say 1890 is worth an evening in the theatre? Really. Think of them, . . . It is all very well to say that we were a young people seventy-five years ago; but did we not have Poe and Hawthorne and Emerson?"[114] Clark's pride is doubly significant when we realize that his enthusiasm caused him to forget that hardly anyone anywhere was writing good plays back in those years, but he is justified in no longer wanting to listen to all the reminiscing (and lying) about those good old days when our theatre had "grandeur." The genteel tradition still had its spokesmen after the crash of 1929, but it was dead as a moving force in the theatre.

3

Realism and Revolution:
1928-39

I

During the mid and late twenties, when the expressionist drama of Germany was arousing interest on the New York stage, it had long passed its peak in its native land. There was no single powerful dramatic movement that replaced expressionism in Germany after 1923, for the fifteen years that followed and led to World War II were politically and artistically chaotic. In those years the German drama followed essentially three lines of development: social realism, which was a topical outgrowth of naturalism and social satire; the theatre of Brecht and Piscator, the new departure in experimental drama; and the nationalist drama, a utilitarian genre that played into the hands of the rising National Socialists who, after their modest beginnings in 1920, had become a formidable power by the end of the decade. After 1935 there was little remaining of social realism, and Brecht had left the country the day after the Reichstag fire.

The German drama of the Weimar Republic and the early Nazi years was a direct outgrowth of the war itself and the revolution that followed it. The years of rebellion, inflation, recovery, and depression nurtured a generation of playwrights some of whom were most deeply affected by the social problems of postwar Germany. Much of their work had a decidedly leftist tone, but in the main their concern was with humane responses to human problems. There were also some writers who saw a new nationalistic spirit as the only answer to the faltering Weimar Republic. These dramatists were fewer in number and far less gifted, but there came a day when their work was, in fact, the only German theatre remaining. "The Nazi revolution of 1933 erased at one stroke, with a completeness unprecedented in history, all the cultural achievements of the republican era, including the drama."[1] Despite their cries of the revival of a truly Germanic *Kultur*, the Nazis were manifestly unproductive in the twelve years that followed, and there was no one left in Germany who was in a position to oppose them on stage or page.

"When the storm of revolution [after World War I] had blown over, the drama reverted to a new realism, known as *Neue Sachlichkeit,* which was suffused with a sense of disillusionment and sober recognition of fact."[2] The height of these plays that held a mirror to society came during the interim years of illusory economic recovery between the inflation and the depression of 1929, the same time that the Nazis were amassing their strength.

The drama of the *Neue Sachlichkeit* avoided the harsh melodramatics of naturalism and took advantage of many of the techniques introduced by expressionism, combining them with its own essential verisimilitude of plot and character. The new realism actually had terse speech, stylized staging, and a deep concern for ethical problems. It was a pessimistic drama reflecting the anarchy and decay of the postrevolution disillusionment. These plays emphasized the gulf between the poor and the *nouveau riche* and the aloofness of the old aristocracy and the bourgeoisie to the whole problem. The new realism was one of those overly inclusive labels of which German critics have always been so fond. However, they decided upon a series of subgenres, each of which was determined by the general milieu of the plays written.

The *Zeitstück* was a development of the twenties and early thirties. It dealt exclusively with contemporary issues and was probably the most significant German drama of the immediate pre-Hitler years. It was, for all of its immediate pertinence, too topical to survive, and it defied exportation to the stages of other countries. The *Zeitstück* was almost unknown in the United States, where plays of the same kind were immensely popular but were also concerned with native problems. The best example of the American *Zeitstück* is our depression drama of the thirties, particularly the work of the Group Theatre and the Federal Theatre Projects.

The *Heimkehrer* play is the natural product of all wars since the Trojan, the drama of the returning soldier. In Germany, these plays underwent a peculiar metamorphosis after World War I. The first of the *Heimkehrer* were young idealists facing readjustment and disillusion in a world which a war had not really changed, although it had changed them. As the nation drifted toward National Socialism, the plays began to deal with the nostalgia of the old days at the front and the dignity of heroic death. By 1930, *Heimkehrer* plays had romanticized the horrors of war, in fact had made them seem desirable as proof of manhood. By 1933 those horrors were being glorified. The official Nazi drama was born.

The "school plays" were an outgrowth of both the drama of social criticism and the naturalistic and expressionistic tragedies of adolescence. They all owed some debt to Wedekind's *Frühlings Erwachen*. Most of them were set in German secondary schools where the conflict of the generations and of the old Germany and the new could be emphasized.

The "law plays" concerned themselves with the inhumane aspects of German jurisprudence and were strong condemnations of both the old imperial state and the Weimar Republic at the same time that they strenuously opposed the advent of the Nazis. Most of them showed leftist sympathies and derived their main dramatic impact from courtroom scenes. The chief trials concerned murder, rape, and illegal abortion and were, for all their documentary touches, not averse to sensationalism. Both the "school" and "law" plays were dominantly realistic in style, although there were vestiges of expressionism to be seen in their staging devices.

The "history plays" provided thin disguises for contemporary figures and problems. The focus of most of these dramas was on the psychological motivation of the pseudohistorical protagonists. Giving men of the past the benefit of Freud and current sociopolitical situations pleased a substantial public. The Nazis, often the victims of the playwrights' attacks in the mid-twenties, eventually put an end to the history play. The type is not to be confused with the Hitler-supported historical drama with Wagnerian overtones.

The playwrights of the era of expressionism who had attained world-wide recognition had done so before the decline of the Republic, but the writers who had come into prominence during the period of *Neue Sachlichkeit* in Germany were cut short by the Nazis. They emigrated and never rose to international stature. They had lost all the stages save the Swiss, from which they could speak in their native tongue. Disillusioned and desperate, they escaped from the reign of terror to freedom and a concomitant literary oblivion outside their homeland.

Between 1928 and 1939, the essentially realistic play of social consciousness dominated the New York as well as the German stage. Modified expressionistic techniques and the established forms of naturalism were clearly present in the plays of this era as were some of the newer stylistic departures on both sides of the Atlantic, but in the main it was a decade of realism. Both the United States and Germany were, at this time, deeply preoccupied with their own problems, one with its great depression, the other with its drift through chaos to fascism. Consequently there was a rising disparity between German and American realistic plays and the audiences for which they were intended. For this reason, the American theatregoer never saw many outstanding modern German plays, for they were from a world too far from New York. Age of dogged devotion to photographic duplication of social detail in drama that the thirties was, it tended to be provincial and overly enamored of details indigenous to its own milieu, German or American. However, a number of German dramas, chiefly those of the various branches of the *Neue Sachlichkeit*, were imported by the New York managers, as were some of the more experimental plays.

The first German plays of the *Neue Sachlichkeit*, chiefly historical and comic in nature, were seen on Broadway in 1928. On January 19 of that year, Gilbert Miller produced *The Patriot*, the work of a minor dramatist, Alfred Neumann, which Ashley Dukes had translated from the German for British production. *Der Patriot* was an attempt to deal realistically with a historical situation that was pertinent for the Weimar Republic, the decline and fall of Czar Paul I of Russia and the rise of the Grand Duke Alexander. The play was very well received in Germany and had been quite successful in London, but its American production, despite a highly praised performance by John Gielgud, closed after only twelve performances. It seems that the New York audience and reviewers were still incapable of seeing a historically set play as anything but a period piece, meaningless for the present. *The Patriot* received even less attention than had Werfel's *Juarez and Maximilian* the season before.

On March 12, 1928, the Garrick Players of New York presented *12,000*, William A. Drake's adaptation of Bruno Frank's *Zwölftausend*, another piece of historical realism but with enough melodramatics to give it a chance for Broadway survival. Frank's play, which had first appeared in Germany in 1926, was a dramatic appeal for democracy in his homeland, although the play was set in the historical frame of the American Revolution. The story concerns the decision of a courageous man to block the use of 12,000 German mercenary troops from aiding the British against the colonists. The play, in both its original form and in adaptation, is forthright and without dramaturgic trickery. Its inherent propaganda is never heavy-handed until the resolution of the dramatic suspense. The *New York Times* reviewer saw this lack of heroic tone as a shortcoming of the play which he said had "too little invention . . . [and] uneasy transitions" although it was an entertaining enough show.[3] Joseph T. Shipley felt that the characterization and dialogue were strong enough to carry the play even without its sermon on democracy,[4] and George Jean Nathan thought the work a good production of a good play that was mercifully not expressionistic.[5] Most reviewers agreed with Joseph Wood Krutch that *12,000* was a nice entertainment,[6] and with *Theatre Arts Monthly*'s commentator that the basic idea was stretched further than

it could go.[7] The play had sixty-four performances before it was withdrawn.

In addition to these two realistic history plays, there were also two
German high comedies performed on Broadway in the early months of
1928. *Improvisationen im Juni,* which had its German premiere in
1922, exhibited a mixture of expressionistic and realistic techniques. A
mood of doom pervades this satire, yet its ending is hopeful, an ambiguity not uncommon in German comedy of the early twenties, written
as it was at a time when the country vacillated between despair and
optimism. The playwright, Max Mohr, a close friend of Thomas
Mann, was neither Jewish nor a leftist but was one of the earliest
German artists to emigrate. A physician by profession, Mohr went to
Shanghai to practice among the poor and disease ridden. He died there
of one of the illnesses he was treating. His correspondence with
Thomas Mann is most interesting and deeply moving. His play was
translated by Suzanne Behn and Cecil Lewis and presented by Eva
Le Gallienne's Civic Repertory Theatre on March 5, 1928, as *Improvisations in June.* The play is set in a tradition-filled old German castle
which is sold to an American millionaire by its aged and debt-ridden
princess who peacefully commits suicide at the time of the transac-
tion. In the midst of this old world splendor, admittedly dead, the
millionaire appears as the stereotyped *nouveau riche* American of the
German comedy of the twenties. However, the focus of the play is
upon his son, a morose young man who is totally disillusioned by the
old world and the new alike. His father, determined to divert the boy
with anything money can buy, hires a traveling comedian to stay with
them. The great talent of this entertainer is that he can improvise
anything on command. When asked to do so, he mimes his impression
of the last man on earth, a bizarre expressionistic charade of the end
of the world which plays right into the hand of the melancholy young
man. The son is finally regenerated after he notes that all the people
around him are victims of their own greed, and that the only way not
to be defeated by this world is not to get caught up in its shabby
values. The play indicates that the only salvation for man lies in
personal integrity rather than in public panacea.

Despite its extreme popularity in Europe, where it received over
two thousand performances, *Improvisations in June* closed in New
York after less than two weeks. High comedy has never been wel-
comed by Broadway's audiences, but descriptions of the production
by numerous reviewers give ample evidence that Miss Le Gallienne,
who staged the play, fell prey, as she had so many times before, to her
tendency to play for sentiment and pathos. Also, the unanimity with
which the notices saw the boorish father as the central character, and

a caricature at that, indicates a case of completely mistaken emphasis
in this production. Joseph Wood Krutch called *Improvisations in June*
a "thin and feeble satire which goes through a number of fantastic
antics to prove that money can't buy everything."[8] John Mason Brown
saw it as one of those tiresome European burlesques on the American
millionaire.[9] The critic for the *Times* apparently saw that there was
more to the play than Miss Le Gallienne's production revealed when
he said that it employed "a translation which, one suspects, is only
so-so" and that the actors tread heavily where lightness is
demanded.[10] Mohr's play deserved better treatment than it got in
New York, but the fault lay primarily with the production rather than
with the original play, the critical reception, or the audience response.

On April 9, 1928, the Theatre Guild presented what its historian,
Walter P. Eaton, called "an unacademic Elizabethan revival."[11] The
play was *Volpone*, but it was Stefan Zweig's German adaptation of it,
translated into English by Ruth Langner, not Ben Jonson's comedy.
Zweig's *Volpone* had deleted the Elizabethan esoterica from the original, had concentrated on plot and character, had interpolated some
distinctly twentieth-century people, and had built to an ironic and
bitter climax in which virtue was not rewarded nor vice punished, but
in which Mosca got all the money and liberated it by squandering it.
The public apparently approved of this modernized text with all of its
boisterously farcical liberties. The play was neither better nor funnier
than Jonson's, but the consensus was that it was just as delightful,
only with a shift in emphasis. Its cruelty was in keeping with modern
comic tendencies as well as with the spirit of Jonson, and the absence
of classical references and archaisms made it eminently playable. In
Dudley Digges and Alfred Lunt, the Guild had two consummate
comedians for the leading roles. The settings also were highly praised,
and few people noticed that designer Lee Simonson (who had learned
much stage trickery in Germany) used the same set, only with different dressing, that was being employed by the production the Guild
was alternating with *Volpone*, O'Neill's *Marco Millions*.

The play is even funnier in German than in English, for Miss
Langner's translation (as in her Werfel efforts) missed much of the wit,
but the critical reception of *Volpone* was gratifying to the Guild. John
Mason Brown actually liked it better than the original,[12] and Brooks
Atkinson thought Zweig's results to be very good despite the fact that
he had turned comedy into farce and poetry into prose.[13] Stark Young
said that he missed Jonson's language and thought, but he felt that for
the present day the Zweig version rings true and does not get lost in
the extraneous details of Jonson's text.[14] Zweig's play was clearly a
comment on greed in Germany in the 1920's, which was not far re-

moved from greed elsewhere. It was another play that tried to make the past meaningful for the present, except that Zweig had turned to literature rather than to history for his source. The New York production was successful enough for the Guild to take it on the road and to revive it several years later.

Imported drama in 1928-29 showed an interest in modern classics seldom before exhibited on Broadway. There were entries by Shaw and by Chekhov and no fewer than four by Ibsen. German drama was represented in its native language not only by the continuation of the Reinhardt repertory but by a second venture embarked upon by the man who had brought Reinhardt here, Morris Gest. Gest engaged the Hippodrome Theatre and on April 29, 1929, presented the *Freiburg Passion Play* for forty-eight performances. The Fassnacht family of Freiburg had supplied the leading players for this passion play ever since 1760, and it was produced in Germany every three years. Although not as celebrated as the *Oberammergau Passion Play*, the Freiburg company was well received in New York.

Only one interesting modern German play, and that a minor one, was presented in English during that season. *The Phantom Lover* opened on September 4, 1928. It was a translation by Herman Bernstein and Adolph E. Meyer of Georg Kaiser's *Oktobertag*, one of his nonexpressionistic plays. The plot concerns a pregnant girl of good family who sincerely believes that the father of her child is a young army officer who in actuality does not even know her. She had seen the young man in front of a jewelry store, then in church where she saw his name in his hat, and finally at the opera. From this sequence of events she created the illusion that they had been married in civil ceremony, then in religious ritual, and had then celebrated. Only the consummation of the union remained. That night, she pulls a butcher boy, on his way to see the family chambermaid, into her room. Although her hallucination is complete for her, all the other characters involved know the boy to be the father of the child. The officer denies his guilt at first but eventually begins to believe that he was in fact the girl's lover. He kills the butcher boy who has resorted to blackmailing the family.

Oktobertag was one of Kaiser's plays which was so cerebral in conception that he neglected to notice how preposterously contrived and romantic the plot appeared on its immediate level. Actually, the play deals with two of Kaiser's favorite themes: the Pirandello-like tenet that belief determines what is real, that the line between reality and illusion is not clearly definable, and that regeneration for the man at odds with his society can come through love. "The regeneration comes about through the absolute union of two lovers, insulated from the outside world. In order to preserve the purity of their love, they transgress the laws that bind society, even to the point of committing a crime, destroying any intruder who dares to break into their magic circle."[15] An understanding of Kaiser's thought tends to explain the play and lend significance to its themes, but a play must be able to stand independent of such support, and *Oktobertag* fails to do this. It is not at all a convincing play, particularly in the realistic style in which it is written, and no one can be blamed for interpreting the piece as melodramatic nonsense. Also, the belief that the love of the lieutenant and the girl divorces them from the morality of the outside world is more tenable in theory than in fact.

The Bernstein-Meyer translation is excellent and must share none of the blame for *The Phantom Lover*'s failure. Even idiomatic usage was given parallel expression in their English rendition; there were no juxtapositions or interpolations; the only deletions were of explicit sexual references which might have offended the patrons of Broadway some years before, but for which they had been amply prepared by 1928.

Reviews of the play clearly indicated that even intelligent viewers, expecting serious work from Kaiser, were unable to make sense out of *The Phantom Lover*. Brooks Atkinson said, "The current production is no fair match for the play," but he felt that this was so because it is a high comedy with a need to be suavely played.[16] Joseph Wood Krutch felt that "it would be kinder to the author to intimate that the play was doubtless better in the original, but at best it can hardly have been other than very silly indeed."[17] It is unfortunate that with so many of Kaiser's fine plays never given a hearing in New York, *Oktobertag* had to be one of the few produced.

The Broadway season of 1929-30 was deeply affected by the market crash in October. Producers were certain after November 1 that no one wanted to see anything other than escapist entertainment. The Viennese operetta was an obvious antidote for depression blues, and the theatrical entrepreneurs quickly began to exhume old favorites: *Die Fledermaus* (this time as *A Wonderful Night*, with one of the leading roles played by a young actor named Archie Leach, later known as Cary Grant), *The Merry Widow*, *The Chocolate Soldier*, *Sari*, and *The Count of Luxembourg*. While other managers languished, the Shuberts, Milton Aborn, and Al Jolson had found that the way to keep the audience was to transport it into a world of waltztime fancy.

The three serious German plays that were seen in New York in 1929-30 were both critical and commercial failures. The first of them opened on October 7, 1929, before the collapse of the economy, when the Theatre Guild presented a play that had been an immense success in Germany the year before, *Karl and Anna* by Leonhard Frank. The drama had been Frank's own adaptation from his novel of the same name which had also enjoyed a warm reception on the Continent. *Karl and Anna* is a variation on the Enoch Arden legend, a *Heimkehrer* play which concentrates on individuals rather than on the social aspects of the world in which they struggle. The story of the escaped prisoner of war who passes himself off to his friend's wife as her husband is difficult to accept, but not so the genuine love that develops between the pair and the wife's decision to remain with her new mate when her husband returns from the war. The *Heimkehrer* play always held great appeal for the German public, but it seems pertinent to Americans only during and immediately after wars. A ten-year lapse since the end of World War I, and that a decade of "roaring," had helped men forget the domestic pathos that often results from wartime situations. War itself is far removed from Broadway. Even after World War II, a conflict that hit Americans much more closely than the first war, most of our native *Heimkehrer* plays were comedies or sentimental romances.

The reviews of *Karl and Anna* were uniformly negative. Stark Young thought the play disastrous on all counts although he had liked Frank's novel,[18] and Joseph Wood Krutch said that the play was "flat . . . spiritless, and [that] it leaves the spectator not so much unconvinced as simply unconcerned."[19] *Karl and Anna* was realistic in style but too contrived in plot to appeal to any but the most sentimental.

Josef Suss, which opened in New York on January 20, 1930, was also an adaptation of a novel, Lion Feuchtwanger's *Jud Süss*, known in English as *Power*. In Germany, the book had been dramatized by Paul Kornfeld after he had ceased to be an expressionist, but the version seen at the Erlanger Theatre was an adaptation directly from the novel made by Ashley Dukes for the London stage where it had been well received under the title *Jew Süss*. The American producers changed the name of the play, for they feared it would sound offensive, despite the fact that a Yiddish version starring Maurice Schwartz had been performed only a few months before in New York with no change in title.

Critical reaction to *Josef Suss* was mixed, but chiefly unenthusiastic. Stark Young thought the historically set melodrama of passion and prejudice was an interesting story but was without "penetrating reality of any kind."[20] Young further objected to the presentation of Jews as caricatures, and he thought the acting extremely bad. Brooks Atkinson, on the other hand, thought the play impressively staged and acted but felt that the drama itself lacked substance,[21] although the canvas of Feuchtwanger's novel was really too broad to be done on the stage. The production was essentially an intact importation of the company that had been lauded in London, but *Josef Suss* closed after forty performances. A German movie was made of *Jud Süss* after Hitler's rise to power. It was a vicious distortion of Feuchtwanger's novel and was violently anti-Semitic.

Hans Chlumberg was known for only one play, *Wunder um Verdun*. Some outstanding historians of the German drama such as Fechter and Garten have gone so far as to say that it was the only play he ever wrote, but before the appearance of the pacifistic drama that brought him fame, Chlumberg had composed a whimsical stunt that owed much of its charm to its resemblance to the work of both Molnár and Pirandello. The comedy was *Das Blaue vom Himmel,* and it opened on February 8, 1930, in New York as *Out of a Blue Sky*. It had been a popular pastiche in Europe, but the adaptation by the English actor Leslie Howard was very free, so that *Out of a Blue Sky* became "virtually a new piece of work."[22] As the play opens, a Viennese stage director appears to announce to the audience that he is dreadfully sorry but that he has neither play nor cast to present. So that the evening will not be a total loss, he asks the cooperation of the audience. Would some customers please volunteer to come up and improvise from a given plot situation. A young man and woman agree to play a pair of lovers deceiving her husband. The couple involved, it turns out, really is having a liaison, and the cuckold himself is in the audience, joining the charade on stage and innocently enjoying the joke. Such a dramatic prank is hardly enough to sustain a full-length play. Mr. Howard was aware of this and consequently interpolated more contrivance in order to fend off the eventual boredom that Chlumberg's original text invited. The additions and changes failed to achieve their purpose.

The Nation's reviewer thought it a rather silly business;[23] Stark Young called the play witless in its imitation of Pirandello;[24] and Brooks Atkinson felt that *Out of a Blue Sky* grew more boring as the evening grew older.[25] Chlumberg's comedy was thin to begin with, and Howard's contribution failed to save a play that should have been confined to one act.

Chlumberg, born of Austrian nobility, had been sent to a military academy in his youth. It was here that he rebelled against the old Teutonic order and began to write poems and stories under various pseudonyms. He saw action during the war and was impressed by its horror and futility. When he returned after 1918, he was impoverished and joined the radical opposition to the imperial government. His writings of the early twenties were largely realistic, but he finally decided to cull all that he found useful from realism, expressionism, and the new epic technique of Piscator and put it into one play that would unify all the current styles of dramatic writing into a passionately pacifistic play. The result was *Wunder um Verdun*, at the dress rehearsal of which, in Leipzig in October, 1930, Chlumberg fell into the orchestra pit and injured his skull and spine. He died a week later.

In Julian Leigh's translation, *Miracle at Verdun*, Chlumberg's play was presented by the Theatre Guild on March 16, 1931, less than six months after its Leipzig premiere, so impressed with it was the Guild and so urgent did they think it was.

Miracle at Verdun is a stylized mass-*Heimkehrer* play. Its mammoth cast is Reinhardtian. The scene is a Verdun graveyard in which both French and Germans are buried in what was then the future, 1939. The miracle is an expressionistic vision which a French caretaker has while sitting in the cemetery after he has given a guided tour to some Germans. The dramatic envelope is realistic. In the hallucination, the dead of both sides rise from their graves and return to their homes where they collide with the reality of a world that has forgotten them and is again choosing up sides. The play attacks governments, church officials, materialists, and the impervious masses alike. Everyone—French, English, German—wants the dead to disappear again. Disgusted, the corpses return to the cemetery and climb into a common grave. The play ends with the awakening of the caretaker and his conversation with the one remaining German tourist. It turns out that these two were the only survivors of the ironic battle in which all of the French and German soldiers were killed in the same trench by fire from both sides.

The German production of the play was a spectacle in which earth spewed from graves, memorial statuary burst spontaneously, and film and slide sequences served as background for many of the scenes in which the dead accost the living. The German audience, partial to vehemence and dramatic chaos and undisturbed by a clashing mixture of styles, was enthusiastic about *Wunder um Verdun*, which was, incidentally, the last emphatic antiwar play before the Hitler coup. (Others were written later, but by Germans in exile. In any case, *Wunder um Verdun* was the last pacifistic play to receive major production. Hitler forbade all drama decrying war and particularly any that proposed that World War I was madness or did not blame the "November Criminals" for the Treaty of Versailles.) The Broadway public, and most critics alike, were quite harsh in their condemnation of Chlumberg's play, for it seemed to them to be an uncontrolled hodgepodge. Complaints were voiced against the mixture of styles and the unrelieved expressionistic shrieking, but the most violent opposition was to the newest dramatic departure, the Piscator techniques of montage, film, and loudspeakers. Americans thought *Miracle at Verdun* a noisy, patchworked muddle.

Julian Leigh did not change too much from the original, but he did cut it somewhat (which did not necessarily hurt the play), rearranged the sequence of a few of the scenes, and diligently cleaned up the dialogue. In essence, the play was unchanged, but there is little doubt that the pressure of the brief rehearsal time that harasses the professional American theatre contributed to a production that was sloppy and uncontrolled when compared with the painstaking German methods of mounting spectacle plays.

Among American critics, only Joseph T. Shipley heaped praise upon Chlumberg's play. He called it "the best symbolic drama of war's human cost and wan futility to come out of World War I."[26] The play has since been included in a number of American anthologies of outstanding modern European drama, but at the time of the Guild production, the verdict was almost completely negative. Francis Fergusson called it a heavy-handed, noisy yelling debate which was not too good a play to begin with,[27] while Mark Van Doren said it was a "stunt . . . [that] leaves me deathly cold. . . . The idea of the play . . . seems to have nothing in it," and it tells us nothing that we did not already know in 1931.[28] Edmund Wilson found *Miracle at Verdun* disappointing despite some excellent scenes. Chiefly, he saw the realization of the play as inferior to the idea. Furthermore, Wilson remarked, the Guild production was sloppy in direction, although the performance and the play were both better than the reviews led one to believe.[29] Barrett H. Clark objected to the excessive emotionalism, noise, and inflated rhetoric,[30] and Brooks Atkinson said that the play was "overwrought," laden with "ostentatious stage contrivances," and full of surface platitudes.[31]

Despite the cold reception, it was clear that the play had impressed some people. The obvious resemblance of Irwin Shaw's *Bury the Dead* (1935-36) to *Miracle at Verdun* was noticed by most critics, despite the fact that Shaw, in an article in the *Times* on the background of his play,[32] makes no mention whatever of Chlumberg's. Also, in the scene in *Miracle at Verdun* in which a meeting of heads of state degenerates into a madhouse brawl, we find clear kinship to the broadly satiric sequence in Dr. Frewd's asylum for people who think they are great historical figures which Paul Green included in his 1936-37 pacifistic play, *Johnny Johnson*. The Green drama was assuredly influenced by German sources, for the playwright employed quite a few devices of expressionism and epic-film-scenario scene division in his antiwar piece. Also, the musical score for *Johnny Johnson* was composed by Kurt Weill who, unlike Brecht, had come to terms with Broadway and raised its music by a substantial notch. *Miracle at Verdun* was an obvious and frenetic play, possibly not an outstanding one, but nevertheless an important one. Popularity was denied all antiwar plays on Broadway in the early thirties. No one wanted to be reminded that World War I had been for nothing, and in the midst of the depression no one wanted to face the possibility of yet another world war.

It was also in 1931 that the press began to pay more attention to European drama. The *New York Times* in particular devoted a good deal of comment to continental productions, many of which were then adapted for the New York stage within a few years. There is no evidence to support the belief that journalistic coverage helped to create a demand for foreign drama, but it unquestionably aroused interest. In the December, 1931, issue of *Theatre Arts Monthly*, Ashley Dukes's adaptation of Ferdinand Bruckner's *Elizabeth von England,* one of the realistic histories of the *Neue Sachlichkeit,* appeared in its full text despite the fact that it had yet to be given in New York.[33] There were also numerous newspaper reports that both Herman Shumlin and Bela Blau intended to produce Carl Zuckmayer's *Der Hauptmann von Köpenick* during the following season, but neither of them ever did.

There was ample *Kitsch,* both new and revived, which was imported from Germany and Austria to supply depression diversion. Not only the inevitable operettas but even two more attempts at Schnitzler were seen in 1930-31. Eva Le Gallienne included *The Green Cockatoo* in her repertory, and Bela Blau revived the Barker adaptation of *Anatol* as a vehicle for Joseph Schildkraut. *Anatol* survived for forty-five performances after lukewarm notices. Schildkraut, in the spirit of the thirties, had apparently tried to play the role more realistically than Schnitzler's old-world comedy would allow, and the production was dull. Edmund Wilson liked it, but only because it was from a tradition of high comedy that he loved, and because it made Philip Barry seem so naïve and banal by comparison.[34] Mark Van Doren, on the other hand, found *Anatol* stale, sophomoric, and badly played, a pleasant memory that should have been allowed to rest in peace.[35]

On October 27, 1930, the Theatre Guild presented an interesting if critically and commercially unsuccessful experiment in leftist drama with epic staging devices, *Roar China,* translated by Ruth Langner from Leo Lania's German adaptation of Sergei Tretyakov's Russian play on the theme of anticolonialism. Most of the personnel involved with the production were instrumental in founding the Group Theatre, the home of the best American social realism in the 1930's.[36]

The first critical and commercial success of the new German realism in New York may have been well received here because despite
its realistic paraphernalia, its substance was a most romantic slice of
life. *Grand Hotel,* which Herman Shumlin produced and directed,
opened on November 13, 1930, and ran for 459 performances. William
A. Drake had translated it excellently from *Menschen im Hotel* which
Vicki Baum had adapted from her novel of the same name for Berlin
production. Miss Baum had been helped by Max Reinhardt, whose
stage magic was largely responsible for the success of the play in
Germany. *Grand Hotel* is divided into eighteen short scenes and thus
was one of the first plays to employ the movie-scenario technique
which was to become quite popular with playwrights everywhere who
saw the motion picture not as an enemy but as a kindred art from
which much could be learned. *Grand Hotel* presents a cross-section of
people coming and going in a huge Berlin hotel. We get glimpses—
some deep, others fleeting—of all of their lives. The dramatic glue that
holds the sequences together is the voice of the desk switchboard
operator, the many extras who give the play a constant sense of motion and transience, and a few central plot threads that involve a
number of the patrons. The script's stage directions are minutely explicit for movements of characters, overlapping of scenes, appearances
of extras, and sounds. All of this gives the real effect of the flux of the
hotel clientele. The staging of *Grand Hotel* demands choreography as
much as direction, and it was Max Reinhardt who was responsible for
this entire realistic conception and for the exploitation of movie technique (although he hated films). The name of Reinhardt even appears
in the text of the play. He is mentioned as one of the celebrities in the
hotel.

It was the stagecraft of *Grand Hotel,* its sheer trickery and invention, always calling attention to itself, that accounted for the play's
success in both Berlin and New York. The realistic effect of the hotel
(the actual "hero" of the play) itself overshadowed the improbable
and lean drama that was performed within it. Shumlin's direction and
the performances of Sam Jaffe, Henry Hull, Hortense Alden, and
Eugenie Leontovich received much of the credit also; but when Hollywood inevitably turned *Grand Hotel* into a film, starring Greta
Garbo and several Barrymores, the motion-picture techniques became
a matter of course and exposed the thin tinsel romance that the substance of the play actually was.

Francis Fergusson praised the New York production highly for its
creation of mood, objectivity, sense of *mittel-Europa* gloom, direction,

and fine acting,[37] and *Theatre* liked its "atmosphere that is electric and crackling with tension."[38] However, Stark Young, although impressed with the mounting of *Grand Hotel,* saw through its melodramatic shallowness,[39] and Barrett H. Clark, while admiring its theatricality, saw it for the slick, meaningless, and superficial comment that it was.[40] *Grand Hotel* was an unimportant play, but a good example of the type of German pseudorealism that appealed to Americans much more than the brutal social realism. The basically unreal plot catered to the American demand for romance and melodrama.

There was little German drama presented in New York in 1931-32 other than the *Kitsch* that the depression economy had inspired. Besides Georg Kaiser, a production of whose *From Morn to Midnight* was presented in Yiddish in September, the only significant German playwright to be represented was Ernst Toller. Maurice Schwartz, the leading actor of the Yiddish theatre, turned to Broadway where he produced, directed, and starred in *Bloody Laughter,* adapted by Forrest Wilson and William Schack from Toller's *Hinkemann.* The German play was first seen in Germany in 1922 and had been written while its author was in Niederschönfeld jail for his revolutionary activities. Almost all of Toller's major works were written during his various jail sentences. Imprisonment seemed to provide him the only time he ever found to write.

Although Hinkemann, the name of the protagonist, could best be translated as "Gimpy," the plot concerns the return from the war of an incredibly strong man whom an injury has rendered impotent. However, the bizarre approach that Toller takes in dealing with the unsexed man makes Hinkemann more like Laurence Sterne's Uncle Toby than like Ernest Hemingway's Jake Barnes. Although Hinkemann's wife wants desperately to remain faithful to her crippled husband who is constantly tormented by the memory of his former dynamic self, she is seduced by an ambitious, irresponsible, but outwardly appealing weakling. Hinkemann, who has been able to gain employment only as a freak show performer, induces his wife to commit suicide. As the curtain falls, the audience is led to believe that he will take the same course. The parallel between the story of Hinkemann and the political history of Germany in the early twenties is apparent.

Despite a large cast, an expressionistic dream sequence, and characters' names such as Immergleich (Consistent), Singegott (Pious), and Unbeschwert (Unconcerned), *Hinkemann* is far more realistic than any of Toller's previous plays and is one of those more modified efforts that many expressionists made after the movement had passed its peak. The central character is not a prophet, and the drama, although intense and overwrought, is almost theatrically convincing.

The dialogue is unrelieved but not rhapsodic. There are touches of humor uncommon to Toller, and a nice sense of detail, frequently absent in the author's bold dramatic strokes, gives dimension to the play. Expressionism is not an end unto itself in *Hinkemann;* it emphasizes the internal horror of the hero in its grotesquerie, and for once Toller has developed his characters quite fully.

Hinkemann is a *Heimkehrer* play that makes more use of stylized technique than did most of the returning soldier plays, and it is not really a part of the *Neue Sachlichkeit.* The protagonist is a symbol of the crushed and impotent Germany of 1918 as well as of the individual victim of war. In the man who once was unable to harm any living creature despite his strength, and who now bites living rats and mice in order to survive and save his public image while destroying his sense of self, Toller has personified the desperate Germany of his day which sought an outlet in brutality. Hinkemann is hurt worst by the laughter of those who come to mock him and who think his plight does not concern them.

When the play was translated for British production by Vera Mendel, the dialect was transposed into cockney, so a new version was needed to give a sense of immediacy in New York. A Yiddish version of *Hinkemann* had been done entitled *The Red Laugh,* and it was probably this that Schwartz had in mind when he commissioned *Bloody Laughter.*[41] It opened on December 4, 1931, and closed after thirty-five performances. *Bloody Laughter* was still excessive for American tastes, and once again it appeared in New York too long after the fact of the war, to an audience unattuned to the German political parallels, and at a time when the public was unreceptive to war-inspired drama. Brooks Atkinson referred to the play as "incohate [*sic*] and dated . . . [despite its] vigorous translation," and that "it belongs to a dying school of thought . . . [and is] overwrought."[42] Richard Dana Skinner, speaking for the liberal Catholic *Commonweal,* said that *Bloody Laughter* was powerful but clumsily symbol laden. His chief objection was to Toller's theory that the artist is responsible for the soul of society.[43] The most interesting review of *Bloody Laughter* appeared in *Theatre Arts,* where John Hutchens, although highly enthusiastic about Schwartz's acting, called the play "screamingly empty . . . hysterical in its symbolism."[44] As an afterthought, Hutchens noted that *Bloody Laughter* had lost all immediacy by 1931 and would be even more remote ten years hence. He would probably have been glad to retract that dictum in 1941, but there is no doubt that at the time of its New York production, *Bloody Laughter* was a play too late in both theme and style and too decidedly Tolleresque to stand independent of its time.

Two other plays by Toller appeared in New York in the thirties, both produced by the Federal Theatre. *The Machine Wreckers,* which opened at the Henry Street Settlement on April 11, 1937, was Ashley Dukes's translation of *Die Maschinenstürmer.* It closed after three days. The German play, which was first produced in Berlin by Reinhardt in 1922 and which Toller had also written while he was in jail, was based on the Luddite revolt of 1815 in Nottingham. The hero, Jimmy Cobbett, accepts the new machinery of the Industrial Revolution as an irrevocable part of human progress, and he warns men that they will prevail only if they control the machines rather than become ruled by them. The masses denounce him as an intellectual, and the very men he wanted to liberate kill him. The manufacturer, Ure, is unfortunately drawn as so black a villain that the conflict between enslaving capital and liberating labor becomes a false dilemma. The play has many excesses of expressionism, and its didacticism overstates a case that would have had ample strength without it. The only objectivity shown by Toller is his insistence that the masses and their potential ignorant violence are a monster as much to be feared as the exploitation by capital. The real object of Toller's attack is blind rage and violence wherever they originate. As Fechter points out, *Die Maschinenstürmer* is not without resemblance to Hauptmann's *Die Weber* and Kaiser's *Gas*.[45] In its dramatic construction, Toller's play is better than most of his other efforts because he builds to a climax and he does not sustain his usual pitch of passion. The crowd as a force is excellently handled and eminently stageworthy, and his main characters, except for his archvillain, come off believably. The oppressed arouse genuine sympathy; they are not the downtrodden mass just because the author says so; they are assuredly abused.

Die Maschinenstürmer was shown all over Europe after its Berlin premiere, but it was never done in the United States before Carnegie Institute of Technology presented it in Pittsburgh in 1926. Its first professional American production came on October 24, 1927, as a pre-Broadway tryout in Boston. The reviews at that time were so damaging that the play was withdrawn before its scheduled New York opening, and it was not seen there until the Federal Theatre presentation of 1937. Thematically, *The Machine Wreckers* should have appealed to the depression audience, but Toller's style was, at this late date, already woefully outmoded. The playwright was living in New York and attended the opening performance. It was one of the many disappointments which converged on Toller in the last years of his life. Two years later he committed suicide.

The review that appeared in the *Times* the morning after the

opening summed up the situation. The play was powerful and timely
in 1922 when the murder of the visionary Cobbett paralleled the
assassination of Walter Rathenau, but despite the undeniable strength
that *The Machine Wreckers* still had, its sense of immediacy was
gone. Furthermore, the play was "suffused in considerable rhetoric"
and was overwrought despite good acting and direction.[46]

No More Peace reached New York the following season. A fantastic and cumbersome comedy based on the Nazi problem, it was written by a man whose anger and depression had overwhelmed what
sense of humor he ever had. The play's first appearance in both print
and production was in English, and the German title, *Nie Wieder
Friede!* was translated from English, which Toller spoke fluently.[47]
However, he wrote the play in German and the translation performed
was by Edward Crankshaw. The lyrics to Herbert Murrill's music
were rendered into English by W. H. Auden, who during the years of
his marriage to Erika Mann had extensive contact with the German
émigré artists. *No More Peace* was first given in February, 1937, by
the Experimental Theatre at Vassar College, at which time the *New
York Times* reviewed it favorably and noted touches in the play
which resembled *Of Thee I Sing, Johnny Johnson,* and *It Can't Happen Here.* The option on *No More Peace* was then picked up by the
Federal Theatre which produced it in early 1938 as part of a repertory. Toller's play had only four performances.

The thesis of *No More Peace* is that although men profess peace
they practice war. In a prologue on Mt. Olympus, almost a parody of
Faust or the Book of Job, Napoleon and St. Francis raise the question:
Do men really want peace or war? The two opponents propose a test
case for the state of Dunkelstein, a thinly veiled Germany, which is
turned from a peaceful country into a militant dictatorship under the
leadership of a hairdresser named Cain. The Olympian plot is eventually discovered and a peace, purposely delineated as preposterous and
humanly impossible, is established. The humor is unwieldy and lacks
all subtlety. The songs are clear imitation of Brecht and Weill, but
they lack the allegorical finesse and touches of wit that mark their
models. Nevertheless there are some genuinely funny moments in
Toller's lyrics, and Auden's translation of them is commendable and
bears some resemblance to the styles of both W. S. Gilbert and Ira
Gershwin, but there the humor ends.

By the spring of 1938, Nazi Germany was no longer a fit subject
for burlesque. In his review, John Gassner said that *No More Peace*
was "thin . . . sophomoric," and lacking in characters. It had been
written by an expressionist out of his element. Gassner continued that
No More Peace was nothing more than a clumsy attempt to lend

fancy to well-known generalizations and clichés.[48] Brooks Atkinson also said that the play was not really very funny, that it was inhuman, and that its heavily underscored message was only a "pretentious platitude."[49] *No More Peace* was a feeble attempt to achieve the end that Charlie Chaplin attained in his film, *The Great Dictator*.

Jeremiah, translated from Stefan Zweig's *Jeremias* of 1917 by Eden and Cedar Paul, and rendered into an acting version by John Gassner and Worthington Miner, was presented in New York during the following season. As *No More Peace* was by a playwright in decline so *Jeremiah* was a pacifistic play in a style long out of favor.

Jeremiah, which had been banned in Germany (even the 1917 production had been in Zurich), is a semi-expressionistic antiwar play in biblical garb. The lengthy and wordy drama is in nine *Stationen*, and the prophet-hero is the only developed character. The rest of the huge cast serves as a chorus to his rhapsodic speeches. *Jeremiah* tells the scriptural story from the outbreak of the war against the Assyrians to the destruction of Jerusalem. Jeremiah suffers martyrdom for his pacifistic beliefs, and the king has him imprisoned. The populace finally turns against the governmental warmongers, but when the prophet is freed, he accuses all the citizens of a common guilt for allowing themselves to be whipped into a war frenzy in the first place. He warns that it would be easy to so manipulate them again. The play ends on a typically expressionistic note of love, brotherhood, and redemption through suffering. After the destruction of the city, Jeremiah exclaims that defeat is a blessing of God that purifies the human heart. Germany had not learned Zweig's lesson in 1917, and it seemed to bear repetition in 1939, if only to show again the teaching that had gone unheeded. But *Jeremiah* declaims against all self-righteous combat. In the second scene, the prophet says, "Strike the name of God from the war, for war is not waged by God, but by man! No war is holy; no death is holy; only life is holy!" (trans. mine). The great thematic weakness of Zweig's play in 1939 must assuredly have been his dictum that no matter what the circumstances peace is better than honor (as if the two were mutually exclusive). The peace of even the year before was with questionable honor, and certainly without justice, to which any Czechoslovakian could attest. With Hitler on the march, the idealism of Zweig's play must have appeared absurd.

Jeremiah lacks all subtlety, and it is overwrought and repetitious in its expressionistic sledge-hammer rhetoric. Pious pronouncements that war is idiotic were still able to arouse sympathy in 1939, but they no longer seemed pertinent. After the opening of the Theatre Guild's production on February 3, Rosamond Gilder said that *Jeremiah* was "ponderous," a good idea that was bad theatre in a production that

did not live up to its potential.[50] Joseph Wood Krutch thought it a
fine play which was too somber to have audience appeal and too
lavish in production to strike home as anything but a clumsy spectacle.[51] The *Times* commended *Jeremiah* for its "admirable motives,"
but found it "hackneyed," produced as it was so many years after its
style had become outmoded.[52] The reviewer also noted that the situation of the play actually no longer applied. King Zedekiah had submitted to waging war at the exhortation of his people. That situation
was reversed in Germany in 1939. Co-adapter John Gassner, in writing of the Guild's troubles in cutting, staging, and preparing the play,
said it "got greatly mangled during the last desperate rehearsals,"[53]
but *Jeremiah*, even done well, would have had inherent difficulties
that were insurmountable. Pure expressionism, be it Toller's or
Zweig's, was an ineffective look backward on the eve of World War
II.

The season of 1932-33 had been one of great caution by producers
who ventured mostly into safe revivals and formula comedy. The
Group Theatre and some lesser organizations were giving mainly
propagandistic plays inspired by the depression, and from a negligible
musical, *Americana*, came the most telling song lyric of the year,
"Brother, Can You Spare a Dime?" During that season, two representatives of the *Neue Sachlichkeit* received little attention in New York.

Christa Winsloe's "school play," *Gestern und Heute*, had been
quite successful in Germany in 1931 despite its anti-Prussian sentiments, but it attained real fame only when it was turned into a
motion picture shortly thereafter as *Mädchen in Uniform*. The film
was part of the last spurt of energy by the German studios to oppose
the impending Nazi coup, and it was generally picked as the best
German screenplay of 1931.[54] The success of the film was international, and it was widely acclaimed in both Great Britain and the
United States. Yet it was also strongly attacked by socially oriented
critics who felt it was not firm enough a condemnation of Prussianism
despite the fact that had *Mädchen in Uniform* been a better polemic,
it would have been a worse play.

Barbara Burnham's adaptation of the German text was produced
in London in October, 1932, and two months later at the Booth Theatre in New York under its film title, *Girls in Uniform*.[55] Producer
Sidney Phillips apparently felt that the success of the movie warranted stage presentation, particularly since the only objections to the
film were based on its significantly changed ending. The tormented
young heroine, Manuela, kills herself in the play, and the entire affair
is hushed up so that the school authorities can save face. In the film,
Manuela's schoolmates stop her from jumping down the stair well in

the last minute, and the dramatic action ends with the old headmistress (who is Frederick the Great in a tailored skirt) receiving the scorn of all the now enlightened children. *Girls in Uniform* closed after twelve performances.

The story, which takes place in an exclusive school for officers' daughters of Prussian nobility, is the plight of those who are trained to become "Mothers of Soldiers." The headmistress accepts a grant from the detested Weimar Republic against her will, but the school would be forced to close if she refuses it. The school's educational system is militaristic and reactionary, and it is designed to inculcate in its pupils the veneration of imperial Germany. A nonpolitical but humanistically inclined teacher and one of the students who develops a schoolgirl crush on her rebel against the system. An unfounded charge of lesbianism precipitates the teacher's open conflict with the administration; the distraught pupil commits suicide. In its limited way, the play is an outspoken attack upon the old Prussian motives and mores. With hindsight at our bidding, it is also an examination of the frame of mind that made the nobility as well as the working class easy prey for fascism.

Whether the film had saturated the potential audience of the play before it opened in New York or whether viewers were just unconcerned about this little corner of German life remains unknown. In any case, the reviews did not warrant so brief a run. Brooks Atkinson thought *Girls in Uniform* a good and "deeply moving" play despite the fact that he preferred the film, ending notwithstanding, because of its superb photography and the way in which it unified the episodic structure of the play.[56] (Miss Winsloe's drama, written in ten scenes, was also patterned after the scenario technique.) The reviewer for *Catholic World* felt that something had been lost in translation, but he approved of the decidedly unsentimental tone of the play although he referred to it as northern Germany's *Uncle Tom's Cabin*.[57] Joseph Wood Krutch objected to the fact that the girl was "pure victim, and therefore the play is pure pathos," but on the whole, he also liked it with a specific reservation about a flat translation, and a general one that the play had gone through too many uninspired hands before it reached New York.[58]

In the late spring of 1933, Paul Gilmore produced a series of limited engagements of noncommercial plays at the Cherry Lane Theatre. One of them was an uncredited adaptation of Ferdinand Bruckner's *Zeitstück, Krankheit der Jugend* as *Sickness of Youth*. Bruckner's drama had had its premiere in 1926 and was one of the plays of the *Neue Sachlichkeit* that concentrated on the problems of young people in a world out of joint. Bruckner's work was entirely nihilistic and thus may have appealed to the depression-conscious little theatre. Bruckner was not a major dramatist, but with nihilism again in vogue after World War II, a German edition of three of his plays, including this one, appeared in 1947 under the title *Jugend Zweier Kriege (Youth of Two Wars)*.

Sickness of Youth is a play suffused with an atmosphere of decay, disillusion, and lack of personal direction. In examining the actions of a group of young intellectuals who have squandered their potential in decadent escapism, Bruckner shows how the young people contaminate each other and eventually destroy each other. The chief merit of the play is its crisp, witty, and incisive dialogue. Bruckner's characters reveal themselves almost entirely by what they say; a bad translation would destroy the play. The sordid and perverted actions of the characters in *Sickness of Youth* are not as repellent for the actions themselves as they are for the total absence of feeling. Yet despite the constant talk of suicide, homosexuality, and heterosexual experimentation, there is little sensationalism in this play. Its dominant theme is ennui. The characters are even bored with their own corruption and perversion. Unfortunately, *Sickness of Youth* does end unconvincingly in a wild farrago of total character disintegration, but before this it is a strong statement of belief that youth itself is a disease in a world without values or goals. The play is, for all of its valid points, an overstatement because Bruckner blames everything on "the times." But who makes "the times"? This is typical of the German dodging of individual moral responsibility for community action which so many post-World War II social historians have pointed out.

Sickness of Youth is one of the most brutally outspoken plays of the *Neue Sachlichkeit*. A faithful adaptation of it would have been impossible on Broadway in 1933 without creating a public outrage. Even the comfortably obscure and critically ignored version produced at the Cherry Lane was substantially bowdlerized. Bruckner's play went almost unnoticed.

Another play by Bruckner which appeared in New York before the outbreak of the war in Europe was also unsuccessful. In the fall of 1938, Theatre House, an off-Broadway group, presented *Elizabeth von England* in an uncredited adaptation, *Gloriana*. This history piece of the *Neue Sachlichkeit* was intended as a comment on modern times, but the little-noticed production was not even reviewed in most newspapers. Atkinson said that both the play and the performance were weak.[59]

Two German *Zeitstücke* were scheduled for New York performance in 1933-34, but neither of them opened. In the spring of 1933, John Gassner's adaptation of Emil Ludwig's *Versailles* was given a

summer stock tryout in Westchester County under the auspices of the
Theatre Guild as *Peace Palace*. It was withdrawn from the Guild's
projected Broadway schedule. The Guild chose instead to present
Ferdinand Bruckner's anti-Nazi play, *Die Rassen*, which had been
produced successfully in Zurich, Vienna, Paris, and London. At the
same time that the American company was preparing, the opening of
Die Rassen scheduled in Prague was canceled for fear of Nazi reprisal
against the actors and management. Despite the interest that such a
history unquestionably aroused, the Guild's *Races* was withdrawn
after its tryout in Philadelphia in March, 1934. It was not seen again
except for a brief run at the Hekscher Theatre in 1935 where it again
became apparent, as it had in Philadelphia, that the translation was
painstakingly literal and unspeakable. Bruckner had a keen ear and
was an avowed realist. The Guild version lost this quality. If *Die
Rassen* were to have succeeded on Broadway, it would have required
the services of an organization such as the Group Theatre.

Of the German plays that did reach New York in 1933-34, none
was important. The operetta revivals continued, and there was even a
new adaptation of *Die Fledermaus*, known this time as *Champagne,
Sec*. In August, 1933, an amateur group, the Playmillers, presented
Klabund's oriental parable *Der Kreidekreis* in a translation, *The
Chalk Circle*, by I. S. Richter, but the play was not given professionally in New York until 1941.

Walter Hasenclever, one of the most extreme of the expressionists,
was also one of those who retreated from the style most sharply. One
of his later comedies, *Napoleon Greift Ein*, is a delightful political
satire. In it, a wax statue of Napoleon accepts the wager of a neighboring museum figure to come to life, change into modern dress, and
attempt to bring order to twentieth-century chaos by typically Napoleonic means. He fails miserably and sheepishly returns to the wax-
works. Hasenclever's play about the inadequacy of tyranny is obvious
in thesis but inventive and funny. Lee Shubert produced Julian
Thompson's adaptation of it on October 11, 1933. The American version, *Her Man of Wax*, was a total distortion intended as a vehicle for
the aging Lenore Ulric which emphasized the wax Napoleon's amo-
rous rather than his political adventures. The satire was turned into a
banal bedroom farce which closed after fourteen performances.

Joseph Wood Krutch referred to *Her Man of Wax* as a pretty
wretched affair "so thoroughly 'adapted' as to have lost whatever
meaning it may once have had."[60] Brooks Atkinson thought that the
play was an excellent idea that should have been executed with equal
excellence, as it may well have been in Germany, but that the dialogue of the Thompson version was so trivial, so poorly written, and

so miserably acted that the play appeared to be a work of "outmoded silliness . . . [and] posturing."[61] *Her Man of Wax* bore little resemblance to Hasenclever's comedy.

By 1934, there were fewer revivals of operettas than there had been, a trend more attributable to the interest in the new American musicals than to public enlightenment, for nonmusical *Kitsch,* although mostly native, was still in demand. With the exception of *The Great Waltz,* all the lightweight German imports of the season failed. The one serious German play of the year ran for only ninety-six performances despite a generally laudatory critical reception.

Sailors of Cattaro was adapted by Michael Blankfort from a translation by Keene Wallis of Friedrich Wolf's *Die Matrosen von Cattaro,* and was produced by the Theatre Union on December 10, 1934. The action of the play, a sailors' mutiny aboard an Austrian ship during the waning days of World War I, is based on fact, and the cast names are those of the historical figures. The mutineers are successful but are then tricked into submission. The four rebel leaders, despite a pledge against reprisals, are executed, but the play closes with the hope of eventual victory for the revolution. The Cattaro mutiny was more against the futility of war, militarism, and tyrannical abuses than it was a red uprising, and Wolf, albeit a leftist, is faithful to the facts. The German play is a very moving one by a master of the realistic craft. Of American dramatists, the one Friedrich Wolf most closely resembles is Clifford Odets, for he has the same unerring ear for the colloquial that gives his dialogue a musical rhythm without sacrificing real speech.

The American rendition of the lines was doggedly literal, carefully cleaned up, and bereft of all of its idiomatic bite. In other respects, the adaptation was commendable. Brooks Atkinson noted this in his review and said that the "too literary" text hurt the production, but that on the whole it was good and went far beyond propaganda.[62] Krutch also lauded *Sailors of Cattaro* and Wolf who "managed somehow to avoid that dreadful two-dimensional flatness which makes so many plays with a purpose palpable cardboard."[63] Stark Young called it "one of the best things in town,"[64] and compared it to Sergei Eisenstein's film, *Potemkin. Sailors of Cattaro* was a play in the style that was winning audiences and reviewers at the Group Theatre, but still the drama of social consciousness that did not treat a local problem was at a disadvantage.

Two seasons later on April 13, 1937, the Jewish Theatre Project of the Federal Theatre presented Anne Bromberger's translation of Wolf's *Professor Mamlock,* a tensely realistic play which he had written in Paris in 1933 in the heated anger of his exile after the Reichstag fire. *Professor Mamlock* is the story of a Jewish doctor,[65] a chief of surgery, who was a hero during World War I. The play takes place between May, 1932, and April, 1933, and concentrates on the early anti-Semitic campaigns and atrocities. Mamlock, who is married to a non-Jewess, is torn between his honest patriotism for Germany and the horrors of the reality that he thought could never be. Ironically, this Jew, in his very ideals, his intellect, his courage, and his professional competence, is the only character in the play who personifies all of the qualities that the Nazis held praiseworthy in a man. Wolf's play is not in black-and-white tones, for he shows attitudes toward National Socialism as varied as those of the man who does not know whether it is better to fight or to flee, and the woman who recants her early idealistic nazism when she sees her dreams going wrong. At the end of the play, Mamlock is given an opportunity to save himself by signing a confession in which he admits to having lied in a public anti-Nazi statement he has made. This last of many humiliations is beyond his endurance, and in a scene closely resembling the climax of Arthur Miller's *The Crucible*, the doctor chooses to die and to preserve his dignity and the integrity of his name. The most deeply horrifying aspect of the play is that Mamlock himself, the proud German, did not accept the reality of the Nazi rule until it was too late.

Despite its painstakingly realistic technique, the play must have seemed preposterous to an audience that still wanted to believe that the persecutions were more fantasy than fact. It is possible that the exiled playwrights were too close to events in Germany to retain any dramatic objectivity, but it is equally possible that an honest presentation of Nazi terror was too incredible to make a convincing play. Also, as Atkinson pointed out in his generally negative review of *Professor Mamlock*, the story of the Nazi brutalities to Jews had at this time never been more than a horror play in stage treatments. The subject cried out for a significant play, but no one seemed capable of writing it.[66] It is to this day understandably impossible to write both honestly and dispassionately about Nazi Germany. Even Shirer's detailed account of the Third Reich, for all of its efforts to be scholarly and objective, cannot hide the revulsion that fills any sane man who deals with the subject. Wolf's play was, unfortunately, also filled with gratuitous leftist propaganda that added nothing to the drama. Indeed, under the circumstances it seemed to be both opportunistic and tasteless. The Federal Theatre production of *Professor Mamlock* ran for seventy-six performances. It was later revived in a Yiddish translation in which it played both in New York and on a tour of major cities, but the play became best known in its film version, made by the Soviet Union. During the early weeks of the Federal Theatre production, an actual Professor Mamlock, former head of the Department of Dentistry at the University of Berlin, came to the United States as a refugee. Many of the details of his life, including the winning of the Iron Cross in World War I, directly paralleled the Mamlock of the play. Whether or not Wolf knew the real Mamlock, or at least knew of him, has never been learned. In any case, there was something Pirandelloishly frightening about the coincidence of 1937.[67]

II

Of the generation of German playwrights that grew up and arrived in the twenties, only two are well known today. Both were famous in Germany long before January, 1933, but neither commanded much attention elsewhere until after World War II. The chaos of geopolitics in the past thirty years, the unpredictability of public taste in all countries, and the American theatregoer's penchant for "the latest" have contributed to obscuring the fact that Carl Zuckmayer and Bertolt Brecht are playwrights who belonged to the German dramatic generation between the wars. They are the only two whose reputations have survived. At the time of their pre-Hitler fame in Germany, the American theatre ignored these men, as it ignores Zuckmayer to this day, and it has discovered Brecht only since the 1950's when his disciples, particularly Eric Bentley, finally made New York aware of the poet's work. The plays of Brecht have been exploited out of context ever since on the New York stage.[68]

Carl Zuckmayer, who was born in 1896, wrote expressionistic verse in his youth, and his first few plays were also in that style, but he soon dropped the technique, for expressionism was already on the wane. After some time as a cabaret entertainer, Zuckmayer began to write plays of social realism, and he soon became Germany's chief exponent of that form. It is a style to which he adhered for the next forty years. "His significance lies not in a complicated, deeply intellectual, or symbolic representation of man's problems. Rather it is to be found in his awareness of the world about him."[69] Zuckmayer attained fame in 1925 with his commercially successful and immensely funny satire, *Der Fröhliche Weinberg (The Happy Vineyard)*. The play is a merciless attack on German provincialism, bureaucracy, and middle-class respectability disguised as morality. But chiefly, it mocks the rising nationalist movement and its attendant insane anti-Semitism. The Nazis, who had suffered serious political setbacks in 1924, were unable to suppress the play a year later, although their newspapers and rabble-rousers railed loudly against Zuckmayer's play as obscene, decadent "Jewish filth." This epithet, popular since the days of the anti-Schnitzler press, was also ascribed to the work of both Brecht and Wolf. The Nazis, who never allowed facts to get in the way of their dicta, conveniently ignored that none of the three was Jewish.

Even Zuckmayer's historical plays were written from a modern point of view, and all of his characters, whether sympathetic or ludicrous, were realistically delineated. His most famous prewar play, *Der Hauptmann von Köpenick (The Captain from Köpenick)*, first appeared in 1931. It is also a satire on militarism and bureaucracy and not only held the German stages but also succeeded as a motion picture, both in the thirties and then after the war in a new filming. Carl Zuckmayer left Germany soon after Hitler's rise to the chancellorship. After a sojourn in Austria, he came to the United States and settled in Hollywood shortly before the outbreak of the war. It was there that he hoped to make a new career for himself, since many German emigrants of years before had established themselves in the motion-picture industry. Furthermore, what little reputation Zuckmayer had in America was based completely on his work as a screenwriter, not only for *Der Hauptmann von Köpenick* but even more so for his dramatization of Heinrich Mann's novella, *Professor Unrath*, which became one of the most celebrated films of all time as *Der Blaue Engel (The Blue Angel)*. In Hollywood, Zuckmayer wrote the scenario for *Rembrandt*, a screen biography of the artist, but he soon left the film capital to seek solitude on a farm in Vermont where he remained during the war and for some years thereafter.

Zuckmayer even wrote some things in English while he was in this country. He is reputed to have said at one time that he could say anything he wanted to in English; he just could not say it in the *way* he wanted to. Neither these English plays nor the ones he wrote in German during his American residence ever reached the New York stage. When his work was being performed in Switzerland and soon thereafter on the stages of West Germany, Zuckmayer returned to his homeland, accepted there as the dean of German playwrights after almost twenty years of exile. He thinks no more of Broadway than do most European playwrights, but holds fond memories of his life in the United States. He returned to Germany only because he needed a stage on which to practice his art. During those anonymous years in Vermont, Zuckmayer wrote what many consider his finest play, *Des Teufels General (The Devil's General)*. Although it was presented once in this country in German, he was unable to find an American producer for a translation. The play was eventually presented in Switzerland in 1946 and then in Germany, where it became the first important postwar play. Again, the drama was made into a successful film which, when exported to the United States, was very well received. Although the new generation of German dramatists sees Zuckmayer's work as outmoded, it treats him with the honest respect due this man who continued to be quite productive once he had returned. Carl Zuckmayer's plays deal with men who must make responsible judgments in the face of the intellectual and spiritual crises of our time. The tragedy of General Harras in *The Devil's General* is precipitated by his insistent belief that a man is responsible for what he does. Maybe this is why not even off-Broadway in the 1960's discovered Zuckmayer, for his plays do not conform to the vogue of drama about "stranger[s] . . . afraid, in a world [they] never made." Zuckmayer is one of the modern drama's most capable realists. That his work has not been performed on the New York stage has not denied Americans an influential dramatist, for Zuckmayer's strength lies in his execution of an established form rather than in any new conception, but it has deprived America of the plays of a man who writes with insight and power, and who, ironically, lived and worked in the United States for many years.

No German playwright of the twentieth century has evoked as much critical and scholarly interest or inspired as much controversy as has Bertolt Brecht. Ignored in the United States during the years of his great productivity, he is currently in peril of becoming a myth to be exploited by the commercial and little theatres alike, both of whom have lighted upon him as a craftsman and spokesman of the anxious world that evolved from World War II. The art of Brecht is no more pertinent today than it was in the thirties and forties, but neither is it less important. Eric Bentley, the man responsible for finally forcing Brecht onto the American theatre, maintains that the cult of Brecht is obscuring the artist Brecht, even as Ibsenism hid Ibsen for so many years.[70]

Brecht was drafted out of medical school during World War I, and his experiences as a field hospital orderly crystallized his hatred for war even as his youth in his burgherly home in Augsburg had developed his deep-rooted hatred for the bourgeois morality. After the war, Brecht abandoned his medical career and turned to writing. Like Wedekind and Zuckmayer, and even like so many of the Brecht cultists of today, he supported himself by performing witty and bawdy ballads of his own creation to the accompaniment of his crude guitar strumming in the cabarets of revolution-torn Germany. He gained a reputation as a "character," complete with strange social habits, strange attire, and a strange haircut; he accumulated an entourage of disciples. (Any of the good books on Brecht by Esslin, Willett, or

Bentley will supply ample evidence from the central to the peripheral for the poet's appeal to the young men and women of the fifties and sixties.)

Brecht's first play, *Baal*, written in 1918, owes a great debt to expressionism; his nihilistic *Heimkehrer* play of the same year, *Trommeln in der Nacht (Drums in the Night)*, owes a lesser one. The debt is, however, a technical one, for Brecht's point of view was radically different. The expressionists believed that man was inherently good, capable of regeneration; Brecht, like Peachum in his *Dreigroschenoper*, always felt "Die Welt ist arm, der Mensch ist schlecht."

The conclusion of the war and the termination of the German monarchy had brought with them the end of the *Hoftheater*. Among the municipal theatres that then became prominent was the *Berliner Volksbühne*, the home of socialistic drama in the era of naturalism. Its new director was Erwin Piscator, a *Regisseur* who held strong leftist sympathies and was greatly influenced by the Russian staging techniques of constructivism. Piscator saw the theatre as a social force and envisioned a new stagecraft which combined the use of drama, narration, loudspeakers, recordings, films, slides, cartoons, and mass spectacle. It was Piscator who coined the term "Epic Theatre" which is always associated with Brecht. The two men worked together in Berlin and elsewhere, and they developed the form known as the *Lehrstück*, the play intended to teach the audience something rather than amuse it. In essence, the *Lehrstück* is didactic drama that makes no pretense of disguising its didacticism. It was also Piscator's theatre that first made use of the very effective grotesque drawings, cartoons, and set designs of Georg Grosz.

When Bertolt Brecht wrote a play, he always had a theatre and a viewer in mind, not a script and a reader. Brecht wrote voluminously of the nature of epic drama, and all of his theorizing tends to overintellectualize, becloud, and inflate out of all proportion what is not essentially a complex concept. The epic drama, like the adventures of Odysseus, and indeed like the *Stationendrama* of expressionism, develops its theme in a series of self-contained units rather than in a line of rising action to be resolved in a climax and denouement. The actor's responsibility as well as the director's is to demonstrate the characters to the audience rather than to create the illusion of impersonation, to *tell* a story rather than to make it seem to happen for the first time. Epic theatre makes no effort to arouse an empathic response from the audience. The trouble with conventional drama, said Brecht, is that no matter how complete its tragedy, the involvement of the audience in stage action by means of a bond of identification brings about catharsis and release. The viewer, thus purged, leaves the theatre feeling cleansed. Brecht wanted his audience to feel dirty. He does not resolve the problem of the play, but examines it, then drops it in the viewer's lap, exhorting him to go out and do something about it. The purpose of epic theatre is to evoke an intellectual rather than an emotional response and to impel the viewer to make a moral decision rather than to indulge his feelings. Brecht desired an objective audience rather than an arena of emotional consumers, what he called a "wide awake" theatre rather than a "culinary" one. There is little creation of plot suspense in an epic drama. The emphasis is on the analysis of a situation, not on its resolution.

Brecht's essays acknowledge the influence of Arthur Waley's translations of Japanese Noh drama and of oriental staging and acting techniques in general on his dramaturgy. He liked the effect of detachment, of aesthetic distance. It was among Brecht's many purposes to use the stage as stage. He maintained that no one minded the unhidden spotlight on a boxing match and that there was no more purpose in concealing stage apparatus, for the audience should be constantly aware of dramatic illusion, that it is not watching an imitation of life but a comment upon it in a theatre. In short, these theories are really little more than expansions of what is usually called theatricalism or anti-illusionist drama, along with an insistence on episodic rather than conventionally dramatic plot delineation. Wedekind and Toller had used such a technique, albeit more moderately, long before Brecht, and an anti-Brechtian in spirit, Thornton Wilder, arrived at it independently and for different reasons. The chief difference is that Brecht hoped to achieve a *Verfremdungseffekt,* the effect of the emotional alienation of the audience so that it could concentrate on its intellectual response. Despite Brecht's avowal that he took the greatest pains to keep his characterizations inhuman so that he could keep his audience at a distance, most of his great characters and a vast gallery of his *Lumpenproletariat* do involve the viewer.

It is fallacious to maintain that all of Brechtian dramaturgy is original; he actually made liberal use of all styles of drama, traditional or modern, that he found useful; he was even accused of plagiarism on occasion. His originality lies in the proportions in which he used older methods and material, in his skilful mixture of colloquial and poetic diction, in his use of song and uninhibited imagination, and in his ironic vision of the human condition. Reality is a grim business, Brecht maintained; while he commented upon it ceaselessly, he refused to be its slave. If his plays had no substance beyond their form, they would hardly have earned him his stature in the modern drama. Much of Brecht's writing on acting, directing, and staging techniques is mere explanation of the obvious and the splitting of dramatic hair.

Brechtian playing is actually a mood and a harshness of tone and an aggressiveness which the actors and directors of the *Theater-am-Schiffbauerdamm* and the *Berliner Ensemble* (which, of course, included Brecht himself) developed for themselves, having found that an intelligent reading of the scripts defied other forms of presentation. A check of production dates of plays against times of publication of Brecht's essays, gives good reason to believe that he often rationalized his techniques into a "theory" after the fact. To overemphasize the endless Brechtian dicta and to ignore the essential artist is to fall into the trap against which Bentley warns us.

Brecht thought that his analytical style of composition was ideally suited for Marxist purposes. Yet the officially approved party drama has always leaned more toward the realism of the Stanislavski method, and of all of the German leftist playwrights of the thirties, Moscow officials thought Friedrich Wolf to be the best. The Stalin regime saw Brecht as an unenlightened Marxist who had not broken his ties with bourgeois sentimentality. Furthermore, Brecht was outspokenly outraged by the nonaggression pact and the nominal alliance of the Soviet Union and Nazi Germany until the spring of 1941. Even today, after the denunciation of Stalin and the reinstatement to grace of the party's schismatics of the late thirties, Brecht's plays are in disfavor in Russia. His latter-day fame flourishes only in East Berlin and in the countries of the Western alliance. Good communist writers must realize that dialectic is a process of reconciling antithetical concepts. Brecht analyzed and revealed antitheses; he never resolved them. What political preachments he made in his plays were really quite subordinate to his overriding sympathy for the poor, the exploited, and the oppressed, a sympathy he was able to express with a minimum of sentimentality and a maximum of honesty. Brecht's humanistic variety of German communism was a very personal code. It pervades all of his work, but with few exceptions his art far transcends politics. It is, however, foolish to try to evade the Marxism in Brecht. His politics make New York producers wary even when there is demand for his plays. Consequently, efforts to excise communism from Brechtian texts sometimes results in a *potpourri* of vignettes such as the 1962 off-Broadway *Brecht on Brecht,* a commercially inspired distortion of the poet's work that makes him appear to be a highbrow Harry Golden.

Brecht's collaboration with Kurt Weill on the 1928 *Dreigroschenoper* brought to full flower his use of the intrusive song to achieve the *Verfremdungseffekt.* His early plays, all angry and rebellious attacks on the social values of the audience, brought Brecht his pre-Hitler fame and are also the chief sources of his success in recent years on the New York stage. Brecht fled Germany in 1933. His plays were banned and his citizenship was revoked. He spent time in Denmark, Sweden, and Finland, and finally came to the United States, settling in California but living in semi-isolation. His years of exile were fruitful, for it was during them that he wrote his greatest plays. However, he could not get them performed in the United States except by the universities. Most of the premieres were in Zurich. Only Brecht's association with the actor Charles Laughton brought about an off-Broadway performance of *Galileo* in 1947. In October of that year, Brecht was called as a witness by the House Un-American Activities Committee. This humiliation coupled with his intense need for a theatre in which he could work prompted him to return to Europe, first to Switzerland, and finally to settle in East Berlin in 1949 where the authorities had offered him an ideal situation: his own theatre and ample funds to do with as he pleased. The result was the *Berliner Ensemble,* today considered by many to be Europe's finest repertory company. Brecht had learned survival tactics well in the years since 1933. At the time of his death in 1956, he still adhered to his belief that a wise man enters no house that does not have a back door. He had taken out an Austrian passport; his publisher was in West Germany; his money, even the receipts from the Stalin Peace Prize which he had won in 1955 (though the Russians still did not perform his plays), was deposited in a Swiss bank.

Brecht's international reputation was late in coming, and his representation on the New York stage as a major writer was delayed until the 1950's and 60's. But despite the failure of his own work in the United States, his impact on certain American dramatists was felt back in the thirties (the decade in which he also belongs in German dramatic history), even though his best work was done during his exile and his art transcended that of the rest of his generation.

On April 13, 1933, *The Three-Penny Opera* opened at the Empire Theatre and succumbed after twelve performances. The next time that it was presented in New York, twenty-five years later, it exceeded that record by 2,599. The adaptation that Gifford Cochran and Jerrold Krimsky made of Bertolt Brecht and Kurt Weill's *Die Dreigroschenoper* has not survived and is therefore impossible to evaluate. The production was directed by Francesco von Mendelssohn and Zeke Colvan, the former an assistant of Reinhardt, and Cleon Throckmorton's sets were an exact duplication of Caspar Neher's epic mounting in Berlin. The score by Weill fell on unprepared ears, and the purposely shabby staging must have impressed the audience as amateurish and incompetent. With few exceptions, criticism of *The Three-Penny Opera* was uncomprehending. Many ignored it completely. Burns Mantle did not even refer to it in his résumé of the season except to list its credits and call it "a German version of The Beggar's Opera."[71] The *New York Times* did not even print a review. *Time* merely stated who was in it, that it was not quite Gay's play, and that it was "often sullen, often merely dirtily proletarian, often obscure."[72] There followed some derision concerning the staging devices, the use of placards, the sparse scenery.

Although *The Three-Penny Opera* was Brecht's most popular play on the Continent, both London and New York were cool to it. The consensus in both England and the United States was that it simply was not as good as John Gay's original. Very few seemed to understand that *Die Dreigroschenoper* was an entirely different play, that it owed as much to Kipling, Villon, and 1920's jazz and tango crazes as to Gay, and that it was about the mores of the generation of the twenties and that it attacked them mercilessly. That the references to indigenously German problems of this time went unnoticed is understandable, but the failure to see the originality of Brecht and Weill that the entire Continent had perceived is particularly hard to believe. Academic critics were appalled by the New York reception, but only one newspaper or periodical critic came to the defense of the performance at the Empire: Joseph Wood Krutch, whose background was academic rather than journalistic. In the one paragraph that he was allotted in *The Nation*, he said that he needed more time and space to discuss this "brilliant work" and that the reviewers who damned it had "missed the point of its deliberate dissonances . . . [and that] it is not in competition with the ordinary operetta."[73] One week later, Krutch stated that there was no further purpose in his discussing *The Three-Penny Opera* at length; it had already closed.[74] The 1933 production of *The Three-Penny Opera* was the first of Brecht's plays to be performed on Broadway; it was also the last for thirty years. Until the presentation of *Mother Courage and Her Children*, which also closed quickly in the spring of 1963, all productions of Brecht in New York were off-Broadway.

Der Jasager was a Marxist *Lehrstück* which Brecht had based on Arthur Waley's translation of the Japanese Noh play, *Taniko*. Rendered into English by Alice Mattulath as *The Yea-Sayer*, it played a limited engagement at the Grand Street Playhouse under the auspices of the Music School of the Henry Street Settlement which was later known as the Neighborhood Playhouse. *The Yea-Sayer* opened in the little theatre on April 25, 1933, immediately after the closing of *The Three-Penny Opera*. Sanford Meisner, one of the men affiliated with the Group Theatre, staged the play, and the capable music director, Lehman Engel, conducted the score by Kurt Weill. Since the production was the effort of an experimental group that functioned chiefly as a school, *The Yea-Sayer* received no critical attention. Indeed, this work which was first performed in Germany in 1930 was what Brecht called a "school opera," a play designed for easy but experimental performance. This obscure production of this minor work was the first of Brecht done off-Broadway.

On November 19, 1935, the Theatre Union, which had done *Sailors of Cattaro* the previous year, presented a play that received more vehement critical condemnation than any other German play to appear in New York within memory. When Brecht's *Die Mutter* was first presented by Piscator in Germany on January 17, 1932, the liberal *Berliner Tageblatt* had called it a primitive play by a primitive playwright for primitive audiences. Other notices concurred, and even in experiment-prone Germany the play was thoroughly denounced. It was Brecht's last play to be performed on the German stage before Hitler became chancellor. *Die Mutter* is based on a historical novel by Maxim Gorki which tells the story of Pelagea Vlassova, the old woman who led the proletarian uprising in Twersk during the Russian Revolution of 1905. Brecht wrote extensive commentary on this play in German editions, using it as an object lesson in epic drama. He also delighted in martyring himself by quoting adverse reviews to the piece. In the *Versuche*, he cites his favorite American comment which appeared in the *New York Evening Journal* after the 1935 production: "His method is as naive as a blackboard, as childish as a set of nursery blocks. . . . 'I am Pelagea Vlassova,' says the old woman, speaking directly to the audience. 'I am making soup for my son, a worker. The soup gets thinner and thinner all the time. . . . He will get discontented and get into trouble. He reads books all the time.' . . . She might as well have added the significant news that c-a-t spells 'cat.' "

The New York production, for which Paul Peters had done the translation, aroused a good deal of critical interest, and the reaction was uniformly damning although a few were intrigued by the style, which even then was referred to as *Piscatorei*. On the morning after *The Mother* opened, the following comments were typical: "Poor stuff amateurishly presented" (*New York Daily Mirror*); "a sort of seminar in class struggle tactics from 1905 to 1917" (*New York Daily Herald*); "The point is, of course, that Pelagea Vlassova, the Mother, started out by believing in God, the Tsar and private property, and was gradually converted, chiefly by precept. It was all explained to her very carefully, and after she understood she explained it all very carefully to others. Then she, and all the others, stood up and explained it, still very slowly and carefully, to the audience." (*New York Sun*) Of the newspaper reviewers, only Brooks Atkinson had some kind words. He saw the Piscator influence and thought the style "technically interesting . . . eccentric [but] . . . thoroughly logical in the theatre, and in its free confession of stage mechanics it has a refreshing frankness. All the bars are down between the actor and the audience." Atkinson thought epic drama to have "educational value" but saw it as an "emotionally tepid exercise . . . [and] desultory theatre."[75] *Time*'s reviewer said *The Mother* was "solemnly, insufferably pretentious,"[76] and Edith J. R. Isaacs called it "straight-forward Communist preachment . . . [with] no purpose except to insult any audience's intelligence."[77] Joseph Wood Krutch[78] and Stark Young[79] saw the Brecht technique as having great possibilities, but the play itself as a weak effort. The consensus, summed up by Joseph T. Shipley, was that the play was "an overstrained, hyper-emotional kindergarten for Communists."[80] It was unmercifully parodied in the musical review *Pins and Needles*. Even *The Daily Worker* panned *The Mother*.

Brecht himself was unhappy with the American production of his play and disclaimed it because he felt it to have paid too much attention to character, verisimilitude, details, and props. This, he said, stopped it from being epic enough and destroyed the *Verfremdungseffekt;* it evoked too much feeling. Apparently he was just playing the bad boy again, but he honestly believed that the only reason for the condemnation of *The Mother* was that uncomprehending critics would not accept what he called a "non-Aristotelian" play. Brecht refused to see that the attack was against the blatant and naïve propaganda. On November 24, the Sunday edition of the *Times* ran a six-column article by Brecht (translator anonymous) about the nature of epic theatre and German drama in the years immediately preceding Hitler. It was too late for explanations. *The Mother* had offended too many. It is assuredly one of the poet's lesser works, but his major plays were either ignored or else fared no better in New York before the late 1950's.

In the thirties, departures from the forms of social realism, even if not from the themes, had little chance for survival. A case in point, in the mode of, though not by, Brecht, was *The Case of Clyde Griffiths*, which the Group Theatre presented on March 13, 1936. A translation by L. Campbell of *Eine Amerikanische Tragödie*, the play was a dramatization of Dreiser's novel which Erwin Piscator had written with the help of Lina Goldschmitt and which had received a successful Berlin production in the epic style. The cast was huge, and scene followed scene as in a motion picture. The *Piscatorei* made it eminently stageworthy. The 1936 performance in New York, however, was not well received despite some nice words for director Lee Strasberg and the actors, the listing of whose names, even those of the extras, reads like a catalog of Broadway and Hollywood stars of the 1960's. Berlin theatregoers had come to expect originality and Marxist propaganda from Piscator, but New York audiences and reviewers expected a play based on *An American Tragedy* to resemble Dreiser's novel. The Piscator version was a completely Marxist interpretation of the book.[81] It soon closed. An American dramatization, faithful to Dreiser, had had no better luck a few years earlier.

The last German play to be produced in New York before the war seasons was *Justice*, one of four experimental one-acters presented in April, 1939, by the New York Players, a minor off-Broadway group under the direction of Anne Gerlette. *Justice* was listed as being by Bertolt Brecht. Nothing further is known of the production. No title in the Brecht canon of one-act plays resembles *Justice*. However, the date of this performance suggests that the play was one of the sequences of *Furcht und Elend des Dritten Reiches*, which has often been and may easily be played independently of the rest of the larger work which had already been written and was printed in Prague in 1938, although never distributed there because of the Nazi takeover. It first appeared in the United States in an English edition in 1948. The title had by then been changed by its translator, Eric Bentley, from the literal *Fear and Misery of the Third Reich* to *The Private Life of the Master Race*, which was also used for the first full-length English performance in 1945. The acting version of the play had fewer scenes than the twenty-four of Brecht's text, many of which could be cut, for they were merely blackouts or independent vignettes. One of the original twenty-four scenes (there were actually twenty-eight, but four remained unpublished and unproduced by Brecht) was entitled *Rechtsfindung*. It was one of the longer sequences of the drama and could easily serve as a one-act play under the title *Justice*. It was fitting that the last German play of the 1938-39 season should be an obscure little mystery, and an unimportant one. The history of the drama of Bertolt Brecht on the New York stage in the 1930's was indeed undistinguished.

III

By the fall of 1936, the era of *Neue Sachlichkeit* and even of epic theatre had ended in Germany. Not one important play of either movement had received major acclaim in New York. It was in the closing years of the decade that German-American dramatic relations took on an entirely new aspect. By 1936 there was no German theatre other than the National Socialist, and except for the aged Hauptmann, there was not one major playwright who had not left Germany.

The National Socialist drama had its roots in the patriotic plays of World War I. Fascism was latent in the drama in the years when expressionism and the *Neue Sachlichkeit* flourished, for the chief playwrights and managers who dominated the German stage in those years were all passionately anti-Nazi, but in the late twenties, the fascists made significant inroads as the opposition began bit by bit to leave Germany. The first Nazi plays were historical, romantic, militant, nationalistic, and racist. Their point of view became more pronounced as the years passed, and the bombastic blank verse in which they were written gave way to carefully distorted realism. The chief dramatist of National Socialism was Hanns Johst, whose two most influential dramas appeared even before Hitler's chancellorship. *Thomas Paine* (1927) was an outrageous piece which presented the American proponent of freedom as a prototype of Nazi philosophy whose passionate beliefs inspired rebellion against a detested rule. *Schlageter* (1932), set in the present, had for its hero an early Hitlerite martyr who was not at all disguised. The historical Leo Schlageter had been executed by the French for sabotage in the Ruhr. It was the dictator's hope that German drama would reach new heights under his regime once the theatre had been purged of Jews, Bolsheviks, and democratic humanists. The drama on stage, screen, and radio was an important part of the techniques of Propaganda Minister Dr. Goebbels, who, like Italian dictator Benito Mussolini, was himself an unsuccessful playwright in his youth. One of his verse tragedies, *The Wanderer,* was poorly received even after the advent of the Third Reich. *The Wanderer* was a play about Jesus. Goebbels was also responsible for staging outdoor spectacles of Nazi power and unity. With the help of Leni Riefenstahl, a former ski champion who was Hitler's ideal of womanhood and who had a talent for directing motion pictures, Goebbels turned the annual Nürnberg revels into a National Socialist version of Wagner's Valhalla. Riefenstahl's film *Triumph des Willens (Triumph of the Will)* is a terrifying record of a Nürnberg *Parteitag.* The cult of war, nationalism, heroism, and racial superiority besieged the public eye wherever it sought entertainment, particularly in the movie houses. Soon after the proclamation of the Nürnberg Laws in 1935, attendance at public spectacles and all dramatic performances was forbidden to non-Aryans. To be a member of the audience was then to belong to the elite of the cast, a race of Teutonic heroes.

Adolf Hitler foresaw enough heroic drama to keep the audience indoctrinated and enough *Kitsch* to keep it amused. He was keenly disappointed, for even the most avid Nazis in the theatre dried up before the outbreak of the war. Nevertheless, the playhouses of Germany were lit almost throughout the Nazi hegemony. Hitler insisted that they remain open even during the early saturation bombings, and they did not close until the fall of 1944.

The Nazis deprived the German drama of every one of its major playwrights and a substantial number of its greatest actors and directors. Men of the theater fled to France, Scandinavia, England, South America, and elsewhere, but most of them emigrated to Switzerland or the United States, where they either went into anonymous isolation or affiliated themselves with the *Zürich Schauspielhaus*, Hollywood, or the New York stage, on and off Broadway. The German drama as a creative force within the confines of that country perished in the mid-thirties; it has only recently shown signs of rebirth, although the German theatre became active almost immediately after the war. "The assertion that Hitler destroyed the culture of Weimar is neither one of his idle boasts nor a hyperbolical accusation of his enemies. It is the truth."[82]

With anti-German feeling running high in the United States by 1936, it was natural that the production of plays from that country would decline sharply. But in contrast to the boycott during and after World War I, a time when Germany was still dramatically productive, there were no more plays to be imported. The years between 1930 and 1945 in New York were actually without much European drama of any kind, but the German offered the least likely choice. The anti-Nazi plays which were imported in the thirties found no audience here. For all of their topical value and emotional immediacy, they were hardly ever first-rate drama. Furthermore, depression-limp America was feeling far too sorry for itself to seek problems elsewhere. The climate of Broadway being what it was in the late thirties, it would have been silly to revive older German drama, for the times made the drama of any time but the present irrelevant. There was nothing new to which theatrical managers could turn, and the men from whom they could have expected significant work were either on the run or else had settled in the United States with the hope of becoming part of the American theatre.

The years from the late thirties to the end of the war were the years of German émigré drama on the New York stage. The only exceptions were a few innocuous comedies and an occasional *Kitsch* operetta, which, if it was lavish enough, was still in demand. A long run was afforded *White Horse Inn*, which at the time had the reputation for being the most popular musical in European history: more than a thousand performances in Vienna, over four hundred in Berlin, over six hundred in London, over two years in Paris, and lengthy runs even in Palestine, Africa, and Australia. Of the production which opened on October 1, 1936, Joseph T. Shipley said:

> The Center Theatre spread the Inn and its Tyrolean surroundings across its wide stage and out along the sides. Everywhere the spectacle has been colorfully and lavishly adorned. Robert Coleman fitly warned his readers: "Bring along your St. Bernard and your skis." . . . There was a cow-milking scene . . . with real cows . . . the visitors for the Tyrolean festival arrived in a real, full size motor omnibus . . . the Emperor arrived by steamer. . . . John Mason Brown said, "The real heroine of the evening is the wardrobe mistress."[83]

As always, no serious play fared so well on Broadway.

Bruno Frank's *Sturm im Wasserglas* was one of Germany's most successful comedies in the years immediately before Nazi domination. It is a political satire that attacks the hypocrisy of windbag municipal officials but goes even further by not sparing the petty, indifferent, and ignorant public that allows such corruption because it believes it to be inevitable. The pompous politician of the piece is finally deflated by a series of farcical circumstances precipitated by his refusal to take any interest in a constituent's impounded dog. Frank's play was also successful in London as *Storm in a Teacup*. The adaptation by James Bridie (O. H. Mavor) was remarkably adroit. He reset the play in Scotland, but changed neither plot nor characters. Yet Bridie's keen sense of common speech, which his own plays always exhibited, allowed him to render the German dialect into truly parallel Scotch diction. For each of the details that lent credibility to Frank's comedy, Bridie found a Scotch equivalent. *Storm in a Teacup* had all the freshness of an original play and none of the stilted mannerisms of translated comedy. When the Theatre Guild presented the play in New York on March 8, 1937, the only change it made in the Bridie text was the title, which became *Storm over Patsy* (Patsy is the name of the dog).

The play is predictable, not devoid of clichés, and even quite mild in its satire. Most reviewers agreed with Krutch that it was good fun and little more, but that it achieved exactly what it had set out to do.[84] *Time* called it "small but perfect in its way. . . . keeping a theatrical puffball slyly in the air,"[85] and Stark Young and Brooks Atkinson also found *Storm over Patsy* entertaining, amusing, and funny.[86] Although thin, it was a good cut above *Kitsch*. Yet despite its good reviews, it closed after only forty-eight performances. Another play by Frank, a melodrama known in English as *Young Madame Conti*, opened in New York three weeks after *Storm over Patsy*. It was undistinguished and closed after twenty-two performances.

Although Adolf Hitler was unquestionably the chief world problem of 1937, the depression still served as a theme for popular plays,
particularly those of the Federal Theatre, two of whose productions
during the season were from German sources. In addition to Toller's
The Machine Wreckers, it presented *Help Yourself,* John J. Coman's
free adaptation of an obscure farce by Paul Vulpius which tells the
story of an unemployed man who walks into a bank, sits down at an
empty executive desk, and behaves as if he belonged there. Before
anyone discovers the hoax, he has become vice-president of the bank
and the husband-to-be of the president's daughter. This dramatic
prank delighted audiences at the Federal Theatre's Popular Price Unit
for eighty-two performances. Vulpius' play might never have succeeded had it not been thoroughly Americanized.

In 1938-39, Reinhardt returned from California to direct Thornton
Wilder's new play, *The Merchant of Yonkers,* a farce freely adapted
from the Austrian Johann Nestroy's comedy of 1842, *Einen Jux Will
Er Sich Machen,* which Nestroy, in turn, had based on an 1835 English comedy, *A Day Well Spent* by John Oxenford. The Wilder play
closed after thirty-nine performances. It was later revised and successfully produced during the 1955-56 season as *The Matchmaker,* and
then, in what must cap the longest string of adaptation and re-
adaptation on record, became a motion picture, followed by yet another reworking into the banal and noisy (but lucrative) musical
comedy *Hello, Dolly!* which even as of this writing is being turned
into a motion picture. Joseph Wood Krutch said that "most of the
amusement which the play furnishes (and it is often quite laughable)
is the result of the honest farce of the original author, to which neither
the rewriting nor the stylized production contributes very much."[87]
Time's reviewer felt that the play went along quite well for a while in
its funny and outdated fashion, but that it broke down when the
author turned "a little cute" and the plot turned "a little silly."[88]
Theatre Arts objected to Reinhardt's "rococo detail,"[89] and Atkinson
lamented that "the fun runs on heavy feet."[90]

During the 1936-37 season, the presence of the immigrants from
Germany was felt for the first time, and the imminent disaster that
Hitler had wrought was finally faced. Many of the actors who had
arrived in this country were unable to speak English well enough to
perform on the New York stage, and there was not yet a demand for
them in Hollywood where, only a few years later, they would be
playing either pathetic Hitler victims or caricature Nazis. Some of
them organized refugee theatre groups which performed for each
other and for other immigrants in German in rented halls and church
basements. One of the organizations, the *Deutsche Schauspiel-Bühne,*

presented Hauptmann's *Die Versunkene Glocke* in 1936-37. However, many of the writers, directors, and performers soon worked in the American theatre.

The first interesting work of German émigré drama to appear in English in New York was *The Pepper Mill* which opened off-Broadway in the Chanin Auditorium on January 5, 1937, and closed after six performances. No major newspaper or periodical reviewed it, and the only detailed record of it is in *Escape to Life*, a book by Erika and Klaus Mann which was published in 1939 and recounts the story of some of the intellectuals exiled from Germany. *"Die Pfeffermühle"* had been a politico-literary cabaret founded and operated by Erika Mann across from the back of the *Hofbräuhaus* in Munich. It was in the best traditions of the *Überbrettl*, but its opening on January 1, 1933, came only twenty-nine days before the Hitler coup. Nevertheless, the cabaret continued to operate until February 27, Shrove Tuesday, when in the midst of the frenetic German *Fasching* celebration, the Reichstag burned. Effective the following morning, the performance of anti-Hitler humor was no longer safe for its authors or players. *"Die Pfeffermühle"* closed and its performers went on an enforced tour outside the country. The company was constantly on the run, but gave 1,034 performances throughout Europe until official protests from the German government had it stopped in numerous countries.[91] In Switzerland, a performance was raided and physically broken up by the Frontists, a fanatical Swiss group which was pro-Nazi. They threw gas bombs and indiscriminately fired live rounds of ammunition until the police quelled the riot. Despite the illegality of the pro-Nazi group's actions, the Swiss authorities, in order to keep the peace, revoked the company's license. Many of its performers, authors, and composers came to the United States after the cabaret disbanded.

The original intimate German review had been written by Erika Mann, Klaus Mann, Ernst Toller, and Erich Mühsam, and there were later additions by W. H. Auden. Mühsam, arrested and tortured by the Nazis, was the only one of the authors not to get out of Germany. His captors pulled his beard out hair by hair, and when he refused to sing the Horst Wessel Song, they condemned him to death. He was compelled to dig his own grave, but he refused to obey the command to kill himself. The Nazis murdered Mühsam in 1937.[92]

The adaptation of the cabaret review which appeared in New York was made by John Latouche (who also appeared in it, as did Erika Mann) and Edwin Denby, and the musical numbers were reworked by Aaron Copland in order to fit their new lyrics. The production was directed by Therese Giehse, who years later was to become Switzerland's most celebrated actress. The failure of *The Pepper*

Mill to find an audience in the United States in 1937 was understandable. The genre of the satirical cabaret was totally foreign to New York and continued to be so for twenty more years. But even more important, translation of the original sketches was almost impossible (many of the humorous allusions were meaningless to those unfamiliar with the intricacies of Nazi Germany), and most of the players had insurmountable trouble playing comedy in English. As Miss Mann herself said, "The enterprise came to grief over the question of language."[93] After the closing, the script was revised, and not long thereafter the performers' English had improved sufficiently to warrant a reopening, but the revival never took place.

The first artistically successful, although financially disastrous German émigré drama opened two days after *The Pepper Mill*. Franz Werfel's biblical spectacle, *The Eternal Road*, had its premiere one year, fifteen days, and ten postponements after its originally announced production date.[94] It had never been performed in German for political, technical, and monetary reasons. The original idea for *The Eternal Road* was that of Meyer W. Weisgal, one of the American producers, who told it to Max Reinhardt who, in turn, transmitted it to Franz Werfel and Kurt Weill.[95] Werfel was once quoted as saying, "The production of plays is as a rule no concern of mine. I am a poet."[96] But in a letter to his wife, dated early in March, 1934, he had said:

> Der vorliegende Versuch will keine Dichtung sein, sondern ein dienendes Werk. Es wurde unternommen, um Gott durch sein eigenes Wort zu loben und vor der Welt den ewigen Plan darzustellen, der Israel auferlegt ist. [The project which lies before me is not intended to be a work of poetry but one of service. It was undertaken in order to praise God through His own word and to present to the world the eternal plan that is the burden of Israel. (trans. mine)]

It was clearly not Werfel's intent to write a profound play, but *Der Weg der Verheissung* was a timely and deeply moving spectacle.

The play opens in a synagogue where a group of frightened Jews in an undesignated land have sought refuge. An angry mob threatens outside the house of worship, and the ruler, in a distant castle, is debating whether to banish or to annihilate the Jews. During the night's vigil, a rabbi reads pertinent Old Testament stories to those gathered, and the dramatization of these tales makes up the bulk of the spectacle. The theological point of view of the play is an example of Werfel's own peculiarly mystical faith, a fusion of Judaism and Catholicism, but for those not looking for Werfelian religious thought, the play's chief power lies in its evocation of a tradition of physical courage, moral integrity, and intellectual strength. The Jews of the play are nameless, referred to only as "The Religious One," "The Cynic," "The Boy," and so forth, and there are some other expressionistic touches, but in the main, The Eternal Road is a spectacle play, climaxed by the oppressed people's reaffirmation of their faith and their determination to survive, here or elsewhere.

The New York version, adapted by William A. Drake from Ludwig Lewisohn's translation, lost Werfel's gift for language which was omnipresent in the German text despite the playwright's decision to renounce the role of poet for this work, but since the production emphasized musical and visual effects, the absence of poetry was not a grievous loss. What need there was for impassioned language was amply fulfilled by the biblical and talmudic texts which made up the rabbi's speeches. Norman Bel Geddes' settings were built on five levels, and the enormous cast was impressively handled by Reinhardt. The Eternal Road was a mammoth production, and despite a year of ballyhoo which made reviewers justifiably suspicious, the play was favorably received. It ran for 153 performances, but the deficit imposed by the half-million dollars it cost to present the play was too much to overcome. Broadway could not afford the lavishness of Reinhardtian technique. There were also those who felt that it was not even necessary. Brooks Atkinson, who found The Eternal Road a "deeply moving [play with] . . . great dignity, power and beauty,"[98] said that it could have been just as good, albeit different, had it been played on a bare stage.[99]

The reviews were almost unanimously laudatory. Krutch thought that the movies could not do this sort of drama better because Hollywood spectacles strained for reality while Reinhardt achieved symbol, groupings that were not just mobs, and the aura of a medieval mystery play. The Eternal Road, Krutch continued, was an idea more than an event, and he found the play "quite genuinely magnificent."[100] Time, usually averse to emotional displays, heaped praise upon Reinhardt and Bel Geddes.[101] Atkinson called The Eternal Road a great and moving spectacle which was given a tone of "exaltation" by Weill's sensitive score.[102] Qualified approval came from Stark Young, who thought that Reinhardt's "expert engineering" crowded itself between play and audience,[103] and George Jean Nathan, who said that "a true poet like Werfel cannot be guided by other men's fancies," that he was not the sort of man who could write a play to order, even on measurements given by Reinhardt, and that the author was far too good for hack work à la Hollywood.[104] Despite some of these aesthetic differences with the production, critics thought highly of *The Eternal Road*, a play that had both immediacy and the splendor of the Reinhardtian extravaganza of a day gone by.

An interesting sidelight of the American drama of the thirties was the native play of undisputed hokum about Nazi Germany. These insufferably melodramatic efforts merely exploited the German horror. Some of them were such romantic wishful thinking that their anti-Nazi sentiments were quite feeble, and they often ended on a self-deluding note that Hitler would soon disappear. Even after that dream exploded, and well into the war years, most American plays set in the Nazi milieu were preposterous. Almost all of them missed the true gravity of the situation.

Early in the 1930-31 season, the first of these plays appeared. William Bolitho's *Overture* revolved around a post-World War I "people's revolution," and it presaged what no one cared to take seriously in New York in 1930, Adolf Hitler. The play was mildly received. In 1933-34, *Kultur*, which was withdrawn after ten performances, was listed as an adaptation by Adolf Phillipp from a play of the same name by Theodor Wächter. Wächter was an obscure German hack who had come to the United States before January, 1933. Rumor had it that Adolf Phillipp, whom no one ever knew, was Wächter himself trying to lend the play an aura of refugee authenticity. No one cared enough to pursue the matter.

Of the American anti-Hitler plays of 1934-35 a few were a cut above the usual romantic rubbish, but with the exception of S. N. Behrman's *Rain from Heaven* they had a tendency to be vehemently propagandistic, and though passionately sincere they were dramatically unconvincing. Chief among these efforts were Elmer Rice's *Judgment Day*, concerning the burning of the Reichstag, and Odets' *Till the Day I Die*, which was more pro-Marx than it was anti-Hitler. Significantly, almost all of the Americans writing anti-Nazi plays were Jewish. Their deep involvement hurt their objectivity, but no one else in theatrical circles was taking Hitler too seriously in 1934.

During the 1938-39 season, the last before the outbreak of war in Europe, an increased awareness of the Nazi situation became apparent in some new American plays. Behrman, who had been one of the first to deal intelligently with the problem, stated his case in *No Time for Comedy*. Clare Booth's *Kiss the Boys Goodbye* was set in the South but was "meant to be a political allegory about Fascism in America."[105] Irwin Shaw's *The Gentle People* was a parable exhorting the oppressed to rise up against tyranny. However, the commercial stage still gave a showplace to numerous efforts of superficial anti-Nazi melodrama, totally divorced from the real issues. Oliver H. P.

Garrett's *Waltz in Goose Step* and Jacques Deval's *Lorelei* were both clumsy and weak, and Burnett Hershey's *The Brown Danube* was a very mild anti-Nazi play despite the fact that it inspired vandals to deface the theatre with swastikas on May 28, 1939.

In the decade preceding World War II, the techniques of German drama and theatre exerted perceptibly less influence on the American stage than had the forms of expressionism. Yet, though the plays of the epic method which were imported were largely failures, their stagecraft was reflected in numerous native ventures.

The Federal Theatre Project of the WPA was an antidepression measure responsible for some new plays as well as for revivals, but its chief contribution, in addition to supplying employment for many people and inexpensive entertainment for a poverty-stricken audience, was the development of the type of play known as the "Living Newspaper." Productions of the next few years such as *Power, One-Third of a Nation, Spirochete,* and $E = MC^2$ were the work of many hands. Their content was derived from current news and social problems, and they were presented on sparse and highly stylized sets that drew greatly from the epic technique of Piscator's theatre in Berlin. The "Living Newspaper" was usually made up of a series of independent vignettes with a common theme. The scenes were held together by headlines projected on screens and by loudspeaker announcements. They bore a marked resemblance also to the fiction of John Dos Passos. Their dramatic effect was cumulative rather than unified, and their dialogue was often directed at the audience rather than at other actors. It was anti-illusionist drama that owed much, and admitted its debt, to Brecht and Piscator. The critical consensus that the "Living Newspaper" was not good drama but effective didactic use of the theatre would have pleased the German theorists of epic drama.

In 1936-37, Paul Green's *Johnny Johnson,* with its music by Kurt Weill, its story of a small man's struggle against war, and its succession of many short scenes some of which indulged in caricature and fantasy, was strongly reminiscent not only of expressionism but of epic theatre. More than one critic noted its similarity to Piscator's dramatization of Hasek's *The Good Soldier Schweik.*

Thornton Wilder's *Our Town,* which won the Pulitzer Prize for 1937-38, was the best of a number of sceneryless or otherwise anti-illusionist plays that year. Its bare stage was a far more conscious device than the more practically enforced barren settings of other productions, particularly those of Orson Welles and John Houseman's Mercury Theatre. There was artistic method in the Mercury's modern-dress *Julius Caesar* which was intended to be pertinent in the day of fascist revolutions, but there was little more than financial justification for the season's other presentations of Shakespeare in mufti. Shakespearean tragedy to serve the current political scene was also the motive of the Federal Theatre's *Coriolanus,* seldom done in this country (but always a favorite in Germany). The Federal Theatre also revived John Howard Lawson's *Processional* in this season and continued its "Living Newspaper" project with what is usually considered the best work in the form, *One-Third of a Nation,* which made extensive use of the techniques that Piscator had devised for Ernst Toller's *Hoppla, Wir Leben!,* wherein the expressionist had come very close to writing an epic drama.

The incidental music for the Welles-Houseman *Julius Caesar* was composed by Marc Blitzstein, a young musician and lyricist who had studied in Germany and had become deeply involved with the experiments of German drama during the twenties and thirties and with the attempts made there at writing opera in a modern idiom, a major interest of Kurt Weill. In the summer of 1937, Blitzstein's first major and most debated work, *The Cradle Will Rock,* had its premiere, sponsored by the Federal Theatre which then dropped its option on the strange musical. The Mercury Theatre then undertook to produce it, and Blitzstein, together with Welles and Houseman, designed the staging. In the last days before the opening, trouble developed with actors, stagehands, musicians, the unions, and the government. There was even some question whether or not the play would have a theatre. When *The Cradle Will Rock* opened on January 3, 1938, the only musician with an instrument was Blitzstein himself. There was no scenery, there were no costumes, and there were very few actors. Blitzstein often jumped up from his on-stage piano to take over a part or two himself, then returned to the keyboard to accompany his own singing. The entire production had an air of spontaneity, anger, and energy that intrigued many who were in the audience that night, while others booed or stormed out, outraged by what they thought to be a fraudulent production. Actually, this almost improvised performance of *The Cradle Will Rock* with its atmosphere of despair and shabbiness did not hurt the musical at all, for it was a cacophonous and harsh attack on the American socio-economic situation that had yielded poverty, depression, and exploitation. The songs were sung right at the audience, and the dramatic scenes, each almost sufficient unto itself, were demonstrated to the opening night audience rather than played for it. There was no illusion that the spectator was anywhere but in a theatre and watching an angrily didactic play with music. Had it been planned that way, it could not have been more akin to the theatre of Brecht and Weill, both of whom Blitzstein regarded with adoration. A program note stated that Blitzstein's *The*

Cradle Will Rock was dedicated to Bertolt Brecht. *The Cradle Will Rock* was briefly revived in December, 1947, and later had a performance in a concert version given by Leonard Bernstein. The incidental music that Blitzstein was to write for many plays in the future owed much to Weill, as did some of his operatic efforts such as *Regina,* based on Lillian Hellman's *The Little Foxes.* When *The Three-Penny Opera* finally became a hit in America in the 1950's, it was in an adaptation by Marc Blitzstein.

There was no more German drama after the mid-thirties. An entire generation of creative and performing artists was either exiled or murdered. By the outbreak of World War II, the German drama existed only outside of Germany, where its practitioners were concerned with more pressing problems.

In both Germany and the United States, as indeed in all of the civilized world in 1939, life had become bigger than art.

4

War and Exile:
1939-45

I

World War II brought a temporary end to the dominance of the social drama of verisimilitude in New York. During the years of conflict, the best of Broadway was largely romantic escapism and wise-cracking situation comedy. The best plays inspired by the war, like the best novels, came after there had been time to reflect and gain perspective. There would have been little public animosity to overcome, as there had been during World War I, had many German plays been produced in New York between 1939 and 1945, for it was common knowledge that the men of German drama were exiles, most of them living in the United States, who were enemies and victims of Nazi hegemony. However, the chaos of their lives had limited the productivity of the émigré artists, and there were few German plays on the New York stage during the war. Of even these, only a small proportion was not the revival of older work. And in addition to the myriad other adjustments that the émigré artists had to make in their violently displaced lives, they were thrown into a theatrical system the structure of which was far different from any they had ever known.

There was not a single important play of German origin presented on the New York stage in 1939-40. Older plays seemed suddenly more outdated than ever; even the new realism was about matters that already appeared historical. The epic experiments had never found their way into favor, and the American venture on which they exerted influence, the Federal Theatre of the WPA, had ceased operations on June 30, 1939. The only Germanic importation was restricted to the lightest Viennese theatrical pastry. On June 20, 1939, a musical review produced by the Refugee Artists Group opened at the Music Box Theatre. It was a synthetic show, made up of material by various Austrian refugees, which was written in German, adapted by John Latouche, Eva Frankin, and Hugo Hauff, and presented under the catch-all title, *From Vienna*. The ensemble was directed by Herbert

Berghof, also a recent immigrant. Language was not so great a problem as it had been with *The Pepper Mill,* for the performers all spoke
English quite well by this time and retained only a charming and
light Viennese accent which lent flavor to the production. Hard-boiled
American reviewers accustomed to the brutal comedy of native origin
were not attuned to *From Vienna,* but they were kind to the performance because of obvious sympathy. *Time* recommended it despite
what it felt was a slow first half,[1] and Franz Hoellring, in *The Nation,* unashamedly partisan, said that *From Vienna* had "not a dull or
tasteless moment."[2] After doing nicely at the box office for seventy-nine
performances and fighting the summer heat to which the Austrians
were unaccustomed, the review closed. However, the company remained intact, changing its name to the American Viennese Group,
and after some additions, deletions, and revisions in sketches and
music, reopened the review at the Little Theatre on February 21,
1940, as *Reunion in New York.* The new version emphasized more
recent events, particularly the humor inherent in the process of the
Americanization of the immigrant, and it ran for eighty-nine performances. The cabaret style was still foreign to Americans, but there were
many refugees who were glad to have a touch of their pre-Hitler life
divert them from their hardships. The removal of the revue to a
smaller theatre was also more conducive to an intimate performance.
These Viennese efforts were not serious drama, but they were testi-
mony to a hardy group who, though deprived of so much, had retained their sense of humor and were game enough to try to laugh
through their tears.

The most significant event in the German émigré drama in New
York during 1940-41 was the establishment of the Studio Theatre by
the New School for Social Research which had made its facilities
available to many exiled artists and to scholars in all disciplines. The
Studio Theatre, which anticipated the resurgence of the off-Broadway
theatre after the war, was made up of both American and refugee
players under the direction of Erwin Piscator, whose exile had led
him also to the United States. The Studio Theatre presented some of
the most interesting drama in New York during the ten years of its
existence. Piscator's repertory was not restricted to the experiments
that had brought him fame in Berlin. His selections were varied and
included many plays of German origin. In a decade when the New
York stage and Broadway were synonymous, and when even the university drama groups were doing largely "hit" plays warmed over,
Piscator's theatre was one of the few that presented noncommercial
drama of quality.

The first German play done by Piscator was *The Circle of Chalk,*

James Laver's translation of *Der Kreidekreis* by Klabund (pseudonym of Alfred Henschke, poet, essayist, and sometime playwright of the twenties). The piece was originally one of a cycle of one hundred plays written during the Chinese Yuan Dynasty (1259-1368). During the nineteenth century, Stanislas Julien had rendered it into French, partly in verse, partly in prose. Klabund's German version, written in 1924, was an adaptation of Julien's work, and it was produced by Reinhardt the following year with Elisabeth Bergner in the leading role.

The Circle of Chalk is the story of Hai Tang, who suffers many tests of her integrity and is finally elevated to the imperial throne. At the rise of the curtain, her father, far in arrears in his taxes, kills himself, and Hai Tang is sold into a brothel from which she is bought by Ma, a tax official, despite the opposition of Prince Po who wants to protect the unfortunate young girl. Ma's wife, a nasty and childless woman, poisons her husband and not only blames Hai Tang for the crime but also says that the child Hai Tang has borne is really hers and that the girl has stolen it. In the midst of various attempts of bribery and corruption to rectify the situation, a trial is ordered. It is presided over by a judge whose unsavory reputation is based largely on his cynical attitude toward the law and his habitual drunkenness. The judge resolves to put the two women to the test of the magic chalk circle: The child is placed in the middle of the circle drawn by the chalk, and only the true mother can lead it out. The murderess tugs desperately, but to no avail; Hai Tang, afraid to hurt the child, refuses to touch it. The result is the same as that of the biblical tale of Solomon and the disputed infant. Hai Tang not only gets her baby, but the Prince announces that he is its father and that he will marry the long-suffering heroine.

There had been an amateur performance of the play done in New York in 1933, but in a different translation. The Laver version which Piscator chose and entrusted to James Light, the director of the performance which opened at the New School on March 24, 1941, had been used for a spectacular production of *The Circle of Chalk* in London in 1931, starring Anna May Wong and Laurence Olivier. At that time it ran for more than a year, but London critics ascribed its appeal largely to its lavish stagecraft in which the prostitutes were suspended from the gridiron in gilded cages. The pageantry and costuming were excessively lush, and a bizarre character was interpolated, a sadistic eunuch headsman who watched over the brothel. The London staging of the play was a commercially inspired venture that was not the fragile fantasy of Klabund but a banal peep-show in oriental decor. The Piscator staging was simple and straightforward, a choice probably inspired as much by the company's lack of funds as it was by its producer and director's good taste. After the opening, the reviewer from the *New York Post* praised *The Circle of Chalk* for its "quaintness and delicacy,"[3] and Brooks Atkinson gave the play a warm notice, calling it a "charming" play well done.[4] Piscator kept the Klabund work in his repertory and revived it every once in a while. *The Circle of Chalk* was also one of the last plays done by the Studio Theatre in its closing season ten years later. The play is a delightful fantasy whose fairy tale quality is accompanied by a substantial amount of humor and social satire which applied to the present as much as it did to the Yuan Dynasty. Indeed, that is what had appealed most not only to Klabund but also to Bertolt Brecht, one of whose finest plays, *The Caucasian Chalk Circle*, is based largely on this work.

The only German play to be produced on Broadway in 1941-42 was a revival of William Gillette's completely Americanized adaptation of Carl Laufs's farce, *Ein Toller Einfall,* which had been a commercial success in 1890 as *All the Comforts of Home.* Although Helen Jerome revised the dated Gillette text, this piece of *Kitsch* lasted for only eight performances. The only other production of a German play to reach Broadway that season was a classic that had opened in a little theatre before its move uptown. This was a cut and streamlined version by Ferdinand Bruckner of Lessing's *Nathan the Wise,* also a quick failure after twenty-eight performances.

Of the two modern German plays to be done off-Broadway that year, one was in its native language. In May, 1942, a group of refugee actors presented a few of the scenes from *Furcht und Elend des Dritten Reiches,* Brecht's synthesis of playlets about life in Hitler's Germany. Each individual scene is naturalistically written; only the chalkfaced chorus which supplies transitions between scenes by singing verse after verse of a parody of the "Horst Wessel Song" resembles Brecht's major style. Piscator had originally intended to do the play, but after he changed his plans, the production was undertaken by the émigré performers under the direction of Brecht's friend, Berthold Viertel (who was also the model for the hero of Christopher Isherwood's *Prater Violet*). Since the selected scenes were played in German, both audience and critical comment were limited.

The other modern German drama, the only one done in English that season, was *The Criminals,* Edwin Denby and Rita Matthias' translation of Ferdinand Bruckner's *Zeitstück* "law play," *Die Verbrecher,* which had first been presented in 1928 in Berlin by Reinhardt. Bruckner, who had also come to the United States, had excellent command of English and translated his own plays, yet his own renditions were never used in production. He even did some original writing in English while here. Apparently, his idiom was that of all educated Germans, the Oxford English taught in the schools. Bruckner's German dialogue was written with a keen sense of the colloquial, and it seems that he could not duplicate that diction in English.

The production which Sanford Meisner staged for Piscator at the New School opened on December 20, 1941, two weeks after American entry into World War II. It closed after fifteen performances, curtailed by the climate of wartime as well as by the nature of Piscator's repertory. Its critical reception was very good, particularly for the acting of Lili Darvas, the former Reinhardt star and wife of Ferenc Molnár, who made her American debut in *The Criminals*. Bruckner's play is a courtroom drama treating simultaneously a cross-section of Berliners living in an apartment house. Each of the main characters is involved in a legal case, and in each instance the trial ends in a miscarriage of justice. The play presents the German courts of the twenties as petrified, inhumane, and rigid institutions created in all their impersonal intransigence by men who wanted to escape from the responsibility that should have been the burden of their own consciences. Bruckner lumps the German legal system together with the entire Teutonic frame of mind which refuses to accept individual responsibility for community action. But this was not the only reason for which *The Criminals* seemed even more pertinent in the days of the Third Reich than it had during the era of *Neue Sachlichkeit*. Bruckner shows "the confusion of the people, the uncertainty of the nation's thoughtful men, the slow breaking down of the ideal of abstract justice. He tells of a boy sucked into nazism and made a murderer, of a young woman who kills a baby she cannot feed, and of a cook who strangles her lover's paramour and lays the blame on the lover himself. And he shows us these people brought to trial before bewildered judges, while the real criminals escape."[5] *The Criminals* is a faithfully sordid picture of Berlin in the twenties, a place and time ripe for the corruption that was Hitler. The play demonstrates that "the true criminals of present-day society are . . . [those] who sit idly by while social forces are being directed by stronger hands into channels that lead to . . . international murder and national suicide."[6] The English version of Bruckner's drama was toned down considerably. Euphemisms replaced direct references to things that to the translators seemed too horrible for an American audience, numerous references to the brutalities perpetrated by Nazi street brawlers of the twenties were toned down, and all intimations of homosexuality were excised from the script.[7] Among the generally favorable reviews of

The Criminals was one by Rosamond Gilder, who found faults in the production but saw it as an interesting and illuminating play about pre-Nazi Germany in which "actors speak directly to the audience, sometimes in the form of an address on abstract themes such as the meaning of justice."[8] Bruckner's play was not without didactic speeches, but this performing technique in the epic style seems to have been the conception of Piscator's new theatre.

Every work of Germanic origin but one to reach New York in 1942-43 was an operetta. There were revivals of *The Student Prince, The Beggar Student, The Merry Widow,* and *The Chocolate Soldier.* Despite the comment about the latter by George Jean Nathan that "liberal slices of the comedy have become arteriosclerotic,"[9] these tired operettas fared well with the wartime audience. *Rosalinda,* yet another reworking of *Die Fledermaus,* this one by Max Reinhardt's son, Gottfried, ran for 521 performances. The only nonmusical play of German origin was S. N. Behrman's *The Pirate,* based on Ludwig Fulda's *Kitsch* romantic comedy, *Der Seeräuber.* The performances of Lunt and Fontanne sustained the comedy for 177 performances. *The Pirate* was the type of play that cried for music; not too many years later, Cole Porter answered.

The resuscitated operetta continued to flourish during the third wartime season. *Blossom Time* was produced by the Shuberts; Gottfried Reinhardt modernized his father's version of Offenbach's *La Belle Helene,* which was presented in lavish form as *Helen Goes to Troy;* and *The Merry Widow* returned with benefit of a slightly revised script to run for 322 performances. In 1943-44, Kurt Weill again adjusted admirably to the needs of an American text and composed a pleasant score for *One Touch of Venus.* On October 31, 1943, an era of great German theatre which had long ago declined, finally passed; Max Reinhardt died in New York at the age of seventy, after his European triumphs had culminated in American failures in his last years.

The only major play by an important modern German dramatist to reach Broadway during the years that the United States was in World War II opened on March 14, 1944, under the auspices of the Theatre Guild. Franz Werfel had gotten the idea for *Jacobowsky und der Oberst* from Stephan S. Jakobowicz, a neighboring guest during the playwright's stay at Lourdes. Werfel later told the story at a party in Max Reinhardt's home in Hollywood, and some of the guests, S. N. Behrman among them, suggested that he turn it into a play. Werfel maintained that he was too busy with a novel, *The Star of the Unborn,* his last great work, and asked Gottfried Reinhardt to try to write the play. The *Regisseur's* son tried but found himself unable, whereupon Werfel undertook the task in his usual painstaking fashion, writing numerous drafts in the hope that he could both please Broadway and be faithful to himself.[10] The play was finished in 1942, and the Guild, eager to produce it, asked Werfel to adapt it into English himself. For reasons which will be obvious in a comparison of the German and the final English texts, the Guild rejected Werfel's translation and gave it to Clifford Odets who wrote his own version only to have the Guild turn that down as well. The next man to try his hand at Werfel's play met with the Guild's approval, S. N. Behrman, and it was his *Jacobowsky and the Colonel* which won the Drama Critics' Circle Award for the best foreign play of 1943-44 and ran for 417 performances. Despite the fact that Werfel never made a public statement to the effect and that the play's publicity said otherwise, he was extremely displeased with Behrman's adaptation.[11] Even before the Behrman version was published, a faithful translation of Werfel's play by Gustave O. Arlt appeared in print. Although the play was first given in New York in Behrman's version, it also attained fame in Europe in its original text after its continental premiere in Basel on October 17, 1944.

Nowhere is the Broadway attitude that comedy is buffoonery and dare not deal with sensitive issues more clearly seen than in the Behrman adaptation, despite the fact that his own plays are probably the best high comedies by an American. It is possible that no one felt the audience of 1944 to be ready for a serious and objective comedy about Nazi tyranny, or for a play which included with its humor an honest representation of the horrors of Hitler's persecution. *Jacobowsky and the Colonel* follows the adventures of the title characters, a clever, charming, level-headed Jew and an overemotional, arrogant, declassé aristocrat who is a colonel in the Polish army, as they escape across western Europe. The two are constantly in conflict but need each other in order to survive. They are accompanied by Colonel Stjerbinsky's beloved, Marianne, and his delightfully funny batman, Szabuniewicz. The differences between Behrman's play and Werfel's are many. The refugees in Behrman's hotel cellar are the stock pathetic figures of a Hollywood film; the ones in Werfel's cellar have a wise, accepting worldliness and a brittle pungency in their dialogue. They are not an attempt to engage the sympathy of the underdog-partial American as Behrman's are. Behrman's Jacobowsky is one of the humble and blessed meek with a natural gift for the craft of survival that defeats the cruelty of the world about him. Werfel's Jacobowsky, though also soft-spoken, is a Viennese cavalier, witty and often caustic. Werfel's Jacobowsky is funnier (as is his Szabuniewicz), and in his strength, admirable, where Behrman's hero is only sympathetic. Werfel deals with philosophical problems; Behrman weaves homey philosophy. Werfel's hero is quicker, more energetic, and he equates the whole world's evils with Hitler, who is more symbol than individual oppressor to him. Behrman's protagonist is pure victim of nazism. The original Jacobowsky retains an objective respect for German culture and is a learned man; the American Jacobowsky is a simple and nonintellectual soul, a Jewish Will Rogers.

The following items do not occur at all in Behrman's play, possibly because he or the Guild thought them too strong for the American stomach of 1944: the plight of the homeless and fleeing, for this was a sensitive subject in the United States, where some social critics maintained that a more enlightened immigration policy in the late thirties might have saved many lives; the hypocrisy of the Colonel who is compulsive in the discharging of all of his ritualistic Catholic obligations, yet behaves in a most unchristian way toward his fellow-men; the nonrealistic scenes of the play, particularly that in which the symbolic characters of the Eternal Jew and the Franciscan Friar appear on a tandem bicycle; satire on American commercialism; the presentation of the Gestapo man who is terrifying and has no compunction about killing children (Behrman's Gestapo man is a stuttering caricature, and he spares the children, à la Hollywood); the humorous dialogue in the duel scene between Jacobowsky and the Colonel which is an exchange of the precepts of Judaism and Catholicism concerning the nature of death, even though Werfel takes no sides. The list could go on. Behrman deleted most serious references and removed all shades of gray or else turned them into black and white. His only justified excisions were of the intrusive nonrealistic scenes and of humorous references to things meaningless to an American audience and not necessary to the play: the BDM, *Rassenschande*, the metamorphosis of Jewish family names. Werfel's play was subtitled "The Comedy of a Tragedy"; Behrman's adaptation was simply a comedy, often funny, often melodramatic, and always superficial.

Despite its award for the best foreign play of the year, *Jacobowsky and the Colonel* "got sparse praise from the critics, whose main objections were aimed at the weaknesses that resulted from too much adaptation of the original."[12] Yet there were reviewers who preferred Behrman's text to Werfel's. How they were able to compare the two, since neither had yet been printed and the original never performed, is unknown. The most damning remarks about the play, in both German and English, were made by Eric Bentley in 1946. He objected to the characters of "St. Francis and the Wandering Jew, two gentlemen whom Mr. Werfel loves to pose as," and summed up his case by saying that "adapted or restored, acted or printed, it is a dreadful play

. . . [an] utterly banal and sentimental piece that parades its pretensions to art."[13] No one was quite that harsh when the play opened.
Margaret Marshall thought *Jacobowsky and the Colonel* a good
comedy chiefly because of the character of the resourceful Viennese
Jew, but that the serious aspects of the play got in the way of the
humor.[14] She would obviously have disapproved of Werfel's text, as
did George Jean Nathan who openly preferred Behrman's in a review
as noteworthy for its own quiet little anti-Semitism as for its wit.[15]
Time's commentator said the play was quite entertaining despite the
fact that "so much third-act gunfire and goo not only mar an otherwise enjoyable play; they also keep it from meaning anything."[16]
Stark Young had the highest praise for Oscar Karlweis' performance
as Jacobowsky but found the play itself "without unity of tone and
without taste and without style," adding that this may well not be so
in Werfel's play, which he did not know.[17] Kappo Phelan of *Commonweal* objected angrily and with unconvincing defensiveness to the
character of the Colonel as "simply laughable" and showing "ignorance of both the history and the spirit of Christianity," but added that
the play was well worth seeing.[18] Lewis Nichols noted that the play
was as much Behrman's as Werfel's, and although not great it was
certainly very good, chiefly because of the character of Jacobowsky
and the acting of Karlweis.[19] In a later article, Nichols stated that
Behrman was responsible for the "tommy gun melodrama" and for
making Werfel's characters "nicer" people.[20] On the whole, the *Times*
preferred Behrman's rendition. *Jacobowsky and the Colonel* received
more attention than any other émigré German drama to reach New
York during the war. Despite its flaws in both German and English, it
was Werfel's most warmly approved play on Broadway, though not
nearly his most significant. It is also particularly interesting to note
that never before had so much care been taken by New York's critics
and reviewers to examine the difference between a German play and
its American adaptation. After the war, this consideration again became important. The off-Broadway movement, which devotes so much
of its energy to imported plays, became a moving force in presenting
European drama in adaptations which made no concessions to Broadway's commercial pressures to Americanize plays and make them suitable entertainment for the "tired businessman."

Piscator's Dramatic Workshop at the New School gave a series of
revivals of important plays during 1943-44 which was arranged by
John Gassner and Paolo Milano. Included in the repertory were
Bruckner's revision of *Nathan the Wise* and the first New York production of Kaiser's *Gas*. The adaptation and editing of the trilogy so
that it could be performed in one evening was uncredited. The fre-

netic play which had reflected the chaos and holocaust of World War
I had its first English performance in Great Britain in 1923, but its
only previous professional production in the United States was in
Chicago in 1926. By the time the New School's theatre presented *Gas*,
it had become an overwrought museum piece of expressionism, and its
picture of annihilation resulting from the technical monsters that
spring from the perversion of human knowledge had not yet acquired
the meaning it would again have after Hiroshima. It was both too late
and too early for a revival of Kaiser's play, and the off-Broadway
performance went almost unnoticed.

In the fall of 1943, the Equity Library Theatre (ELT) was established on the simple stages that the WPA had built in some of the
branches of the New York Public Library. One of the stipulations
made in the incorporation of ELT was that it would present no new
plays or pre-Broadway tryouts; productions had to be of classics, revivals, or foreign plays at least a few years old on which Broadway
producers held no options. The actors were almost all professionals,
and though ELT was to give many commercial plays warmed over in
the ensuing years, it also presented a number of good dramas untouched by Broadway. Staging was simple, but the playing was good.
Equity Library Theatre and Piscator's Workshop were the opening
wedges for the postwar professional off-Broadway theatre and the presentation of important European plays in New York which were considered unsuitable for the commercial stage.

On June 12, 1945, shortly after the end of the war in Europe, the
Theatre of All Nations, a group made up largely of refugees from
nazism, presented *The Private Life of the Master Race* at the Pauline
Edwards Theatre of the City College of New York. The play was Eric
Bentley's translation, sensitive in mood and language, of Brecht's
Furcht und Elend des Dritten Reiches. The first full-length production of the piece in English had been given the previous week in
Berkeley, California, although some of the scenes had been done in
German in New York. Inclusion or deletion of scenes is optional, for
each is sufficient unto itself; the total effect is the same no matter
which selection a director decides upon. Although Brecht eschewed
his usual style in *The Private Life of the Master Race*, the purpose of
the play is still to jolt the audience into action rather than to let it sit
back and watch. As such, the production was ill timed. As Lewis
Nichols commented, "it sounded like the echo of a call to arms rather
than the call itself,"[21] a play that should have been done years before
rather than in 1945, when it suffered from the fact that "history goes
faster than the theatre."[22]

Timing was not the only problem encountered by this passionate anti-Nazi play. The English of many of the refugee members of the cast was almost unintelligible,[23] and director Berthold Viertel had, after much conflict with the cast, been replaced during the final rehearsals by Mr. Bentley. These intramural differences among Brecht's own friends undermined the morale and the ensemble mood of the company. Some reviewers tried to be kind to *The Private Life of the Master Race* because of what it was trying to do, but it seemed that there were many to whom the Nazi persecutions were already semiforgotten history; their objections to both the play and its production were complemented by an obvious indifference to the subject matter. Burton Rascoe, in the *World-Telegram*, dismissed the play peremptorily: "It was perfectly awful."[24] George Jean Nathan took the opportunity to attack not only the play but also Brecht himself, a playwright whom Nathan thought to be negligible, with "more the power of lungs than of the spirit."[25] Of the production, Nathan said "the direction of Berthold Viertel and the acting were of the sort that would have been hooted out of even the German provincial Wandertheater."[26] Stark Young and Kappo Phelan were among the few who said that *The Private Life of the Master Race* was a good play which had been butchered in the playing, and who noted that the vagaries of the theatre could destroy an inherently good work.[27] Although *The Private Life of the Master Race* is not one of the poet's major plays and was appreciably different from the rest of Brecht previously played in New York, its reception was no less hostile. With the exception of the off-Broadway presentation of *Galileo* in 1947-48, it was to be the last of Brecht's plays produced in New York before the unprecedented critical and commercial success of the Blitzstein adaptation of *The Three-Penny Opera*.

The only other plays from German sources to be performed in New York during the last wartime season were an unsuccessful dramatization of Werfel's novel *Der Veruntreute Himmel* as *Embezzled Heaven*, yet another revival of *The Merry Widow*, and Equity Library Theatre's restaging of *Mädchen in Uniform*.

II

Throughout the years of conflict, the effect of war was sharply reflected in the New York theatre. The first season of World War II, 1939-40, seemed to present a playbill trying to overcompensate for the situation in Europe. Almost every play of any interest was a romantic comedy: *The Time of Your Life, The Male Animal, The Man Who Came to Dinner.* Although they were beginning to wear out their long-extended welcome, *Life with Father* and *Tobacco Road* were still running. Native anti-Nazi plays increased in frequency, the best of them being Sherwood's *There Shall Be No Night* which opened so late in the spring that it was considered one of the next season's offerings (in fact, it won the Pulitzer Prize for the later season). Most of the anti-Nazi plays were hastily manufactured melodramas written to accommodate what producers thought to be a ready market, but Clare Booth's comedy *Margin for Error* was well received. One anti-Nazi play of 1939-40 was a collaboration by columnist Dorothy Thompson, who had befriended many refugees, and Fritz Kortner, the noted actor, writer, and director who had worked with Reinhardt for many years. Their joint effort, *Another Sun*, was a contrived piece which closed after eleven performances.

The New York theatre lapsed even further into escapist drama during the 1940-41 season as the entrepreneurs of Broadway hoped to offer the public diversion from reality with such efforts as *George Washington Slept Here, Arsenic and Old Lace, My Sister Eileen, Pal Joey,* and a revival of *Charley's Aunt.* The American anti-Nazi plays also continued, most of them still very weak, even Elmer Rice's *Flight to the West,* but there was one outstanding entry, Lillian Hellman's *Watch on the Rhine,* which won the Drama Critics' Circle Award for the best play of the year.

The émigré influence was felt in *Lady in the Dark,* a play by Moss Hart which made extensive use of expressionistic dream sequences with music which had lyrics by Ira Gershwin and score by Kurt Weill. The music reflected some of the protean Weill's older power. Among the other émigré artists to attempt a contribution to Broadway this season were Fritz Kortner and Carl Zuckmayer. They collaborated on a play in English, *Somewhere in France,* a war drama which was presented in Washington, D.C., in April, 1941, but was withdrawn before it was to be presented in New York. Little is known of this otherwise unproduced and unpublished play. Even the coverage given it by the *New York Times* in its one engagement was more of a news item than a review and devoted most of its space to reporting the names of the Washington dignitaries in the audience. There were also continued efforts by some of the refugee groups. One of them, Theatre Friendship House, presented a brief run of Hofmannsthal's *Jedermann* in George Sterling's translation.

During the 1941-42 season, the United States entered World War II, and the New York theatre received little attention, not only because of the obvious focus of public interest elsewhere, but also because there was not a single good modern play to be seen that year. Both the Pulitzer committee and the Drama Critics' Circle refrained from presenting any awards to American plays. Most productions

were either of farcical and musical froth totally oblivious to world
events and which, for once, the public was too serious minded to
patronize, or else of preposterously contrived war and anti-Nazi plays.
In the latter group were such efforts as *Letters to Lucerne,* by Allen
Vincent and Fritz Rotter (a Viennese lyricist who had gone to Hollywood); *Candle in the Wind,* an absurdly romantic anti-Nazi piece by
Maxwell Anderson; *The Man with the Blond Hair* by Norman Krasna,
a silly melodrama about a Nazi war prisoner who escapes from
Canada to the United States and hides with a Jewish family on the
East Side of New York where, after two days, he has a sentimental
change of heart; *Plan M* by Hollywood scriptwriter James Edward
Grant, in which a member of the German High Command, a perfect
double for the head of the War Office in London, takes over the
British position. Even the most substantial of the American anti-Nazi
plays of the season, John Steinbeck's *The Moon Is Down,* adapted
from his novel, was second-rate at best. Broadway's war drama was no
better than the romantic contrivances of Hollywood.

The second wartime season, 1942-43, was artistically far better
than the first, but the business record of Broadway indicated that
playgoers refused to support serious plays about World War II with
the exception of the often melodramatic *Tomorrow the World* by Gow
and d'Usseau. There were actually few plays of substance concerning
the war but many superficial ones. One drama that tried to be more
than it was, Irwin Shaw's *Sons and Soldiers,* was directed by Max
Reinhardt and mounted by Norman Bel Geddes, but the cumbersome
and hyperemotional production floundered, was poorly received, and
closed within three weeks. The year's Pulitzer Prize went to Thornton
Wilder's *The Skin of Our Teeth,* a play inspired by the war almost as
much as it was by Joyce's *Finnegans Wake* and the movement of anti-
illusionist drama. Yet Wilder was never much in sympathy with
Bertolt Brecht; their points of view on the human condition could
hardly be more opposite. When Wilder, whose German is excellent,
was asked by the poet to do a translation of his *Der Gute Mensch von
Setzuan,* he flatly refused although he had done translations of infinitely lesser works. Nonetheless, Wilder shares Brecht's desire to
break down the proscenium and to destroy the illusion that the theatre is a place where life is imitated rather than commented upon. *The
Skin of Our Teeth* constantly draws attention to itself as a play. For
this it was attacked as often as praised, but on the whole, Wilder's
supercute hodgepodge of philosophy, theology, and anthropology was
far more favorably received than had been any of Brecht's or anyone
else's anti-illusionist dramas. The reason for the appeal of *The Skin of
Our Teeth* may well have been that its tone was so pleasantly opti-

mistic, that it said that no matter how horrid the past or present, the future will somehow work itself out. This theme without doubt was a major reason for the play's phenomenal popularity on the postwar German stage, where it was played far more seriously than Wilder had intended and is significantly known as *Wir Sind Nocheinmal Davon Gekommen,* which loosely translated means "We managed to pull through again." This title is far more cocky than the title in English and, as some German critics have pointed out, almost blasphemous in the light of the German situation. *The Skin of Our Teeth* has lost much of the stature it once held in critical eyes. The optimism so appealing during the war no longer rings true. To say that man will somehow survive because he has always outlasted what seemed to be total catastrophe before, has become meaningless in the age of thermonuclear weapons. The jaded perspective of Brecht seems far more pertinent in the 1960's, although in 1942 he was an almost unnoticed figure in Hollywood. In that year, he wrote the plot line for the movie *Hangmen Also Die,* based on the assassination of Reinhard Heydrich by the Czech resistance. However, Brecht dissociated himself from the film and refused to be listed in the credits when he saw that the finished product had strayed far from his script.

In 1944-45, there were still war plays, romantic and patriotic pieces, and anti-Nazi dramas, most of them as silly as ever, but their incidence decreased. They were beginning to be replaced by American *Heimkehrer* plays even before the end of the war in Europe. Broadway, ever anxious to anticipate the market, fatuously declared an early and lasting peace. With few important exceptions, the commercial American plays of the first few postwar years concerning the readjustment of the homecoming soldier were comedies or farces, but this phenomenon may well have been nothing more than one of the spoils of victory.

5

Out of the Rubble:
1945-65

I (1945-53)

The rapid financial and physical reconstruction of Germany after the war brought with it a resurrection of the theatre, something that Germans, in war or peace, with fascism or with freedom, seem unable to do without. As Kenneth Tynan has pointed out, "Drama in Germany is a wounded art, still recovering from the casualties it suffered between 1933 and 1945 . . . something is missing . . . a whole age group has almost disappeared; there are hardly any actors in their forties."[1] Most of the German theatres were destroyed during the latter years of the war; the German drama itself had been destroyed long before. After 1945, plays were produced in halls, schools, back rooms, and cellars. Then came the rebuilding of the German theatres and the construction of hundreds of new ones throughout the country. The system of decentralization has persisted, and there are first-rate companies in each of West Germany's major cities and in some of East Germany's. The *Berliner Ensemble*, which Brecht established in East Berlin, is not the only great postwar repertory but certainly the most celebrated one.

The Third Reich and its downfall created an intellectual vacuum in Germany. There was no great upsurge of art as after World War I. Germany was dry. The Nazis, who had kept out everything foreign since the late thirties, thus created the conditions for the first obvious theatrical revival after the war; Germany had to catch up on what it had missed in world drama during the Hitler years. The German stages of the late forties were deluged by foreign drama, mostly French and American. The realistic American plays in particular achieved great popularity and critical acclaim, but the more stylized work of Miller, Williams, and Wilder aroused the most avid intellectual discussions on the revitalized campuses and in the literary journals. The German theatres also continued their tradition of producing more Shakespeare than any other country. They also gave many German classics.

But there were no notable new German dramatists to appear after the Nazi collapse. There were few older playwrights who returned in the postwar years; for most of those who were still alive, Germany held no enticement. The exceptions were: Zuckmayer, the only pre-war dramatist to retain any of his old power; Brecht, who organized his theatre in Berlin but wrote no more important plays and died in 1956; Wolf, a shell of the writer he once was, totally disillusioned, unproductive, and dead by 1953; Bruckner, who never regained his stature and died in 1958. Hauptmann, the only major dramatist to remain in Nazi Germany, atoned for his indiscretions with his *Atreiad,* but the old man died in 1946. Toller, Zweig, and Hasen-clever had committed suicide. Werfel and Kaiser were both still writing significantly until their deaths in 1945, one in California, the other in Switzerland. Germany would have to start anew in the development of a native drama. The young men to come out of the war were bewildered and had first to gain a world perspective denied them in Hitlerian isolation; the older men who were unable to speak before had to establish themselves as new writers when they were already middle-aged. There were few names to appear for the first time in the German playbills during the late forties other than those of Wolfgang Borchert, a promising talent who died at the age of twenty-six on the night before the opening of his one play, and Günther Weisenborn, already in his mid-forties at the war's end, who was the first nonexile to write a significant play dealing with the German anti-Nazis, *Die Illegalen* (*The Illegal Ones,* 1948). Weisen-born, for whom playwriting would have been futile for so many years before, had turned to other media. His reputation is based on his fiction and poetry. New German dramatists were not to make their presence felt until the late fifties and the sixties, and even those who have each written a significant play or two have shown no indications as yet of becoming major playwrights. The two most celebrated writers of German drama since the end of World War II are both Swiss, Friedrich Dürrenmatt and Max Frisch. Among the Germans themselves, the most promising playwrights at this time seem to be Rolf Hochhuth and Peter Weiss. Weiss is no longer a young man, and though he writes in German, he is a Jewish exile and a citizen of Sweden where he has lived since the late thirties. It was almost a decade after the war before the new drama from Germany and Switzerland established itself, received any international attention, and was produced on the New York stage. The German theatre, in all its technical excellence, recovered with amazing alacrity after the war, but the German drama, destroyed by Hitler, had no hope of recovery. It had to be reborn.

After the dramatic doldrums of the war years, the American theatre underwent numerous changes, chiefly the result of a new prosperity-conditioned audience, commercial production problems, the advent of some important new American playwrights, and the gradual emergence of the off-Broadway stages. The years of transition lasted from 1945 to 1953, years that in the main yielded better new American plays than Broadway was to present for the ten years following, because commercialism stifled it completely and placed the burden of serious drama on the little theatres.

There was little of interest in 1945-46 which was German in origin. Some of the older émigré artists were still presenting special performances off-Broadway in German, usually of older modern classics (such as this season's *Ghosts* at the Barbizon Plaza, produced by Albert and Elsa Bassermann and Ernst Deitsch). Equity Library Theatre revived Schnitzler's *The Affairs of Anatol* under the direction of Mady Christians, daughter of Rudolf Christians. She had appeared in the Schnitzler comedy under Reinhardt's direction in 1924, and her staging of it for ELT was considered by the group's leaders to be their outstanding production of the year. Broadway itself dipped into the *Kitsch* of a day long gone for its German plays. *Mr. Strauss Goes to Boston* was a ludicrous attempt to Americanize a Viennese operetta. Not even Robert Stolz's pleasant score was able to save the text which the *Times* said was "old . . . tired" and generally awful,[2] and the musical closed after twelve performances. Another effort to resuscitate *Alt Wien* resulted in 165 showings. *Marinka* was based on the mysterious and romantic incident at Mayerling, and it used the music of Emmerich Kálmán, now long in the United States, but for all of its Hapsburgiana, *Marinka* was *ersatz* Vienna. The only other play from a German source was a foolish venture. Jean and Walter Kerr had dramatized Werfel's most popular novel in the United States, *The Song of Bernadette,* for presentation at Catholic University in Washington. Now they took it to Broadway after Hollywood had turned the novel into a highly acclaimed motion picture. The consensus of reviews was that the Kerrs' stage version was lifeless, amateurish, and overloaded with Catholic propaganda that was suitable for its church-sponsored college production but not for the popular theatre. Many plays are adapted into commendable motion pictures; few films have ever been followed up by a good stage version. *The Song of Bernadette* was withdrawn after three performances.

In 1946-47, foreign plays, most of them French, began to reach Broadway again. Experimental Theatre, a group inactive off-Broadway since 1941, reorganized its company, and Equity Library Theatre continued its operations. The émigré influence was represented only by Kurt Weill's scores for Ben Hecht's *A Flag Is Born* and a semi-operatic version of Elmer Rice's *Street Scene*. Eva Le Gallienne established the American Repertory Company, but could find no audience; the general public insisted on new plays, and in the coming years, producers would accommodate that demand. On Broadway it has become axiomatic that a new play, no matter how feeble, is a better risk than an old play, no matter how good. Here also, off-Broadway would steal a march on the commercial entrepreneurs in the years to come.

Although the native sentimental musical comedy still flourished, the 1946-47 season marked the belated death of the imported operetta, although its ghost still occasionally stumbles across a Broadway stage or through a summer stock tent. On September 5, 1947, *Yours Is My Heart*, an adaptation of Franz Lehar's *Das Land des Lächelns*, opened as a vehicle for Richard Tauber, once the darling of the Viennese operetta. Tauber became ill shortly after the premiere and died soon thereafter. The operetta closed. Brooks Atkinson's question in his review was pertinent: "Why not treat the score as good [light] concert music and spare the theatre?"[3] The trend since has been to save the good songs and to dispense with the operettas. It was about this time that "musical comedy" and "operetta" ceased to be interchangeable terms in Broadway parlance. The new American musicals were largely responsible for that.

The 1947-48 season was the one in which production expenses began to soar with the general inflation and in which Broadway began its pattern of producing fewer plays each year (only forty-three new plays in 1947-48). Lightweight material was still very much on the scene, but obvious *Kitsch* began to disappear unless its box-office potential was almost certain. 1947-48 was also the year in which the little theatre resurgence began. Experimental Theatre, a young off-Broadway group, specialized in foreign plays during that season and aroused a great deal of public opposition, expressed in letters to the drama editors of all the major newspapers. For each of these vituperative attacks on non-American drama, there were answers written which stated the hope that the naïve old chauvinism of Broadway would not reassert itself as it did in the anti-European feeling of the days of World War I. The problem of imported drama was thus constantly kept in front of the public that followed journalistic coverage of current theatrical events.

It is off-Broadway that has given Americans an opportunity to see neglected foreign drama and experiments that the shopkeepers of Broadway would not dare risk. The Brecht discovery is an off-Broadway product, as is much of the American playing of the important work of the Theatre of the Absurd by Genêt, Beckett, Ionesco, Pinter, and lesser practitioners. The off-Broadway playhouses frequently collapse financially, move to other quarters like vagabond players, or change hands. They are all over New York City, not only in Greenwich Village. In recent years, they have become almost too big a business. Their popular success has brought them financial problems: rising salaries for stagehands (much more so than for actors), tickets too expensive for the audience to which off-Broadway has its greatest appeal, new expenses for air conditioning to prevent warm-weather closings in stuffy quarters, rising rents imposed by real-estate men who have seen a good thing, necessity for physical improvements required to compete successfully with more comfortable little theatres, and advertising. Off-Broadway, expanding at an overaccelerated rate, will, if not prudently managed, be in peril of going the way of Broadway or else of becoming nothing more than another littered beach on the seacoast of Bohemia, forsaking substance for pretentiousness. Off-Broadway has been a courageous venture, often giving foolish plays, but at least seldom afraid to run a risk. That courage has yielded the noteworthy results as well as the inferior ones. Admittedly, the theatres are often uncomfortable and shabby, the staging is frequently pathetic, the acting and direction are sometimes embarrassingly bad, too great a number of the new plays are simply awful, there is a superabundance of arty self-indulgence, and the general tenor of the entire district is too much a uniform wail of self-pity. Decentralization and professional regional companies may be the ultimate hope of the American theatre, but in the main, New York is still the home of this country's drama, and off-Broadway has undertaken a responsibility that Broadway has abrogated.

Of course, the most glaring shortcoming of the movement has been its inability to emulate the post-World War I little theatres in developing young native playwriting talent, but in turning to European drama in order to establish itself, off-Broadway has given the American theatre many important plays. Periods of experiment in the New York theatre have always been the time when German drama, so avid in its own experimentation, has fared best on our stage. Off-Broadway is responsible for the reintroduction of good German drama after the war.[4]

In those seasons between 1946 and 1953 there was not one German play produced on Broadway, and only one even had a German source, Sidney Kingsley's *Darkness at Noon* which won the Drama Critics' Circle Award for 1950-51. It can hardly be considered other than an American play, since Mr. Kingsley had adapted it from Daphne Hardy's popular translation of the novel by Arthur Koestler,

which though German in manuscript was first published in English
and in this country. The few German plays seen here in those seven
seasons were all produced off-Broadway, and almost all of these were
written quite a few years before or else were outright revivals.

During 1946-47, Piscator's Dramatic Workshop included Hauptmann's *Hannele* in its repertory and it went unnoticed. Not so a play
entitled *Crown Colony,* given an amateur performance by Fordham
University at the Penthouse Theatre. There was some comment in the
newspapers about the professional potential of this play. The play
concerned the failure of a Jesuit colony in South America, and was
adapted from *Das Heilige Experiment* by Fritz Hochwälder, a native
Austrian who had been residing in Switzerland since the *Anschluss* in
1938. In 1953, this play was to be the first serious German drama to
reach Broadway since the war's end as *The Strong Are Lonely.*

In 1947-48, Piscator produced *Chaff,* based on one of Bruckner's
realistic but dated plays. On Stage, a dramatic group "seeking to
bridge the gap between the university theater and Broadway,"[5] attempted to capitalize on the relevance of Kaiser to the atomic bomb
by presenting *Gas* at the Cherry Lane. Neither *Chaff* nor *Gas* received
critical attention or audience response, and both of them succumbed
before two weeks had passed. Bruckner's subject matter was always
too topical to survive the years, and unbridled expressionism was too
noisy and unrestrained for an audience even less accustomed to its
shriek than had been the public of the twenties.

Brecht's *Leben des Galilei* was written in 1938 and 1939 and had
its first performance at the *Zürich Schauspielhaus* on September 9,
1943. The play does not pretend to be historically accurate; like most
of Brecht's works, it was written to prove a point and to arouse the
inert to action. The Galileo of the piece is sensual, gluttonous, and
unscrupulous, a man given to the easy path, one who will forsake that
which is right for that which is expedient. Shown instruments of torture by the Grand Inquisitor, Galileo recants his scientific assertions
to the dismay of his highly principled disciples. When his chief pupil
reproaches him, "Pity the country that has no heroes!" Galileo replies
with the most famous line in the play: "No. Pity the country that
needs heroes!" The scientist then goes into seclusion and silence.
Years later, a pupil visits the old man, now showing visible signs of
his self-indulgent life. The pupil states his disgust with Galileo's cowardice, but begs forgiveness when the scientist hands him the completed manuscript of the *Discorsi,* finished in his seclusion. But after
all this careful construction comes the lesson of the play: Galileo
refuses to see himself as a hero; rather he considers himself a social
criminal, a traitor who sold his integrity for comfort and who fears he

has set a pattern for scientists to follow in the future. "He has made science the servant of authority rather than asserting its right to transform the world for the benefit of mankind."[6] This lesson is a point which Brecht actually added in a second and authorized version. The original manuscript praises Galileo's recanting as a cunning act of survival that allows him to work. Galileo is one of the protagonists Brecht conceived as he did Mother Courage and Mack the Knife— heroes who are to have little charm or appeal, who do not arouse the sympathy of the audience, and who, in fact, should evoke the viewer's indignation at the bourgeois morality displayed in their unheroic actions. In American renditions of Brecht's plays concerning ideologically detestable heroes, the protagonists are almost always played sympathetically. The possibility for such interpretation lies within the texts, so the responsibility is in part the author's, but in arousing pity for Courage, Galileo, Puntila, or Mack, a performance will undermine Brecht's very thesis. Even the *Berliner Ensemble* has played *Galileo* with empathetic gusto and direct, traditional audience appeal.

While Brecht was living in California, his play came to the attention of Charles Laughton, who saw not only the original genius of the playwright but also a succulent role for himself. With the assistance of Brecht and a good dictionary to supplement his admittedly weak German, Laughton translated the drama as *Galileo* and starred in its English premiere on July 30, 1947, at the Coronet Theatre in Beverly Hills. Audience and reviewers thought the play dull and as oppressive as the summer heat of the theatre without air conditioning. But Laughton, convinced of the value of *Galileo*, took it to New York, where it opened at Maxine Elliott's Theatre on December 7, 1947, under the auspices of the Experimental Theatre. The Laughton text cut Brecht's lengthy play freely, but the poet approved, for he never considered his scripts sacrosanct. The peculiar idiom of Brecht was totally lost in translation, and what the play gained in concentration by Laughton's deletions and more prosaic diction it lost in texture, wit, and gift of expression. Brecht's play itself has far fewer passages of irrelevant didacticism than do most of his other major dramas, but Laughton excised most such passages as those along with all the original's purposeful vulgarity. The result was much the same as when a play by Shaw is drastically cut. For the sake of dramatic tightness, much bright talk must be sacrificed. Furthermore, in *Galileo*, some of the dimension of character was lost in the interest of verbal economy. Neither in its original form nor in Laughton's version is *Galileo* a Marxist play. As Bentley points out, the dialectic is hardly scientific, for who would believe that had Galileo not recanted, an age of reason would have begun and today's troubles been avoided? The tendency to read Marxism into everything Brecht wrote is dangerous, particularly when used as a weapon against his work. He always spoke for himself, never for the party with which he was always at odds. Brecht seems even more of a preacher to many than he really is for the simple reason that much of what he says appears to be patently self-evident, particularly to an audience seeing his plays as much as twenty years after they were written. Consequently, the insightful social comment of 1940 easily becomes the socio-economic cliché of 1960. Furthermore, there is an easy logical fallacy into which many fall: Brecht is didactic; Brecht was a Communist; therefore, when Brecht preaches, he is preaching communism. There is no such necessary connection between the two facts.

Despite the topical quality in the early nuclear age of the problem of the responsibility of the scientist to society, *Galileo* got a resounding thumping from most critics and reviewers and had no audience appeal whatsoever. It closed after six performances. The play was thought to be dull and episodic. "Even critics who rather liked *Galileo* had nothing to say about the form of the play except that it seemed rambling."[7] Brecht, judged not on the basis of his goals but on the conventions of popular dramaturgy, was still completely misunderstood. Reviewers and audiences were outraged by the techniques of anti-illusionism. What was considered particularly offensive was that a very dirty Galileo destroyed all illusion by first putting on and then changing his costumes in clear view of the audience. This device was to be exactly repeated fifteen years later by the very Brechtian character, The Common Man, in Robert Bolt's *A Man for All Seasons* —the young English playwright received accolades for his inventive genius. Some of the very men who solemnly proclaim its greatness in the 1960's abhorred *Galileo* in 1947, almost ten years after it had been written and a decade before the American theatre would be ready for it.

At the time of ET's production, "the play was too cool, too cold. . . . It was written with the intention of exposing a situation rather than emotionally involving the spectators; we are not made to sympathize with Galileo but to understand his problem."[8] Typical comment in 1947 included Brooks Atkinson's: "loose and episodic . . . puts form ahead of contents. . . . The production is stuffed to the ears with hokum."[9] George Jean Nathan, historically a Brechtophobe, said that *Galileo* was "entirely lacking in any distinction . . . static. . . . It is difficult to make out any experimental value whatsoever . . . offers an opportunity to piscator it almost out of recognition."[10] Irwin Shaw fell into the common trap of misinterpretation that Brecht had unfortunately set himself. Even Shaw, like many intelligent people, saw the

play as the story of Galileo's martyrdom at the hands of authority.[11]
The 1947 *Galileo* was the last of Brecht in New York before the
totally unexpected and belated success of *The Three-Penny Opera*.
The postwar history of Brecht in New York went through three stages
of development: (1) the rejection of the late forties and early fifties;
(2) the discovery of the mid-fifties; (3) the cult of the late fifties and
the sixties. The second and third stages must be discussed in their
chronological places. To understand their significance demands historical perspective.

Equity Library Theatre, apparently not frightened by the fate of
the revival of *Gas* of the previous season, produced *From Morn Till
[sic] Midnight* in December, 1948. It prompted Brooks Atkinson to
say that the play was "gibberish out of a period of romantic despair
that fortunately is now finished."[12] To this, John Gassner retorted that
"one may well wonder whether the play is gibberish and whether the
period of romantic or any other kind of despair is actually finished,
although the faults of Kaiser's dramatic nightmare are transparent
enough in the text and can be exaggerated in inexpert stage productions."[13] There was truth on both sides. Pure expressionism was dead,
but the "gibberish of romantic despair" was to reassert itself mightily
in the fifties and sixties.

On March 1, 1949, the Dramatic Workshop of the New School
presented the first New York production of any German play written
since the end of the war. *Outside the Door* was a translation by Erwin
Piscator and Zoe Lund-Schiller of *Draussen vor der Tür*, the only play
written by Wolfgang Borchert. *Outside the Door* is a *Heimkehrer*
play about a desperate, disillusioned alien to society who upon his
return from a Siberian prison camp attempts to drown himself in the
Elbe. The river refuses to accept him, and he is forced to face life
again. Beckmann, the young veteran who is obviously an autobiographical creation of the playwright, who knew that he himself was
dying, tries to make contact with his fellow-men but always fails. He
is constantly "outside the door." He says, "I am merely a bad joke the
war has made, a ghost from yesterday." The text of the play is unrelieved from beginning to end, a passionate cry of despair written in a
style much closer to World War I expressionism than to any more
restrained technique. *Outside the Door* is intensely subjective. Only
its hero is a fully developed character while all the others are allegorical types. The River Elbe appears in the form of an old woman; God
is an old beggar powerless to help and incapable of evoking belief
from anyone; Death is a gluttonous, belching, blasé undertaker who is
getting rich and whom everyone admires. Later in the play, Death
reappears as a street sweeper, exactly the form he takes in Tennessee

Williams' derivative hodgepodge, *Camino Real* (1952-53). Beckmann
argues throughout the play with his Tolleresque alter ego, known as
The Other One, who can give him no courage at all. *Outside the Door*
was precisely the mood of postwar Germany. When the Federal Republic became prosperous, that mood disappeared and Borchert's play
with it.[14] But for a while, the unfortunate young writer was wrong in
the phrase which he placed under the title of his manuscript, written
in an eight-day frenzy in the fall of 1946: "Ein Stück das kein Theater
spielen und kein Publikum sehen will." ("A play that no theatre wants
to perform and no audience wants to see." [trans. mine])

Borchert's play is not without glaring weaknesses despite its moments of great power. In his short stories, the young writer made
effective use of repeated words and phrases (e.g., *Der Kaffee ist Unde-
finierbar*), but the repetitiousness in his play is overextended. Furthermore, there are too many rhapsodical speeches. The drama
unfolds at a constant level of passion; it tends to wear out an audience
rather than move it. There is too much shouting. Thematically, *Outside the Door* is distressing not for what it says but for what it neglects to say. Only the most insensitive audience in its native land
could fail to notice that all of the play's references to suffering concern
the hardship *endured* by, not *caused* by, the Germans. Borchert was
not a Nazi, but all mention within the play of mass death and muti-
lated bodies refers to combat; there is not one word about the mur-
ders and atrocities of the Hitler regime. Even when Beckmann finally
sees that he himself caused murder and horror, it is only the bloodshed he has wreaked among Germans of which he becomes cognizant.
It is this tone of narcissistic self-pity as much as the latter-day expressionism that must make *Outside the Door* a distasteful play to anyone
but the most chauvinistic German. It would assuredly alienate an
American audience. Yet the few reviewers of the Piscator production
were more offended by the technique. The *Times* said that *Outside
the Door* exhibited "a genuine intensity possessed only by those who
have known torment and pain," and that the chief flaw of the play
was its interminable repetitiousness despite the fact that the translation was "vivid and often powerful."[15] John Gassner's evaluation of
Outside the Door is fair: "Inept in spite of flashes of inspired
writing."[16] Had Borchert lived, he might have become an important
dramatist, but his only play is too limited in time, place, and point of
view to allow it to survive.

The only significant work of Germanic origin to appear in New
York during the 1949-50 season was again produced and directed by
Piscator. On April 19, he presented the first performance of a brief
run of *The Scapegoat*, Columbia University teacher John F. Mathews'

dramatization of Franz Kafka's *The Trial*. The tormented Czech artist was receiving much attention in campus and literary circles, and the Mathews script was the first of several American attempts to reproduce Kafka's nightmare world on the stage. The task is apparently impossible and has frustrated a man as gifted as André Gide. The mystical and mysterious vision of Joseph K. in his awareness of guilt and his compulsion to expiate is so subjective that it can most effectively be dramatized by an imaginative motion picture. The film, *The Trial*, released in 1963, was the work of Orson Welles and is in most ways, particularly those that are visual and elicit a sensory response, the finest dramatic adaptation of Kafka's novel. The Welles script places the action in the present and is full of current allusions not found in Kafka. The Mathews adaptation had done the same. In both cases, however, the general design and intent of the novel are not violated. When Atkinson reviewed *The Scapegoat*, he called it "one of the most original dramas of the season—hovering between reality and insanity where so much of our life seems to be today. . . . [It is] an imaginative, stinging and pertinent play."[17] He further praised Piscator's direction as well as the settings and the acting. Very few people paid any attention to *The Scapegoat;* they were too busy trying to get tickets for *South Pacific.*

The only production of an actual German play that season came on June 6, 1950, when Studio 7, a new and short-lived off-Broadway group rented the Provincetown and presented an undistinguished revival of Wedekind's *Erdgeist*, this time called *Earth Spirit*. A few reviewers mildly approved that Wedekind was being done at all, but the *Times* reflected the consensus that despite the fact that *Erdgeist* is still interesting, it shows its age ungraciously. It was forty years too late for even a good performance of the adventures of Lulu. Eight years after the Studio 7 production, Wedekind's dramatic mayhem was to be revived again, hopefully for the last time, when Eva Gabor put the quietus on the earth spirit.

1950-51 was the last season in which Piscator's Dramatic Workshop performed. The repertory included two German plays. The first, opening on December 1, was a revival of Klabund's *The Circle of Chalk*, which Atkinson said was still an enchanting and lovely ceremony of make-believe whose "morality is so timeless, basic and simple."[18] The production may well have been a sentimental farewell for Piscator who had given the Klabund fantasy in 1941, his first season, with the same star, Dolly Haas.

The second Piscator effort was the first American performance of a work by Max Frisch. *A House in Berlin* was an adaptation by Vernon Brooks and William Kennedy of *Als der Krieg zu Ende War* (1949) and opened at the New School on December 26, 1950. The play is more conventional in form than most others by Frisch, but there is ample evidence of the influence of Brecht, as there is in almost all of the new Swiss drama, particularly in the characters' direct addresses to the audience. The plot of A House in Berlin concerns a German woman torn between her love for a Russian officer who is billeted in her house and her husband who is hidden in the cellar. The husband is a war criminal who has connived to create this possible assignation in order to have a hold on a man who could help him to escape. The wife is presented as a heroic figure. Because she has actually fallen in love with the Russian colonel she may provide freedom for her despicable husband who had told her of the sadistic pleasure he derived from slaughtering Jews in Poland. She renounces her love and kills herself rather than allow her husband's crimes against humanity to go unpunished. What makes her most admirable is her deep regard for human dignity, whether it be that of the unfortunate victims of nazism or for the Russian whom she has learned to accept as a person, not as an instrument of conquest. The Swiss critic Hans Bänzinger compares the restraint and objectivity of Frisch's play with the unrelieved Aufschrei of Borchert's Draussen vor der Tür.[19] George E. Wellwarth, on the other hand, says that Als der Krieg zu Ende War "is the only one of Frisch's plays which is a complete failure."[20] A House in Berlin apparently did not have a fair hearing in New York. Not only had Piscator's theatre fallen out of favor because of pressure exerted by the congressional witch hunts of the early fifties, but the group was almost at the point of dissolution. The production was slapdash, and few reviewers or critics paid it any attention. Brooks Atkinson said that "colorless [and] . . . monotonous" acting had ruined a perceptive play; half of the lines, Atkinson continued, were unintelligible, but it "might be a whale of a play if it were acted."[21] No other play by Frisch was performed on Broadway or off until the 1962-63 season. After the closing of A House in Berlin there were no German plays at all in New York for two years, but beginning in the fall of 1953, the incidence of imported drama, including the German, increased remarkably in the American theatre.

II   (1953-57)

Between 1953 and 1957 the "off" in "off-Broadway" began to be listed with increasing frequency as a capitalized word. The little theatres, spurred on by the success of The Three-Penny Opera, clearly one of their major achievements in the mid-fifties, were soon to give wider hearing to recent experiments from Europe and further rediscovery of Brecht. Whenever the New York theatre finds room for experimentation, the German drama reasserts itself.

During those four seasons between 1953 and 1957, when the leadership in presenting important plays passed from Broadway to off-Broadway, there were a number of interesting productions of German drama in both camps. There was only one play by a new dramatist, Fritz Hochwälder, but there were adaptations of Kafka's fiction, revivals and revisions both on and off Broadway, and most important, the explosive beginning of the cult of Brecht.

Fritz Hochwälder, like so many young German writers on whom Hitler had enforced a silent youth, first attained prominence after the war when he was already approaching middle age, although his first and best-known play, *Das Heilige Experiment*, had its premiere in Switzerland in 1943. Hochwälder, a Jew, had left his native Vienna in 1938 and settled in Switzerland—the only place where the German drama remained alive during the Nazi years, where Brecht's and Zuckmayer's plays were being performed, where Georg Kaiser spent his exile, and where young dramatists had a chance to learn and to practice their craft. All of Hochwälder's plays are concerned with moral rather than sociological issues, and each of his dramas is the story of the awakening of a man's conscience. Although the settings of most of his plays are historical, they are clearly commentary upon the present. Despite the fact that Hochwälder was a friend and a student of Kaiser, his dramas are conventional in form.

Das Heilige Experiment, which Fordham University had produced in 1946-47 as *Crown Colony*, first received attention outside the German-speaking countries when it was produced in postwar Paris as *Sur la Terre comme au Ciel*. An English translation soon followed, and praise was heaped upon the London production, *The Strong Are Lonely*. Eva Le Gallienne's English version was translated from the French rather than from the original and had its New York premiere under Margaret Webster's direction on September 29, 1953. The drama is the story of the fall of the Jesuit state founded in eighteenth-century Paraguay. The conflict of material and spiritual values is centered in the character of the Father Provincial, who is forced against his personal beliefs to accept the interests of the church as taking precedence over the kingdom of God on earth. Commanded by his superiors to dissolve the state, he finds death easier to accept than the destruction of everything he has worked to build in the colony. The lesson that the idealistic Father Provincial must learn is that the kingdom of God on earth is an impossibility so long as men, including those of the church, are cruel, greedy, hungry for power, and willing to place private interest before the public good, no matter how pious their rationalizations. Historically, there are, of course, strong differences of opinion on the virtues of the Jesuit state in Paraguay (see D'Alembert or Voltaire), but in Hochwälder's drama the colony is close to an Eldorado, although with a massive army. Because of political pressures in Spain, the Father must choose between the dissolution of his experiment or of the entire Jesuit order. He is willing to go along with his superiors until he sees that the church itself is behaving out of motives of selfishness and opportunism. The Father decides that he would rather be a heretic than forego his personal integrity in a world in which all men's hands are dirty.

Das Heilige Experiment is a moving, intelligent, and powerfully written play. The French version was excessively rhetorical and repetitious. Miss Le Gallienne's translation magnified the flaws of *Sur la Terre comme au Ciel*. Miss Webster's direction of *The Strong Are Lonely* emphasized the excesses of the translation. The New York reviews were harsh, but their opposition was to the performance rather than to the play. The inadequate translation seemed apparent to most of the critics. Wolcott Gibbs also thought that the climax of the play came far too early in the evening, but saw the chief flaws as the horrid overacting, the unintelligible accent of the Father Provincial, the stuffy translation, and Webster's plodding direction.[22] Richard Hayes said that *The Strong Are Lonely* was "provocative and enthralling [beneath] the glaze of baroque rhetoric and fustian which obscured its New York presentation," and that Miss Le Gallienne had turned a drama into a melodrama and that Miss Webster's direction was "strident and operatic."[23] The reviews of Atkinson and Bentley also noted that the play presented challenging ideas but did not live up to its potential.[24] Perhaps the comment by Harold Clurman was the most significant. His review appeared after the play's closing, and he blamed the commercial failure of Hochwälder's drama not only on the shabby treatment it had received in production but on the climate of Broadway. He said the play's "subject matter, though based on a fundamentally universal theme, is foreign to our theater audiences,"[25] namely the discussion of religion in other than sanctimonious or platitudinous terms. The popular American audience expects all plays about priests to resemble *Going My Way* and becomes irate with anyone who even dares to intimate that he is fed to the teeth with Santa Claus, "White Christmas," or "one nation under God," the American version of the fatuous "*Gott mit Uns!*" Because it was so badly translated and played (though not so badly as the reviews led one to believe), *The Strong Are Lonely* received only seven performances, but one may wonder how well the play would have fared with the Broadway audience had justice been done to Hochwälder. *The*

Strong Are Lonely was the first new German play to appear on Broadway after the war; there was not another one until Dürrenmatt's *The Visit* in 1958.

With the ever-increasing interest in Existentialism and the Theatre of the Absurd off-Broadway, further attempts were made to dramatize the fiction of Franz Kafka, whose art inspired so many of the new generation of writers. On June 14, 1955, Theatre 12 under the direction of Denis Vaughan presented yet another play version of *The Trial*, this one by Aaron Fine and Bert Greene. Arthur Gelb commented in the *Times* that the obscurity "puts an awful strain on the audience,"[26] but he admired the group's courage for doing the baffling play. The new version, decidedly inferior to that by Mathews which Piscator had presented in 1949-50, was an attempt to make Kafka's work acceptable for the "Beat Generation" and consciously magnified the mysteries of the novel. Yet *The Trial* was worth seeing and ran for 131 performances at the Provincetown Playhouse.

The following season, one special performance was given of an experiment integrating acting, music, and movement. Under Anna Sokolow's imaginative dance direction, ANTA presented an adaptation of Kafka's short story, *The Metamorphosis*, and the work was considered admirable by the dance critic of the *Times*.[27] Kafka still defied dramatic treatment on the stage, but interest in his style and themes showed that off-Broadway was willing to try experimental drama of which the German stage had much to offer.

Most of the German drama presented off-Broadway between 1953 and 1957 was either revival or revision. In 1953-54, Equity Library Theatre, whose productions usually ran for one week, returned to the drama of Franz Werfel with presentations of *Goat Song* and *Jacobowsky and the Colonel*, but there were no other German plays in the little theatres that season and none at all in the one following. However, in 1955-56 there were numerous revivals of older German plays. Arthur Schnitzler's *The Gallant Cassian*, a puppet play, served as a curtain-raiser for Genet's *The Maids*, and the already famous Circle-in-the-Square presented Schnitzler's controversial *La Ronde* under José Quintero's direction.

Schnitzler's *Reigen* was a cynical comment on the mores of a dying society. The *Reigen* was a circular dance, closely resembling the medieval dance of death which Strindberg, like Schnitzler, had compared to the game of love at which modern men and women play. *Reigen* had been banned in Austria in 1921 and had never been allowed even a private performance in the United States. Once it was permitted in Europe, it caused riots and required police protection even in Berlin. Each of the scenes depicts the conversation between two people before and after their sexual union. In each liaison, one of the partners is a character from the previous sequence, until the last affair when the Count, representing the highest of all the social orders presented, couples with the lowest of the characters, the prostitute of the first scene. The circle is complete, and each affair has ended in a different species of sordid disillusion. Schnitzler's satire on the debasing of human love by a moribund society is deft and compassionate. There is no leer of sensuality whatsoever behind this bitter comedy, but in tasteless production it could arouse much indignation. Even when expertly performed it would offend those who in essence share the degrading concept of love that Schnitzler opposes. The play was brought back to the public's attention when a French motion-picture version appeared in the early fifties. Its title, *La Ronde,* was then used by Eric Bentley for the Circle-in-the-Square rendition. In a 1954 essay, Mr. Bentley had condemned the French film because in it "Schnitzler's serious sadness has dwindled to a cheap cynicism [and because the movie] has converted a satire into the thing satirized."[28] Consequently, Eric Bentley decided to translate Schnitzler's play into English, and it opened on June 27, 1955, to run for 132 performances. Of the play, Maurice Zolotow said that it "presents right before your eyes what the American theatre is forever hinting at, preluding toward, and retreating from nervously . . . [for] our society feels comfortable with sex only when we can reduce it to statistics, charts, graphs and percentages."[29] The analysis in the *Times* was perceptive. Lewis Funke thought *La Ronde* well done in its treatment of "the game [which] goes along according to the rules. First there is the flirtation, involving the pretenses, the awkwardness, the eagerness of passion. Then comes the consummation, and finally the weariness and the distaste."[30] Undoubtedly the box office for *La Ronde* was bolstered by those who sought titillation, but for once a Schnitzler play in a good translation was given a fair hearing in New York. It would not have been possible on Broadway or even in the little theatres a few years before.

On May 9, 1960, a new translation of Schnitzler's *Reigen* by Hans Weigert and Patricia Newhall opened at the Theatre Marquee, again with the French film title, *La Ronde.* The melancholy picture of the manners of a world that needs the illusion of love so badly that it reduces all emotion to a physical level had become obvious. The once notorious play had worn thin.[31] The new text had some decided improvements over earlier efforts: The irony of the last scene in which the Count bids the prostitute a furtive "good morning," which actually tells the audience to wake up, is effectively handled; the lines have more of the fluency of Schnitzler's German than do most translations of his work; the grotesquerie, the sham, and the jaded feeling of the original are admirably conveyed. However, the Weigert-Newhall text misses the lightness and humor of Schnitzler. According to most reviewers, the performance was dull and heavy-handed. *Reigen* had lost its charm and its usefulness, particularly for a young audience that shares none of the nostalgia for the old days in *mittel-Europa*.

The day after the closing of *The Trial* at the Provincetown, the same staff—Bert Greene, adapter; Denis Vaughan, director; Theatre 12, producer—presented the play that thirty-nine years before had created an outrage in New York: Frank Wedekind's *Frühlings Erwachen*. But when *Spring's Awakening* opened its fifteen-performance run on October 9, 1955, the implication in the newspapers was that it was not worthwhile to review this obvious, clumsy, and quite unsensational piece. Arthur Gelb summed it up by saying that the play is now "an unpleasantly graphic museum piece."[32] He further stated that in this faithful adaptation, it was apparent that Wedekind's characters did not come off as people but only as awkward symbols, personifications, or one of the playwright's points of view. It was an unfortunate end for a play that in both form and content had been so highly influential, had been such a *cause célèbre*, and was finally unable to outlive the generation of its author. But the New York theatre had owed a debt to this play, and off-Broadway paid it in 1955. There was an abortive attempt in May, 1964, to resuscitate Wedekind's play with characters and settings Americanized. At that time, critical consensus was unanimous in suggesting that *Frühlings Erwachen* should be allowed to sleep in peace.

It may well have been the new-found appeal to the off-Broadway audience of Brecht's and O'Casey's *Lumpenproletariat* or the relish with which the "method" actors play them that prompted the Greenwich Mews Theatre to revive Ludwig Lewisohn's translation of Gerhart Hauptmann's worn-out comedy, *Der Biberpelz*, on March 28, 1956, but it soon closed. *The Beaver Coat* was once a good naturalistic study of the fight for survival among the poor Berliners and of the compulsive German bureaucracy that everywhere hampered social progress and justice, but it had paled appreciably by 1956. The crafty but endearing washerwoman who is the heroine of the comedy is still a universal type—aggressive, opportunistic, domineering—but the situation in which she is involved and the manner in which she and her associates speak are no longer pertinent and not at all funny. Lewisohn's translation was almost as dated as Hauptmann's original play by the time *The Beaver Coat* had this, its first New York performance in English. In trying to duplicate the ungrammatical peasant dialect for which Hauptmann had such a keen ear, Lewisohn emerged with a synthetic American argot, an incoherent cross between *Tobacco Road* and an artificial jargon. Atkinson's review was justifiably damning. *The Beaver Coat,* he said, was "not worth the trouble of putting on the stage . . . [and a] performance [which] seems to be a desperate attempt to flog a dead horse into merriment."[33] Again, off-Broadway was to be commended for its sincerity but reproached for its lack of selectivity. In the early years of the resurgent little theatre movement, the too-late presentation of plays once good was common.

On January 7, 1957, under the direction of Gene Frankel, Stefan Zweig's version of *Volpone,* which had been a Guild favorite years before, opened at the Rooftop Theatre and ran for 130 performances. Critical praise was generous, particularly for the lightness of touch in direction and playing, and for the inherently funny text. The Rooftop production made no attempt to please Jonson purists. *Volpone* was played in the sardonic mood of Zweig's version. In its Elizabethan or modern form, the comedy has staying power, for each generation can see its own folly in this caustic attack on materialism.

The last of the revivals between 1953 and 1957 was another tired fling for *The Merry Widow* in a year when operetta had long been considered a quaint relic. The version given at the City Center was the same as that of the revival of 1943-44. Even the stars were the same, much too old for the parts but still in fine voice. John Chapman commented that "Marta Eggerth and Jan Kiepura seem to have made a lifetime career of appearing in *The Merry Widow* in many lands and languages. They sing well and look handsome, but English is not one of their languages."[34] Brooks Atkinson said that the operetta was from "a time of settled values," at least in the theatre, and that it was gone.[35] He added that the music was still endearing but that the words were no longer endurable. The operetta was finished on Broadway and a subject for parody off-Broadway.

Only one of the old favorites survived, *Die Fledermaus,* but it did it by having its status changed. A revival at the City Center ran for only fifteen performances in the spring of 1954, but Rudolf Bing, who had revitalized the Metropolitan Opera Company, had also commissioned a new English version of the Strauss operetta. This text emerged as so far superior to those of the operetta adapters that, coupled with the seemingly indestructible score, it became part of the repertory of the leading American opera company. All the other operettas faded, but *Die Fledermaus,* still the favorite in Europe as well, graduated to the category of light but serious music. The last futile effort to modernize it was *Oh, Rosalinda,* a 1955 international film version which reset the plot in postwar Vienna under four-power occupation.

The only Broadway attempt between 1953 and 1957 of revival or revision of a play from a German source was *The Matchmaker*, which opened under Theatre Guild auspices on December 5, 1955. It had had a successful premiere at the Edinburgh Festival, and it ran for 486 performances in New York. The comedy was a revision by Thornton Wilder of his earlier failure, *The Merchant of Yonkers* which had been based on Nestroy's 1842 adaptation of an 1835 farce by John Oxenford. The success of the new version was ascribed largely to the imaginative direction of Tyrone Guthrie and Wilder's creation of a mood which was obviously not to be taken seriously. Wilder never let his audience forget that it was in a theatre. Characters stepped out of the story and spoke directly to the public. The Brechtian touch was unmistakable in technique, but Wilder's good-natured kindness bore no resemblance to the German poet's sardonic anger. Those unattuned to Wilder's sentiments feel that in its metamorphosis into the crass *Hello, Dolly!*, *The Matchmaker* was not desecrated; it got what it deserved.

The most significant event in the history of the German drama on the New York stage in the fifties was the belated discovery of Bertolt Brecht, precipitated by the production of *The Three-Penny Opera*, which opened at the Theatre de Lys on March 10, 1954. Almost overnight, a man who had for years been dismissed by both the audiences and the makers of the American theatre and who was championed by only a few literary critics became recognized as one of the great dramatists of the twentieth century. Why, after all these years, the sudden artistic beatification of Brecht, and at the height of anti-communist feeling in the United States?

The potential obstacle of Brecht's Marxism can easily be dismissed. His most emphatically communistic *Lehrstücke* are not being performed professionally in New York; after all, most of the Brecht plays which have enjoyed recent success are from the poet's early canon in which his social theories exhibit a generally acceptable humanism more than a party line which only eager investigators would take the trouble to ferret out. Even in the evening of vignette selections which include later work, *Brecht on Brecht*, the political bombshells are egregiously avoided. It is still safe to be opposed to war, poverty, crime, injustice, greed, exploitation, and middle-class Philistinism. It is a commonly accepted fact that Brecht's plays have no capability of converting anyone to outright communism and that his compassion for the small man's suffering far outweighs his dialectic.

Furthermore, the playwright's technique no longer seems as radical as it did when it intruded on the compulsive social realism of the thirties. Not only the imported nonrealistic plays from Europe but also the most significant American drama since the war has drifted ever further away from verisimilitude. In their dramaturgy, Williams and Miller are anything but realistic. With the off-Broadway audience receptive to experiments in drama as drastic as those of Beckett and Ionesco, Brecht's anti-illusionism could hardly be an outrage. Furthermore, an audience which accepts theatre-in-the-round and poverty-imposed settings (which are only indicated) would not rebel against the Brechtian stage no matter how much of the machinery was in plain view. As audiences of years before had grown tired of artificiality, so a substantial segment of the new generation of postwar playgoers was weary of photographic realism. Many plays seen in the years since 1935 borrowed liberally from the epic technique. By 1954, Brecht's theatre was no longer an iconoclastic outrage.

Another reason for the Brecht cult is unquestionably that angry young people enjoy listening to an articulate man who happens to be angry about the same things that they are. Brecht's audience in America is today essentially an audience of intelligent, politically liberal, young people who find Brecht saying what they want to hear in productions that emphasize his agreeable dicta. The devotees easily ignore the poet's indiscreet attacks on Churchill as a political gangster, or his support of Walter Ulbricht, or his one-time implication in *Rundköpfe und Spitzköpfe* that the Nazis and the rich Jews would eventually combine to wipe out the German workers, or his dust jacket of *Das Kapital* which he used as a cover for the thrillers he was usually reading, or the whistles with which he supplied the Baden-Baden cast of one of his plays so that they could hoot back at the audience. To his off-Broadway admirers today, Brecht is the irate voice which cries out against injustice. The fallible man, the poet, the heavy-handed preacher, the impetuous "bad boy" of the literary world, the dialectician—these are conveniently sidestepped. In this selective appraisal of Brecht, his true genius is also frequently ignored. And, in all honesty, it is not so much what Brecht says as how he says it that has elicited the most admiration in academic circles.

The Brecht cult has alighted only on the useful Brecht. The current age is one of anxiety and despair, and it is this very tone in the plays, the one that shouts "Die Welt ist arm, der Mensch ist schlecht," rather than the one that proposes crude social theories that accounts for much of Brecht's popularity today.[36] Ironically, it is in the Western camp rather than the communist, with the exception of East Berlin, in which he enjoys fame today. The Brecht plays which have been most warmly received in New York to date are *The Three-Penny Opera, In the Jungle of Cities,* and *A Man's a Man,* all early plays which attack the social values of the New York audience of the fifties and sixties as they attacked those of the German public of the twenties. It is the part of Brecht's drama which destroys the public value system rather than that which offers a substitute for it that has the widest appeal today. In both theme and form, the early Brecht closely resembles the nihilism of the Theatre of the Absurd even as those early plays held much in common with expressionism, often called the forerunner of the Absurd. It is impossible not to ask whether much of the cult of Brecht results not from an appreciation of the poet's work but from its uncanny resemblance to the moods of Genêt, Ionesco, Beckett, and Adamov.

The great plays of Brecht's maturity, whether we share their tenets or not, propose a philosophy of social responsibility. Little wonder that the cult of Brecht has stayed away from these plays; how much more convenient to exploit the youthful Brecht whose work joins in the cry, "I didn't make this lousy world, Daddy-O! *You* keep it. I refuse to be a part of it. I don't accept its values, so I don't accept any responsibility to it or for it." The credo is more violent but essentially it is still Housman's crybaby stranger, "afraid in a world I never made." We dare not ascribe too much meaning to the American discovery of Brecht. He has been exploited out of context by those for whom rebellion and escape are synonymous. Only that part of his work which corroborates current notions of romantic negation receives popular acclaim when on view. The appreciation of his drama has become fashionable, and so it would be well for those who attribute Brecht's popularity to a new cultural enlightenment to remember that a large percentage of the poet's audience today is made up of faddists and dilettantes. But for as long as it lasts, those whose appreciation of Brecht's work probes beneath the present superficial selectivity may rejoice that some of his plays are at least being staged, though not a single one of his substantial later works has been a commercial success on Broadway. His popularity in academic and professional regional theatres is extended to the major plays.

It is important to note, however, that no matter what the motives of the off-Broadway Brecht fad may be, serious interest in the poet has increased sharply in scholarly circles. Beginning in 1956, the year of his death, we find for the first time a substantial list of entries under his name in the bibliographies of the learned literary journals. Indeed, it is in the universities that Brecht was kept alive in the years of his obscurity in the United States. He first "established himself in

America through . . . amateur performances by student players,"[37] and in a letter to Eric Bentley, dated November 12, 1949, Brecht wrote, "I prefer the university productions to the commercial ones."[38] The list of Brecht plays performed in American colleges even before the advent of the cult is impressive.[39] It would be unfair to say that the entire Brecht revival is suspect. The poet's work and reputation have become firmly entrenched in the serious study of the modern drama, and there he will survive long after the New York theatre has switched its allegiance to a newer and more expedient hero.

The pattern for the distorted view of Brecht which the American theatre presents was established by the production that began the movement. Marc Blitzstein had been at work for some time on a new adaptation of *Die Dreigroschenoper*. His version was first given in concert form at Brandeis University in 1952. The production of March, 1954, ran for ninety-five performances but closed only because the Theatre de Lys went into receivership. When *The Three-Penny Opera*'s producers bought the de Lys, they reopened the play on September 20, 1955, with essentially the same cast. *The Three-Penny Opera* finally closed after the longest run of any German play ever to appear in New York, 2,611 performances, a spectacular achievement even though the Theatre de Lys seats fewer than three hundred people.

Blitzstein was devoted to Brecht and Weill, but his text and lyrics, though excellent in their own right, are appreciably different from those of the original. In order to understand the disparity between Brecht and Blitzstein, we must first examine the difference between Brecht and Gay, on whose *The Beggar's Opera* the German work was based. In addition to satirizing Italian operatic plots, Handel's oratorios, and the fetish for folk song current in eighteenth-century London, Gay also made sport of the mores of the aristocracy and the professions. Brecht used the same material to attack the values of the bourgeoisie. He criticized an "amoral and predatory *laissez-faire* philosophy."[40] Weill's music, on the other hand, was in large part a parody of the metallic jazz and popular tangos of the twenties. It was also part of the musical genius of both Brecht and Weill to be able to set lyrics to melodies whose moods were diametrically opposite to those of the text, thus heightening the satire. Weill's score is as haunting as it is jarring. As Judith Sherwin points out, "Gay speaks of social injustice, Brecht of the universal injustice of life."[41] Gay's Macheath is a resourceful, amoral hero; Brecht's Mack the Knife represents every detestable trait of the middle-class morality, no better and no worse than those who oppose him, connive with him, love him, or despise him. It is Mack's very lack of social responsibility that makes him one of Brecht's hero-villains with whom the audience should not become emotionally involved. To present him as a charming rascal is to negate Brecht's intention. The Blitzstein version was not nearly so guilty of this as all the popular recordings of the "Moritat" ("The Ballad of Mack the Knife") in which voices of finger-snapping teen-age idols proclaimed gleefully that all would be fun now that Mack was back in town, even though the lyrics asserted that he was a thief, murderer, blackmailer, profligate, liar, and adulterer. Taking delight in Mack's return rather than being horrified at his very existence is exactly what Brecht was attacking. Mackie Messer looks, for all the world, like a minor bank official, not a Hollywood hero. The world of Gay's play is that depicted by William Hogarth; the world of Brecht's play is the harsh caricature of Georg Grosz, set in nineteenth-century London (one hundred years later than Gay's), but reflecting pre-Hitler Berlin. Blitzstein's *The Three-Penny Opera* resembles Hogarth more than it does Grosz.

Barnard Hewitt has pointed out that Blitzstein's text "romanticized considerably Brecht's mordant script and softened somewhat the irony of Weill's score, [but] it hardly concealed the shocking bitterness of the piece, and one can account for its popularity only by assuming that under the bright surface of peace, prosperity, and a record national income, which seemed to sum up American life, lay a dark and angry core of disillusion and cynicism."[42] Blitzstein, like Gay, attacked social injustice, not the inherent injustice of life and human nature, as Brecht had.

In his lyrics, Brecht had borrowed freely from Rudyard Kipling and François Villon in German translation. Miss Sherwin has observed that Blitzstein, whenever he knew Brecht's source, returned to the original for his lyrics rather than to Brecht. The result is a far less bitter and less graphic text.[43] Blitzstein's tactics can be justified because Brecht's peculiar colloquial diction always defies translation. The lyrics of Eric Bentley's faithful early rendition of *The Three-Penny Opera* are unsingable (Mr. Bentley got much better at lyrics as the years passed). But the Blitzstein words, although they alter "more of tone than of substance,"[44] have effected perceptible changes in the songs to the extent that total meanings are sometimes altered. The cuteness of Mack's song, "The Bulging Pocket Makes the Easy Life" is not the bitterness of "Nur wer in Wohlstand lebt, lebt angenehm" ("Only the affluent live pleasantly" [trans. mine]). Although it captures the antimilitarism, the happy Kiplingesque camaraderie of Blitzstein's "Cannon Song" is not the vicious mock ode to genocide that appears in Brecht's "Kanonensong." But the most distorted song of all is "Pirate Jenny," which in Blitzstein's folk-song lyric, beautiful though it assuredly is in its own right, has nothing to do with the original. The "Black Freighter" of the English lyric is "ein Schiff mit acht Segeln und mit fünfzig Kanonen"—"an eight-sailed ship with fifty cannons"—in German. Blitzstein's Jenny dreams of release from her sordid life of prostitution and sings plaintively of the ship that will take her away from the horrors of reality. Brecht's Jenny is a whore who sells out Mack and who sings neither of salvation here or beyond nor of family, home, or fortune as release from the existence of the *Kleinbürger*. She dreams of a pirate ship with eight black sails—a swastika!—that will annihilate everything that she hates, and then will carry her off with it. When the people appeal to her, the absolute power in league with the swastika, the whore that becomes *Führer*, she denies them and commands that they be killed. Jenny sees force and slaughter as her means of release. She is the political whore that was the German people of the 1920's who put their faith in a pirate with eight black sails. Even Hitler and Goebbels clearly understood the Brecht-Weill song; the Nazi attack on *Die Dreigroschenoper* was vehement. An entire room of Hitler's Museum of Degenerate Art in Nürnberg was devoted to Weill's music, including a recording of this score. Cleverly symbolic songs about the advent of National Socialism had assuredly lost their meaning, particularly for an American audience in the 1950's, but Blitzstein, in his rendition, made little effort to turn "Pirate Jenny" into anything more than a pseudo-folk song that contemplated, as do so many of the Greenwich Village favorites, how pleasant it would be to get away from this mess of a world.

It would be unfair to imply that because Blitzstein's *The Three-Penny Opera* is not Brecht's that it is therefore not good. On the contrary, his version was so successful largely because it was meaningful in the 1950's, maybe more meaningful than Brecht's play could have been in the same place and time, for much of what the German was talking about in 1928 would have had no pertinence for Americans in 1955. All the bitter disillusion and youthful anger were still there, and many critics are unconvinced that a *Three-Penny Opera* with *Verfremdungseffekt* would be superior to one that is emotionally involving. The magic of Weill's music alone virtually forbids detachment. Furthermore, in some of his lyrics and dialogue, Blitzstein displayed brilliance. His "Solomon Song" is even more biting than the original; the first act Finale is an uncanny duplication of the German; and the line "For even honest folk may act like sinners, unless they've had their customary dinners" is one that Brecht could have been proud to call his own. Whether the de Lys *Three-Penny Opera* was good because of or despite Blitzstein, a question argued by many, is a false dilemma. Probably it was a bit of each.

The reviews of *The Three-Penny Opera* were, with few exceptions, enthusiastic in their approval. Harold Clurman found the acting, staging, and direction awkward with the exception of Lotte Lenya's performance, but he had the highest praise for the play and its adapter. He said that the "inherent superiority of the material survives all hazards."[45] Most critics scored the inadequacy of the performance and were surprised to find that the play held up despite that. They did not take into account that a certain amount of spontaneous sloppiness adds to, rather than detracts from, *The Three-Penny Opera*. Henry Hewes called the play "a masterpiece"[46] although he also objected to the acting, and Brooks Atkinson was uninhibited in the praise he lavished upon the play in numerous articles in the *Times*. The only totally negative comment came from Wolcott Gibbs in *The New Yorker*. In a supercilious review intended to please sophisticates who sneer at anything concerning ill-bred people, Gibbs spoke chiefly of his own ennui. In fact, he said he couldn't tell much about the play because he was so bored that he walked out long before the end. He didn't understand what was going on, he said, and he didn't care.[47] His was decidedly a minority opinion.

When *The Three-Penny Opera* reopened in 1955, the acting and direction were no longer deserving of disapproval. Cast changes were many throughout the seven-season run, but periodic newspaper coverage reported that the play never lost its freshness or spontaneity, and the producers had the good sense to keep it in a state of proper Brechtian shabbiness. When it had opened, Atkinson had called it a "poverty-stricken production."[48] In the case of *The Three-Penny Opera*, that is a virtue. Only three months after the 1955 reopening, there was another Brecht play to be seen off-Broadway; the poet's work was suddenly in demand. In August, 1956, Bertolt Brecht died in East Berlin.

The Private Life of the Master Race was a poor choice for the first Brecht play to follow *The Three-Penny Opera*. It has neither the qualities that account for the author's new-found popularity nor is it one of his major plays. Drama concerning Nazi Germany was unquestionably dated in 1956, and the surge of historical interest in the Hitler years did not begin until the early sixties with the publication of Shirer's *The Rise and Fall of the Third Reich*, the capture and trial of Adolf Eichmann, and the blatant parading of a fashionable and not quite uncomfortable guilt by the then economically very comfortable Germans. The production of the Bentley translation presented by the Open Stage on January 30, 1956, had only a brief run, although for the first time the play was praised by reviewers for its technique and for an adequate performance.

During the following season, one of Brecht's finest plays received its first New York production although it had been one of the favorites of the university groups for years. On December 18, 1956, the Phoenix Theatre, the largest off-Broadway enterprise, presented *The Good Woman of Setzuan*, Eric Bentley's translation of *Der Gute Mensch von Setzuan*. The play had had its premiere in Zurich in 1943. Its title is beyond translation, for English has no suitable equivalent for "Mensch," and the distinction is important since the title character, the good Shen Te, commits her necessary evil acts in the guise of her fictitious male cousin, Shui Ta. She is a good person who devises a wicked alter ego of the opposite sex. The China in which the play is set is as unrestricted by fidelity to place as is the Chicago of Brecht's plays that were set in America, but the oriental mood gives the author a chance to employ all the acting techniques he found admirable in Eastern theatre. Attention to details outside the dramatic action of a play were never Brecht's concern; he considered them encumbrances. The quality of exotic fable also enhances the effect of parable in this play, the theme of which is that it is impossible to be completely good and still manage to survive in this world. Because we ask no realistic delineation of character from Brecht, we do not even question the logic of the dialectic that makes his heroine so gullible when she is Shen Te and so shrewd when she becomes Shui Ta. The theme is a geometrical "given" of the play; the purpose of its presentation is once more to get the public to do something about it. Although Bentley's version for the Phoenix inexplicably deleted it, the original play ends with Shen Te's plea for help from the audience. She can find no way out of her dilemma. Not even the gods who put her in her predicament can help her out of it. They are naïve and powerless, capable only of spouting sanctimonious clichés. Solution to the problem is the audience's responsibility. Brecht assumes again that "Die Welt ist arm, der Mensch ist schlecht," but that the situation could be improved.

While Brecht was in the United States he had tried to get Thornton Wilder to translate this play but was rebuffed.[49] The Bentley text which the Phoenix used was a revision of the one he had published eight years before. By 1956, foreign drama had reasserted itself in New York, particularly off-Broadway. It had actually become fashionable, so reviewers displeased with what they saw assumed the fault to be the translator's. Often it was, but in the case of *The Good Woman of Setzuan*, Bentley came under harsh attack only because of a current critical ploy. His version is excellent, not only faithful to Brecht but devoid of the idiomatic clumsiness that usually mars English renditions of his plays. Yet the Phoenix' *The Good Woman of*

Setzuan was not a good performance, and the fault actually seemed to be Bentley's, not for his text but for his direction. Bentley had spent much time with Brecht, and though he tends to be overly enamored of the poet, his understanding of his work is paralleled by few, most notably Esslin. But Eric Bentley's ability as critic, scholar, and translator is not matched by his talent for theatrical direction. As Henry Hewes pointed out, Bentley is so intent on Brechtian theory that he loses sight of the playing of the piece. Even Brecht himself frequently forsook his dicta when he directed at his own theatre, a practice which he shared with Stanislavski. Bentley "removed the passion and inhibited the actor."[50]

John Gassner blamed the reviewers who disapproved of *The Good Woman of Setzuan* for not being attuned to Brecht, for expecting the dramatist to do something that he had never set out to do,[51] but the notices were almost unanimously poor. Yet it is significant that few critics or reviewers blamed Brecht's play. The flaws were attributed to performance and translation. In the case of *The Good Woman of Setzuan*, that happened to be half true although the reviewers clearly wanted to "get" Bentley who had been attacking them for years, not without justification. Ten years before, the play itself would have been held just as culpable.

John Chapman said that "the Phoenix Theatre did little to further its hard-won reputation as an important playhouse. . . . [The play is] completely non-realistic theatre, quite badly acted."[52] There is an implication in his comments that all nonrealistic drama is inherently inferior, an attitude no longer shared by many in 1957. Robert Hatch felt that the performance was "boring . . . [but] the fault is with the production, not with the play."[53] Hatch also stated that the chief flaw was Bentley's fumbling attempt to squeeze out epic acting that made the actors look "like a crowd of extras on their lunch hour." *Theatre Arts* also found the play boring,[54] as did most other popular and theatrical periodicals. However, Gibbs outdid himself in *The New Yorker*. His sophisticated weariness was even more pronounced than it had been in his review of *The Three-Penny Opera*. The purpose of the play, Gibbs said, was "to discover how far a production can go in the direction of sheer, staggering dullness without quite emptying the theatre at the end of the first act."[55] Again, most of Gibbs's review is about Gibbs and why he walked out rather than about the play. By the time *The Three-Penny Opera* closed, Gibbs had died, after which even *The New Yorker* staff of reviewers became mild supporters of Brecht.

The Good Woman of Setzuan was admittedly poorly played, though not uniformly so. However, it is one of that group of Brecht's later plays that has not captured the New York audience despite the fact that serious critics of drama are unanimous in calling them Brecht's best work. With two such failures after *The Three-Penny Opera,* the Brecht cult might well have subsided quickly, but after 1957, the off-Broadway groups realized that it was the early Brecht, the one who resembled the absurdists and who was at home in Bohemia, who was in demand. When that realization was implemented, the New York theatre entered upon its third stage of postwar Brecht revival.

III   (1957-65)

With the exception of a few off-Broadway revivals or an occasionally exhumed operetta, the German plays performed in New York between 1957 and 1965 fall into three distinct categories: the continuation of the Brecht cult, the advent of the Swiss tragicomedy, and the presentation of new works by Germany's new (though not necessarily young) dramatists. To greater or lesser degree, the spirit of Bertolt Brecht hovers over almost all of these plays.

Brecht had written the text and Weill the music for a ballet-cantata, *Die Sieben Todsünden der Kleinbürger,* first produced in Paris in June, 1933. A London performance followed a few days later under the title *Anna Anna.* It was never published until 1959 when it appeared on the jacket of a recording (Columbia KL 5175) and in a German edition in Frankfurt. The text with the record was in both German and English, and the translation was by W. H. Auden and Chester Kallmann, a version which had been used earlier in 1959 when the New York City Center produced the ballet-cantata as *The Seven Deadly Sins.* The text of the piece is a series of poems by Brecht and tells the story of a pair of sisters, both named Anna, who represent halves of the same personality. The first Anna, the reasoning self, sings; the second Anna, the emotional self, dances. The ballet-cantata is a satire on middle-class hypocrisy. Anna supports her self-righteous family and builds it a new house with the profits of prostitution, the portion of her life she leads with a total absence of feeling. To be successful in her enterprise, she must avoid all the deadly sins. By not committing any of the seven, she makes her career far more profitable than it would be should she give in to pride, anger, sloth, lechery, and the rest. She leads an existence which by commercial standards follows all the rules of decency, and thereby demonstrates that morality and respectability are not synonymous. In the New York production, a limited engagement, Weill's widow, Lotte Lenya, played the singing Anna and the City Center Ballet's Allegra Kent her dancing alter ego. *The Seven Deadly Sins* is not a play, but its performance in 1959 was highly praised and would probably never have taken place had it not been for the new interest in Brecht.

On December 20, 1960, the Living Theatre, one of off-Broadway's most polished and imaginative companies, presented *In the Jungle of Cities*, a translation by Gerhard Nellhaus of *Im Dickicht der Städte* (Brecht's 1927 revision of his 1923 play, *Im Dickicht*). This is the most difficult and obscure of Brecht's early works and owes much of its technique to the interest the young poet had in surrealism, Dada, and expressionism. Brecht said that the piece was also greatly influenced by J. V. Jensen's bizarre Danish novel laid in a mythical Chicago, *The Wheel*, a story of two powerful men who wish to control each other's souls, and by Arthur Rimbaud's *A Season in Hell*.[56] The relationship between the two antagonists in Brecht's play closely resembles that between Rimbaud and Paul Verlaine.

In the Jungle of Cities is the story of an unmotivated fight between two men: Shlink, a wealthy Malayan lumber merchant, and Garga, a desk clerk in a lending library. In his foreword to the play, Brecht said, "You find yourself in the year 1912 in the city of Chicago. You observe the inexplicable boxing match between two men. . . . Do not rack your brains over the motives for this fight but note the human stakes, judge without prejudice the style of each contestant, and direct your interest to the finish." (Eric Bentley's translation.) The fight begins when Shlink wants to buy Garga's opinion about a book and the young man says that this cannot be done. The struggle continues in symbolic and metaphysical terms. The ostensible hatred which the two men have for each other is part of a continuum that also includes love and respect. The relationship is always violently emotional, and neither of them really understands it, yet each feels compelled to go on with the "fight." During the entire love-hate conflict, which is rife with overtones of a destructive homosexuality, both men attempt to communicate with each other but find it impossible to do so. As Shlink says, in the last great confrontation, "If you crammed a ship full of human bodies till it burst, the loneliness inside it would be so great that they would turn to ice. . . . So great is our isolation that even conflict is impossible." (Gerhard Nellhaus' translation.) Interpersonal communication in our world has broken down to the point where there can no longer even be a meaningful fight. As Ernst Borneman has pointed out, there really is no fight in the play—only a series of surrenders with each character accepting without protest his defeat and his humiliation.[57] Esslin adds that it "is always a matter of making the one man acknowledge the other's superiority through forcing him into either gratitude or aggression."[58] There is a marked resemblance between the Shlink-Garga relationship and that between Jerry and Peter in Edward Albee's *The Zoo Story*.

Eric Bentley has observed that *In the Jungle of Cities* is a drama of passive action and negative dynamics—like a donkey refusing to budge[59]—and he has said that "critics have not been slow to see the connection between the Brecht of 1920 and the plays of Beckett in the fifties."[60] He further states that "as in Genêt, eros is subordinated to the struggle for power; in which struggle Brecht's characters tend to wish to lose."[61] In its deliberate rejection of motivation and insistence on human incapacity for communication, *In the Jungle of Cities* also anticipates the drama of Ionesco and Adamov.

After the opening of *In the Jungle of Cities* there were many letters written to the drama editors of the New York dailies. There were as many interpretations of the play as there were contributors to the papers, and the reaction of the writers ranged from condemnation through confusion to adulation. The play became a controversial conversation piece and did much to enhance the reputation of the Living Theatre which was invited to present Brecht's play at the *Théâtre des Nations*. Of course, for the privilege of playing in Paris, the gallant Gauls requested that the struggling little theatre do so at its own expense. The United States also offered no financial help.

Critical opinion of the production was far from unanimous. Whitney Balliett of *The New Yorker* said that *In the Jungle of Cities* was confusing but impressive, "way out but very good."[62] Harold Clurman was one of the few who felt that the drama was clearly a product of post-World War I Germany in its presentation of the world as "a place of mutual and universal torture, of aloneness for each individual."[63] He added that he found the play "mordantly eloquent . . . grotesquely witty" and baffling, but that it is better to be baffled by this than "to be lucid about the safe commodities proferred elsewhere." Howard Taubman lamented that it took a long time for him to find out what Brecht was trying to say and that afterwards he did not feel it was worth the effort. Taubman saw the play as interesting and challenging, but as an arty bore that was not Brecht at his best.[64] Clearly, it was Brecht at his most fashionable.

George Tabori's arrangement of scenes, songs, sayings, and snippets of Brechtiana which opened in November, 1961, as *Brecht on Brecht* was a shamelessly superficial exploitation of the poet intended to show how he was everything a great angry writer should be: tough, trenchant, passionate, pithy, idiosyncratic, cute. It was Broadway plying its wares off-Broadway. The performers sat around on stools, taking turns at pompously dispensing The Word or some pretentiously hoked-up business. Only when Lotte Lenya stood up to sing was there the electricity generated when Brecht is *echt*. The whole wretched affair was insufferably smug and condescending, but this was box-office Brecht, and it ran for 424 performances, toured to general acclaim, and enjoyed a return engagement of fifty-five more evenings.

Brecht once said that a man could be dismantled and reassembled like an automobile engine. *Mann ist Mann*, written in 1924, is the story of Galy Gay, a mild and acquiescent little porter who is incapable of saying "no." The setting is a cartooned Kipling India where the priests are Chinese; the time is the 1920's, though Victoria is queen. Through a series of grotesquely funny adventures, carefully planned by the gang of soldiers who have inveigled him, Galy is transformed into a human fighting machine: a shooting, shouting, bandolier-laden, machine-gun toting one-man army. The soldiers have done this to poor Galy because one of their squad is missing, and if they cannot be all present at roll call, they will be discovered as the sackers of a temple. One man is as good as any other, they maintain. Even Galy will do, for it isn't all that hard to mold a man's personality to fit the whims of those who want to use him. The play demonstrates that individual identity is at best a slippery and transient thing, that war dehumanizes, and that the machine-men that war creates blithely perpetuate the waging of senseless wars. *Mann ist Mann* also has a subplot that allows Brecht to delineate the frustrating ambiguity that the play poses. A sergeant known as Bloody Five, the fiercest man in the entire regiment and an inflexible dispenser of military discipline, is constantly humiliated by his own inability to resist seductive women (though only when it rains). In order to live up to his terrifying reputation as a soldier's soldier and to earn his name, like some demented Odysseus, he decides that to be the one man that he really is, Bloody Five must castrate himself. Brecht implies that rigid individualism may be as destructive as the replaceable personality. *Mann ist Mann* is the play that marks Brecht's transition from his early nihilism to the bitter irony and harsh lyricism that pervade *The Three-Penny Opera*, yet it is much closer to the early works than it is to the mature dramas.

In a time of political and commercial brainwashing, *Mann ist Mann* seemed stingingly pertinent. Productions of two different versions opened off-Broadway on successive evenings. On September 18, 1962, the Living Theatre presented *Man Is Man*, Gerhard Nellhaus' translation of Brecht's more heavily Marxist 1953 revision of the original script. On September 19, the Masque Theatre gave *A Man's a Man*, the 1924 version, in an adaptation by Eric Bentley which interpolated a good deal in the style of the later Brecht and featured some

additional songs with very good Brechtian lyrics by Mr. Bentley. It
was an unusual situation, and many reviewers could not resist comparing the two scripts and the two productions, each of which ran for
175 performances.

Most critics preferred *A Man's a Man* because it was a sparser,
sharper, less didactically top-heavy script, though still emphatically
instructive enough to irk Howard Taubman and Edith Oliver[65] among
others. Harold Clurman was not alone in calling the Living Theatre's
Man Is Man a "wretched"[66] production, though some reviewers
thought the Masque presentation also to be quite weak. Nevertheless,
the usually carping *Time* considered the Bentley version to have had
a "taut and inventive"[67] performance, and Robert Brustein liked the
cabaret style of *A Man's a Man* despite weak acting.[68] Clurman and
Brustein agreed that *Mann ist Mann* is not one of Brecht's great plays
but certainly a very good one, meaningful in the sixties as it was in
the twenties, and clearly a play with texture and a complex ambiguity
that far outweighs whatever blatant preachment Brecht's detractors
found disturbing. However, the *Time* review expressed the dominant
sentiment that pervades so much of the recent acceptance of Brecht's
work: the ideas, though often obvious, are sound, but the play is
really exciting because of the author's gifts as a playmaker and his
"poison-*cum*-laughing gas." What seemed so amazingly intuitive at
the time it was written may appear to be a bit jaded in the shadow of
the rubble of recent history, but the way in which Brecht said it was
as immediate as the news of 1962.

When *Mother Courage and Her Children* opened at the Martin
Beck Theatre on March 28, 1963, exactly thirty years had elapsed
since the last production of Brecht on Broadway. There is an inadver-
tent irony in the play's subtitle: "A Chronicle of the Thirty Years'
War." Brecht had written *Mutter Courage und Ihre Kinder* in 1939,
and it was first produced in Zurich in 1941, although the standard
musical score by Paul Dessau was not introduced until the Berliner
Ensemble production.

Anna Fierling, nicknamed "Mother Courage" when she braved a
bombardment to rescue some bread she feared would turn moldy and
thereby cost her a business investment, is based on a character from
the seventeenth-century tales by Grimmelshausen. She is a wandering
trader whose wagon offers wares to any and all participants in the
Thirty Years' War, the source of both her livelihood and her misery.
The Thirty Years' War was the historical epitome of senseless wars,
for by the end of that conflict of incalculable bloodshed, hardly anyone still knew with whom, against whom, to what end, or for what
cause he was fighting. But Anna Fierling knew; she was fighting for

survival. Her survival exacts a terrible price, the cost of which she determines largely by her own actions, and the paying of which teaches her almost nothing. Mother Courage sets out with her wagon and three children (by three different fathers). When the curtain falls, she has only her battered wagon left. Her older son is killed; he might have survived had he not been courageous. Her younger son is killed; he might have survived had he not been honest. Her daughter is killed; she might have survived had she not been compassionate. Anna Fierling is neither courageous, nor honest, nor compassionate. Each of her children is shot while she is haggling elsewhere.

The songs are Brecht at his biting, ironic, and poetic best. The tapestry of *Mother Courage* is rich in complex themes and brilliantly realized characters beyond Anna and her children: the chaplain, the cook, the camp follower, the soldiers. The war serves as an ever-present backdrop to the play while the main action concentrates on the daily activities of those who struggle to live through it—the people, not the heroes of history. The dramatic conflicts spring from the commerce of war, not the combat. As Brustein has observed, the play demonstrates war to be an extension not so much of diplomacy as of free enterprise,[69] and that the ideals that men spout so piously are mere rationalizations for greed, pettiness, and exploitation. All Mother Courage really learns is that the human "capacity for suffering is limitless" and that "the cruelty of men, the venality of society, and the indifference of the gods seem immutable conditions of life."[70]

Mother Courage has already disposed of her horse when the play begins. Her children pull the wagon. When the play ends, the old woman, now alone, drags what is left of her cart as she sings the refrain of her song:

> *Christians, awake! The winter's gone!*
> *The snows depart. The dead sleep on.*
> *And though you may not long survive*
> *Get out of bed and look alive!*
>   (trans. by Eric Bentley)

The scenery, though sparse, indicates the total devastation of the war. It turns slowly on its revolving stage. Anna, as if on an eternal treadmill, pulls her wagon against the course of the revolver and its set. The lights go down, and her song continues in the dark. What a challenge for an actress to play this role as Brecht said she should: *not* to gain the sympathy of the audience. Mother Courage is one of the great, complex characters of modern drama, maybe greater and more complex than Brecht intended her to be, and the response that she elicits when well played is a frustratingly ambivalent one. She is

selfish and cunning, yet she is strong and resourceful. She is infuriat-
ingly callous, yet she has the sensitivity to see through the world's
hypocrisies and to explode its sanctimonious clichés and shibboleths.
She is a moral coward, but like Falstaff, she is a coward not by nature
but on principle. The attitudes she represents—the resilience, the ability to make the best of a bad business, and the stoic acceptance of a
world that is evil in root and fiber—are the very attitudes that have
always made war thinkable, and therefore possible. Nevertheless,
there is an ineluctable strength in this doggedly stubborn cynic, and
to some extent we must admire her reserve of misguided guts. She
may be a contributory executioner of her children, but it is almost
impossible not to be moved by her fate. It is, after all, forged on the
anvil of the world on which the ideals of even the best of us have
been somewhat battered into compromise.

The Broadway production of this masterpiece was an almost total
disaster. After nineteen previews, it had fifty-two regular performances, then closed. It is hard to believe that so great a play could
have been so brutally butchered by allegedly professional hands. The
adaptation is blameless, for Eric Bentley's text is more than just a
skilful translation; it is, in its own right, a work of art. Except for that,
and a few good performances, just about everything else went wrong,
and in ways that could happen nowhere but on Broadway.

Mother Courage cannot be adequately prepared in the time allowed a Broadway show, four weeks of rehearsal. The actors were
uncomfortable; there was neither unity of style nor rapport among
players; the mechanical procedures of production went awry. The
play opened during a newspaper strike, although that ended before
the closing. The box office would have had to gross $29,000 a week to
meet expenses, and hardly anything but a *Kitsch* musical in a large
house can do that kind of business. Had the songs not been cut to a
bare minimum, the production would have cost even more. Regula-
tions of the musicians' union dictate that any show devoting more
than twenty-four minutes to music must be listed as a "musical" and
employ twenty-four musicians at exorbitant rates. However, the economy of Broadway was far from the only culprit. In the rush of
preparation, Jerome Robbins' direction emphasized nothing but the
already obvious antiwar preaching while it ignored every subtlety of
the text. The result was a ponderous, labored, heavy-handed, monotonous, immobile performance staged by a man whose other work,
mainly in musical comedy, has often been brilliant. The ironies and
nuances of Brecht's play were seldom communicated. The whole thing
was so superficially and naïvely conceived that it was "intellectually
spineless."[71] Clearly, the production wanted to satisfy the Broadway

audience, an audience too largely dominated by the vulgar affluent who respond to all the wrong things, will not accept a serious play if it is too complex, and have "a Yahoo's appetite only for blunt obscenities."[72] In catering to that audience, the production betrayed the play.

Whether the backers or theatre owners pressured the director into hiring a big name as a hedge for this risky venture or whether the casting of the title role was a monstrous indiscretion on Robbins' part is not really known, but Anne Bancroft, really quite gifted in roles suited to her, was a preposterous Mother Courage. She was not only much too young, but she also played the part for unbridled pathos, softness, and warmth. It was a direct appeal for the audience's sympathy, and it missed the crux of the character, its range, and its toughness. Harold Clurman was kindly euphemistic when he said that Miss Bancroft was "too locally urban."[73] The less gracious reviewers and critics had no trouble seeing an Italian girl from the Bronx making believe that she was a "tired Jewish housewife"[74] playing Anna Fierling. Miss Bancroft would have looked more convincing hanging onto a strap on the Eighth Avenue Express than onto that wagon. At the very best it was acceptable Odets, but it wasn't Brecht.

The production did not employ a revolving stage, so the wagon was not pulled against the passing scene. Courage had to lug it all around the stage, and this distorted the focus of the last scene. Robbins interpolated a totally unnecessary, gimmicky, pseudo-Brechtian opening: All the actors came out and introduced themselves and told what parts they would play (shades of *Brecht on Brecht!*). Many in the audience complained that the words of the songs were inaudible, and Dessau's music and Bentley's lyrics were not always tailored to blend.

The tactful newspaper reviewers and periodical critics tried to be kind by being either bland and superficial or by speaking well of the play and minimally of the production. There were, of course, those infuriated enough by the performance (and its audiences) to vent their anger, and there were even some who seemed so stunned that they began to wonder if *Mother Courage* was, after all, that good a play. The general critical consensus was, "Oh, well; better than nothing," but the tone of sadness was inescapable in the intelligent reviews: finally, after all these years, is this the best that Broadway can do?

Brecht's *Der Aufhaltsame Aufsteig des Arturo Ui* was an attempt to tell the story of Adolf Hitler from his beginnings to the *Anschluss* of Austria in terms of caricature Chicago gangsters, each one analogous to and looking like a member of the Nazi upper echelon. The thugs are trying to gain control of the vegetable market. Brecht had a great gift for parody, and the victims of his talent were often the sacred cows of German culture: Luther's hymns, anthems, and Bible; Shakespeare; Goethe. *Arturo Ui*, written in 1941, was in mock-heroic blank verse, and Arturo's character, though Hitler, is openly based on Richard III. His courting of Betty Dullfeet after the killing of her husband (clearly Dollfuss) parodies Schlegel's translation of Richard's wooing of Lady Anne, while the murder of the Roehm character closely parallels the fall of Buckingham. All this may be spritely and inventive, and Brecht had fun with it, but it is buried beneath the overwhelming mass of the play which is neither spritely nor inventive. Indeed it is a woefully clumsy affair which is based on a silly, taste- less, and totally illogical analogy. To depict Hitler's rise as nothing but an economic problem created by gangsters and to say nothing at all of the political madness or even the maniacal anti-Semitism invali- dates the Arturo-Hitler parallel. It is a naïve play, a blatant oversim- plification. Robert Brustein is not alone in calling it a satire "inade- quate to its subject."[75] In so much of his work of the forties and fifties, Brecht, who had foreseen nazism so clearly twenty years be- fore, seemed incapable of dealing with it as it really was.

David Merrick, Midas-touched producer of extravagant *Kitsch*, imported the gifted but erratic British director Tony Richardson, whose work on both stage and screen has usually been either bril- liantly inspired or chaotically unrestrained, to stage *Arturo Ui*. On November 11, 1963, it opened at the Lunt-Fontanne Theatre and closed after eight performances. It is one of Brecht's weakest efforts to begin with, a play both gross and flimsy, but Merrick, master of the gross and flimsy, must have seen possibilities for a spectacular carnival of a play, particularly if it was stuffed with enough flashy hokum, brassy noise, and beerhall humor to conform with that Yahoo audi- ence's definition of fun. Neither the critics nor the audience liked *Arturo Ui*, and for one of very few times, Merrick, long-time sub- scriber to Mencken's law that no one ever went broke underestimat- ing the taste of the American public, was wrong.

George Tabori, of the tin ear and leaden sentence, adapted Brecht's play, leaving out that part of the title that said Arturo's rise was resistible, and interpolating numerous local and anachronistic jokes. The music was Jule Styne's idea of what Weill might have written had Merrick been able to ask him to. It was almost as if producer, director, and adapter alike had decided that all Brecht needed to be a Broadway hit was the appropriate salesmanship and showmanship. Richardson could not keep his actors in one style for more than a few minutes at a time; the mechanical gimmicks para- lyzed the eye; and the noise desensitized the ear. Lights flashed around the proscenium during the entire performance. The costumes looked like leftovers from *Guys and Dolls*. Christopher Plummer struggled valiantly with the Arturo-Hitler role, but what little was good in *Arturo Ui* was obliterated by glare and blare.

The reviews were uniformly damning. Brustein said that "the evening took on the aspect of a Shriner's convention."[76] Clurman noted that were the play done as a horror that could happen again (though the script hardly allows it), *Arturo Ui* might be good, but that the Merrick-Richardson-Tabori version was only a bad cartoon.[77] Richard Gilman was forced to conclude that "Brecht is simply not wanted on Broadway and there is no way to make him palatable," least of all this way.[78] Broadway had, for the second time, recognized Brecht, but had still not learned how to perform his work, or even to select it judiciously. *Arturo Ui* tried so hard to be funny. Adolf Hitler was not funny from the point of view Brecht had used to examine him, and the play as written was no longer pertinent. The performance merely compounded the felony.

The Circle-in-the-Square presented *Baal*, Brecht's first play, on May 6, 1965, at the Martinique Theatre where it ran for fifty-nine performances in an adaptation by Eric Bentley and Martin Esslin. This violent, unrestrained drama, close to expressionism and suffused with nihilism, is the story of a completely amoral man following the dictates of nature. Baal is a repellent character, but by the end, one almost admires this monstrous man who believes that life and the world are totally and irrevocably sordid, but that if we use this belief as our premise rather than our conclusion, we may make something of our lives. The 1964-65 production of *Baal* was generally well received, and its violence, its chaos, and its despair again found a responsive audience among the cultists of the early Brecht.

The Exception and the Rule (1930) is a short *Lehrstück* in which a merchant and the coolie he abuses shamelessly (the typical *Lehrstück* capitalist-worker situation) are crossing a desert while trying to beat a competitor to a big city. They run out of water, but the coolie has hoarded some, and he offers the merchant a drink. Mistaking the act of kindness for a threat to his life, the merchant shoots the coolie. At the trial the killer is acquitted. After all, how could he have known that the coolie meant no harm? One naturally fears people he has injured. When violence is the rule, we expect violence. Kindness is the exception. Therefore violence is the norm of human conduct. Eric Bentley's adaptation of *Die Ausnahme und Die Regel* was performed at the Greenwich Mews Theatre beginning in May of 1965. Most reviewers agreed that it was "transparently dogmatic" but that before it was over, the viewer could not but be "touched by its truth and humanity."[79] There was nothing spectacular about the performances

of either this play or *Baal*, but they were solidly and honestly presented. Early Brecht done off-Broadway was still the better part of
valor.

Plays by Brecht were also being performed by semi-professional,
peripherally professional, and dramatic school groups in New York.
They were seldom reviewed by the press, but among those to be seen
in 1963 alone were *The Elephant Calf, The Good Woman of Setzuan,*
and *Saint Joan of the Stockyards.* Regional professional theatres of
stature were also playing several of Brecht's plays. *The Caucasian
Chalk Circle,*[80] directed by Alan Schneider, was excellently reviewed
and received at the Arena Stage of Washington, D.C., in October,
1961; the Actors' Workshop of San Francisco mounted a highly successful *Galileo* in January, 1963; the Goodman Theatre in Chicago
gave a sound performance of *Mother Courage* in 1964. Brecht
abounded in the university theatres. In New York, there were not only
many new plays that showed the clear influence of Brecht (e.g., the
imports *A Man for All Seasons* and *Irma La Douce*), but there were
also performances of works tangential to his theatre: an ill-conceived
reworking of *The Good Soldier Schweik* in 1963, a production of the
Piscator-Neumann *War and Peace* in 1965, and a highly successful
program, *The World of Kurt Weill in Song*, which was performed by
Will Holt and Martha Schlamme and ran for 245 performances in
1964.

Because Brecht was not always subtle, many of his detractors for-
got that being unsubtle does not exclude complexity or intricacy or
depth. His work is generally admired more than it is liked, but his
impact on the American theatre has been strongly felt in the fifties
and sixties, and the techniques of epic theatre in themselves are no
longer a hindrance to acceptance. The best of Brecht is still not in
favor in New York. Broadway seldom touches it, and when it does,
cannot resist "improving" on it. Off-Broadway is not in sympathy with
the major works as it is with the early plays that are in phase with the
Theatre of the Absurd. That the poet's work is being performed at all
is indeed a boon, but the essential Brecht is as foreign to the New
York theatre as ever. His best work is yet to be done well, on Broadway or off. Being fashionable is not enough; the fashionable writer is
always at the mercy of fickle audiences and incompetent exploiters.

The cultural life of Switzerland was not destroyed by the war; it
was hardly interrupted. Except for a sharp decline in the tourist
trade, it was business as usual in the beautiful little country. For the
most part, the Swiss remained smugly aloof of all that was transpiring

around them, an attitude of unconcern that has come under sharp
attack by Switzerland's new generation of writers. It was in Switzerland alone, however, that the German-speaking theatre's tradition remained unbroken. During the Hitler years, the German drama went
underground in the superb municipal theatre on the bank of the
Zürichsee. It was at the *Schauspielhaus* that most of the exiles had
their plays first produced in German and where the essential Brecht
was premiered. The new Swiss drama is the product of men who
spent their artistically formative years in Zurich.

Martin Esslin has said that "[Max] Frisch and his compatriot,
Friedrich Dürrenmatt, without doubt the leading dramatists of the
German-speaking world today, have developed a dramatic idiom of
their own, a style that owes a great deal to Bernard Shaw, Thornton
Wilder, and Bertolt Brecht, and one that might perhaps most aptly be
described as a theatre of intellectual fantasy, airing contemporary
problems in a vein of disillusioned tragicomedy."[81] In his excellent
1955 essay, *Theaterprobleme,* Dürrenmatt himself stated that he
thought the age of tragedy to be past, for great tragedy is produced in
an ordered world with a stable code by which men can measure their
conduct.

> Tragedy presupposes guilt, despair, moderation, lucidity, vision,
> a sense of responsibility. In the Punch-and-Judy show of our cen-
> tury . . . we are all collectively guilty. . . . Comedy alone is
> suitable for us. Our world has led to the grotesque as well as to
> the atom bomb. . . . But the tragic is still possible even if pure
> tragedy is not.[82]

Our world is disintegrating, says Dürrenmatt. It calls not for a Sophocles but for a Swift. The new Swiss drama is one of cruel and bitter
comedy, actually a scornful view of a tragically irresponsible world
that cannot measure up to its own tragedy.

Friedrich Dürrenmatt has been prolific since the war. In addition
to his plays, he has written mystery tales, serious novels, numerous
essays which have already appeared in many anthologies of contemporary criticism because of their power and insight, and radio dramas
(still a viable form in Europe). Dürrenmatt's early plays were usually
set in the past, but by 1952, he turned to contemporary settings with
Die Ehe des Herrn Mississippi (The Marriage of Mr. Mississippi), a
total smashing of theatrical illusion in which the last scene is played
first, then stopped so that the audience can be told of the events
leading up to it.

Dürrenmatt sometimes asserts that he has no further objectives
than to tell a good theatrical tale, but this disclaimer is not to be
taken seriously, for he also says that "the world, for me, stands as

something monstrous, an enigma of calamity that has to be accepted
but to which there must be no surrender."[83] One of the main features
of Dürrenmatt's effectiveness is that he deals with ethical problems of
the most searching and serious nature with both wit and humor, a
departure in German drama almost the exclusive province of Brecht
and the two Swiss tragicomedians of whom Dürrenmatt is much the
funnier and Frisch the more didactic. Dürrenmatt has said that if he
felt that nothing had meaning or value, he would not bother to write—
nor would the Absurdists, for they would thereby be giving the lie to
their own theories. Dürrenmatt, who comes from a family of poets and
Protestant ministers, is always concerned with moral values. From his
early interest in Kierkegaard and Kafka comes his devotion to the
theme of sin, suffering, and the quest for redemption.[84] Dürrenmatt
shares the Existentialist belief that the world is indifferent to the
individual and that a man must alienate himself from the values of the
world. Yet though the world be absurd, Dürrenmatt believes that a
man may, indeed must, make responsible decisions within it. Because
that decision is rarely made within his plays, and the consequences of
irresponsibility are studied is no reason to agree with Wellwarth's
statement that "Dürrenmatt sees life only as a long futility working up
to an ultimate futility."[85]

The plays of both Frisch and Dürrenmatt transcend reality, but
they employ the techniques of realism within scenes, romance in their
ironic fancy, expressionism in some of their symbolic sequences, epic
theatre in their over-all structure, and social drama in their thematic
material. The balance is not always carefully struck, but in these plays
that have, along with the work of numerous other men, broken down
all distinctions between comedy and tragedy in recent drama, Dürrenmatt and Frisch have emerged with a distinctly original style,
though one making liberal use of established forms. Their pessimistic
comedy reflects much of the mood of today and should therefore have
appeal for the audience prepared by Brecht and off-Broadway. Yet, in
their insistence on responsible decisions in human conduct, Dürrenmatt and Frisch are in direct opposition to the philosophy of most of
the work achieving popularity off-Broadway. Critical praise has been
accorded a few Swiss plays, but to date, only Dürrenmatt's *The Visit*
has had a substantial run.

The first of Friedrich Dürrenmatt's plays to be given a performance in New York was *Die Ehe des Herrn Mississippi*, presented at
the Jan Hus Auditorium for twenty-four performances beginning on
April 2, 1958, under the inexplicable title *Fools Are Passing Through*.
The adaptation was by Maximilian Slater, who also directed the production. Mr. Slater had been a pupil of Max Reinhardt's and was for

six years a director of Vienna's *Theater in der Josefstadt*.[86] Dürrenmatt's play is a grotesque, nightmarish story of a judge whose passion
for absolute justice leads him to the excessive desire of wanting to re-
establish jurisprudence by direct vengeance. His theories are those of
the *Oresteia* in reverse. The political, philosophical, and criminal
machinations of the plot are extremely involved and are played out in
bizarre comic sequences of absurd behavior by the characters. There
is no attempt at credibility. Dürrenmatt seems to be experimenting
with various forms which are only half realized and ideas which are
only half formed. The play is an interesting portent of more coherent
work to come on similar themes.

"Mr. Slater's English often sounded very German,"[87] and there was
a conspicuous lack of clarity in the entire text as well as in the
production. Apparently, the acting was also very bad.[88] Atkinson
thought that the play started out interestingly enough but that it
became tedious, maybe because the direction should have been more
à la Beckett or Ionesco's work, a "madder style."[89] *Fools Are Passing
Through* got very little critical or popular attention.

The Visit, which opened on May 5, 1958, at the Lunt-Fontanne
Theatre, was Maurice Valency's adaptation from a French translation
of Dürrenmatt's *Der Besuch der Alten Dame*. It was the first German
drama to be performed on Broadway since *The Strong Are Lonely*,
and it won the Critics' Circle Award for the best foreign play of 1958-
59. The play was first produced in Zurich in 1956. In it, Dürrenmatt
employed a fusion of theatricalist, epic, naturalistic, and expressionistic techniques to present his tragicomedy. The various styles were so
well integrated that the forms never drew attention to themselves.
The Visit is a macabre fable set in an impoverished Swiss town,
Güllen, a colloquialism which can be translated as "dungheap." The
burghers expect relief from their penury, for they are to be visited by
Mme. Claire Zachanassian, the wealthiest woman in the world whose
reputation for generosity is unparalleled. Dürrenmatt derived her
name from those of the billionaires Zacharoff, Onassis, and Gulben-
kian. He says that Mme. Zachanassian's resemblance to Sarah Bernhardt—travelling with a coffin, having a wooden leg, keeping a pet
panther—is accidental. Mme. Zachanassian had been born in Güllen
and spent her youth there; the burghers are sure she will not turn her
back on her own townfolk. But they do not know that it is the old
lady who has caused the decay of the village so that she could have it
at her mercy. As a girl, Claire had been in love with Anton Schill,
now the most respected member of the community and surely its next
Bürgermeister. Claire arrives amid confusion and with an incredibly
grotesque entourage. She says that she will give Güllen one billion

Marks—half for the town; half to be divided among the citizens—on one condition: that she receive justice from them. She wants the burghers to kill Anton Schill, her old lover, who had bribed witnesses to his advantage in a paternity suit Claire had brought against him in their youth. The current mayor refuses the offer. Justice, he says, cannot be bought in a civilized country. To this, Claire replies that anything can be bought, and she can wait. Soon a dreadful change comes over the people. They live on credit; they become optimistic. They run up a bill, and it must be paid in the only way they can pay it. The reputation of Schill declines gradually, and the rationalizing populace begins its hypocritical justification of the murder they know they must commit collectively no matter how much they protest individually.

In its values and in the behavior of its citizenry, Güllen is a microcosm of modern society, the dungheap that is "Everytown," the cesspit of the decayed ideals of our civilization that has only its slogans left. It is the village more than any one character that determines the course of Claire's horrible prank. Schill is the scapegoat on whom are heaped all the petty vices and selfish indulgences of the community. He is killed to cleanse that community, but the act instead besmirches it. Schill's death marks the moral and spiritual death of Güllen, for in killing him and accepting the redeeming billion which brings them prosperity, the Güllners have killed their own consciences. As a final irony, they do it in good democratic fashion—in a town meeting with full radio and television coverage. Anton Schill is human and therefore has weaknesses and is tainted with sin, but he has integrity and he alone accepts responsibility for his own actions. This is not a strong enough weapon against the corruption and self-delusion of society. The townspeople construct an elaborate series of rituals, thus helping themselves to commit the murder by invoking every platitude of Western morality. One wag has said that the play should have been called *The Price Is Right*. One by one, everyone forsakes Schill: the common man, the law, the doctor, the priest, the teacher. They, and by implication we, are all to blame for the execution of Schill. Humanity has a collective guilt for its actions and for the ills it has inherited and done nothing about. Because Güllen has no standards of guilt and retribution and responsibility but only of expediency, it can have no tragedy by Dürrenmatt's definition.[90] It can have only the grotesque "Punch-and-Judy show" of today. In a postscript to the play, Dürrenmatt said that nothing could hurt the performance of this comedy that ends tragically more than to play it in an unrelieved serious tone. Randolph Goodman has pointed out that "Dürrenmatt's philosophy [in *The Visit*] shows the strong influence of the existentialism of Kierkegaard; in this hollow, hopeless

world, a man's character is his fate. . . . Man is free to choose his
path but once the first step is taken, everything that follows is inevitable."[91] That would describe a character in Sophocles as well, but as
long as there is no ordered cosmos with stable values, the result is
tragicomedy. *Der Besuch der Alten Dame* has been played in more
than fifteen languages and in more than twenty-five countries.[92]

There are many differences between Valency's text and the original. Not all of the changes are praiseworthy, although Dürrenmatt
approved them all in order to accommodate what Valency thought to
be American taste. The scapegoat's name was changed to Anton Schill
from Alfred Ill, both to satisfy Alfred Lunt and to avoid the connotations of the surname. The character of Claire was appreciably softened; she was given an air of aristocratic attractiveness in the adaptation, primarily to please Lynn Fontanne. The original Claire is a
dumpy and grotesque hag, a shrewd whore who struck it rich. Half of
her body is made of artificial parts. She is bedecked with all that
money can buy. This makes the German love scenes grisly where the
American ones are nostalgic. Some of Dürrenmatt's staccato dialogue
of expressionist derivation is filled out by Valency. Much of the humor and satiric comment are deleted for fear that American audiences
would not accept too much wit in a serious play. In the forest scenes
of the original, the trees are played by citizens—everything, the ani-
mate and the inanimate, is a citizen of the dungheap. This was
thought to be too stylized for Broadway. In the German text, Claire
has a new husband in each act, all played by the same actor; she has
one fiancé in *The Visit*. All topical jokes about things such as bad
German movies, Graham Greene's religious fanaticism, Dwight Eisen-
hower's good-natured dullness, America's mass culture, and Hollywood's bosom cult are deleted. Most of Dürrenmatt's bizarre hyper-
bolic situations do not appear in the American version (*e.g.*, CLAIRE:
"Call the Russians, Bobby. Tell them their offer is satisfactory."). The
ironic scene in which Schill's son takes the family for a ride in his new
Opel (after all, *anyone* can have a Volkswagen, says the lazy lout)
resembles Wilder's *Happy Journey to Trenton and Camden* in its
staging. It does not appear in the Broadway text, despite the fact that
it is the scene in which the glories of the reborn town are pointed out
to the man who is about to be sacrificed for them. The original play
also had a pseudo-Greek epilogue in verse in which the people ask for
divine grace for their new happiness and prosperity. "The sell-out of
Schill was a slower, more insidious process in Dürrenmatt's text."[93]
There is a horrifying unawareness on the part of the Güllners in the
original; Valency's townfolk are clearly out to "get" Schill. "The original version of *The Visit* was thought to be too fantastic . . . to suit

the tastes of American audiences."[94] Most of the changes were of details, and the larger frame of the play was untouched, but somehow a good deal of Dürrenmatt's irony, wit, texture, and highly allusive condemnation of Western culture were lost. Valency's adaptation was not always faithful in spirit, but it was eminently effective on the stage. However, a translation of *The Visit* by Patrick Bowles, who does not tamper with Dürrenmatt's play, is much the better English version than Valency's.

George E. Wellwarth has maintained that the American success of *The Visit* "has been due mainly to its sensationalism rather than to its more solid dramatic and philosophical qualities,"[95] and there is little question that this, in addition to the drawing power of the starring Lunts, contributed to what limited popularity the play enjoyed. It was still too strange a play for the general theatregoer, despite high praise from many respected reviewers and critics. It ran for a comfortable but hardly spectacular 189 performances, after which the Lunts took it on the road for a year and played a return engagement in New York in March, 1960. At that time, *The Visit* received even better reviews than it had in 1958.

The reviews were unanimously favorable about the acting of the play and the new theatre named for its stars, but not about the drama. John Gassner found Dürrenmatt's controlled use of expressionism the "most impressive factor" of the play.[96] Wolcott Gibbs called it a work he was "certainly not . . . likely to forget,"[97] and one that was quite disturbing. *Time* thought *The Visit* a superior version of Twain's *The Man That Corrupted Hadleyburg*, an "acrid, eerie, fiendish—and wonderful [picture of] a fanged and carnivorous world."[98] Brooks Atkinson, in several articles in the *Times*, found new reasons to praise Dürrenmatt's play.[99] He particularly approved of the drama's progression from broad fun to hard cruelty. The spectator knows what is going to happen. It is the *way* in which it happens that is terrifying. Atkinson said that *The Visit* was easily the best play of the year. Although its run was modest, it was without doubt the most successful German play to appear on Broadway since 1945. It is also one of the few really important German plays written since the end of World War II.

On February 2, 1960, *The Deadly Game* opened at the Longacre Theatre and ran for thirty-nine performances. The play was an adaptation by James Yaffe of Dürrenmatt's novella, *Trapps*. Also concerned with the concept of justice, as is most of his fiction and drama, it is the story of a small group of retired Swiss jurists who gather periodically to practice their former craft by trying famous people of history *in absentia*. But if by chance a visitor should happen to come along, they put him before the bar. If they probe long enough, they can find anyone guilty of some crime or other. A salesman named Trapps (Trapp in the play) seeks refuge from a winter storm. He plays the deadly game with the old men. At first it seems rather a good-natured pastime, but soon he finds that the lawyers are not merely playing. The salesman is convicted of murder for a death he indirectly caused by practicing greedy business tactics and by stepping on people to achieve commercial success. He is condemned to death, and in bizarre fashion the sentence is implemented. When Trapp's widow pays a call on the old men the following day, they remember how she contributed to her husband's behavior. The old lawyers look at each other meaningfully, ask Mrs. Trapp to sit down, and the curtain falls. Dürrenmatt has again held all men responsible for the corruption of society.

The Deadly Game presents, as Henry Hewes has observed, more of a kangaroo court than did the novella.[100] The play is more obvious; the machinery is everywhere apparent and Dürrenmatt's subtle and macabre analysis of human guilt is missing. The Deadly Game is also more melodramatic than Trapps. In the play, the salesman runs away from the house and inadvertently falls off a cliff in the snowstorm. In the story, his guilt is more than he can bear and he hangs himself, to the horror of the old men who are much more playful and kind than are the jurists of the play. They really consider it a game; it is the guilty Trapps who takes it seriously. The characters in the play are always in earnest. Howard Trapp is presented by Yaffe as a crass, brash American; in Dürrenmatt's tale he is one of those smug, detached Swiss who prosper from other people's suffering. Dürrenmatt's novella is an ironic and sardonic comment on man's behavior; Yaffe's play is an ordinary thriller, albeit an eerie one. As Atkinson said in his review, the play made "commercial fiction" out of serious material.[101] Reviewers were unanimous in preferring the novella. An off-Broadway revival in 1966 ran for 105 performances, but The Deadly Game is actually Yaffe's play. It only takes its basic plot from Trapps.

Another of Dürrenmatt's works presented off-Broadway was The Jackass, adapted by George White from Der Prozess um des Esels Schatten, and performed twice at the Barbizon Plaza Theatre in March, 1960. The original is one of Dürrenmatt's radio plays and actually defies transplanting to the stage. The German text is peppered with witty dialogue, and although its thesis is obvious the author's caustic humor carries the play. The Jackass takes place in a fringe province of ancient Greece where a dentist named Anthrax rents a jackass in order to visit a patient. He rides the beast into a blazing hot plain. Finding that the shadow cast by the jackass is the

only shade in sight, Anthrax sits down in it. The animal's owner is
furious. He has rented Anthrax a jackass but not its shadow, and he
demands further payment which the dentist refuses. The owner takes
him to court. The situation then becomes very much like the famous
vaudeville routine in which a lawyer impoverishes a friend for whom
he is trying to fix a two-dollar fine by going to successively higher
and more expensive courts of appeal while the weary victim keeps
wailing, "Please, pay the two dollars, Charlie!" Dürrenmatt's play attacks greedy and corrupt lawyers and governmental bureaucracy but
does not stop there. Anthrax's case becomes a national issue, and the
entire population (all of it, of course, eminently corruptible) is in
upheaval over all of the commercial, philosophical, political, and religious implications of the trial. Two political parties develop, those
who support the owner and those who sympathize with the dentist. It
becomes a class struggle of the haves and the have-nots. The parties
arm. Dürrenmatt has reduced modern geopolitics to an ultimate
absurdity. The parties go to war while the neutrals sell arms to both
sides. Both camps bribe a drunken sea captain, apparently a symbol
of thermonuclear warfare, to burn down the enemy stronghold. The
old salt accepts both offers and burns down the entire province. The
people, having lost everything and having forgotten the original issue,
look for someone to blame. They decide that it was all the fault of the
jackass itself in the first place. The people, again united in common
cause, stone, beat, and knife the beast to death. The play ends as the
fleeing animal, just short of his end, becomes vocal and asks the audience to consider exactly who is and who is not a jackass.

What makes Dürrenmatt's radio play delightful is his gift of wit.
The parable is far from subtle, but it is written by a master of language. Unfortunately, most of what is commendable in Dürrenmatt's
script is not translatable. Even the talented George White was unable
to achieve a parallel effect, so that all that remained in *The Jackass*
was the obvious and clumsy architecture of a play not intended for
the stage. *The Jackass* was mercifully ignored by most reviewers and
critics.

An early Dürrenmatt play, *Romulus der Grosse*, presents the dramatist's whimsical conception of the last of the Roman emperors.
Romulus has carefully weighed the history of his forefathers and their
empire in the balance, and he has found them wanting. He retires to
his villa to pursue his beloved hobby, breeding chickens, and to await
the advancing Goths whom he believes to deserve a chance at ruling
the world now that Rome has irrevocably botched the job. His glory,
Romulus maintains, will be in his wisdom rather than in the stupid
and vain valor that surrounds him, and he chooses to preside over the

well-deserved defeat of the corrupt empire. In a world of preposterously inflated illusions, Romulus sees himself as the only true realist.
To his final and utter amazement, Romulus learns that there is another such man, Odoaker the feared Gothic chieftain. Odoaker is devoted to classical culture, completely disillusioned with his empire's
shabby values and bestial violence, and terrified of his brutal
nephew, Theodoric, who will succeed him and destroy all that is
valuable in the civilized world. Odoaker came to Rome in order to
surrender to Romulus before it is too late. They face each other in the
decrepit villa, each determined to capitulate to the other. The two
leaders discover that they share their great passion, and they determine, under Teutonic leadership and Roman abdication, to make the
world safe for breeding chickens. Only the audience knows that never
yet has the world come to that blessed state. The play's twentieth-
century relevance is obvious, and Dürrenmatt's Goths are very modern Germans.

The play is not nearly as good as its idea, but it has many moments of sparklingly witty dialogue. Most of what is admirable in
Dürrenmatt's comedy was lost in Gore Vidal's flippant adaptation
which opened as *Romulus* on January 10, 1962, and closed after sixty-
nine performances. Most reviewers blamed Dürrenmatt and Vidal
equally. *Time* said that it was a shallow play to begin with, "a wispy
heap of intellectual shavings,"[102] but Robert Brustein thought that
Dürrenmatt should have defended himself by not giving Vidal permission to take the excessive liberties he did.[103] Brustein decried Vidal's
emasculation of the intellectual content of the play and for turning it
into an exercise in fey cuteness. Harold Clurman was angered by the
adaptation's "aimless sophistication" clearly intended to prime it for
Broadway, particularly with its heavy-handed anachronisms and
"feeble topical jokes."[104] (e.g., "The international menace of Gothi-
cism.") Vidal's play, like Dürrenmatt's, is much better during the second half, but Taubman of the *Times* was among the few who felt that
half a play was better than none.[105] Cyril Ritchard was quite funny as
Romulus (though far too narcissistic, foppish, and smart-alecky) and
Howard DaSilva was excellent as the Gothic chieftain, but Romulus'
original weaknesses coupled with Vidal's Broadwayese adaptation
yielded a disappointing performance.

The action of one of Dürrenmatt's most popular successes on the
Continent, *Die Physiker*, is set in that most favorite of recent German
dramatic locales: a madhouse. Specifically, the scene is the decayed
old wing of a villa, microcosm of the slag heap of Western culture,
where all the social amenities are observed but barbaric violence is an
everyday occurrence. Presiding over this private sanitarium is a

crippled, megalomaniacal, lady psychiatrist. Residing in the old wing
are three ostensibly mad nuclear physicists. One (Beutler) thinks he is
Newton, another (Ernesti) that he is Einstein, and a third (Möbius)
claims that he communicates directly with King Solomon. The plot
and the theme of the play both raise its basic questions: Who, exactly,
is mad? What is the responsibility of the scientist? Can a world that
places its destiny in the very hands that hold the means of destroying
it hope to survive? What, or who, in this corroded civilization is
worth saving? Can a thought, once thought, be unthought? These
heady questions are asked and answered in the bizarre charade that
takes place in the madhouse. Each of the three inmates kills his nurse
for fear of being exposed; each physicist ultimately has no choice but
to remain in the asylum; two of the three scientists turn out to be
espionage agents as well; and the psychiatrist reveals herself as the
most dangerously insane of them all. The intricacies of the plot twist
and turn ironically with each successive scene.

The Physicists, an adaptation by James Kirkup which respects the
play but petrifies its language, opened at the Martin Beck Theatre on
October 13, 1964, under the direction of Peter Brook. The cast was
solid: Jessica Tandy as the psychiatrist, Hume Cronyn as "Newton,"
George Voskovec as "Einstein," and Robert Shaw as Möbius. The
notices were lukewarm, and The Physicists, respected but not really
liked, closed after fifty-five performances. The reviewers, almost to a
man, thought the play far better in conception than in execution and
objected to the script's preachiness. Time, far harsher than most, said
that The Physicists was full of "fat, fuzzy thoughts," a piece of "intellectual Swiss cheese."[106] Clurman felt that the play should be frightening but wasn't;[107] Wilfrid Sheed commented that while Dürrenmatt's problems were well posed, and his questions needed to be
asked, the play resolved those problems badly, and the answers to the
questions are what crumbled the play.[108] The Physicists is a fable;
fables should not come with explanations. The tastes of the New York
reviewers and audiences are not receptive to plays laden with
Teutonic intellectual discussions, not even witty ones. The general
response to The Physicists was that it was too grotesque to be serious,
too serious to be funny, too analytical to be entertaining, too distant
to be moving, and too didactic to be stimulating. This reception has
greeted the play nowhere but in the United States.

It is almost impossible to find any American critical statement
concerning contemporary German drama that does not somewhere say
that Friedrich Dürrenmatt is the most important playwright writing
in his language today. Nevertheless, his only drama to have found

favor on this country's professional stage is *The Visit,* and that in Valency's distorted adaptation.

European critics have frequently observed that the work of Max Frisch loses meaning for men who have not personally experienced the holocausts of the twentieth century, who have not seen their neighbors murdered or the roofs blown off their own houses. There is no question that Frisch's plays are often pedantically didactic, maddeningly repetitious, or ponderously ironic, but they are also frequently imaginative, intelligent, and insightful. Two of his dramas were performed in New York in February of 1963; both were critical and commercial failures.

Frisch's major plays deal with two essential themes: guilt and responsibility. Maybe that is really one theme. *Andorra* is one of the many works in what Robert Brustein has called the Germanic *mea culpa* syndrome, the fashionable public breast beating which has accompanied postwar prosperity.[109] The setting of *Andorra* is a mythical country adjacent to, and threatened by, the fascist land of the Blacks. Andri, a young Andorran is thought to be of Jewish parentage, and he is persecuted even in righteous Andorra because of the spectre of the anti-Semitic Blacks whom the populace would like to appease. It turns out that Andri is not a Jew; indeed, his mother was a Black and his father a respected member of the Andorran community. When the Blacks arrive, they bring a "Jew Detector" who readily ferrets out Andri (by the gait of his Jewish feet, one of the most preposterous of the Nazis' racial myths). The young man accepts the role of Jew no matter what the facts. Andri has, in spirit, identified himself with the Jews. Claiming his moral and spiritual rather than his physical identity, he is executed.

George Tabori's clumsy English version played for only nine performances. The newspaper strike did not help, but the periodical reviews were so damaging that it probably made little difference. *Time* said that Frisch had "dropped a couple tons of irony on the New York theater," but crushed only himself.[110] The review further noted that Frisch was proposing that people are beasts, then trying to arouse the conscience of those beasts after proving that beasts had no conscience—all a very circular argument with a big hole in the middle. There is also a hole in *Time's* logic; nowhere does Frisch say that *all* men are beasts. John McCarten objected because the play's propositions are "self-evident to any civilized man."[111] Most comment concerning the production agreed that the sets were bad, the direction static, the acting mediocre, and the adaptation stiff. *Andorra* is an unsubtle play and a self-righteous one. It lacks the texture that a

Dürrenmatt might have given it. Brustein's comment is incisive:
Frisch seems unable "to keep two ideas in his mind at the same
time."[112] The playwright's moral passion was simply not enough to
sustain *Andorra*.

There were commentators who said that *Andorra* might have fared
better off-Broadway, but there was no evidence to substantiate this
guess. Quite the contrary. *The Firebugs*, Mordecai Gorelik's adaptation of Frisch's *Biedermann und die Brandstifter*, opened at the off-
Broadway Maidman Playhouse only two days after the premiere of
Andorra. *The Firebugs* is the much better play; it closed after eight
performances.

Herr Biedermann (the word means "common man"), manufacturer
of a useless and misrepresented hair oil, lives in a town that has been
victimized by prolific arsonists. He refuses to believe that anyone
would ever burn down *his* house. When the two firebugs—one satanic,
the other thuggish—insinuate themselves into Biedermann's home, the
nasty but naïve little man laughs congenially, invites the men to
accept his hospitality, allows them to store gasoline in his attic, helps
them to lay the fuse, and even gives them the matches they need to
incinerate the Biedermann household. The scenes of the play are con-
nected by mock-heroic choruses by the town's Keystone Kop-like fire-
men who chant panegyrics to their own superb preparedness while
fires rage round about. In an epilogue, the dead Biedermann and his
wife still have not understood their own complicity in their destruction. The common man, as well as the nebulous circumstances he is
always blaming, is largely responsible for his own undoing. Frisch's
play was an expanded version of his earlier, highly successful radio
script.

The Firebugs is a rather blatant allegory, and in its blaming of the
Biedermänner it oversimplifies about as recklessly as those works that
have totally exonerated the common man from any culpability for his
own destiny. The reviews of *The Firebugs* were almost in total agreement with Howard Taubman that "the material is thin and the moral
transparent."[113] The play is appreciably better than most of its judges
seemed able to see, but it was certainly not helped by a too farcically
directed production, an amateurish set, and the sort of inexcusably
bad acting of which off-Broadway has too often been guilty. In November, 1963, the Seattle Repertory Company presented *The Firebugs* under André Gregory's direction. The *Times* said that it was
much better than it had been in New York.[114] *The Firebugs* has since
been performed by several regional professional companies and by
numerous university theatres.

The feeling in the New York drama district is that Frisch just is

not as good as Dürrenmatt while being too much like him, both of
which are fair assessment. Nevertheless, neither of Frisch's two plays
given in New York in 1963 was fairly treated by its production.

The *Wirtschaftswunder,* the "economic miracle" that is West Germany's remarkable recovery from World War II, has brought with it
two phenomena that might, at first glance, seem antithetical. A closer
look shows that they are inextricably joined. Prosperity has yielded a
certain air of the crass and the brash: callous pride in material
achievement and smug delight in material gratification. Some German minds and consciences are as metaphysically oriented as ever,
but the values of the middle class are almost exclusively physical.
After the war, the great mass of German people, with few outspoken
exceptions, were determined to forget or to repress the age of Hitler.
However, once the first busy work of recovery was under control,
many began to struggle with the guilt-laden memory of the sheer
malevolence that was National Socialism, whether they had contributed to it or only stood idly by. A dominant theme of postwar
German literature became: Not to choose is also a choice. Some writers began to see themselves as the new nation's conscience, and they
bitterly scorned the new German utilitarianism while they scored a
people who seemed capable of developing their consciences only after
it became a luxury they could afford. And there was a hard core of
Germans with only one regret about the Nazi era—its failure. The
Germans had re-established themselves as men in the world's market-
place; they could now admit that they had for quite a while been
beasts. And so, the arrogantly insensitive mood of prosperity and the
loud, public self-flagellation for savage misdeeds spring from the same
source. It is far easier to sit in the square in sackcloth and ashes when
you know that a hot bath, a clean shirt, and an expensive suit are
waiting at home. It did not take all that long for West Germany to go
from total devastation to Europe's chief exporter of goods. Along with
the Volkswagens and the precision instruments, Germany began to
peddle to the world the product of what seems to have become one of
its major industries: guilt.
   Though the methods of expression vary greatly, the central
thematic concern of most continental dramatists since 1945 has been
that man lives in an indifferent universe that has no discernible meaning. In it, he has created societies that have no viable direction. Man
himself is an individual isolated from his fellows with whom he shares
only his mortality, and he can discover no definable purpose for his
own existence. In such a given world, any god that may have existed

must be dead if he was a good god, for if he is still alive, he has abdicated, and is therefore an irresponsible god. What, then, is left to a human being who somehow has retained a raging need for meaning, for purpose, and for direction where there are none? He has two alternatives: nihilism, accepting that all is meaningless and that one ethic or action is as good or bad as any other; or responsibility, deciding that in the absence of external values, a man creates meaning by ascribing it to his own life. The tormented dramatists of post-*Wirtschaftswunder* Germany have largely opted for the second choice, in which a man admits to bearing the burden of his own dust and accepts the guilt and the responsibility of individual conduct in the quest for a meaningful existence.

In 1956, Harold Clurman, having recently returned from a European tour, wrote that "there is no escaping the fact: in quality of production, in scenic invention, in variety of repertory, in solidity of organization, the German theatre at this moment (and Berlin is by no means the single nor even the most signal instance of it) makes the American, English, French stages look like little-theatre activities."[115] Good theatre was to be seen throughout the country, not only at Brecht's *Ensemble*.

The artistic vacuum which Hitler had created in Germany left the country without a generation of dramatists, but some of the new ones now emerging, though their canon is not large, bear watching. More than a few of the new voices belong to middle-aged men, but there are also young men writing plays. Among the most promising in both groups are: Karl Wittlinger, Hermann Gressieker, Guenter Rutenborn, Rolf Hochhuth, and Peter Weiss. There have also been some interesting plays written by men who are better known for work in other genres. Among these are Wolfgang Hildesheimer and Günter Grass. Not one of these men restricts himself to the limits imposed by verisimilitude. They are all to some degree anti-illusionist playwrights, and of their work, only Hochhuth's one piece is essentially realistic in style despite its epic scene sequence, rhapsodically Schillerian bravado, and verse dialogue which is actually more orthographic than poetic except for one episode in the last act. The influence of Brechtian theatre is everywhere apparent in their efforts.

Royal Gambit, which opened at the Sullivan Street Playhouse on March 4, 1959, and ran for eighty-seven performances, was George White's excellent translation of Hermann Gressieker's *Heinrich VIII und Seine Frauen*, which had enjoyed high critical praise at the time of its premiere in Berlin in 1957. It presents Henry VIII as the prototype of the modern man, and though the king remains constant in his sixteenth-century costume, the topics of conversation between Henry and his wives cover the time span from the Renaissance to the present. Each of his six wives represents another stage of development from the world of the Tudors to the twentieth century and is costumed to indicate the age of which she is a product. In his introduction, Gressieker states that he intends to show how modern value systems are reflected in the "erotic and moral tragi-comedy" of Henry's life. The characters of the drama are aware of the historical consequences that stem from their actions within the play. There is no sense of stage trickery; Henry and his wives do not jump recklessly through the centuries, but step outside their historical identities to comment upon their actions. Most of Gressieker's work has been purposefully anachronistic, allowing historical characters to serve as commentators on the present day.

Henry marks the end of God's age and the beginning of man's, but he destroys man for the sake of civilization. His first step is to free himself from the bondage of Rome and from Luther. The reasons, he says, are unimportant. It is only important that he makes the break. Henry praises himself for his "modern" accomplishments: allowing reason to free the mind and the senses, and questioning both authority and nature. However, in overcoming the fear of God, the monarch has established the age of human anxiety. This is the price for an existence in which mind is master. But rather than develop that mind, Henry becomes more interested in self-gratification. Anne's execution shows that Henry prefers expediency to justice, an attitude that becomes a permanent part of his nature in his relationship with Jane Seymour. Henry develops the habit of making up a set of standards after the fact in order to justify his behavior. Gressieker's hero discusses the development of humanism and an age of reason which, for all its ideals, bred wars in the name of faith which were actually ventures for profit. After Jane's death while bearing a son, Henry marries Anna of Cleves in order to cement relations with the Lutheran forces. She represents the age of materialism, of gold and state and power. She is a lusty and independent woman whom Henry admires greatly, but she is ugly and ungainly, so he pensions her off and marries Katharine Howard, who likes the world Henry has created but is a wanton within it. We are now in the twentieth century, and the criticism of the play hits closer and closer to the audience itself in a careful and logical development of the drama's argument. The final wife, and the one who outlives Henry, is the devilishly enticing Kate Parr, the spirit of the post-World War II age, a prophetess of learned skepticism. She believes that "to calculate is bliss," and it is her frame of mind that makes a war thinkable, a machine lovable, and material gratification the greatest good.

The play ends on an unfortunately sentimental and wishful note that man will come full cycle and return to the idealism that he lost when he discarded his deocentric life in the Renaissance. Power, wealth, freedom, love, and knowledge have all failed Henry. Maybe he was better off before. Gressieker's play is a moral and philosophical history of modern Western civilization seen in microcosm. As such, it is necessarily sketchy and often vague or confusing, but *Royal Gambit* raises many important questions and presents them dramatically. The play would have been stronger had Gressieker not been presumptuous enough to answer his questions with a platitude.

Reviewers' reactions to *Royal Gambit* were varied, but no one was offended by the didacticism or by the Brechtian "demonstrating" and direct addresses to the audience. Harold Clurman saw the play as a *Lehrstück*, "forthright . . . controversial . . . [but] intellectually too vague."[116] Its ideas, Clurman said, are not crisp enough. Brooks Atkinson found *Royal Gambit* "original, stimulating and mature." He added that "what he [Henry] thinks sounds a good deal like the pious rationalizations of today."[117] Gressieker's play was unanimously praised for its performance. It has become a favorite of the university theatres and has already been revived by Equity Library Theatre.

The Emperor, George White's adaptation of a Gressieker play about the early years of Nero's reign, did not fare nearly so well. It asks whether those of us who judge the ways of the past are actually doing much better, but its story of an emperor who could not control his passion for killing (Nero's parallel is more than obvious) is developed in words alone. There is no drama. Howard Taubman noted that a lot of the talk was good, but by the end there was just a superabundance of talk, a lot of it philosophical and too much of it lacking focus and definition.[118] *The Emperor* opened on April 16, 1963, at the Maidman Playhouse and closed after twenty-four performances.

Guenter Rutenborn is a Protestant pastor in East Germany whose play, *Das Zeichen des Jona*, was first produced in Germany in 1947. It was adapted into English as *The Sign of Jonah* by the highly competent George White. A theatricalist play that owes much of its technique to Wilder, Brecht, and Pirandello (though only Wilder would sympathize with its point of view), it is set in a theatre in West Berlin in which actors are trying to present the story of Jonah, but members of the audience keep interrupting, asking questions, arguing, contradicting, and making personal statements of belief. The play is consequently an analysis of a biblical play by modern men rather than the play itself. *The Sign of Jonah* is too self-righteously religious, and Rutenborn's background as a minister is everywhere apparent, but the piece is theatrically effective in its presentation of old truths in twentieth-century terms. The thesis of the play is that all of us (and maybe even God) share the guilt for our modern horrors. We are responsible for our actions, and when we condemn God or fate or other men or circumstances or "the times," we are only re-echoing an old cry and are, in effect, condemning ourselves. One need not accept Rutenborn's theology in order to be moved by the play.

Rutenborn's drama had approximately five hundred performances in small towns in East Germany alone, where the troupe of players was constantly on the run so as not to be forced to answer questions by the communist authorities.[119] Its first performance in the United States was at Union Theological Seminary in 1957, but *The Sign of Jonah* was first produced professionally on September 8, 1960, at the Players' Theatre. White's translation beautifully captured Rutenborn's gift for language, and *The Sign of Jonah* is an articulate play. It received too little critical attention and not enough publicity in New York. Consequently it was forced to close after only fifty-three performances despite some excellent reviews, among them that of Howard Taubman of the *Times* who said that one could disagree with Rutenborn's conclusions or think that he doesn't go far enough, but that *The Sign of Jonah* is a "stimulating and moving" play, beautifully performed, and written by a man who is both a poet and a thinker.[120] The chief opposition to the play expressed by a few reviewers was that its frame of reference was so clearly Germany right after World War II that the piece had to lose both meaning and power in another place at a later time. Rutenborn is a preacher as much as he is a playwright, but he writes with a strength that derives from dramatic traditions as well as from ecclesiastical ones.

Karl Wittlinger is a young dramatist whose *Kennen Sie die Milchstrasse?* has been performed in Europe more than two thousand times, often in the intimate cabaret style that he intended for the two-player piece. The basic situation is a psychiatrist's interview of an asylum inmate, a war veteran, officially listed as dead, who is trying to return to life in the opportunistic and competitive *Bundesrepublik*. The scene, indicated only sparsely or by costume changes, shifts quickly for each psychodrama from his life that the inmate acts out, and in each such scene, the psychiatrist plays a different one of the young man's antagonists. The veteran's "job" at the asylum is driving a milkwagon; he ends up as a daredevil motorcycle rider in a carnival where he is billed as Nemo—no one, a man without name or identity, officially dead and now actually courting death daily.

The veteran is tormented by his need, as one of the innocent Germans, to atone for his nation's guilt. He is convinced that only when all men bear the responsibility for conduct, and not just the wicked share the blame for evil, will there be any real morality. The play's answer to the question of responsibility seems to be that if a man retains his integrity in a mad world, he will also retain his sanity, and maybe hitch himself to a star instead of a milkwagon. Or maybe there is nothing left but to become Nemo. The implication that the members of the audience are fellow asylum inmates is almost as clear as in Peter Weiss's somewhat different use of the same device. *Kennen Sie die Milchstrasse?* is too gimmick laden and too foggy where it needs a gem-hard clarity, but the excesses are the sort of youthful mistakes that only a gifted man makes, and Wittlinger has a talent which, if disciplined, could yield significant plays.

Considering the intimate cabaret style of *Do You Know the Milky Way?* it seems particularly foolish for it to have been produced in a large Broadway theatre where it played for sixteen performances in October, 1961. Not even the solid acting of Hal Holbrook as the veteran and the brilliant virtuoso achievement of George Voskovec as the other eleven characters could save the production. John McCarten said that the quick changes and self-conscious devices often made the play look like a vaudeville act and blotted out the drama's philosophical import.[121] The general tenor of most reviews was that *Do You Know the Milky Way?* was murky in its symbolism and too full of self-pity in its thematic development. The play failed to engage the emotions while it befogged the intellect. Not atypical was Marya Mannes's comment that it was too Germanic, that "even the light touch taps too hard."[122]

Actors' Equity Association has a rule that a play which closes on Broadway must wait at least six months before it reopens off-Broadway. An unscrupulous producer might move his play to the little theatre district in order to cut actors' salaries. The producers of Wittlinger's piece, seeing their error in not mounting it in a small house and sure that the play could be successful in a cabaret setting, asked that the rule be waived, but they were denied permission to reopen after three weeks. In the spring of 1963, *Do You Know the Milky Way?* was revived at the small Gramercy Arts Theatre. The cast was not as good, but the simpler, more intimate production was quite well received and ran for ninety-four performances.

From the moment of its first performance in West Berlin in 1963, Rolf Hochhuth's *Der Stellvertreter* raised the wildest tempest of controversy of any drama within memory. Very little of the storm has had anything to do with the play as play; the furor rages over what Hochhuth says—or what his supporters as well as his assailants say he says. Production of the play has generated riots in many countries.

Pressure has been exerted by church, state, press, and private organizations to force its closing. Actors playing it have been pelted and even physically attacked on stage by outraged members of the audience. Theatres have been filled with the side-by-side noises of hooting and cheering. *Der Stellvertreter* has spawned endless comment, counter-comment, articles, and reviews already appearing on both sides of the Atlantic in fat anthologies. The commentators' views range from virulent denunciation to passionate praise. Hochhuth has been attacked by even Pope Paul VI; he has been lauded by no less a person than Albert Schweitzer.

Der Stellvertreter, known in the American production and edition as *The Deputy* (elsewhere as *The Representative* or *The Vicar*), is a gargantuan play. An uncut performance would last seven hours, and even in its fully printed version, complete with Herr Hochhuth's lengthy appendix of historical documentation and commentary, it undertakes a herculean task: making the monstrously unbelievable believable. Consequently, productions of *The Deputy* must invariably reduce the play, but many have so severely chopped it that only the bare bones of its central situation remain. This is unfair to the integrity of the drama, for it makes shadowy sketches of both characters and events which are fully developed and realized in the complete text. Hochhuth's enormous tapestry has dimension, texture, subtlety, and a panoramic overview of the many ramifications of his story; as performed, *The Deputy* can all too easily be distorted into nothing more than an isolated attack on Pope Pius XII, far from the intention of the total work which sees Pacelli as ultimate symbol rather than sole perpetrator of the moral cowardice that the play condemns. Unfortunate as this distortion is (and it has caused much of the anger leveled at *The Deputy*), the blame for it ultimately rests with the playwright himself for asking the impossible of a working theatre. *The Deputy* cannot be cut without changing its meaning, for it is not inflated in the way of O'Neill's elephantine dramas, although there are surely long passages of expansive and somewhat unconvincing rhetorical bombast in Hochhuth's work. Rolf Hochhuth is a gifted young dramatist, but *The Deputy,* more of a dramatic novel than a drama, defies the stage and therefore fails to meet a primary obligation of a good play. A fair evaluation of the work can result only from reading it in its entirety, and for all the agitation that productions have elicited, the stature of *Der Stellvertreter* must inevitably rest with its existence on the page rather than the stage.

The hero of the piece, Father Riccardo Fontana, is fictitious but loosely based on two clergymen: Provost Lichtenberg, who prayed publicly in Germany for the Jews and volunteered to accompany them to Dachau, enroute to which he died; and Father Kolbe, who took a Jew's place in a starvation cell at Auschwitz and died after long agony. Exhorted by Kurt Gerstein, a historical figure of heroic dimensions who joined the SS in order to fight the Nazis from the inside, Father Riccardo, who has family connections in the Vatican, appeals to the Pope to take a strong public stand against the German atrocities. At the very moment of the confrontation between the two men, Jews are being rounded up directly under the windows of the Vatican. The Pope refuses, for all the well-known reasons ascribed to Pius' decision: direct intervention by the church into secular matters of state might bring even worse reprisals—better to do what one can behind the scenes; millions of Catholic Germans are fighting for Hitler, and they should not be confused because there is still time to save their souls; Hitler may be reprehensible, but he is Europe's last buffer against the menace of Bolshevism; if the church remains neutral, it may have a chance of negotiating the peace to come; individual prelates are free to act on their own, and are often encouraged to do so. The character of Pius also argues another motive that Hochhuth has scrupulously documented: An early collapse for Hitler imperils Vatican investments. The Pope speaks of Italy's economy *"mit brennender Sorge"* ("with burning concern"), ironically the title of Pius XI's encyclical about the Nazis. Pacelli is presented as cold, aloof, vain, inhuman, a master of *Realpolitik*. He is also a Germanophile and maybe even a lukewarm Nazi sympathizer. Hochhuth does not go so far as some of Pius XII's severest critics who say that he was quite possibly a bit of an anti-Semite himself, no matter how many Jews have jumped to his defense. The words the character speaks are often the actual words of Pius XII as recorded and as published in *L'Osservatore Romano*. It seems to be a historical fact that the only deed of the entire era of World War II that Pius condemned specifically in a public statement was the American bombing of Monte Cassino. In any event, he never once spoke out against the massacres mentioning Nazis or Jews by name, he never ordered priests to pray for the afflicted, he never threatened to break the Concordat with Hitler (as its framer, Pacelli's predecessor Pius XI, had) or even to excommunicate the Nazis who were baptized Catholics—among them, Himmler, Goebbels, and Hitler himself. Pius did not even take a stand against Catholic priests, whoever or wherever they may have been, who were open supporters of Hitler.

After the Pope refuses Father Riccardo's request, he signs the famous generalized platitude that was published in *L'Osservatore Romano* at the time of the arrests of the Italian Jews—a fatuous, flowery pronouncement devoid of any specifics or power. Hochhuth's

Pius gets ink on his fingers in the process of signing; the Pope-as-Pilate washes his hands while Fontana accuses him of the crime of silence. The young priest, under Pius' gaze, pins a Star of David on his own cassock and goes to Auschwitz to die. The true Vicar of Christ is the man who assumes the responsibility of acting as Jesus would have. If the Pope evades the responsibility of being the Lord's representative, then for God, for church, and for humanity, another man must go as the Pope's deputy.

Surrounding this central conflict of the play, and integrated with it, are the story of Gerstein, studies of Jews and Nazis great and small, analyses of various churchmen, the private life of the Nazi industrialists and SS terrorists, and the play's ever-present symbol of the satanic in nazism, the Doctor, based on Joseph Mengele, the final selector of Auschwitz' victims. These are the skeletonized casualties of the cut productions, and their sketchiness not only nullifies the overview of the play, but also puts the Pius scene into an overblown perspective.

There is neither time nor need here to discuss all of the elegantly elaborate arguments that have raged around the moral, philosophical, historical, artistic, and emotional issues raised by *The Deputy*. These may be read in proliferation elsewhere.[123] However, a few of the major points of controversy cannot go unnoticed. Hochhuth has been accused of whitewashing the Germans at the expense of Pius and the Church of Rome. This charge is manifestly unjust. As the playwright himself has reputedly said, one does not exonerate the arsonist by calling attention to the ineptitude of the fire department. It is impossible to read *The Deputy* and say that it does not hold the Germans guilty. To assert that the play is anti-Catholic is to ignore that its hero as well as the two men to whom it is dedicated are priests. One could hardly accuse Dante Alighieri of anti-Catholicism, yet he singled out popes who betrayed the Vicarage of Christ. The entire controversy also glosses over the play's clear statement (in print, at least) that Pius is not an isolated manifestation of moral passivity, but rather the one high-ranking leader of the Hitler years who by the very exalted nature of his charge most forcefully symbolizes the failure of nerve and abject hypocrisy of the entirety of Western civilization. *The Deputy* goes to great pains to explicate the courage and the beneficence of individual prelates throughout Europe. The play spares none of the culpable among the many who shared in the guilt of the exterminations, whether it be the German people, the Nazis, the Poles and Ukrainians more than willing to join in the slaughters, the British prime minister who for political reasons did not respond to the reports from his diplomats in the Reich, or the cagily evasive American government. It is Hochhuth's very point that all who chose not to choose thereby made an immoral choice, and that all who were uncommitted in a crisis that cried for commitment were accomplices in the "final solution."

There are those who maintain that Hochhuth speaks with hindsight at his bidding and that his central premise is conjectural. Would an open protest by the Vatican indeed have saved lives? No one will ever know, and it is for history to judge Pacelli, but Hitler historically feared the animosity of the church, and where local churchmen opposed the Nazis, there are documented records of the palpable benefits that came from such opposition. Is not Pope Paul VI, in saying that intervention would have made matters worse, being as conjectural as Hochhuth? Furthermore, if Hitler's intention to exterminate every living Jew was clear, and it most emphatically was, how on earth could matters possibly have gotten worse? A protest from the Holy See might at least have exerted influence on the populace of Catholic countries such as Poland and Hungary where local citizens helped to kill Jews. There is no telling what influence an early protest might have had on the staunchly Catholic Bavarians. Might it not even have given courage to men of good but weak wills who sat at the head of states? The grave questions raised by *The Deputy* are at the very heart of the central horrendous act witnessed and perpetrated by modern man—the murder of six million Jews—an act so central not only because of its own monstrousness but also because it is a screaming indication of the unfathomable depravity to which allegedly civilized man has sunk, and may sink again. It is precisely because the Nazi atrocities were not an isolated instance but only the most signal manifestation of man's capacity for evil that these atrocities must be understood if man is ever to understand himself, even to the point of recognizing his own complicity.

Although the vacant words and baroque rhetoric were actually the Pope's, it is assuredly unfortunate that Hochhuth's Pius comes off as a quite unbelievable character in the play. He is too cold, too calculating, an open invitation to a caricature performance. Even if the characterization is truthful, literal truth does not necessarily make good drama. The Pius of the play is not the formidable antagonist he should be, convinced of his own righteousness; he is a hateful and crafty hypocrite, and this weakens *The Deputy* immeasurably. Rolf Hochhuth may well be far more historically accurate than his detractors will allow, but there is good reason to question some of his interpretation of that history, his exaggeration by selection, and certainly his mode of dramatic presentation. However, *The Deputy* flings a stingingly cogent *J'accuse* in the face of the entire world, and one fact is inescapable: no matter what the merits or inadequacies of

Hochhuth's drama, it has engendered more emotional, moral, and maybe even intellectual excitement than any European play since the war. Had it been less impassioned, *The Deputy* might have been a better play, though it is doubtful that any drama could measure up to the requirements imposed by Hochhuth's subject. A more finely wrought work of art might never have aroused heads, hearts, or viscera as this play has. If it has engaged its readers and viewers in the moral issues that it poses, that alone is enough to make it a play of the first importance that not only puts the past into perspective but challenges the present and the future.

Jerome Rothenberg's adaptation of *Der Stellvertreter*, produced and directed by Herman Shumlin, opened in New York at the Brooks Atkinson Theatre on February 26, 1964. The sheer controversy that had already been generated by the play kept it running for 316 performances despite the abysmally bad production. Robert Brustein epitomized the most intelligent critical responses when he called the performance "beneath discussion," saying that the adaptation had not cut the play but butchered it, carving out its intellectual heart and leaving only the "melodramatic bones."[124] *The Deputy* was presented without any integrity, a shameless exploitation of its sensational reputation. Rothenberg not only cut; he changed scenes, interpolated material, and rewrote dialogue. The horror was so mollified for fear of offending that there was no genuine horror at all. The characters of Gerstein and the Doctor were shaved to bit parts. The fifth act almost completely disappeared. Brustein added that the director and actors finished off what scraps the adapter had left. "Broadway may have had the initial courage to produce *The Deputy*," he continued, "but it has not finally been able to transcend its ingrained cowardice and artistic inadequacy." To be fair to Mr. Shumlin, he faced tremendous opposition in putting on the play, which may have hurt the production even though it assuredly helped business. Shumlin accused the Hearst papers of fomenting a conspiracy to close *The Deputy*, and the *New York Journal-American* did actually ask the mayor to prevent the performance. Ironically, it was the *Journal-American*'s critic who gave *The Deputy* a better review than it received in any other daily paper.

Most of the press comment was in substantial agreement: a production unequal to the interest surrounding the play, a mangled script, bad casting (except for Emlyn Williams as Pius), and slovenly direction. Most serious reviewers saw the inherent flaws of the original text, or knew them from reading it, but even those who disliked the play itself were willing to admit the abusive distortions of this presentation. The great bulk of what was written about *The Deputy* had to do only with the moral issues it raised, and the importance of raising

them. The best discussions were about the translation of the complete
work by Richard and Clara Winston which was published almost
simultaneously with the New York performance of the corrupted version. There was talk of a national tour of *The Deputy* in a completely
revised playing text, but nothing ever came of it.

Rolf Hochhuth, author of the most debated literary work to
emerge from the new Germany, was in New York for the opening of
what was billed as his play. Broadway failed him, as he quite possibly
failed his own monumental task, but *The Deputy*, whatever its flaws
as a play, is one of the central documents of our age.

Peter Weiss, born in 1916, left Germany in the thirties and settled
in Sweden. He has been a painter and film director as well as a
novelist and dramatist writing in German. Weiss was late in com-
manding international attention, but when his first major play premiered in Berlin in 1964, it brought him instantaneous fame and
accolades as lavish as that he was the most important German playwright since Brecht. *The Deputy* is the most thematically provocative
play to come out of Germany since the war, but no drama from that
country in the past twenty-five years has generated as much sheer
theatrical excitement as has Weiss's *Die Verfolgung und Ermordung
Jean Paul Marats Dargestellt Durch Die Schauspielergruppe des Hos-
pizes zu Charenton Unter Anleitung des Herrn de Sade*. The title is
only the first and possibly the least jarring of its calculated shock
effects. The literal English translation of the title, which synopsizes
the main action of the play, was quickly reduced by all who commented upon the work, and it became known as *Marat/Sade*.

When the Marquis de Sade was an inmate at the asylum of
Charenton, he wrote and directed plays that were presented by the
patients for each other, their overseers, and selected guests. These
performances were intended to have a therapeutic effect on their actors. There is no known Sade script of such a play about Marat, but
there is nothing subterfugeous about Weiss's play within a play, for he
does not pretend that it is the Marquis', and it does give him an arena
in which to explore the antitheses represented by his two main characters, Sade himself and Marat as played by one of the inmates.

The scene is the stark, sterile bath house of the asylum. The patients enter—spastic, drooling, demented, repulsive. They elicit neither
pity nor sentiment. As the director of Charenton and his family take
their places to watch, and burly sisters post themselves in anticipation
of trouble, Sade begins to put his "actors" through their paces of
playing the persecution of the festering and scabby Jean-Paul Marat
in his bathtub, and his eventual assassination by Charlotte Corday.
The Marat story is important only as a vehicle; it is the commentary

about the Revolution and the performing of the bizarre charade itself that constitute the heart of Weiss's play.

Marat/Sade is alternately serious and comic, elevated and crude, verbal and physical, pantomimic and rhapsodic, intellectual and emotional, abstract and concrete, violent and reflective, graphic and allusive, ritualistic and improvised, historical and anachronistic. Sometimes it looks like *commedia dell' arte;* at other times like a political cabaret or a medieval dance of death. At all times, it looks like exactly what it—and by implication, our world—is: a grotesque madhouse. By constantly shifting his style and his focus, by teasing the brain and startling the nervous system with his clashing contrasts, Weiss repeatedly jolts and unbalances his audience into a sense of apprehensive alertness. He puts it at sufficient distance to make it reflect, then brings it in close to kick it in the groin. It has become a commonplace to observe that what Weiss has done is to combine the theatres of Brecht and Artaud. The viewer is always aware of the play as play and the play within the play, for he is watching people watching the action. There are intrusive Weillish songs, miming, stop-action, backtracking, interruptions, violent distractions. *Marat/Sade* commands all the objectivity desired by anti-illusionist drama. At the same time, it is a relentless assault on the senses which yields that direct engagement and subjective response to immediate stimuli which Artaud said were essential to the dramatic event. The viewer's mind and viscera both become conditioned to tense anticipation of the next attack. The intermittent periods of relief are short lived. The sounds of the play are usually cacophonous; its rhythms are invariably driving, frenetic, irregular. In its style of composition, *Marat/Sade* may owe more to Brecht, but in its totality of theatrical effect, it is the very incarnation of the aims of Artaud. Most of the time, the spectacular assault overpowers the intellectual distancing.

The performing of Sade's play within his own allows Weiss to give distinct representation to a number of points of view concerning the central question of his play: Where along the continuum between total commitment to mass social action and completely alienated individualism do man's best hopes lie? Marat is the extreme provoker of public revolution in quest of a perfect world. His impassioned arguments are convincing (to both the inmates and the audience) while flaunted, but they crumble under the weight of Sade's icy logic. The activities of the historical Marat were, after all, a signal example of the self-defeating aspects of the French Revolution—its massacres, horrors, deceptions, frustrations, and perversions of altruistic goals. The Marquis, on the other hand, is weary of action and has become a proponent of introspective isolation, of the world of the imagination rather than the social arena. He distrusts the material, and he has faith neither in human knowledge nor in any romantic notion of human perfectibility. However, his arguments are also incapable of withstanding attack. His individualism is a self-deception masking personal gratification. Weiss shows both Marat and Sade's rigidly immutable ideologies to be inadequate. Because these two points of view are untenable extremes, Weiss is able to be fair to both sides. The playwright says that he is a Marxist, and that his play is dialectical. Where, then, is the synthesis of Marat and Sade? Surely, it is not in the other voiced points of view: the bourgeois, as represented by the director, Coulmier; the proletarian, as represented by the singing quartet of inmates; the splinter-group lunacies, as represented by the cross-section of the insane who are acting out Marat's murder; the authoritarian, as represented by the established government, the restraining nuns, and the play's many references to organized churches. These are, in the actuality of the play as well as in its implications, the solutions of madmen.

Marat/Sade seems to be saying that mankind is incapable of an answer, or at least has proved itself incapable thus far. The Marquis' play at Charenton is performed in 1808, after the debacles of the Revolution and Marat's murder, and at a time when the follies of the Napoleonic era were already clear. There is also the Herald, the Brechtian narrator of the play within the play, who is the voice of the twentieth century. Past, present, and future—it was, and is, and is to be forever the same. But a strange thing happens to the audience of *Marat/Sade* in two hours. It begins to feel that it too is a part of the asylum world, inmates of that unreal theatrical madhouse, the actual world—where actors play lunatics pretending to be sane, and where madmen play at barbarism in an allegedly rational universe gone barbarically mad. If Weiss has no answer, he at least has a question: What will *you* do? The burden is ultimately placed on the play's perceiver. Maybe some audience, now or in the future, will achieve a synthesis that yields the good life. *Marat/Sade* is a call for commitment to examine, to re-evaluate afresh, to attempt to answer what may be unanswerable, because only in the continued attempt is there any hope. In its own way, Weiss's play is a plea for that mad, necessary illusion that sustains man and makes him endure all horror: that somehow life *does* have meaning, and that there may be a sanity that lies, like Lear's, on the far side of madness.

The production of *Marat/Sade* that opened in New York on December 27, 1965, was an intact importation of the spectacular London mounting of the play by the Royal Shakespeare Company directed by Peter Brook. The excellent English text was by Geoffrey Skelton, with verse passages adapted by Adrian Mitchell and music by Richard Peaslee. It was to be a limited engagement only, but *Marat/Sade*, which won the Drama Critics' Circle Award, became such a "hot ticket" that the run had to be extended and eventually taken over by an American company which then also toured the country. It was an expensive play to produce, if only because of the many highly skilled actors needed to play even the smallest parts and to serve as extras. Several analysts of the Broadway business scene have said that had the *Marat/Sade* company not been subsidized as an international cultural enterprise, it could not have made expenses despite completely soldout houses. Left to its own devices, Broadway might never even have attempted the play.

The success of *Marat/Sade* in New York is attributable to its immediate reputation as a tour de force, an extravagant spectacle, and an exercise in what few of the hack reviewers could resist calling "total theatre." The substance of the play was either overlooked or peremptorily dismissed by most of the press and the audience alike. With such a well-known success on the ledgers, it is interesting to go back to the days after the opening and see how many negative reviews met the play in the newspapers and popular magazines. Even some of the more respected arbiters in the dailies objected to it strenuously, among them Walter Kerr (never able to evaluate fairly any play even slightly critical of the Catholic church). It was not uncommon to call *Marat/Sade* thin in substance and stale in thought, but good because it was "quintessentially theatrical,"[125] full of lolling heads, slabbering mouths, gushing blood, nakedness, masturbation, sexual assaults, and guttural expletives. There was a significant play for those willing to see and hear it, but there was also enough to bring in the Yahoos. *Time* praised the terrifying production and the precise craftsmanship of the London company in its "sustained barrage on the senses,"[126] but felt the play to be "largely inspired sensationalism." John McCarten said it was a pretentious and self-indulgent play, interesting for the bizarre effects by the lunatics and bad because of the deleterious influence of Brecht and interruptions "by bits of doggerel and foolish jingles."[127] His was the most scathing of the popular reviews. Harold Clurman observed that there was much of a hectic muchness that almost buried the play, but he was one of the few who saw the drama beneath the spectacle.[128] Clurman also noted that the audience was not ultimately engaged by the play but only by the display—which, of course, may be the audience's fault as much as *Marat/Sade*'s. Almost all reviewers approached the production as if it were by Peter Brook instead of Peter Weiss. There is no question of the brilliance of the company and its inspired director, but

Marat/Sade had, after all, been quite an artistic success in Berlin and Stockholm without benefit of Mr. Brook.

Weiss is a playwright who knows how to bring a stage to life; his script invites theatrical pyrotechnics; his own experience as a director is everywhere apparent. If *Marat/Sade* suffers from excess and does not finally make its substance clear in production, the fault is too much rather than too little creative energy by its author. The success of *Marat/Sade* in New York may well have been a fortuitous fluke. For some it was the total play, for others it was only the masterful showmanship, but real excitement was the response of almost everyone who saw it.

The German drama, which had virtually disappeared during and immediately after the Hitler years, has again become an energetic influence and forceful presence not only in the theatres of Europe, but also in those of the United States. The American theatre, in New York and throughout the land, is immeasurably richer for its discovery of Brecht, the Swiss tragicomedians, and a promising new generation of German playwrights.

The eagle is still hooded, but he peers out on occasion. The owls are still blinking, but they are beginning to understand what they see.

Notes

Chapter I

1. John Gassner, ed., *Twenty Best European Plays on the American Stage*, 7.
2. H. F. Garten, *Modern German Drama*, 11.
3. *Ibid.*, 18.
4. Arthur Hobson Quinn, *A History of the American Drama from the Civil War to the Present Day*, 6, 7.
5. Ironically, it was not long after 1932 that Hauptmann, who has since been excused for his actions by incipient senility, lent his support, albeit with feeble mouth honor, to Adolf Hitler. For a man allegedly senile during the years of World War II however, he wrote a remarkable tetralogy concerning the House of Atreus. It showed a change of heart. The four plays are distinctly and passionately antifascist. They were first produced in postwar Berlin by Erwin Piscator.
6. Helen Emerson, "A Criticism of Meltzer's Translations of *Hanneles Himmelfahrt* and *Die Versunkene Glocke*," *German Quarterly*, Vol. XXI (1948), 163-74.
7. Edith Cappel, "The Reception of Gerhart Hauptmann in the United States" (unpublished Ph.D. dissertation, Columbia University, 1953), *passim*.
8. As a youth, he was an avid reader of Cooper, and he later expressed great enthusiasm about Whitman. He also read widely in Emerson, Longfellow, and Poe and was an admirer of Sinclair Lewis, Theodore Dreiser, and particularly of Eugene O'Neill, whose works he delighted in seeing as well as reading. See Siegfried H. Muller, "Gerhart Hauptmann's Relation to American Literature and His Concept of America," *Monatshefte für deutschen Unterricht*, Vol. XLIV (1952), 333.
9. John C. Blankenagel, "Early Reception of Hauptmann's *Die Weber* in the United States," *Modern Language Notes*, Vol. LXVIII (May, 1953), 335.
10. Joseph T. Shipley, *Guide to Great Plays*, 759. See also James G. Huneker, *Iconoclasts: A Book of Dramatists*, 291.
11. *Nation*, Vol. CXXII (February 17, 1926), 187.
12. See K. W. H. Scholz, *The Art of Translation, With Special Reference to English Renditions of the Prose Dramas of Gerhart Hauptmann and Hermann Sudermann, passim*, for play-by-play analysis.
13. *Ibid.*, 23-25.
14. As quoted in Shipley, *Guide to Great Plays*, 760.
15. *Ibid.*, 761.
16. *Bookman*, Vol. XXXI (June, 1910), 418.
17. *Theatre Magazine*, Vol. XI (May 10, 1910), xxxi.
18. *New York Dramatic Mirror*, Vol. LXIII (April 23, 1910), 7.

19. *Ibid.*, Vol. LXV (June 14, 1911), 6.

20. *Theatre*, Vol. XIV (July, 1911), viii.

21. *New Republic*, Vol. I (January 2, 1915), 25.

22. *Nation*, Vol. C (January 21, 1915), 87.

23. "Essential Difference Between an American Play and a European Play," *Current Opinion*, Vol. LVIII (February, 1915), 97.

24. Barry Ulanov, *Makers of the Modern Theater*, 136.

25. Eric Bentley, *The Playwright as Thinker*, 316.

26. As quoted in Shipley, *Guide to Great Plays*, 296.

27. *Nation*, Vol. CI (December 30, 1915), 786.

28. *New Republic*, Vol. V (December 25, 1915), 200.

29. Gassner, *Twenty Best European Plays*, Introduction.

30. Emerson, "A Criticism of Meltzer's Translations . . .," *German Quarterly*, Vol. XXI (1948), 168-74.

31. Edwin H. Zeydel, "The German Theatre in New York City," *Jahrbuch der deutsch-amerikanischen Historischen Gesellschaft von Illinois*, Vol. XV (1915), 290.

32. Charles C. Ayer, "Foreign Drama on the English and American Stage: II. German Drama," *University of Colorado Studies*, Vol. VII, No. 1 (December, 1909), 70.

33. *Ibid.*, 67.

34. Schwabing is the artists' quarter of Munich.

35. *New York Dramatic Mirror*, Vol. LXXIV (November 13, 1915), 8.

36. *New York Times*, November 10, 1915, 13:5.

37. *New York Dramatic Mirror*, Vol. LXIII (April 23, 1910), 7.

38. *Bookman*, Vol. XXXI (June, 1910), 418.

39. *Theatre*, Vol. XI (May 10, 1910), xxix.

40. Garten, *Modern German Drama*, 56.

41. As quoted in Shipley, *Guide to Great Plays*, 588.

42. Any number of the first six in addition to the seventh may be used to combine the sketches into a coherent full-length play.

43. *Life*, Vol. LX (October 24, 1912), 2051.

44. *Theatre*, Vol. XVI (October, 1912), 110.

45. As quoted in Shipley, *Guide to Great Plays*, 588.

46. *New York Times*, March 22, 1917, 9:3.

47. *Theatre*, Vol. XXV (January, 1917), 24.

48. *New York Times*, December 6, 1917, 7:1.

49. See Chapter II for detailed discussion of Wedekind.

50. *New York Dramatic Mirror*, Vol. LXXV (January 22, 1916), 8.

51. *New York Times*, January 11, 1916, 11:3.

52. *New Republic*, Vol. VI (April 22, 1916), 320.

53. *New York Times*, November 14, 1916, 8:2.

54. Garten, *Modern German Drama*, 64.

55. See Chapter II for detailed discussion of Reinhardt at the time of his major trip to the United States.

56. E.g. "Max Reinhardt, the Maker of a New Mimic World," *Current Literature*, Vol. LI (September, 1911), 311-15. The adulation in this article is typical.

57. Barnard Hewitt, *Theatre U. S. A., 1668-1957*, 313.

58. *New York Dramatic Mirror*, Vol. LXVII (January 24, 1912), 6.

59. Hewitt, *Theatre U. S. A.*, 313.

60. Ayer, "Foreign Drama on the English and American Stage," *University of Colorado Studies*, Vol. VII, No. 1 (December, 1909), 70.

61. These casters were actually invented by an American man of the theatre, Steele MacKaye, but the Germans were the first to build and use them.

62. For a detailed study of these theatrical experiments see Hiram K. Moderwell, *The Theatre of Today;* Kenneth Macgowan and Robert Edmond Jones, *The Theatre of Tomorrow;* Huntley Carter, *The Theatre of Max Reinhardt;* and Mordecai Gorelik, *New Theatres for Old.*

63. Norman Hapgood, *The Stage in America, 1897-1900,* 143.

CHAPTER II

1. As quoted in *New York Dramatic Mirror,* Vol. LXXVII (April 7, 1917), 9.

2. *Ibid.*

3. As quoted in Shipley, *Guide to Great Plays,* 809.

4. See discussion of *The Pepper Mill* in Chapter III.

5. O. Seidlin, "Frank Wedekind's German-American Parents," *American-German Review,* Vol. XII, No. 6 (1946), 26.

6. *New Republic,* Vol. XLIII (May 27, 1925), 20-21.

7. *New York Times,* May 12, 1925, 26:1.

8. Haskell M. Block and Robert G. Shedd, eds., *Masters of Modern Drama,* 271.

9. Garten, *Modern German Drama,* 101.

10. *Ibid.,* 100.

11. *American Mercury,* Vol. VII (February, 1926), 249-50.

12. *Nation,* Vol. CXXI (December 16, 1925), 713.

13. *New York Times,* December 6, 1925, VIII, 5:1.

14. *Ibid.,* November 16, 1920, 19:1.

15. *Nation,* Vol. CXI (November 10, 1920), 539.

16. *New York Times,* October 27, 1920, 14:3.

17. Oliver M. Sayler, "Translation and the Theatre," *North American Review,* Vol. CCXV (January, 1922), 115.

18. *New York Times,* October 12, 1921, 18:2.

19. *Theatre,* Vol. XXXVI (December, 1922), 375.

20. *New York Times,* September 27, 1922, 17:1.

21. *Ibid.,* October 1, 1922, VII, 1:2, 3, 4.

22. *New Republic,* Vol. XXXII (November 1, 1922), 251-52.

23. *Dial,* Vol. LXXIII (November, 1922), 584-85.

24. *New York Times,* October 8, 1922, VI, 1:2, 3, 4.

25. *American Mercury,* Vol. I (April, 1924), 503.

26. *New York Times,* February 16, 1924, 16:2.

27. *Ibid.,* February 17, 1924, VII, 4:2.

28. *American Mercury,* Vol. V (June, 1925), 245-46.

29. *New York Times,* April 15, 1925, 16:2.

30. Walter Pritchard Eaton, *The Theatre Guild: The First Ten Years,* 116.

31. *American Mercury,* Vol. III (October 24, 1924), 247-48.

32. *New York Times,* August 26, 1924, 6:1, 2.

33. *Ibid.,* August 31, 1924, VII, 1:1.

34. *Nation,* Vol. CXIX (December 31, 1924), 736.

35. *New York Times,* December 16, 1924, 28:2.

36. *New Republic,* Vol. XLIV (October 28, 1925), 256.

37. *Nation,* Vol. CXXI (October 28, 1925), 494.

38. *New Republic,* Vol. XLIV (October 28, 1925), 255-56; and *New York Times,* October 10, 1925, 10:1.

39. Kenneth Macgowan and William Melnitz, *Golden Ages of the Theater,* 151.

40. Burns Mantle, ed., *The Best Plays of 1923-24;* and the *Year Book of the Drama in America,* 7.

41. One of the chief financial problems was created when producer Morris Gest engaged Lady Diana Duff Cooper to play one of the leading roles. Princess Matchabelli (stage name: Maria Carmi) came from Europe, maintaining that Reinhardt had hired her for the part, which he had, and that she would sue Gest for $100,000 if Lady Diana performed. The conflict received daily attention in the press, for never before had two actresses, both members of European nobility, behaved in such unlady-like fashion. The two combatants were finally compelled to draw straws for opening night after Reinhardt had to rehearse with both of them while awaiting a solution to the problem. Lady Diana won, and the Princess promptly sued Gest for $500,000. Both actresses eventually played the role, with Miss Carmi returning to Europe after her contract with Reinhardt ran out. She withdrew her suit against Gest, but the relief was short. Mr. Gest had made some nasty remarks about the Princess which found their way into print. This time she sued for libel, and won. It was a good thing that *The Miracle* broke all receipt records for the Century Theatre.

42. *New York Times,* January 16, 1924, 17:1, 2.

43. *American Mercury,* Vol. I (March, 1924), 369-70.

44. *Theatre,* Vol. XXXIX (March, 1924), 15.

45. *Nation,* Vol. CXVIII (January 30, 1924), 121.

46. *New Republic,* Vol. XXXVII (January 30, 1924), 257.

47. *Nation,* Vol. CXVIII (February 13, 1924), 190.

48. *Ibid.,* (May 7, 1924), 540.

49. The Reinhardt troupe that came to this country in 1927 played a repertory that, technically speaking, does not fall within the limits of this study. The selections were not from the modern drama and the performances were in German, but the impact they made were pronounced and their stagecraft was the only good look that Americans had at the technology of the new German theatres. The Reinhardt productions were also the only successful manifestations here of the German romantic revival. Furthermore, despite the fact that the Reinhardt methodology inspired no Broadway imitation, it exerted enormous influence on the West Coast where Reinhardt hoped to create a regular American Salzburg Festival. After his flight from Hitler, he finally settled on the West Coast, where he became involved with the American motion-picture industry, the logical realm for his techniques.

50. Mantle, *Best Plays of 1927-28,* 7.

51. *Ibid.*

52. Alexander Moissi, who played Jedermann; Paul Hartmann, who was the Voice of the Lord; Vladimir Sokoloff and Lili Darvas, who portrayed Death and Faith, respectively.

53. *New York Times,* May 9, 1941, 19:2.

54. Walter H. Sokel, *The Writer in Extremis: Expressionism in Twentieth-Century German Literature,* 4.

55. Paul Fechter, *Das Europäische Drama: Geist und Kultur im Spiegel des Theatres* (Vol. III,"Vom Expressionismus zur Gegenwart"), 67.

56. Garten, *Modern German Drama*, 103.

57. For an excellent and thorough study of expressionism, see Sokel, *The Writer in Extremis*.

58. Mantle, *Best Plays of 1921-22*, 8.

59. Shipley, *Guide to Great Plays*, 369.

60. Block and Shedd, *Masters of Modern Drama*, 488.

61. *Bookman*, Vol. LV (August, 1922), 600.

62. *Nation*, Vol. CXIV (June 14, 1922), 726.

63. *New Republic*, Vol. XXXI (July 12, 1922), 189-90.

64. *Dial*, Vol. LXXIII (July, 1922), 116-17.

65. *Theatre*, Vol. XXXVI (August, 1922), 94.

66. Macgowan and Jones, *Theatre of Tomorrow*, 261.

67. Block and Shedd, *Masters of Modern Drama*, 488.

68. Gassner, *Twenty Best European Plays*, 19.

69. This title, with its slight variant, appears numerous times in critical commentary, but not as frequently as the title of the Dukes translation.

70. Ulanov, *Makers of the Modern Theater*, 652.

71. J. Wesley Thomas, *Amerikanische Dichter und die deutsche Literatur*, 155.

72. As quoted in Shipley, *Guide to Great Plays*, 99.

73. *Ibid.*, 100.

74. *Ibid.*

75. *Nation*, Vol. CXVI (January 10, 1923), 48.

76. *Bookman*, Vol. LVII (March, 1923), 54.

77. *New York Times*, December 25, 1922, 20:3.

78. *Theatre*, Vol. XXXVII (February, 1923), 15.

79. Toller's plays produced in New York are discussed in detail in their appropriate slots in the American chronology rather than the German.

80. It is interesting to read Fechter, an otherwise astute historian, who throughout his entire work egregiously avoids blaming the Nazis for anything bad in German life or drama. It is particularly interesting to see the short shrift he makes of German Jewish dramatists: Toller, Werfel, Zweig, Beer-Hoffmann, Schnitzler, *et al.*

81. Frank W. Chandler, *Modern Continental Playwrights*, 431.

82. Block and Shedd, *Masters of Modern Drama*, 7.

83. *Nation*, Vol. CXVIII (April 30, 1924), 513.

84. *New Republic*, Vol. XXXVIII (April 30, 1924), 262.

85. *American Mercury*, Vol. II (June, 1924), 244.

86. *Theatre*, Vol. XXXIX (June, 1924), 15.

87. *New York Times*, April 15, 1924, 25:1, 2.

88. *Nation*, Vol. CXX (February 11, 1925), 168-69.

89. *New York Times*, January 27, 1925, 14:1.

90. Fechter, *Das Europäische Drama*, III, 70-71.

91. Adolf D. Klarmann, ed., Introduction to [Franz Werfel] *Gesammelte Werke: Die Dramen*, I, 7.

92. *Ibid., passim.*

93. Eaton, *Theatre Guild*, 90.

94. Garten, *Modern German Drama*, 113.

95. John R. Frey, "America and Franz Werfel," *German Quarterly*, Vol. XIX (March, 1946), 124.

96. *Nation*, Vol. CXXII (February 17, 1926), 187.

97. *New Republic,* Vol. XLVI (February 24, 1926), 17-18.

98. Barrett H. Clark, "Experiments and Fantasies," *Drama,* Vol. XVI (April, 1926), 250.

99. *Theatre,* Vol. XLIII (April, 1926), 16.

100. *New York Times,* January 26, 1926, 18:1.

101. *Ibid.,* February 7, 1926, VII, 1:1, 2.

102. *Bookman,* Vol. LXIII (April, 1926), 213-14.

103. *Life,* Vol. LXXXVII (April 15, 1926), 23.

104. *New York Times,* March 24, 1926, 20:4.

105. Lawrence Langner, "The Magic Curtain," *Theatre Arts,* Vol. XXXIX (October, 1955), 28.

106. *Nation,* Vol. CXXIII (October 27, 1926), 435.

107. *New Republic,* Vol. XLVIII (October 27, 1926), 272.

108. *Dial,* Vol. LXXXI (December, 1926), 522-23.

109. *Theatre,* Vol. XLIV (December, 1926), 15.

110. *New York Times,* October 12, 1926, 31:1.

111. As quoted in Toby Cole, ed., *Playwrights on Playwriting: The Meaning and Making of Modern Drama from Ibsen to Ionesco,* 236.

112. Mantle, *Best Plays of 1922-23,* 15.

113. Quinn, *History of American Drama,* 110.

114. Barrett H. Clark, "Native and Foreign Drama on Broadway," *Drama,* Vol. XV (December, 1924), 52.

CHAPTER III

1. Garten, *Modern German Drama,* 17.

2. *Ibid.,* 16-17.

3. *New York Times,* March 13, 1928, 23:1.

4. Shipley, *Guide to Great Plays,* 240.

5. *American Mercury,* Vol. XIV (May, 1928), 121-22.

6. *Nation,* Vol. CXXVI (March 28, 1928), 356.

7. *Theatre Arts Monthly,* Vol. XII (May, 1928), 318, 321.

8. *Nation,* Vol. CXXVI (March 14, 1928), 303.

9. *Theatre Arts Monthly,* Vol. XII (May, 1928), 317-18.

10. *New York Times,* February 27, 1928, 16:5. (This review appeared before the opening date of the play and was based upon a preview.)

11. Eaton, *The Theatre Guild,* 109.

12. *Theatre Arts Monthly,* Vol. XII (June, 1928), 387-90.

13. *New York Times,* April 10, 1928, 32:1.

14. *New Republic,* Vol. LIV (April 25, 1928), 295-96.

15. Garten, *Modern German Drama,* 162.

16. *New York Times,* September 5, 1928, 25:1.

17. *Nation,* Vol. CXXVII (September 19, 1928), 277.

18. *New Republic,* Vol. LX (October 23, 1929), 269-70.

19. *Nation,* Vol. CXXIX (October 30, 1929), 504.

20. *New Republic,* Vol. LXI (February 5, 1930), 301-302.

21. *New York Times,* January 21, 1930, 28:5.

22. *Ibid.,* February 10, 1930, 20:6,7.

23. *Nation,* Vol. CXXX (February 26, 1930), 254.

24. *New Republic,* Vol. LXII (February 26, 1930), 48.

25. *New York Times*, February 10, 1930, 20:6,7.

26. Shipley, *Guide to Great Plays*, 151.

27. *Bookman*, Vol. LXXIII (June, 1931), 410.

28. *Nation*, Vol. CXXXII (April 1, 1931), 361.

29. *New Republic*, Vol. LXVI (April 1, 1931), 182-83.

30. *Drama*, Vol. XXI (April, 1931), 10-11.

31. *New York Times*, March 17, 1931, 34:6.

32. *Ibid.*, May 3, 1936, X, 1:6.

33. It was done off-Broadway in November, 1938, as *Gloriana*.

34. *New Republic*, Vol. LXV (February 4, 1931), 323.

35. *Nation*, Vol. CXXXII (February 4, 1931), 134-35.

36. Another play given in New York in 1930-31 was also a translation, two steps removed. A production in modern Greek of *Elektra* was actually a translation *into* Greek of Hugo von Hofmannsthal's play.

37. *Bookman*, Vol. LXXII (January, 1931), 515-16.

38. *Theatre*, Vol. LIII (January, 1931), 25.

39. *New Republic*, Vol. LXV (December 3, 1930), 72.

40. *Drama*, Vol. XXI (January, 1931), 12.

41. This English title is from a direct reference that Toller makes in the text of the play to Sterne's Uncle Toby in *Tristram Shandy*. Another British version of the play is known as *Brokenbrow*.

42. *New York Times*, December 5, 1931, 20:6,7.

43. *Commonweal*, Vol. XV (December 23, 1931), 214-15.

44. *Theatre Arts Monthly*, Vol. XVI (February, 1932), 95-96.

45. Fechter, *Das Europäische Drama* (Vol. III, "Vom Expressionismus zur Gegenwart"), 25.

46. *New York Times*, April 12, 1937, 14:2. (Signed "B.C.," probably Bosley Crowther.)

47. Toller's play *Pastor Hall*, written with Denis Johnston and published in 1939, also appeared first in English in a translation by Stephen Spender and Hugh Hunt. The play was based on the life of Pastor Martin Niemöller.

48. *One-Act Play Magazine*, Vol. I (February, 1938), 950.

49. *New York Times*, January 29, 1938, 13:2,3.

50. *Theatre Arts Monthly*, Vol. XXIII (April, 1939), 248.

51. *Nation*, Vol. CXLVIII (February 18, 1939), 212-13.

52. *New York Times*, February 4, 1939, 11:2,3.

53. Gassner, *Twenty Best European Plays*, 44.

54. Siegfried Kracauer, *From Caligari to Hitler: A Psychological Study of the German Film*, 227.

55. In England it was called *Children in Uniform*.

56. *New York Times*, December 31, 1932, 10:3,4,5.

57. *Catholic World*, Vol. CXXXVI (February, 1933), 590-91.

58. *Nation*, Vol. CXXXVI (January 18, 1933), 74-75.

59. *New York Times*, November 26, 1938, 18:4.

60. *Nation*, Vol. CXXXVII (October 25, 1933), 494.

61. *New York Times*, October 12, 1933, 32:3,4.

62. *Ibid.*, December 11, 1934, 28:4.

63. *Nation*, Vol. CXXXIX (December 26, 1934), 749-50.

64. *New Republic*, Vol. LXXXI (January 2, 1935), 223.

65. Wolf was also a doctor, but not Jewish. He came to the United States after his stay in France and remained here throughout the war and after. He eventually returned to Germany, choosing to reside in East Berlin. Although he

was the Communist party's favorite German dramatist, he died totally disillusioned with the rule of Moscow.

66. *New York Times,* April 14, 1937, 30:3.4.

67. See Hallie Flanagan, *Arena: The Story of the Federal Theatre,* 198.

68. See Chapter V.

69. Ian C. Loram, "Carl Zuckmayer: German Playwright in America," *Educational Theater Journal,* Vol. IX (1957), 183.

70. Eric Bentley, ed., *Seven Plays by Bertolt Brecht,* xiii.

71. Mantle, *The Best Plays of 1932-33;* and the *Year Book of the Drama in America,* 484.

72. *Time,* Vol. XXI (April 24, 1933), 21.

73. *Nation,* Vol. CXXXVI (May 3, 1933), 512.

74. *Ibid.,* (May 10, 1933), 540.

75. *New York Times,* November 20, 1935, 26:3,4.

76. *Time,* Vol. XXVI (December 2, 1935), 68.

77. *Theatre Arts Monthly,* Vol. XX (January, 1936), 14.

78. *Nation,* Vol. CXLI (December 4, 1935), 659-60.

79. *New Republic,* Vol. LXXXV (December 18, 1935), 175.

80. Shipley, *Guide to Great Plays,* 120.

81. *New York Times,* March 14, 1936, 10:4.

82. Eric Bentley, "German Writers in Exile, 1933-43," *Books Abroad,* Vol. XVII (Autumn, 1943), 313.

83. Shipley, *Guide to Great Plays,* 455.

84. *Nation,* Vol. CXLIV (March 20, 1937), 333.

85. *Time,* Vol. XXIX (March 22, 1937), 59.

86. *New Republic,* Vol. XC (March 24, 1937), 210-11; and *New York Times,* March 9, 1937, 26:4,5.

87. *Nation,* Vol. CXLVIII (January 14, 1939), 74.

88. *Time,* Vol. XXXIII (January 9, 1939), 25.

89. *Theatre Arts Monthly,* Vol. XXIII (March, 1939), 173-74.

90. *New York Times,* December 29, 1938, 14:2,3.

91. Erika and Klaus Mann, *Escape to Life,* 5.

92. *Ibid.,* 19.

93. *Ibid.,* 324.

94. *Time,* Vol. XXIX (January 18, 1937), 47.

95. Klarmann, ed. [Franz Werfel] *Gesammelte Werke: Die Dramen,* 509.

96. *New York Times,* December 22, 1935, IX, 5:7,8.

97. As quoted in Klarmann, *Gesammelte Werke: Die Dramen,* 509.

98. *New York Times,* January 8, 1937, 14:2,3.

99. *Ibid.,* January 24, 1937; X, 1:1,2.

100. *Nation,* Vol. CXLIV (January 23, 1937), 109.

101. *Time,* Vol. XXIX (January 18, 1937), 47-48.

102. *New York Times,* January 8, 1937, 14:2,3.

103. *New Republic,* Vol. XC (February 10, 1937), 19-20.

104. *Saturday Review,* Vol. XV (February 27, 1937), 17, 19.

105. Miss Booth as quoted by Mantle, *Best Plays of 1938-39,* vi.

CHAPTER IV

1. *Time,* Vol. XXXIV (July 3, 1939), 43.

2. *Nation,* Vol. CXLIX (July 22, 1939), 109.

3. As quoted in Shipley, *Guide to Great Plays,* 850.

4. *New York Times,* March 27, 1941, 28:4, 5.

5. *New York Sun,* as quoted in Shipley, *Guide to Great Plays,* 124.

6. *Cue,* as quoted in Shipley, *ibid.,* 125.

7. Homosexuality, then taboo on the American stage, was a glaring public issue in Germany, particularly since so many of Hitler's early associates who made up the nucleus of leadership in the S.A. were publicly known and legally convicted murderers and/or sexual perverts. It was the homosexuality issue, along with political expediency, that precipitated Hitler's blood purge of the S.A. in 1934, including the murder of its leader who was one of his closest former friends, Ernst Roehm, a notorious homosexual.

8. *Theatre Arts* (formerly *Theatre Arts Monthly*), Vol. XXVI (February, 1942), 86.

9. George Jean Nathan, *Theatre Book of the Year* (1943), 20.

10. Klarmann, ed., [Franz Werfel] *Gesammelte Werke: Die Dramen,* 513.

11. *Ibid.*

12. Frey, "America and Franz Werfel," *German Quarterly,* Vol. XIX (March, 1946), 125.

13. Bentley, *The Playwright as Thinker,* 11.

14. *Nation,* Vol. CLVIII (March 25, 1944), 373.

15. Nathan, *Theatre Book of the Year* (1944), 263-67.

16. *Time,* Vol. XLIII (March 27, 1944), 60, 62.

17. *New Republic,* Vol. CX (March 27, 1944), 407.

18. *Commonweal,* Vol. XXXIX (March 31, 1944), 589-90.

19. *New York Times,* March 15, 1944, 17:2,3; and March 19, 1944, II, 1:1.

20. *Ibid.,* May 21, 1944, II, 1:1.

21. *Ibid.,* June 17, 1945, II, 1:1,2.

22. *Ibid.,* June 13, 1945, 28:3,4.

23. Martin Esslin, *Brecht: The Man and His Work,* 73.

24. Quoted in *ibid.*

25. Nathan, *Theatre Book of the Year* (1945), 28.

26. *Ibid.,* 29.

27. *New Republic,* Vol. CXII (June 25, 1945), 871; and *Commonweal,* Vol. XLII (June 29, 1945), 262-63.

Chapter V

1. Kenneth Tynan, *Curtains,* 454.

2. *New York Times,* September 7, 1945, 20:2,3.

3. *Ibid.,* September 6, 1946, 15:5,6.

4. For a good brief history of the current movement, see introduction to Richard A. Cordell and Lowell Matson, eds., *The Off-Broadway Theatre.*

5. Chapman, *The Burns Mantle Best Plays of 1947-48;* and *The Year Book of the Drama in America* (1948), 424.

6. Esslin, *Brecht,* 303.

7. Eric Bentley, *In Search of Theatre,* 35.

8. John Gassner, *The Theatre in Our Times,* 87.

9. *New York Times,* December 8, 1947, 34:2,3.

10. Nathan, *Theatre Book of the Year* (1948), 178-80.

11. *New Republic,* Vol. CXVII (December 29, 1947), 36-37.

12. *New York Times,* December 7, 1948, 41:6.

13. Gassner, *Twenty Best European Plays,* 51.

14. Garten, *Modern German Drama,* 224.

15. *New York Times,* March 2, 1949, 33:2,3.

16. Gassner, *The Theatre in Our Times,* 15.

17. *New York Times,* April 20, 1950, 36:5.

18. *Ibid.,* December 2, 1950, 8:3,4.

19. Hans Bänzinger, *Frisch und Dürrenmatt,* 65.

20. George E. Wellwarth, "Friedrich Dürrenmatt and Max Frisch: Two Views of the Drama," *Tulane Drama Review,* Vol. VI (Spring, 1962), 28.

21. *New York Times,* December 27, 1950, 32:5,6.

22. *New Yorker,* Vol. XXIX (October 10, 1953), 70-72.

23. *Commonweal,* Vol. LIX (October 23, 1953), 60-61.

24. *New York Times,* September 30, 1953, 38:3,4,5; and *New Republic,* Vol. CXXIX (October 26, 1953), 20.

25. *Nation,* Vol. CLXXVII (October 17, 1953), 317.

26. *New York Times,* June 15, 1955, 35:2,3.

27. *Ibid.,* March 17, 1957, II, 8:5,6,7.

28. *New Republic,* Vol. CXXX (April 5, 1954), 21.

29. *Theatre Arts,* Vol. XL (February, 1956), 77-78.

30. *New York Times,* June 28,1955, 24:2,3,4.

31. *Ibid.,* May 10, 1960, 44:2,3.

32. *Ibid.,* October 10, 1955, 30:2,3.

33. *Ibid.,* March 29, 1956, 22:5,6.

34. John Chapman, *Broadway's Best, 1956-57,* 287.

35. *New York Times,* April 11, 1957, 36:6,7,8.

36. Garten, *Modern German Drama,* 217.

37. Esslin, *Brecht,* 72-73.

38. As quoted in *ibid.,* 340.

39. See *ibid.,* 340-51.

40. Gassner, *The Theatre in Our Times,* 85.

41. Judith J. Sherwin, "The World Is Mean and Man Uncouth," *Virginia Quarterly Review,* Vol. XXXV (Spring, 1959), 265.

42. Barnard Hewitt, *Theatre U.S.A., 1668-1957,* 468.

43. Sherwin, "The World Is Mean and Man Uncouth," *Virginia Quarterly Review,* Vol. XXXV (Spring, 1959), 260.

44. William Becker, "Broadway: Classics and Imports," *Hudson Review,* Vol. VII (Summer, 1954), 268.

45. *Nation,* Vol. CLXXVIII (March 27, 1954), 265-66.

46. *Saturday Review,* Vol. XXXVII (March 27, 1954), 23.

47. *New Yorker,* Vol. XXX (March 20, 1954), 62, 64.

48. *New York Times,* March 21, 1954, II, 1:1.

49. Esslin, *Brecht,* 75.

50. *Saturday Review,* Vol. XL (January 5, 1957), 24.

51. John Gassner, *Theatre at the Crossroads,* 269-70.

52. Chapman, *Broadway's Best* (1957), 237.

53. *Nation,* Vol. CLXXXIV (January 5, 1957), 27.

54. *Theatre Arts,* Vol. XLI (February, 1957), 26.

55. *New Yorker,* Vol. XXXII (December 29, 1956), 46.

56. Bentley, *Seven Plays by Brecht,* 5.

57. Ernst Borneman, "Two Brechtians," *Kenyon Review,* Vol. XXII (Summer, 1960), 476.

58. Martin Esslin, *The Theatre of the Absurd*, 272.

59. Bentley, *Seven Plays by Brecht*, xiv.

60. *Ibid.*, xv.

61. *Ibid.*, xvii.

62. *New Yorker*, Vol. XXXVI (December 31, 1960), 42.

63. *Nation*, Vol. CXCII (January 7, 1961), 18-19.

64. *New York Times*, December 21, 1960, 39:1,2,3.

65. *Ibid.*, September 20, 1962, 30:2-4; and *New Yorker*, Vol. XXXVIII (September 29, 1962), 100-101.

66. *Nation*, Vol. CXCV (October 6. 1962), 207.

67. *Time*, Vol. LXXX (September 28, 1962), 91.

68. *New Republic*, Vol. CXLVII (October 1, 1962), 26, 28.

69. *Ibid.*, Vol. CXLVIII (April 13, 1963), 35-36.

70. *Ibid.*

71. *Ibid.*

72. *Ibid.*

73. *Nation*, Vol. CXCVI (April 13, 1963), 315.

74. *New Republic*, Vol. CXLVIII (April 13, 1963), 36.

75. *Ibid.*, Vol. CXLIX (December 21, 1963), 26.

76. *Ibid.*

77. *Nation*, Vol. CXCVII (December 7, 1963), 403-404.

78. *Commonweal*, Vol. LXXIX (December 6, 1963), 314.

79. *New York Times*, May 21, 1965, 19:1.

80. This play was not performed professionally in New York until the Lincoln Center company presented it in 1966.

81. Esslin, *Theatre of the Absurd*, 191.

82. Friedrich Dürrenmatt, "Problems of the Theatre," trans. Gerhard Nellhaus, *Tulane Drama Review*, Vol. III (October, 1958), 3-26.

83. As quoted in Garten, *Modern German Drama*, 252.

84. Block and Shedd, *Masters of Modern Drama*, 1132.

85. Wellwarth, "Friedrich Dürrenmatt and Max Frisch: Two Views of the Drama," *Tulane Drama Review*, Vol. VI (Spring, 1962), 15.

86. Gordon Rogoff, "Mr. Dürrenmatt Buys New Shoes," *Tulane Drama Review*, Vol. III (October, 1958), 29.

87. *Ibid.*

88. *Ibid.*, 30.

89. *New York Times*, April 3, 1958, 24:2,3.

90. Randolph Goodman, *Drama on Stage*, 380.

91. *Ibid.*, 381.

92. *Ibid.*, 386.

93. Rogoff, "Mr. Dürrenmatt Buys New Shoes," *Tulane Drama Review*, Vol. III (October, 1958), 33.

94. Goodman, *Drama on Stage*, 388.

95. Wellwarth, "Friedrich Dürrenmatt and Max Frisch: Two Views of the Drama," *Tulane Drama Review*, Vol. VI (Spring, 1962), 14.

96. Gassner, *Theatre at the Crossroads*, 272.

97. *New Yorker*, Vol. XXXIV (May 17, 1958), 87.

98. *Time*, Vol. LXXI (May 19, 1958), 83.

99. *New York Times*, May 6, 1958; 40:1,2,3; May 8, 1958, II, 1:1,2; and September 7, 1958, II, 1:1,2,3.

100. *Saturday Review*, Vol. XLIII (February 20, 1960), 28.

101. *New York Times*, February 3, 1960, 27:2,3.

102. *Time*, Vol. LXXIX (January 19, 1962), 68, 70.

103. *New Republic*, Vol. CXLVI (January 29, 1962), 22.

104. *Nation*, Vol. CXCIV (February 3, 1962), 106-107.

105. *New York Times*, January 11, 1962, 27:1-4.

106. *Time*, Vol. LXXXIV (October 23, 1964), 67.

107. *Nation*, Vol. CXCIX (November 9, 1964), 340.

108. *Commonweal*, Vol. LXXXI (November 13, 1964), 237-38.

109. *New Republic*, Vol. CXLVIII (March 9, 1963), 28-29.

110. *Time*, Vol. LXXXI (February 22, 1963), 75.

111. *New Yorker*, Vol. XXXVIII (February 16, 1963), 114.

112. *New Republic*, Vol. CXLVIII (March 9, 1963), 28-29.

113. *New York Times*, February 13, 1963, 7:3.

114. *Ibid.*, November 22, 1963, 41:1,2.

115. Harold Clurman, *Lies Like Truth*, 231.

116. *Nation*, Vol. CLXXXVIII (April 4, 1959), 302.

117. *New York Times*, March 5, 1959, 34:2,3.

118. *Ibid.*, April 17, 1963, 30:1,2,3.

119. *Life*, Vol. XLII (June 10, 1957), 121, 123-24.

120. *New York Times*, September 9, 1960, 35:1.

121. *New Yorker*, Vol. XXXVII (October 28, 1961), 137.

122. *Reporter*, Vol. XXV (November 9, 1961), 58.

123. See Eric Bentley, ed. *The Storm over the Deputy;* and Dolores Barracano Schmidt and Earl Robert Schmidt, eds. *The Deputy Reader: Studies in Moral Responsibility.*

124. *New Republic*, Vol. CL (March 14, 1964), 23-25.

125. *Time*, Vol. LXXXVII (January 7, 1966), 51.

126. *Ibid.*

127. *New Yorker*, Vol. XLI (January 8, 1966), 98, 100.

128. *Nation*, Vol. CCII (January 17, 1966), 82-84.

Appendix

PLAYS ORIGINALLY IN GERMAN WHICH APPEARED IN TRANSLATION OR ADAPTATION ON THE NEW YORK STAGE BETWEEN 1894 AND 1965

This list does not include revivals of the classics of the eighteenth and nineteenth centuries. The theatrical season runs from June 15 to June 15. An asterisk (°) before a title indicates an off-Broadway production. The number of performances, when known, appears in parentheses after the title.

1894-95

A NIGHT OFF (16)

By Augustin Daly. Based on *Der Raub der Sabinerinnen* by Franz and Paul von Schönthan. Revival by Daly. Daly's Theatre, Aug. 27, 1894. Original production at Daly's Theatre, Mar. 4, 1885. Also one performance in repertory at Harlem Opera House, May 18, 1895. Direction by Augustin Daly. Scene and characters Americanized, as were all of Daly's adaptations except *The Countess Gucki.*

SEVEN TWENTY-EIGHT (1)

Adapted by Augustin Daly from *Der Schwabenstreich* by Franz von Schönthan. Revival by Daly. Daly's Theatre, Sept. 13, 1894. First New York production at Daly's Theatre, Feb. 24, 1883.

FRITZ in a MADHOUSE (8)

Adapted by J. K. Emmett. Revival at People's Theatre, Sept. 17, 1894. Revived again for a week at Third Avenue Theatre, Jan. 22, 1889, and for another week at Metropolitan Theatre, Apr. 17, 1889.

THE QUEEN of BRILLIANTS (29)

Musical comedy adapted by H. J. W. Dam from the German by Theodor Taube and Isidor Fuchs. Music by Edward Jakobowski. Abbey's Theatre, Nov. 7, 1894. Starred Lillian Russell.

LOVE on CRUTCHES (11)

Adapted by Augustin Daly. Based on *Ihre Ideale* by Heinrich Stobitzer. Revival by Daly. Daly's Theatre, Dec. 15, 1894. First production at Daly's

Theatre, Nov. 25, 1884. Directed by Augustin Daly. Based on Sardou's *Les Pattes de Mouche,* which in turn was based in part on Poe's *The Purloined Letter.*

THE LITTLE HUSSAR (1 special matinée)
Musical arranged from the German by Elizabeth Stagg. Music by Emma Steiner. Fifth Avenue Theatre, Dec. 21, 1894.

THE RAILROAD of LOVE (8)
Adapted by Augustin Daly from *Goldfische* by Gustav Kadelburg and Franz von Schönthan. Daly's Theatre, Jan. 21, 1895. Revival of Daly production at Daly's Theatre, Nov. 1, 1887. Directed by Augustin Daly.

THE ORIENT EXPRESS (28)
Adapted by Francis C. Burnand from *Orientreise* by Oscar Blumenthal and Gustav Kadelburg. Daly's Theatre, Jan. 31, 1895. Directed by Augustin Daly.

HIS WIFE'S FATHER (104)
By Martha Morton. Central idea taken from the German of Adolph L'Arronge. Produced by Joseph Brooks. Fifth Avenue Theatre, Feb. 25, 1895.

NANCY & CO. (4)
By Augustin Daly. Based on *Halbe Dichter* by Julius Rosen. Revived at Daly's Theatre, Mar. 19, 1895. First production at Daly's Theatre, Feb. 24, 1886. Staged by Augustin Daly.

A BUNDLE of LIES (7)
Adapted by Augustin Daly from *Der Höchste Trumpf* by Carl Laufs and Wilhelm Jacoby. Produced by Daly at Daly's Theatre, Mar. 28, 1895. Also played for one performance in Daly Repertory, Harlem Opera House, May 16, 1895.

1895-96

HANSEL and GRETAL [*sic*] (48)
Opera with libretto by Adelheid Wette, adapted from the tale by the Grimm brothers. Music by Engelbert Humperdinck. Produced by Augustin Daly at Daly's Theatre, Oct. 7, 1895. Also rlayed at Daly's Theatre, Dec. 23, 1895, for sixteen more performances, probably a typical Christmas production of the children's opera. Performance may have been in German.

MAGDA (2)
Uncredited translation of *Heimat* by Hermann Sudermann. Part of Mme. Helena Modjeska's repertory, beginning at Garrick Theatre, Oct. 7, 1895. Modjeska had appeared in first New York production of *Magda* on Jan. 28, 1894, at the Fifth Avenue Theatre.

HONOUR (8)
Uncredited translation of *Die Ehre* by Hermann Sudermann. Standard Theatre, Nov. 11, 1895.

THE TRANSIT of LEO (10)
Adapted by Augustin Daly from *Das Schösskind* by an unknown German.
Produced by Daly. Daly's Theatre, Dec. 10, 1895. Directed by Daly.

THE TWO ESCUTCHEONS (24)
Adapted by Sidney Rosenfeld from *Zwei Wappen* by Oscar Blumenthal and
Gustav Kadelburg. Produced by Augustin Daly. Daly's Theatre, Jan. 7,
1896. Twenty-four more performances at Garden Theatre, Feb. 24, 1896.
Staged by Daly. This play had been acted in German at the Irving Place
Theatre the previous season.

THE COUNTESS GUCKI (32)
Adapted by Augustin Daly from the German of Franz von Schönthan.
Produced and staged by Daly. Daly's Theatre, Jan. 28, 1896.

HIS ABSENT BOY (48)
Adapted by Al Neuman, assisted by Sidney Rosenfeld, from *Der Rabenvater*
by Yarno and Fischer. Produced by A. M. Palmer at Garden Theatre, Apr.
6, 1896. Staged by Max Freeman.

FRITZ in LOVE (?)
By Arthur D. Hall. Although not listed as a German play, it starred J. K.
Emmett, adapter of the previous season's *Fritz in a Madhouse* and played at
the same theatre where the Emmett title was revived again on Jan. 2, 1899
(Third Avenue Theatre). It was originally done Apr. 27, 1889, at the 14th
Street Theatre and seems to have been very popular. This may have been
an American play which cashed in on the other *Fritz* play's popularity and
became a sequel.

1896-97

THE MERRY TRAMPS (40)
By Robert Breitenbach. Music by Carl Pleininger. Produced by Carl and
Theodore Rosenfeld at Star Theatre, Sept. 28, 1896. Judging by the names
of the sixteen actors in the cast, the production may have been in German.
Many German plays were given at the Star. Sixteen further performances at
Star beginning Dec. 21, 1896.

A SUPERFLUOUS HUSBAND (16)
By Clyde Fitch and Leo Ditrichstein. Based on the German of Ludwig
Fulda. Fifth Avenue Theatre, Jan. 4, 1897. Scene and characters American-
ized.

THE LOST PARADISE (one week, matinée daily, probably 12 performances)
adapted by Henry C. DeMille from *Das Verlorene Paradies* by Ludwig
Fulda. Produced by Waite Comedy Co., Murray Hill Theatre, May 3, 1897.
One week revivals on Sept. 5, 1898; Sept. 12, 1898; Dec. 5, 1898. At
Columbus, Star and Third Avenue theatres.

1897-98

LEAH the FORSAKEN (16)

By Augustin Daly from *Deborah* by Solomon Mosenthal. Murray Hill Theatre, Sept. 13, 1897. One further week, People's Theatre, Mar. 7, 1898. Also one week, Columbus Theatre, Oct. 10, 1898 in a revised version by Rev. Oliver J. Booth. First New York production; Niblo's Garden Theatre, Jan. 19, 1863, at which time it was Daly's first play.

THE FAIR in MIDGETTOWN (56)

By Robert Breitenbach. Music by Victor Holländer. Produced by Carl and Theodore Rosenfeld. Star Theatre, Sept. 20, 1897. Eight further performances beginning Nov. 15, 1897, at Harlem Opera House. Author and many of the cast the same as the previous season's *The Merry Tramps*. Probably a sequel and may well have been played in German.

INGOMAR (one week)

Translated by Maria Lovell from *Der Sohn Der Wildnis* by Münch-Bellinghausen (Friedrich Halm). Wallack's Theatre, Nov. 21, 1897.

ALEXANDRA (16)

Adapted by Richard Voss from a play by Victorien Sardou variously known as *Agnes, Andrea, Anselma,* and *In Spite of All.* American adapter of Voss's German version is uncredited. Fifth Avenue Theatre, Nov. 29, 1897. May have been in German.

NUMBER NINE, or THE LADY of OSTEND (20)

Adapted by Francis C. Burnand from *Hans Huckebein* by Oscar Blumenthal and Gustav Kadelburg. Produced and directed by Augustin Daly. Daly's Theatre, Dec. 8, 1897.

DEBORAH (one week)

Adapted by Isaac C. Pray from *Deborah* by Solomon Mosenthal. Fifth Avenue Theatre, Dec. 13, 1897. First New York production: Tripler Hall, May 30, 1863.

THE COUNTESS VALESKA (24)

Uncredited adaptation from *Der Lange Preusse* by Rudolph Stratz. Knickerbocker Theatre, Jan. 10, 1898. With Julia Marlowe.

LILI TSE (35)

One-act operetta adapted by Sidney Rosenfeld from *Lili Tse* by Wolfgang Kirchback. Music by Franz Curti. Produced and staged by Daly. Daly's Theatre, Feb. 11, 1898. One additional performance at Harlem Opera House in repertory, Apr. 18, 1898. Used as curtain-raiser for Daly's adaptation of the Garrick version of Wycherley's *The Country Wife.*

LOVE FINDS the WAY (64)

Adapted by Marguerite Merington from unknown source. Fifth Avenue Theatre, Apr. 11, 1898. Eight more performances in repertory, beginning Feb. 27, 1899. Both productions starred Minnie Maddern Fiske.

1898-99

HIS WIFE'S FATHER (12)
By Martha Morton. Central idea taken from the German of Adolph L'Arronge. Murray Hill Theatre, Feb. 20, 1899.

THE GOLDEN HORSESHOE (32)
Musical with libretto by Robert Breitenbach and music by Carl Pleininger. Produced by Carl and Theodore Rosenfeld. Irving Place Theatre, Sept. 15, 1898. Same cast and staff involved as with *The Merry Tramps* (1896) and *The Fair in Midgettown* (1897). Probably in German.

FANCHON (one week)
Adapted by A. Wildeur from *Die Grille* by Charlotte Birch-Pfeiffer. Columbus Theatre, Oct. 24, 1898. First New York production: Laura Keene's Varieties, June 9, 1862.

A DANGEROUS MAID (65)
Musical comedy translated by Sidney Rosenfeld. Some lyrics by Louis Harrison. Music by Leopold Schenck and Frederick J. Eustis. Produced by George W. Lederer and George B. McLellan. Casino Theatre, Nov. 12, 1898. Eight more performances beginning Feb. 27, 1899. Eight additional performances beginning Mar. 6, 1899, at Harlem Opera House. Seems to have strayed far from its source.

THE HEAD of the FAMILY (31)
"Freely adapted" (according to program) by Clyde Fitch and Leo Ditrichstein from *Hasemanns Töchter* by Adolph L'Arronge. Produced by Joseph Brooks. Knickerbocker Theatre, Dec. 6, 1898. Staged by Clyde Fitch. May be same source as Martha Morton's *His Wife's Father*.

AT the WHITE HORSE TAVERN (64)
Adapted by Sidney Rosenfeld from *Im Weissen Röss'l* by Oscar Blumenthal and Gustav Kadelburg. Incidental music by Frank A. Howson. Later turned into a famous operetta. Produced by Daniel and Charles Frohman. Wallack's Theatre, Feb. 6, 1899.

MAGDA (16)
Uncredited translation of *Heimat* by Hermann Sudermann. Produced by the Minnie Maddern Fiske Repertory. Fifth Avenue Theatre, with entire repertory beginning Feb. 27, 1899.

THE PURPLE LADY (48)
Adapted by Sidney Rosenfeld from uncredited German source. Produced by Rudolph Aronson. Bijou Theatre, April 3, 1899. Scene and characters Americanized.

1899-1900

THE GIRL in the BARRACKS (31)
Uncredited adaptation from the German of Curt Kraatz and Heinrich Stobitzer. Garrick Theatre, Oct. 26, 1899.

A RICH MAN'S SON (36)
> By Michael Morton. Based on *Das Grobe Hemd* by H. Karlweiss. Produced by William H. Crane. Wallack's Theatre, Oct. 21, 1899.

THE SUNKEN BELL (40)
> Translated by Charles Henry Meltzer from *Die Versunkene Glocke* by Gerhart Hauptmann. Knickerbocker Theatre, Mar. 26, 1900. Starred E. H. Sothern and Edith Taliaferro.

TWELVE MONTHS LATER (8)
> Uncredited adaptation from a German comedy by Oscar Blumenthal and Gustav Kadelburg. Madison Square Theatre, Mar. 26, 1900. Starred Richard Bennett and Leo Ditrichstein.

1900-1901

HODGE, PODGE & CO. (73)
> Musical comedy libretto adapted by George V. Hobart from uncredited German source. Lyrics by Walter Ford. Music by John W. Bratton. Interpolated numbers by Gus Edwards, Herman Perlet, Dave Reed, Jr., and MacConnell & Smith. Produced by Frank McKee. Madison Square Theatre, Oct. 23, 1900. The fact that the lyrics, music, and interpolated numbers were all by Americans indicates that this was a German comedy which was turned into a musical review rather than a coherent comedy with music. As indicated by the title and the vaudeville hands involved in the interpolations, it may be assumed that the show took off far from its source.

VIENNA LIFE (35)
> Operetta adapted and with lyrics by Glen MacDonough from libretto by Victor Leon and Leo Stein. Music by Johann Strauss. Broadhurst Theatre, Jan. 23, 1901.

ARE YOU a MASON? (32)
> Adapted by Leo Ditrichstein from *Die Logenbrüder* by Carl Laufs and Curt Kraatz. Produced by Charles Frohman. Wallack's Theatre, April 1, 1901. Staged by Ditrichstein who also starred. Revived for 32 performances, Garrick Theatre, Aug. 19, 1901, and again by producers Rich and Harris for 16 performances beginning Sept. 5, 1904, at the Garrick Theatre.

1901-1902

THE STROLLERS (70)
> Musical comedy adapted by Harry B. Smith from the German of L. Kremm and C. Lindau. Music by Ludwig Englander. Produced by George W. Lederer. Knickerbocker Theatre, June 24, 1901.

MAGDA (?)
> Translated by Louis N. Parker from *Heimat* by Hermann Sudermann. Part of Mrs. Patrick Campbell's Repertory. Produced by Liebler and Co. and George C. Tyler. Republic Theatre. Repertory began Jan. 13, 1902. *Magda* was used by Mrs. Campbell for her New York debut.

THE TWIN SISTER (48)
Translated by Louis N. Parker from *Die Zwillingsschwester* by Ludwig Fulda. Produced by Charles Frohman. Empire Theatre, Mar. 3, 1902.

1902-1903

THE JOY of LIVING (19)
Translated by Edith Wharton from *Es Lebe das Leben* by Hermann Sudermann. Produced by Charles Frohman. Garden Theatre, Oct. 23, 1902. Staged by Mrs. Patrick Campbell, who also starred.

THE CHILDREN of KINGS (14)
Adapted by Frederick Langbridge and A. H. Ferro from *Königskinder* by Ernst Rosmer (pseudonym for Elsa Bernstein). Special music by Engelbert Humperdinck. Produced by Klaw and Erlanger. Herald Square Theatre, Nov. 3, 1902.

MARY of MAGDALA (105)
Adapted by William Winter from *Maria von Magdala* by Paul Heyse. Music by Charles Puerner. Ballet by Carl Marwig. Produced by Harrison Grey Fiske. Manhattan Theatre, Nov. 12, 1902. Staged by Mr. and Mrs. Fiske. Starred Mrs. Fiske and Tyrone Power. Also played three more weeks, Manhattan Theatre, Sept. 14, 1903.

HEIDELBERG (40)
Adapted by Aubrey Boucicault from *Alt Heidelberg* by Wilhelm Meyer-Förster. Produced by Sam S. and Lee Shubert. Princess Theatre, Dec. 15, 1902.

THE BIRD in the CAGE (40)
Adapted by Clyde Fitch from *Die Haubenlerche* by Ernst von Wildenbruch. Produced by Charles Frohman. Bijou Theatre, Jan. 12, 1903.

1903-1904

OLD HEIDELBERG (32)
An uncredited new version of *Alt Heidelberg* by Wilhelm Meyer-Förster. Produced by Richard Mansfield. Lyric Theatre, Oct. 12, 1903.

INGOMAR (1 special matinée)
Translated by Maria Lovell from *Der Sohn der Wildnis* by Münch-Bellinghausen (Friedrich Halm). Revived by Charles Frohman. Empire Theatre, May 16, 1904. Starred Julia Marlowe, Tyrone Power, and Frank Reicher. First New York production in 1851.

1904-1905

MILITARY MAD (16)
Adapted by Leo Ditrichstein from *Im Bunten Rock* by Franz von Schönthan. Garrick Theatre, Aug. 22, 1904. Starred Mr. Ditrichstein.

TAPS (25)
> Translated by Charles Swickard from *Zapfenstreich* by Franz Adam Beyerlein. Produced by Sam S. Shubert. Lyric Theatre, Sept. 17, 1904.

MAGDA (5)
> Uncredited translation of *Heimat* by Hermann Sudermann. Revived by John B. Schoeffel. Daly's Theatre, Nov. 21, 1904.

THE FIRES of ST. JOHN (8)
> Uncredited adaptation from *Johannisfeuer* by Hermann Sudermann. Produced by John B. Schoeffel. Daly's Theatre, Nov. 28, 1904.

FATINIZA (four weeks, presumably 8 performances per week)
> Comic opera adapted by Harry B. Smith from the Viennese *Fatiniza*. Music by Franz von Suppé. Produced by Charles B. Dillingham. Broadway Theatre, Dec. 26, 1904. Two more weeks at the same theatre beginning Feb. 13, 1905. The show was one of a series of revivals for the popular Fritzi Scheff. First New York production was in 1878-79.

°FLIRTATION (?)
> Uncredited adaptation of *Liebelei* by Arthur Schnitzler. Produced by the Progressive Stage Society in February, 1905. First production in English of *Liebelei*.

1905-1906

WONDERLAND (73)
> Musical play by Glen MacDonough. Based on *The Dancing Princess* by the Grimm brothers. Music by Victor Herbert. Produced by Julian Mitchell. Majestic Theatre, Oct. 24, 1905.

THE MOUNTAIN CLIMBER (79)
> By C. Kraatz and M. Neal (program is so listed, but since Curt Kraatz is a German playwright and M. Neal obviously is not, it is probable that Mr. Neal is the adapter of this uncredited play). Produced by Charles Frohman. Criterion Theatre, Mar. 5, 1906.

1906-1907

JOHN the BAPTIST (?)
> Translated by Mary Harned from *Johannes* by Hermann Sudermann. Part of the E. H. Sothern-Julia Marlowe Repertory which began an eight-week stand at the Lyric Theatre on Jan. 21, 1907. Produced by Sam S. and Lee Shubert.

THE SUNKEN BELL (?)
> Translated by Charles Henry Meltzer from *Die Versunkene Glocke* by Gerhart Hauptmann. Part of the same repertory as *John the Baptist*, above.

THE RECKONING (73)
Uncredited translation of *Liebelei* by Arthur Schnitzler. Berkeley Lyceum, Feb. 12, 1907.

1907-1908

THE RECKONING (24)
Uncredited translation of *Liebelei* by Arthur Schnitzler. Revived by Walter N. Laurence. Madison Square Theatre, Jan. 13, 1908.

THE LITERARY SENSE (24)
Adapted by Charles Harvey Genung from *Literatur* by Arthur Schnitzler. Served as curtain-raiser for *The Reckoning*, above.

THE MERRY WIDOW (416)
Adapted and with lyrics by Adrian Ross from *Die Lustige Witwe* by Victor Leon and Leo Stein. Music by Franz Lehár. Produced by Henry W. Savage. New Amsterdam Theatre, Oct. 21, 1907.

A WALTZ DREAM (111)
Operetta with English book and lyrics by Joseph W. Herbert. Adapted from *Ein Walzertraum* by Felix Dörmann and Leopold Jacobson (sometimes listed as Jacks), based on a story by Hans Müller. Music by Oscar Strauss. Produced by the Inter-State Amusement Co., Inc. Broadway Theatre, Jan. 27, 1908.

MAGDA (?)
Uncredited translation of *Heimat* by Hermann Sudermann. One of the plays in the repertory of Olga Nethersole which began three weeks at Daly's Theatre on Feb. 8, 1908.

ELECTRA (9)
Translated by Arthur Symons from *Elektra* by Hugo von Hofmannsthal. Revived at the Garden Theatre, Feb. 11, 1908. Starred Mrs. Patrick Campbell. First New York production in English had been by students of the American Academy of Dramatic Arts on Mar. 11, 1889.

GIRLS (64)
Adapted by Clyde Fitch from *Die Welt Ohne Männer* by Alexander Engel and Julius Horst. Produced by Sam S. and Lee Shubert. Daly's Theatre, Mar. 23, 1908. A program note stated, "The author wishes to acknowledge an indebtedness to a play by Hugo Holtz." This source is unknown. Revived for one week at Hackett's Theatre, Feb. 8, 1909. The scene and characters of this comedy were Americanized.

1908-1909

MLLE. MISCHIEF (96)
Operetta adapted by Sidney Rosenfeld from an unlisted work by Kraatz and von Sterk. Music by E. M. Ziehrer. Produced by Sam S. and Lee Shubert. Lyric Theatre, Sept. 28, 1908.

THE BLUE MOUSE (232)
Adapted by Clyde Fitch from an unlisted farce by Alexander Engel and Julius Horst. Lyric Theatre, Nov. 30, 1908. Moved to Maxine Elliott Theatre, May 3, 1909. Staged by Clyde Fitch.

1909-10

THE GAY HUSSARS (44)
Operetta with libretto adapted by Maurice Brown Kirby and lyrics by Grant Stewart. Based on *Ein Herbstmanöver* by Karl von Bakonyi and Robert Bodansky. Music by Emmerich Kálmán. Produced by Henry W. Savage. Knickerbocker Theatre, July 29, 1909.

THE FLORIST SHOP (40)
Adapted by Oliver Herford from *Glück bei Frauen* by Alexander Engel and Julius Horst. Produced by Henry W. Savage. Liberty Theatre, Aug. 9, 1909.

IS MATRIMONY a FAILURE? (183)
Adapted by Leo Ditrichstein from an unlisted farce by Oscar Blumenthal and Gustav Kadelburg. Produced by David Belasco and staged by him at the Belasco Theatre, Aug. 24, 1909.

THE LOVE CURE (35)
Musical adapted by Oliver Herford from *Künstlerblut* by Leo Stein and Karl Lindau. Music by Edmund Eysler. Produced by Henry W. Savage. New Amsterdam Theatre, Sept. 1, 1909. This was a very free adaptation.

THE DOLLAR PRINCESS (288)
Musical comedy adapted by George Grossmith, Jr., from *Die Dollarprinzessin* by Willner and Grünbaum. Music by Leo Fall. Produced by Charles Frohman. Knickerbocker Theatre, Sept. 6, 1909.

THE CHOCOLATE SOLDIER (296)
Operetta adapted by H. Stanislaus Stange from *Der Tapfere Soldat* by Rudolph Bernauer and Leopold Jacobson, which was based on George Bernard Shaw's *Arms and the Man*. Shaw gave permission to use his work on condition that all playbills read: "With apologies to Bernard Shaw." Music by Oscar Strauss. Produced by F. C. Whitney. Lyric Theatre, Sept. 13, 1909. Moved to Herald Square Theatre, then returned to Lyric, then went on to the Casino. Revived by the Shuberts at the Century Theatre on Dec. 12, 1921.

ON the EVE (24)
Adapted by Martha Morton from an unlisted play by Leopold Kampf. Produced by Henry B. Harris. Hudson Theatre, Oct. 4, 1909.

THE DEBTORS (15)
Adapted by Margaret Mayo (Margaret Mayorga) from an unlisted comedy by Franz von Schönthan. Produced by the Allison-Ziegler Co. Bijou Theatre, Oct. 12, 1909.

THE GIRL HE COULDN'T LEAVE BEHIND HIM (37)
Uncredited adaptation from an unlisted play by Gustav Kadelburg. Produced by William Collier. Garrick Theatre, Mar. 9, 1910.

THE GREEN COCKATOO (16)
Translated by Philip Littel and George Rublee from *Der Grüne Kakadu* by Arthur Schnitzler. Produced by Harrison Grey Fiske. Lyceum Theatre, Apr. 11, 1910. Was curtain-raiser for *Hannele*, below.

HANNELE (16)
Translated by Mary J. Safford from *Hanneles Himmelfahrt* by Gerhart Hauptmann. The metrical passages in this translation were by Percy Mac-Kaye. Starred Mrs. Fiske. Lyceum Theatre, Apr. 11, 1910.

1910-11

THE CHEATER (78)
Adapted by Louis Mann from an unlisted German farce by Wilhelm Jacoby and Arthur Lipshitz. Produced by William A. Brady. Lyric Theatre, June 29, 1910.

WELCOME to OUR CITY (16)
Adapted by George V. Hobart from an uncredited German farce. Produced by Joseph Brooks. Bijou Theatre, Sept. 12, 1910.

THE GIRL in the TRAIN (40)
Operetta adapted by Harry B. Smith from *Die Geschiedene Frau* by Victor Leon. Music by Leo Fall. Produced by Charles Dillingham. Globe Theatre, Oct. 3, 1910.

THE CONCERT (264)
Adapted by Leo Ditrichstein from *Das Konzert* by Hermann Bahr. Produced and staged by David Belasco. Oct. 4, 1910.

THE GIRL and the KAISER (64)
Operetta adapted by Leonard Liebling from *Die Förster-Christel* by Bernhard Buchbinder. Music by Georg Jarno. Produced by the Messrs. Shubert. Herald Square Theatre, Nov. 22, 1910.

THE PRIVATE SECRETARY (14 weeks—probably 112 performances)
Adapted by William Gillette from *Der Bibliothekar* by Gustav von Moser. Produced by Charles Frohman as one of a series of revivals of plays and adaptations by Gillette and starring him. Dec. 12, 1910. Empire Theatre. First New York production: Sept. 29, 1884.

OLD HEIDELBERG (?)
Uncredited adaptation of *Alt Heidelberg* by Wilhelm Meyer-Förster. Revived at the New Theatre, Dec. 19, 1910.

YOUTH (7)
Translated by Herman Bernstein from *Jugend* by Max Halbe. Produced by Julius Hopp. Bijou Theatre, June 11, 1911.

1911-12

THE SIREN (136)

Musical adapted by Harry B. Smith from *Die Sirene* by Leo Stein and A. M. Willner. Music by Leo Fall. Produced by Charles Frohman. Knickerbocker Theatre, Aug. 28, 1911.

THE GREAT NAME (21)

Adapted by James Clarence Harvey from an unlisted comedy by Victor Leon and Leo Feld. Produced by Henry W. Savage. Lyric Theatre, Oct. 4, 1911. Later moved to 39th Street Theatre.

GYPSY LOVE (31)

Operetta adapted by Harry B. and Robert B. Smith from *Zigeunerliebe* by Willner and Bodansky. Music by Franz Lehár. Produced by A. H. Woods. Globe Theatre, Oct. 17, 1911.

VERA VIOLETTA (112)

Musical adapted by Leonard Liebling and Harold Atteridge from an unlisted play by Leo Stein. Music by Edmund Eysler. Produced by the Winter Garden Co. Winter Garden Theatre, Nov. 20, 1911. Al Jolson and Mae West were in the cast.

LITTLE BOY BLUE (176)

Operetta adapted by A. E. Thomas and Edward A. Paulton from an unlisted title by Rudolph Schanzer and Carl Lindau. Music by Henri Bereny. Produced by Henry W. Savage. Lyric Theatre, Nov. 27, 1911.

MODEST SUZANNE (24)

Operetta adapted by Harry B. and Robert B. Smith from an unlisted title by Georg Okonkowsky. Music by Jean Gilbert. Produced by A. H. Woods and H. H. Frazee. Liberty Theatre, Jan. 1, 1912.

SUMURUN (62)

Wordless play in nine tableaux. Plot by Friedrich Freksa from his *Tales of the Arabian Nights*. Music by Victor Holländer. Complete company from *Deutsches Theater* in Berlin under supervision of Max Reinhardt. Produced by Winthrop Ames. Casino Theatre, Jan. 16, 1912.

THE OPERA BALL (32)

Musical adapted by Sidney Rosenfeld and Clare Kummer from *Der Opernball* by Victor Leon and H. von Waldberg. Music by Richard Heuberger. Liberty Theatre, Feb. 12, 1912.

BARON TRENCK (40)

Musical with libretto adapted by Henry Blossom and lyrics by Frederick F. Schrader from *Baron Trenck* by A. M. Willner and Robert Bodansky. Music by Felix Albini. Produced by the Whitney Opera Co. Casino Theatre, Mar. 11, 1912. This adaptation was so free that it was actually a rewriting.

THE ROSE MAID (176)

Operetta adapted by Harry B. Smith and Raymond Peck, with lyrics by

Robert B. Smith, from *Bub Oder Mädel* by Bruno Granichstädten and Felix Dörmann. Produced by Louis F. Werba and Mark A. Luesher. Globe Theatre, April 22, 1912.

TWO LITTLE BIRDIES (63)
Musical adapted by Gustav Kerker, Arthur Anderson, James T. Powers, and Harold Atteridge from an unlisted title by Willner and Wilhelm. Produced by the Messrs. Shubert. Casino Theatre, April 23, 1912.

MAMA'S BABY BOY (9)
Musical adapted by Junie McCree from an uncredited source. Music by Hans S. Linne. Additional numbers by Will H. Becker. Broadway Theatre, May 25, 1912.

1912-13

THE MERRY COUNTESS (135)
Operetta libretto adapted by Gladys Unger and lyrics by Arthur Anderson from *Die Fledermaus* by Carl Haffner and Richard Genée, who had based their text on Meilhac and Halévy's *Le Reveillon*, which in turn was based on Roderich Benedix's German comedy, *Das Gefängnis*. Music by Johann Strauss. Produced by the Messrs. Shubert. Casino Theatre, Aug. 20, 1912.

THE COUNT of LUXEMBOURG (120)
Operetta libretto adapted by Glen MacDonough and lyrics by Adrian Ross and Basil Hood from *Der Graf von Luxemburg* by Willner and Bodansky. Music by Franz Lehár. Produced by Klaw and Erlanger. New Amsterdam Theatre, Sept. 16, 1912.

THE WOMAN HATERS (32)
Operetta adapted and with lyrics by George V. Hobart from *Die Frauenfresser* by Leo Stein and Carl Lindau. Music by Edmund Eysler. Produced by A. H. Woods. Astor Theatre, Oct. 7, 1912.

THE AFFAIRS of ANATOL (72)
Translated by Harley Granville-Barker from *Anatol* by Arthur Schnitzler. Produced by Winthrop Ames. Little Theatre, Oct. 14, 1912. John Barrymore starred.

OUR WIVES (40)
Adapted by Frank Mandel and Helen Kraft from an uncredited German source. Produced by Joseph M. Gaites. Wallack's Theatre, Nov. 4, 1912.

SNOW WHITE and the SEVEN DWARFS (72 matinées)
By Jessie Graham White from *Schneewittchen* by the Grimm brothers. Produced by Winthrop Ames. Little Theatre, Nov. 7, 1912. Moved to Maxine Elliott Theatre, Jan. 27, 1913.

EVA (24)
Musical adapted by Glen MacDonough from an unlisted source by Willner and Bodansky. Music by Franz Lehár. Produced by Klaw and Erlanger. New Amsterdam Theatre, Dec. 30, 1912.

THE MAN with THREE WIVES (52)
   Operetta adapted by Paul M. Potter and Agnes Morgan from an uncredited
   text. Music by Franz Lehár. Produced by the Messrs. Shubert. Weber and
   Fields' Theatre, Jan. 23, 1913.

THE FIVE FRANKFORTERS (88)
   Adapted by Basil Hook from *Die Fünf Frankfurter* by Carl Rössler. Produced by the Messrs. Shubert. 39th Street Theatre, Mar. 3, 1913.

THE BEGGAR STUDENT (33)
   Uncredited adaptation of the operetta, *Der Bettelstudent* by Karl Millöcker.
   Revived by the Messrs. Shubert and William A. Brady. Casino Theatre,
   Mar. 22, 1913.

MY LITTLE FRIEND (24)
   Musical adapted by Harry B. Smith, with lyrics by Robert B. Smith, from
   the unlisted German text by Willner and Stein. Music by Oscar Strauss.
   Produced by F. C. Whitney. New Amsterdam Theatre, May 19, 1913.

1913-14

THE DOLL GIRL (88)
   Musical adapted by Harry B. Smith from an unlisted text by Leo Stein and
   A. M. Willner. Music by Leo Fall. Produced by Charles Frohman. Globe
   Theatre, Aug. 25, 1913. On October 14, during the 55th performance of
   The Doll Girl, a skit by J. M. Barrie was introduced into the second act. It
   remained there for the rest of the run. These scripts were not sacrosanct.

LIEBER AUGUSTIN (37)
   Operetta adapted and with lyrics by Edgar Smith from an uncredited text.
   Music by Leo Fall. Produced by the Messrs. Shubert. Casino Theatre, Sept.
   3, 1913.

THE MARRIAGE MARKET (80)
   Musical play adapted by Gladys Unger, with lyrics by Arthur Anderson and
   Adrian Ross from an unlisted text by M. Brody and F. Martos. Music by
   Victor Jacobi. Produced by Charles Frohman. Knickerbocker Theatre, Sept.
   22, 1913.

THE GIRL on the FILM (64)
   Musical adapted by James T. Tanner, with lyrics by Adrian Ross, from
   Filmzauber by Rudolph Schanzer and Rudolph Bernauer. Music by Walter
   Kollo, Willy Bredschneider and Albert Sirmay. Produced by the Messrs.
   Shubert. 44th Street Theatre, Dec. 29, 1913.

THE QUEEN of the MOVIES (104)
   Musical comedy adapted by Glen MacDonough from *Die Kino-Königin* by
   Julius Freund and Georg Okonkowski. Music by Jean Gilbert. Produced by
   Thomas W. Ryley. Globe Theatre, Jan. 12, 1914.

SARI (151)
> Operetta adapted by C. C. S. Cushing (sometimes called "Alphabet" Cushing) and E. P. Heath from *Der Zigeunerprimas* by Julius Wilhelm and Fritz Grünbaum. Music by Emmerich Kálmán, who came to the United States to live shortly after this show. Produced by Henry W. Savage. Liberty Theatre,. Jan. 13, 1914. Moved to New Amsterdam Theatre, Apr. 13, 1914.

THE LAUGHING HUSBAND (48)
> Musical adapted by Arthur Wimperis from *Der Lachende Ehemann* by Julius Brammer and Alfred Grünwald. Music by Edmund Eysler. Produced by Charles Frohman. Knickerbocker Theatre, Feb. 2, 1914.

MAIDS OF ATHENS (22)
> Operetta adapted by Carolyn Wells from an unlisted text by Victor Leon. Music by Franz Lehár. Produced by Henry W. Savage. New Amsterdam Theatre, Mar. 18, 1914.

1914-15

THE HIGH COST of LOVING (75)
> Adapted by Frank Mandel from an uncredited source. Produced by A. H. Woods. Republic Theatre, Aug. 25, 1914. Moved to 39th Street Theatre, Nov. 16, 1914.

THE ONLY GIRL (240)
> Musical based on the 1912-13 adaptation *Our Wives*. Text by Henry Blossom. Music by Victor Herbert. Produced by Joe Weber. 39th Street Theatre, Nov. 2, 1914. Moved to Lyric Theatre, Nov. 16, 1914.

THE SONG of SONGS (191)
> Adapted by Edward Sheldon from *Das Hohe Lied*, a novel by Hermann Sudermann. Produced by A. H. Woods. Eltinge Theatre, Dec. 22, 1914. Scene and characters Americanized.

THE PEASANT GIRL (111)
> Musical adapted by Edgar Smith, with lyrics by Herbert Reynolds and Harold Atteridge, from an unlisted text by Leo Stein. Music by Oskar Nedbal, with additional numbers by Rudolph Friml. Produced by the Messrs. Shubert. 44th Street Theatre, Mar. 2, 1915.

TAKING CHANCES (85)
> Adapted by Benrimo and Morgan from an unlisted text by Paul Frank and Siegfried Geyer. Produced by the Messrs. Shubert. 39th Street Theatre, Mar. 17, 1915.

A MODERN EVE (56)
> Musical adapted by William H. Hough and Benjamin Hapgood Burt from an unlisted text by Georg Okonkowski and A. Schönfeld. Music by Jean Gilbert and Victor Holländer. Casino Theatre, May 3, 1915.

1915-16

THE BLUE PARADISE (356)
Musical adapted by Edgar Smith, with lyrics by Herbert Reynolds, from an unlisted text by Leo Stein and Bela Jenbasch (sometimes listed as Jenbach). Music by Edmund Eysler, with additional numbers by Sigmund Romberg. Produced by the Messrs. Shubert. Casino Theatre, Aug. 15, 1915. Moved to 44th Street Theatre, May 29, 1916.

°LITERATURE (?)
Translated by Elsie Plaut from *Literatur* by Arthur Schnitzler. Bandbox Theatre, Nov. 8, 1915.

°THE TENOR (?)
Translated by André Tridon from *Der Kammersänger* by Frank Wedekind. Both *Literature* and *The Tenor* were in the one-act play series of the Washington Square Players beginning Oct. 15, 1915, and playing through May 20, 1916. There was a total of 16 plays in the repertory. *The Tenor* opened on Jan. 10, 1916. All were given at the Bandbox Theatre.

ALONE AT LAST (180)
Operetta adapted by Edgar Smith and Joseph Herbert, with lyrics by Matthew Woodward, from *Endlich Allein* by A. M. Willner and Robert Bodansky. Music by Franz Lehár, with additional music by Gaetano Merola. Produced by the Messrs. Shubert. Oct. 14, 1915.

THE WEAVERS (87)
Translated by Mary Morrison from *Die Weber* by Gerhart Hauptmann. Garden Theatre, Dec. 14, 1915. Staged by Augustin Duncan and Emanuel Reicher.

SYBIL (168)
Musical adapted by Harry Graham, with lyrics by Harry B. Smith, from an unlisted text by Max Brody and Frank Martos. Music by Victor Jacobi. Produced by Charles Frohman. Liberty Theatre, Jan. 10, 1916.

1916-17

THE GIRL from BRAZIL (61)
Musical adapted by Edgar Smith from an unlisted text by Julius Brammer and Alfred Grünwald. Music by Robert Winterberg, with additional music by Sigmund Romberg. Produced by the Messrs. Shubert. 44th Street Theatre, Aug. 30, 1916.

°LITERATURE (?)
Same version as previous season's.

°ALTRUISM (?)
Translated by Benjamin F. Glazer from an unlisted text by Karl Ettlinger. Nov. 13, 1916, Comedy Theatre.

°THE POOR FOOL (?)
Translated by Mrs. F. E. Washburn-Freund from *Der Arme Narr* by Hermann Bahr. Mar. 21, 1917. This one-acter, and the two listed above, were on the schedule of the Washington Square Players which began on Aug. 30, 1916, and played through the season. The group gave a total of 22 plays.

FLORA BELLA (112)
Operetta adapted by Cosmo Hamilton from an unlisted text by Felix Dörmann. Music by Charles Cuvillier and Milton Schwarzwald. Produced by John Cort. Casino Theatre, Sept. 11, 1916. Moved to 44th Street Theatre, Nov. 27, 1916.

FOLLOW ME (78)
Musical comedy adapted by Robert B. Smith from an unlisted text by Felix Dörmann and Leo Ascher. Music by Sigmund Romberg. Consequently, this was a play turned into a musical in the adaptation. Produced by the Messrs. Shubert. Casino Theatre, Nov. 29, 1916.

THE MASTER (47)
Translated by Benjamin F. Glazer from *Der Meister* by Hermann Bahr. Produced by the Henry B. Harris Estate. Fulton Theatre, Dec. 5, 1916. Moved to Bandbox Theatre, Jan. 8, 1917.

HER SOLDIER BOY (198)
Musical adapted by Rida Johnson Young from an unlisted text by Victor Leon. Music by Emmerich Kálmán, with additional music by Sigmund Romberg. Produced by the Messrs. Shubert. Astor Theatre, Dec. 6, 1916. Moved to Lyric, Apr. 30, 1917, and to Shubert, May 14, 1917.

THE WANDERER (108)
Translated by Maurice V. Samuels from *Der Verlorene Sohn* by Wilhelm Schmidtbonn. Play based on the parable of the prodigal son. Incidental music by Anselm Götzl. Produced by William Elliott, F. Ray Comstock, and Morris Gest. Manhattan Opera House, Feb. 1, 1917.

THE AWAKENING of SPRING (1)
Uncredited translation of *Frühlings Erwachen* by Frank Wedekind. Membership production under auspices of the Medical Review of Reviews. 39th Street Theatre, Mar. 30, 1917.

GRASSHOPPER (3 matinées)
Adapted by Padraic Colum and Mrs. F. E. Washburn-Freund from a play by Eduard Keyserling. Produced by Iden Payne. Maxine Elliott Theatre, Apr. 7, 1917.

1917-18

MY LADY'S GLOVE (16)
Operetta adapted by Edgar Smith and Edward A. Paulton. No mention of any German source, but music was by Oscar Strauss. Beginning this season producers stop admitting to a play being from the German. There is no

telling how many such uncredited texts there were. Additional music for *My Lady's Glove* by Sigmund Romberg. Produced by the Messrs. Shubert. Lyric Theatre, June 18, 1917.

THE RIVIERA GIRL (78)
Musical adapted by Guy Bolton and P. G. Wodehouse from *Das Schwarz-waldmädel*. Music by Emmerich Kálmán. Produced by Klaw and Erlanger. New Amsterdam Theatre, Sept. 24, 1917. Program did not list indebtedness to source, but music was recognized, even though characters and settings were changed.

THE STAR GAZER (8)
Musical adapted by Cosmo Hamilton, with lyrics by Matthew C. Woodward. No listing of source. Music by Franz Lehár. Produced by the Messrs. Shubert. Plymouth Theatre, Nov. 26, 1917.

°THE FESTIVAL of BACCHUS (?)
Translated by Charles Henry Meltzer from *Das Bacchusfest* by Arthur Schnitzler. Greenwich Village Theatre, Nov. 15, 1917. Directed by Frank Conroy, who together with Meltzer formed an off-Broadway production company.

JOSEPHINE (24)
Adapted by Dr. Washburn-Freund from *Josephine* by Hermann Bahr. Produced by Arnold Daly. Knickerbocker Theatre, Jan. 28, 1918. Staged by Daly who also starred. Play was accused of being German propaganda; the charge was refuted in the *Times* by Daly.

THE MASTER (39)
Adapted by Benjamin F. Glazer from *Der Meister* by Hermann Bahr. Produced by Arnold Daly. Hudson Theatre, Feb. 19, 1918.

°THE BIG SCENE (?)
Translated by Charles Henry Meltzer from *Grosse Szene* by Arthur Schnitzler. Produced by the Greenwich Village Players. Greenwich Village Theatre, Apr. 18, 1918 through May 18, 1918. Was on same program of one-acters with O'Neill's *'Ile*.

1918-19

Not one play this season is admitted to have been derived from a Germanic source, but a few of the operettas sound suspicious.

1919-20

°LAST MASKS (?)
Translated by Grace Isabel Colbron from *Die Letzten Masken* by Arthur Schnitzler. Provincetown Players, Mar. 26, 1920.

1920-21

°YOUTH (7)
Uncredited translation (but probably by Herman Bernstein) from *Jugend* by
Max Halbe. Produced by Conroy and Meltzer. Greenwich Village Theatre,
Oct. 26, 1920. Staged by Emanuel Reicher.

°THE MANDARIN (?)
Adapted by Herman Bernstein from an unlisted play by Paul Frank. Princess Theatre, Nov. 11, 1920.

THY NAME IS WOMAN (120)
Translated by Benjamin F. Glazer from *Der Weibsteufel* by Karl Schönherr
(though the program listed the play as being by "Schoner and Glazer").
Produced by William A. Brady. Playhouse, Nov. 15, 1920.

THE LAST WALTZ (43, but an unknown additional number the next season)
Musical adapted by Harold Atteridge and Edward Delaney Dunn from *Der
Letzte Walzer* by Julius Brammer and Alfred Grünwald. Music by Oscar
Strauss. Produced by the Messrs. Shubert. Century Theatre, May 10, 1921.
Hero changed to an American adventurer abroad.

1921-22

THE MERRY WIDOW (56)
Revival of adaptation of 1907-1908. Produced by Henry W. Savage. Knickerbocker Theatre, Sept. 5, 1921.

BLOSSOM TIME (576)
Musical adapted by Dorothy Donnelly from *Das Dreimäderlhaus* by Willner
and Reichert. Music based on melodies of Franz Schubert by E. Berte,
arranged by Sigmund Romberg. Produced by the Messrs. Shubert. Ambassador Theatre, Sept. 29, 1921.

°THE CHILDREN'S TRAGEDY (8)
Translated by Benjamin F. Glazer from *Kindertragödie* by Karl Schönherr.
Produced by Arnold Daly. Greenwich Village Theatre, Oct. 10, 1921.

THE CHOCOLATE SOLDIER (83)
Revival of adaptation of 1909-10. Produced by the Messrs. Shubert. Century
Theatre, Dec. 12, 1921.

FROM MORN to MIDNIGHT (2 subscription performances)
Translated by Ashley Dukes from *Von Morgens bis Mitternachts* by Georg
Kaiser. Produced by the Theatre Guild. Garrick Theatre, May 14, 1922.
Directed by and starring Frank Reicher.

1922-23

FROM MORN to MIDNIGHT (24)
Same production as previous season's special performance. Produced by the
Theatre Guild. Frazee Theatre, June 26, 1922.

ROSE BERND (87)
Adapted by Ludwig Lewisohn from *Rose Bernd* by Gerhart Hauptmann. Produced by Arthur Hopkins. Longacre Theatre, Sept. 26, 1922. Ethel Barrymore starred.

THE YANKEE PRINCESS (80)
Adapted by William LeBaron, with lyrics by B. G. De Sylva, from *Die Bajadere* by Julius Brammer and Alfred Grünwald. Music by Emmerich Kálmán. Produced by A. L. Erlanger. Knickerbocker Theatre, Oct. 2, 1922.

THE LADY in ERMINE (232)
Musical adapted by Frederick Lonsdale and Cyrus Wood, with lyrics by Harry Graham and Cyrus Wood, from *Die Frau im Hermelin* by Rudolph Schanzer and Ernst Welisch. Music by Jean Gilbert, with additional music by Alfred Goodman. Produced by the Messrs. Shubert. Ambassador Theatre, Oct. 2, 1922.

SPRINGTIME of YOUTH (68)
Musical adapted by Matthew C. Woodward and Cyrus Wood from an unlisted text by Bernauer and Schanzer. Music by Walter Kollo, with additional music by Sigmund Romberg. Produced by the Messrs. Shubert. Broadhurst Theatre, Oct. 26, 1922. Setting transplanted to New England.

JOHANNES KREISLER (65)
Adapted by Louis N. Parker from *Die Wunderlichen Geschichten des Kapellmeisters Kreisler* by Carl Meinhard and Rudolph Bernauer, after E. T. A. Hoffmann. Music by Emil von Rezniczek. Produced by the Selwyns. Apollo Theatre, Dec. 20, 1922. Staged by Frank Reicher and starred Jacob Ben-Ami.

JITTA'S ATONEMENT (37)
Adapted by George Bernard Shaw from *Frau Gitta's Sühne* by Siegfried Trebitsch. Produced by Lee Shubert. Comedy Theatre, Jan. 17, 1923. Far removed from its source.

CAROLINE (149 and an unknown additional number the following season)
Adapted by Harry B. Smith and E. Kunneke from an unlisted text by Hermann Haller and Edward Rideamus (Fritz Oliven). Music by Edward Rideamus, with additional music by Alfred Goodman. Produced by the Messrs. Shubert. Ambassador Theatre, Jan. 31, 1923. Settings and characters Americanized.

1923-24

THE RACE with the SHADOW (?)
Uncredited translation from *Der Wettlauf mit dem Schatten* by Wilhelm von Scholz. Produced by the Theatre Guild. Garrick Theatre, Dec. 14, 1923.

THE MIRACLE (175 and unknown number into next season)
Play without dialogue by Max Reinhardt from *Das Mirakel* by Karl Volmöller. Produced by Ray Comstock and Morris Gest. Century Theatre, Jan. 16, 1924.

BEGGAR on HORSEBACK (144 and unknown number into next season)
By Marc Connelly and George S. Kaufman, freely adapted from *Hans Sonnenstossers Höllenfahrt* by Paul Apel. Produced by Winthrop Ames. Broadhurst Theatre, Feb. 12, 1924.

THE ASSUMPTION of HANNELE (3)
Translated by Charles Henry Meltzer from *Hanneles Himmelfahrt* by Gerhart Hauptmann. Produced by John D. Williams. Cort Theatre, Feb. 15, 1924.

MAN and the MASSES (32)
Translated by Louis H. Untermeyer from *Masse-Mensch* by Ernst Toller. Produced by the Theatre Guild. Garrick Theatre, Apr. 14, 1924. Staged and designed by Lee Simonson.

BLOSSOM TIME (24)
Revival by the Messrs. Shubert of the adaptation of 1921-22. Jolson Theatre, May 19, 1924.

1924-25

THE WEREWOLF (112)
Adapted by Gladys Unger from *Der Werwolf* by Rudolph Lothar. Produced by George B. McLellan. 49th Street Theatre, Aug. 25, 1924.

MME. POMPADOUR (80)
Musical adapted by Clare Kummer from *Madam Pompadour* by Rudolph Schanzer and Ernst Welisch. Music by Leo Fall. Produced by Charles Dillingham and Martin Beck. Martin Beck Theatre, Nov. 11, 1924.

THE STUDENT PRINCE (183)
Operetta with book and lyrics by Dorothy Donnelly. Music by Sigmund Romberg. Based on Wilhelm Meyer-Förster's *Alt Heidelberg*. Produced by the Messrs. Shubert. Jolson Theatre, Dec. 2, 1924.

THE MONGREL (32)
Adapted by Elmer Rice from Frances C. Fay's translation of an unlisted play by Hermann Bahr. Produced by Warren P. Munsell. Longacre Theatre, Dec. 15, 1924.

THE LOVE SONG (135)
Operetta adapted from the Hungarian and German by Harry B. Smith. Unlisted title by Ferago, Nador, Klein, and Bredschneider was source. Music by Jacques Offenbach, arranged by Edward Kunneke. Produced by the Messrs. Shubert. Century Theatre, Jan. 13, 1925. Based on an incident in the life of Offenbach.

°BEYOND (?)
Translated by Rita Matthias from *Jenseits* by Walter Hasenclever. Produced by the Provincetown Players at their theatre, Jan. 26, 1925.

THE DEPTHS (31)

Uncredited translation from an unlisted text by Hans Müller. Produced by
Arch Selwyn in association with Adolph Klauber. Broadhurst Theatre, Jan.
27, 1925. Melodrama in old style about a girl born in sin and poverty who
goes wrong.

LOUIE the 14TH (79)

Musical adapted by Arthur Wimperis from an unlisted text by F. and J.
Wilhelm. Music added by Sigmund Romberg. Produced by Florenz Ziegfeld. Cosmopolitan Theatre, Mar. 3, 1925.

BEGGAR on HORSEBACK (16)

Revival of previous season's production with a few cast changes. Shubert
Theatre, Mar. 23, 1925.

TAPS (32)

Uncredited translation (probably by Charles Swickard) of *Zapfenstreich* by
Franz Adam Beyerlein. Produced by the Messrs. Shubert. Broadhurst Theatre, April 14, 1925.

THE LOVES of LULU (16)

Translated by Samuel A. Eliot, Jr., from *Erdgeist* by Frank Wedekind. 49th
Street Theatre, May 11, 1925.

1925-26

THE CALL of LOVE (19)

Adapted by Dorothy Donnelly from *Der Ruf des Lebens* by Arthur Schnitzler. Produced by the Actors' Theatre. Comedy Theatre, Oct. 9, 1925.

MORALS (40)

Adapted by Charles Recht with assistance by Sidney Howard from *Morale*
by Ludwig Thoma. Produced by the Actors' Theatre. Comedy Theatre, Nov.
30, 1925.

THE LOVE CITY (42)

Uncredited adaptation from an unlisted text by Hans Bachwitz. Little Theatre, Jan. 25, 1926.

GOAT SONG (58)

Translated by Ruth Langner from *Bocksgesang* by Franz Werfel. Produced
by the Theatre Guild. Guild Theatre, Jan. 25, 1926. Staged by Jacob Ben-
Ami. Cast included Alfred Lunt, Lynn Fontanne, Blanche Yurka, and Edward G. Robinson.

MAGDA (24)

Revised translation by C. E. A. Winslow of *Heimat* by Hermann Sudermann. Revived by Lawrence J. Anhalt. 49th Street Theatre, Jan. 26, 1926.

BLOSSOM TIME (16)

Revival of adaptation of 1921-22. Produced by the Messrs. Shubert. Jolson
Theatre, Mar. 8, 1926.

°THE APOTHECARY (27)
>   Adapted by Ann Macdonald from *Der Apotheker* by Joseph Haydn. Score
>   revised by Howard Barlow. Produced by the Neighborhood Playhouse.
>   Neighborhood Theatre, Mar. 16, 1926. Actually a one-act opera, but this
>   production used actors to provide speech and action while the music came
>   from singers behind the scenery. It was an experiment to see if opera could
>   be done without the attendant evil of operatic acting.

SCHWEIGER (30)
>   Translated by Jack Charash and William A. Drake from *Schweiger* by Franz
>   Werfel. Produced by the Fifth Avenue Playhouse. Mansfield Theatre, Mar.
>   23, 1926. Staged by and starred Jacob Ben-Ami.

1926-27

NAUGHTY RIQUETTE (88)
>   Musical adapted by Harry B. Smith from unlisted text by Rudolph Schanzer
>   and Ernst Welisch. Produced by the Messrs. Shubert. Cosmopolitan Theatre,
>   Sept. 13, 1926.

COUNTESS MARITZA (318)
>   Musical adapted by Harry B. Smith from *Gräfin Mariza* by Julius Brammer
>   and Alfred Grünwald. Music by Emmerich Kálmán. Produced by the
>   Messrs. Shubert. Shubert Theatre, Sept. 18, 1926.

JUAREZ and MAXIMILIAN (48)
>   Translated by Ruth Langner from *Juarez und Maximilian* by Franz Werfel.
>   Produced by the Theatre Guild. Guild Theatre, Oct. 11, 1926.

WHAT NEVER DIES (39)
>   Translated by Ernest Boyd from an unlisted comedy by Alexander Engel.
>   Produced by David Belasco. Lyceum Theatre, Dec. 28, 1926. Staged by
>   Belasco and starred E. H. Sothern. The whole production was as if out of
>   the past.

THE CIRCUS PRINCESS (192)
>   Musical adapted by Harry B. Smith from *Die Zirkusprinzessin* by Julius
>   Brammer and Alfred Grünwald. Music by Emmerich Kálmán. Produced by
>   the Messrs. Shubert. Winter Garden, Apr. 25, 1927.

1927-28

THE COMMAND to LOVE (247)
>   Adapted by Herman Bernstein and Brian Marlow from an unlisted text by
>   Rudolph Lothar and Fritz Gottwald. Produced by William A. Brady and
>   Dwight Deere Wiman, in association with John Tuerk. Longacre Theatre,
>   Sept. 20, 1927. This piece of *Kitsch* had to be cleaned up after its opening
>   in order not to be closed by the police.

THE GARDEN of EDEN (23)
Adapted by Avery Hopwood from an unlisted text by Rudolph Bernauer and Rudolph Oesterreicher. Produced by Arch Selwyn. Selwyn Theatre, Sept. 26, 1927.

THE PATRIOT (12)
Adapted by Ashley Dukes from *Der Patriot* by Alfred Neumann. Produced by Gilbert Miller. Majestic Theatre, Jan. 19, 1928. Staged by Mr. Miller and starred John Gielgud.

IMPROVISATIONS in JUNE (14)
Translated by Susanne Behn and Cecil Lewis from *Improvisationen im Juni* by Max Mohr. Produced by the Civic Repertory Theatre, Mar. 5, 1928.

12,000 (64)
Adapted by William A. Drake from *Zwölftausend* by Bruno Frank. Produced by the Garrick Players. Garrick Theatre, Mar. 12, 1928.

VOLPONE (?)
Translated by Ruth Langner from Stefan Zweig's adaptation of Ben Jonson's play. Produced by the Theatre Guild. Guild Theatre, Apr. 9, 1928.

COUNTESS MARITZA (16)
Revival of previous season's adaptation. Produced by the Messrs. Shubert. Century Theatre, April 9, 1928.

ANNA (31)
Adapted by Herman Bernstein and Brian Marlow from an unlisted text by Rudolph Lothar. Produced by Samuel Samach. Lyceum Theatre, May 15, 1928.

1928-29

THE PHANTOM LOVER (15)
Translated by Herman Bernstein and Adolph E. Meyer from *Oktobertag* by Georg Kaiser. Produced by Gustav Blum, who also directed. 49th St. Theatre, Sept. 4, 1928.

WHITE LILACS (136)
Musical adapted by Harry B. Smith from an unlisted text by Sigurd Johannsen which was based on the relationship of Frederic Chopin and George Sand. Music by Karl Hajos from melodies by Chopin. Produced by the Messrs. Shubert. Shubert Theatre, Sept. 10, 1928. An attempt to do with Chopin what *Blossom Time* did with Schubert.

CAPRICE (186)
Translated and adapted by Philip Moeller from an unlisted title by Sil-Vara (Geza Silberer). Produced by the Theatre Guild. Guild Theatre, Dec. 31, 1928. Mr. Moeller staged the production and Lunt and Fontanne starred.

MUSIC in MAY (80)

> Musical adapted by Fanny Todd Mitchell, with lyrics by J. Kiern Brennan, from an unlisted text by Heinz Merley and Kurt Breuer. Music by Emil Berte rearranged by Maury Rubens. Produced by the Messrs. Shubert. Casino Theatre, Apr. 1, 1929.

1929-30

CANDLE LIGHT (128)

> Adapted by P. G. Wodehouse from an unlisted text by Siegfried Geyer. Produced and staged by Gilbert Miller. Empire Theatre, Sept. 30, 1929. Starred Leslie Howard and Gertrude Lawrence.

KARL and ANNA (49)

> Translated by Ruth Langner from *Karl und Anna* by Leonhard Frank. Produced by the Theatre Guild. Guild Theatre, Oct. 7, 1929.

LADIES DON'T LIE (12)

> Translated by Herman Bernstein from an unlisted comedy by Paul Frank. Produced by Radiant Productions, Inc. Gallo Theatre, Oct. 10, 1929.

THE BOOSTER (12)

> Adapted by Nate Reid from an unlisted comedy by Nertz and Friedmann. Produced by Y-DNA, Inc. Bayes Theatre, Oct. 24, 1929.

A WONDERFUL NIGHT (125)

> Adapted by Fanny Todd Mitchell from the Haffner-Genée text of *Die Fledermaus*. Music by Johann Strauss. Previous versions had been known as *The Merry Countess* and *Night Birds*. Produced by the Messrs. Shubert. Majestic Theatre, Oct. 31, 1929. One of the leading roles was played by a young man named Archie Leach, later known as Cary Grant.

THE MERRY WIDOW (16)

> The standard adaptation of 1907-1908. Produced by the Jolson Theatre Musical Comedy Co. Jolson Theatre, Dec. 2, 1929.

JOSEF SUSS (40)

> Adapted by Ashley Dukes from Lion Feuchtwanger's novel, *Jud Süss*, known in English as *Power*. Produced by Charles Dillingham in association with J. C. Williamson, Ltd. Erlanger's Theatre, Jan. 20, 1930.

THE CHOCOLATE SOLDIER (25)

> Revival of the standard adaptation of 1909-10. Revived by the Jolson Theatre Musical Comedy Co. Jolson Theatre, Jan. 27, 1930.

SARI (15)

> Revival of the adaptation of 1913-14. Produced by Eugene Endrey. Liberty Theatre, Jan. 29, 1930.

OUT of a BLUE SKY (17)

> Adapted by Leslie Howard from *Das Blaue vom Himmel* by Hans Chlumberg. Produced by Tom Van Dycke. Booth Theatre, Feb. 8, 1930.

THE COUNT of LUXEMBOURG (16)
Revival of adaptation of 1912-13. Produced by the Jolson Theatre Musical Comedy Co. Jolson Theatre, Feb. 17, 1930. Jolson, and his director, Milton Aborn, were reviving many standard operettas for limited engagements, extendable if business warranted, this season.

VOLPONE (8)
Revival by Theatre Guild of 1927-28 play. Liberty Theatre, Mar. 10, 1930. Cast largely changed from earlier production.

THREE LITTLE GIRLS (104)
Musical adapted by Marie Hecht and Gertrude Purcell, with lyrics by Harry B. Smith, from an unlisted text by Herman Feiner and Bruno Hardt-Warden. Music by Walter Kollo. Produced by the Messrs. Shubert. Shubert Theatre, Apr. 14, 1930.

1930-31

DANCING PARTNER (119)
Adapted by Frederic and Fanny Horton from an unlisted text by Alexander Engel and Alfred Grünwald. Produced and staged by David Belasco. Belasco Theatre, Aug. 5, 1930.

THE GREEN COCKATOO (one week)
Uncredited translation of *Der Grüne Kakadu* by Arthur Schnitzler. Produced by Eva Le Gallienne's Civic Repertory Theatre. Civic Theatre. Repertory began Oct. 6, 1930.

ROAR CHINA (72)
Ruth Langner's translation of Leo Lania's German version of a Russian play by Sergei Tretyakov. Produced by the Theatre Guild. Martin Beck Theatre, Oct. 27, 1930.

GRAND HOTEL (459)
Translated by William A. Drake from *Menschen im Hotel* by Vicki Baum, assisted by Max Reinhardt. Produced by Herman Shumlin, who also directed. National Theatre, Nov. 13, 1930.

ANATOL (45)
Adapted by Harley Granville-Barker from *Anatol* by Arthur Schnitzler. Produced by Bela Blau. Lyceum Theatre, Jan. 16, 1931.

THE STUDENT PRINCE (42)
Revival of the Dorothy Donnelly adaptation of *Alt Heidelberg* with music by Sigmund Romberg. Produced by the Messrs. Shubert. Majestic Theatre, Jan. 29, 1931.

BLOSSOM TIME (29)
Revival of adaptation of 1921-22. Produced by the Messrs. Shubert. Ambassador Theatre, Mar. 4, 1931.

NAPI (21)

Adapted by Brian Marlow from an unlisted comedy by Julius Berstl. Produced by L. Lawrence Weber. Longacre Theatre, Mar. 11, 1931.

MIRACLE at VERDUN (49)

Translated by Julian Leigh from *Wunder um Verdun* by Hans Chlumberg. Produced by the Theatre Guild. Martin Beck Theatre, Mar. 16, 1931.

THE WONDER BAR (76)

"Cabaret Drama" adapted by Irving Caesar and Aben Kandel from an unlisted text by Geza Herczeg and Karl Farkas. Music by Robert Katscher. Produced by the Messrs. Shubert and Morris Gest. Bayes Theatre, Mar. 17, 1931. Starred Al Jolson.

JOY of LIVING (16)

Uncredited adaptation of an unlisted comedy by Rudolph Lothar and Hans Bachwitz. Produced by Fred G. Womrath and George W. Lederer. Masque Theatre, April 6, 1931. Not to be mistaken for the adaptation of Sudermann's *Es Lebe das Leben* which had the same title.

1931-32

THE MERRY WIDOW (32)

Revival of standard adaptation of 1907-1908. Revived by Civic Light Opera Co. Erlanger's Theatre, Sept. 7, 1931. Revived again on Feb. 22, 1932, for 16 more performances.

THE CHOCOLATE SOLDIER (16)

Revival of standard adaptation of 1909-10. Produced by Civic Light Opera Co. Erlanger's Theatre, Sept. 21, 1931. The Company was again producing limited engagements of revivals of operettas.

BLOODY LAUGHTER (35)

Adapted by Forrest Wilson and William Schack from *Hinkemann* by Ernst Toller. Produced by Maurice Schwartz, who also starred and directed. 49th Street Theatre, Dec. 4, 1931.

EXPERIENCE UNNECESSARY (45)

Adapted by Gladys Unger from an unlisted comedy by Wilhelm Sterck. Produced by the Messrs. Shubert. Longacre Theatre, Dec. 30, 1931. Twenty-five more performances at National Theatre, March 26, 1932.

A LITTLE RACKETEER (48)

Musical adapted by Harry Clarke, with lyrics by Edward Eliscu, from an unlisted text by F. Kalbfuss and R. Wilde. Music by Haskell Brown; thus it was a comedy turned into a musical in adaptation. Produced by the Messrs. Shubert. 44th Street Theatre, Jan. 18, 1932.

COLLISION (7)

Adapted by John Anderson from an unlisted comedy by Lothar and Sebesi. Produced by Lewis E. Gensler. Gaiety Theatre, Feb. 16, 1932.

MARCHING BY (12)
Musical adapted by Harry Clarke and Harry B. Smith from an unlisted title by Ernst Neubach. Music by Jean Gilbert, augmented by Gordon and Revel in the adaptation. Produced by the Messrs. Shubert. Chanin's 46th Street Theatre, Mar. 3, 1932.

1932-33

THE STORK IS DEAD (27)
Adapted by Frederic and Fanny Hatton from an unlisted Viennese farce by Hans Kottow. Produced by A. H. Woods. 48th Street Theatre, Sept. 23, 1932.

THE DUBARRY (87)
Operetta adapted by Rowland Leigh and Desmond Carter from *Die Dubarry* by Paul Knepler and J. M. Willeminsky. Music by Carl Millöcker, arranged by Theo Mackeben. Produced by Morris Green and Tillie Leblang. George M. Cohan Theatre, Nov. 22, 1932. This was a vehicle for Grace Moore.

GIRLS in UNIFORM (12)
Adapted by Barbara Burnham from *Gestern und Heute* (*Mädchen in Uniform* in the film version which is better known) by Christa Winsloe. Produced by Sidney Phillips. Booth Theatre, Dec. 30, 1932.

THE THREE-PENNY OPERA (12)
Adapted by Gifford Cochran and Jerrold Krimsky from *Die Dreigroschenoper* by Bertolt Brecht, based on John Gay's *The Beggar's Opera* (but only superficially). Music by Kurt Weill. Produced by John Krimsky and Gifford Cochran. Empire Theatre, April 13, 1933.

°THE YEA-SAYER (?)
Translated by Alice Mattulath from *Der Jasager* by Bertolt Brecht, based on the Japanese Noh play, *Taniko* in Arthur Waley's translation. Music by Kurt Weill. Produced by the Music School of the Henry Street Settlement. Grand Street Playhouse, April 25, 1933.

°SICKNESS of YOUTH (?)
Uncredited adaptation from *Krankheit der Jugend* by Ferdinand Bruckner (Theodor Taggers). Produced by Paul Gilmore. Cherry Lane Theatre. This was one of a series of plays which began on June 18, 1933, but the exact date of production is unknown.

1933-34

°THE CHALK CIRCLE (?)
Adapted by I. S. Richter from *Der Kreidekreis* by Klabund (Alfred Henschke). Produced by the Playmillers. Union Methodist Episcopal Church, Aug. 21, 1933.

HER MAN of WAX (14)

Adapted by Julian Thompson from *Napoleon Greift Ein* by Walter Hasenclever. Produced by Lee Shubert. Shubert Theatre, Oct. 11, 1933.

CHAMPAGNE, SEC (113)

Adapted by Lawrence Langner (under the name of Alan Child), with lyrics by Robert A. Simon, from *Die Fledermaus*. Produced by Dwight Deere Wiman and Lawrence Langner. Morosco Theatre, Oct. 14, 1933.

A HAT, a COAT, a GLOVE (13)

Adapted by William A. Drake from an unlisted title by Wilhelm Speyer. Produced by Crosby Gaige and D. K. Weiskopf. Selwyn Theatre, Jan. 31, 1934. A murder story with settings and characters removed to America.

THE CHOCOLATE SOLDIER (13)

The standard adaptation of 1909-10. Revived by Purcell and Brian. St. James Theatre, May 2, 1934.

KULTUR (10)

Adapted by Adolf Phillipp from *Kultur* by Theodor Wächter (possibly the same man). Produced by J. J. Vincent. Mansfield Theatre.

1934-35

THE RED CAT (13)

Adapted by Jessie Ernst from an unlisted title by Rudolph Lothar and Hans Adler. Produced by A. H. Woods in association with 20th Century Pictures Corp. Broadhurst Theatre, Sept. 19, 1934. This play served as the basis for the 1951 motion picture, *On the Riviera*, a vehicle for Danny Kaye.

THE GREAT WALTZ (298)

Musical adapted by Moss Hart, with lyrics by Desmond Carter, from an unlisted operetta by A. M. Willner, Heinz Reichert, Ernst Marischka and Caswell Garth, based on the lives of the Strausses. Music by Johann Strauss, the elder and the younger. Produced by Max Gordon. Center Theatre, Sept. 22, 1934.

THE CHINESE NIGHTINGALE (8)

Adapted by James L. A. Burrell from an unlisted title by Hans Schuwedel and Lasar Galpern, based on a story by Hans Christian Andersen. Music added by Alan Shulman. Produced by the American Children's Theatre. Theatre of Young America, Oct. 5, 1934.

°SAILORS of CATTARO (96)

Translated by Keene Wallis and adapted by Michael Blankfort from *Die Matrosen von Cattaro* by Friedrich Wolf. Produced by Theatre Union. Civic Repertory Theatre, Dec. 10, 1934.

A JOURNEY by NIGHT (7)

Adapted by Arthur Goodrich from a play by Leo Perutz which is sometimes known as *A Trip to Pressburg* in translation. Produced by the Messrs. Shubert. Shubert Theatre, Apr. 16, 1935.

1935-36

THE GREAT WALTZ (49)
Return of previous season's production. Revived by Max Gordon. Center Theatre, Aug. 5, 1935.

°THE MOTHER (36)
Translated by Paul Peters from *Die Mutter* by Bertolt Brecht, based on Maxim Gorky's novel of the same name. Music by Hanns Eisler. Produced by the Theatre Union. Civic Repertory Theatre, Nov. 19, 1935.

TOMORROW'S a HOLIDAY (8)
Adapted by Romney Brent from an unlisted title by Leo Perutz and Hans Adler. Produced by John Golden in association with Joseph Schildkraut. Golden Theatre, Dec. 30, 1935. Staged by George S. Kaufman.

THE CASE of CLYDE GRIFFITHS (?)
Translated by L. Campbell from *Eine Amerikanische Tragödie* by Erwin Piscator and Lina Goldschmitt, based on Theodore Dreiser's *An American Tragedy*. Produced by the Group Theatre. Ethel Barrymore Theatre, Mar. 13, 1936.

°RACES (?)
Uncredited adaptation from *Die Rassen* by Ferdinand Bruckner (Theodor Taggers). Hekscher Theatre.

1936-37

°HELP YOURSELF (82)
Adapted by John J. Coman from an unlisted title by Paul Vulpius. Produced by the Popular Price Unit of the Federal Theatre Project. Manhattan Theatre, July 14, 1936.

WHITE HORSE INN (223)
Adapted by David Freedman, with lyrics by Irving Caesar, from *Im Weissen Röss'l* by Oscar Blumenthal and Gustav Kadelburg, who had turned their own play into the libretto with music by Ralph Benatsky and Robert Stolz. Produced by Lawrence Rivers, Inc. Center Theatre, Oct. 1, 1936.

°THE PEPPER MILL (6)
Adapted by John Latouche and Edwin Denby from the cabaret review *Die Pfeffermühle* by W. H. Auden, Klaus Mann, Erich Mühsam, Ernst Toller, and Erika Mann. Music by Magnus Henning, Peter Krender, Herbert Murrill, and Werner Kruse. Music reset for adaptation by Aaron Copland. Produced by F. C. Coppicus in association with Columbia Concerts Corp. Chanin Auditorium, Jan. 5, 1937.

THE ETERNAL ROAD (153)
Adapted by William A. Drake from a translation by Ludwig Lewisohn of *Der Weg der Verheissung* by Franz Werfel. Music by Kurt Weill. Produced by Meyer Weisgal and Crosby Gaige. Manhattan Opera House, Jan. 7, 1937. Staged by Max Reinhardt. Sets by Norman Bel Geddes.

FREDERIKA (95)
Operetta adapted by Edward Eliscu from *Friedericke* by Franz Lehár (text uncredited). Produced by the Messrs. Shubert. Imperial Theatre, Feb. 4, 1937. Story based on an incident in the life of Goethe.

STORM over PATSY (48)
Adapted by James Bridie (O. H. Mavor) from *Sturm in Wasserglas* by Bruno Frank. Produced by the Theatre Guild. Guild Theatre, Mar. 8, 1937. Bridie's title was *Storm in a Teacup*. Production title was the Guild's variation.

YOUNG MADAME CONTI (22)
Adapted by Hubert Griffith and Benn W. Levy from an unlisted title by Bruno Frank. Produced by Bernard Klawans. Music Box Theatre, Mar. 31, 1937.

°THE MACHINE WRECKERS (3)
Translated by Ashley Dukes from *Die Maschinenstürmer* by Ernst Toller. Produced at Henry Street Settlement, Apr. 11, 1937.

°PROFESSOR MAMLOCK (76)
Translated by Anne Bromberger from *Professor Mamlock* by Friedrich Wolf. Produced by the Jewish Theatre Project of the Federal Theatre. Daly's 63rd Street Theatre, Apr. 13, 1937.

1937-38

°NO MORE PEACE (4)
Translated by Edward Crankshaw, with lyrics by W. H. Auden, from *Nie Wieder Friede!* by Ernst Toller. Music by Herbert Murrill. Part of the repertory of the WPA Federal Theatre Project at the Maxine Elliott Theatre. Repertory began Jan. 25, 1938, and ran through Feb. 12, 1938.

1938-39

YOU NEVER KNOW (78)
Musical adapted by Cole Porter and Rowland Leigh from an unlisted title by Robert Katscher, Siegfried Geyer, and Karl Farkas. Produced by Lee and J. J. Shubert in association with John Shubert. Winter Garden, Sept. 21, 1938.

°GLORIANA (5)
Uncredited adaptation of *Elizabeth von England* by Ferdinand Bruckner (Theodor Taggers). Songs by Thomas Jefferson Scott were interpolated in the adaptation. Produced by Theatre House, Inc. Little Theatre, Nov. 25, 1938.

BLOSSOM TIME (19)
Revival of standard adaptation of 1921-22. Produced by the Messrs. Shubert. 46th Street Theatre, Dec. 26, 1938.

THE MERCHANT of YONKERS (39)

Very freely adapted by Thornton Wilder from *Einen Jux Will Er Sich Machen* by Johann Nestroy, which was based on *A Day Well Spent* by John Oxenford. Produced by Herman Shumlin. Guild Theatre, Dec. 28, 1938. Directed by Max Reinhardt to whom it was dedicated, as was its revision some years later, *The Matchmaker*.

JEREMIAH (35)

Translated by Eden and Cedar Paul, with acting version by John Gassner and Worthington Miner, from *Jeremias* by Stefan Zweig. Incidental music by Chemjo Vinaver. Produced by the Theatre Guild. Guild Theatre, Feb. 3, 1939.

°JUSTICE (?)

Uncredited adaptation of a "one-act play" by Bertolt Brecht, but probably is taken from the independent segment, *"Rechtsfindung,"* from *Furcht und Elend des Dritten Reiches*. Produced by the New York Players as one of a bill of one-acters. In April of 1939.

1939-40

FROM VIENNA (79)

Musical revue adapted by John Latouche, Eva Frankin and Hugo Hauff from material by Lothar Metzl, Werner Michel, Hans Weigel, Jura Soyfer, Peter Hammerschlag, and David Greggory. Music by Werner Michel, Walter Drix, Otto Andreas, and Jimmy Berg. Produced by the Refugee Artists Group. Music Box, June 20, 1939.

REUNION in NEW YORK (89)

Review conceived by Lothar Metzl and Werner Michel. Sketches by Carl Don, Richard Alma, Richard Holden and Hans Lefebre. Lyrics by David Greggory, Peter Barry, and Stewart Arthur. Music by André Singer, Bert Silving, Berenece Kazounoff, and M. Cooper Paul. Produced by the American Viennese Group. Little Theatre, Feb. 21, 1940. Somewhat of a sequel to *From Vienna*.

A CASE of YOUTH (5)

Adapted by Wesley Towner from an unlisted comedy by Ludwig Hirshfeld and Eugene Wolf. Produced by Courtney Burr. National Theatre, Mar. 23, 1940.

1940-41

°THE CIRCLE of CHALK (?)

Translated by James Laver from *Der Kreiderkreis* by Klabund (Alfred Henschke). Produced by the Studio Theatre of the New School for Social Research under the direction of Erwin Piscator. Mar. 24, 1941.

GABRIELLE (2)

By Leonard Bercovici, based on the short story, *Tristan*, by Thomas Mann. Produced by Rowland Leigh. Maxine Elliott Theatre, Mar. 25, 1941.

°EVERYMAN (?)
Translated by George Sterling from *Jedermann*, Hugo von Hofmannsthal's
adaptation of the medieval play. Produced by Theatre Friendship House,
May 8, 1941.

1941-42

°THE CRIMINALS (15)
Translated by Edwin Denby and Rita Matthias from *Die Verbrecher* by
Ferdinand Bruckner (Theodor Taggers). Produced by the Studio Theatre.
New School for Social Research, Dec. 20, 1941.

ALL the COMFORTS of HOME (8)
Revival of an 1890 adaptation by William Gillette, revised by Helen
Jerome, of *Ein Toller Einfall* by Carl Laufs. Produced by Edith C. Ringling
in association with Mollie B. Steinberg. Longacre Theatre, May 25, 1942.

1942-43

THE CHOCOLATE SOLDIER (24)
Revival of standard adaptation of 1909-10. Produced by Joseph S. Tushinsky
and Hans Bartsch. Carnegie Hall, June 23, 1942.

THE MERRY WIDOW (39)
Revival of standard adaptation of 1907-1908. Produced by Joseph S. Tushinsky and Hans Bartsch. Carnegie Hall, July 15, 1942.

ROSALINDA (521)
Adapted by Gottfried Reinhardt, John Meehan, Jr., and Paul Kerby from
Max Reinhardt's version of *Die Fledermaus*. Produced by Lodewick Vroom
for the New Opera Co. 44th Street Theatre, Oct. 28, 1942.

°THE BEGGAR STUDENT (?)
New adaptation by Don Wilson and Alix Szilasi of *Der Bettelstudent* by
Karl Millöcker. Cosmopolitan Opera House, Sept. 25, 1942.

THE PIRATE (177)
Adapted by S. N. Behrman from *Der Seeräuber* by Ludwig Fulda. Produced
by the Playwrights' Company and the Theatre Guild. Martin Beck Theatre,
Nov. 25, 1942.

THE STUDENT PRINCE (153)
Revival of standard Donnelly-Romberg version. Produced by the Messrs.
Shubert. Broadway Theatre, June 8, 1943.

1943-44

THE MERRY WIDOW (322)
New version of libretto by Sidney Sheldon and Ben Roberts. Adrian Ross's
standard lyrics modernized by Robert Albert. New arrangement of Franz
Lehár's score by Robert Stolz. Produced by Yolanda Mero-Irion for the New
Opera Co. Majestic Theatre, Aug. 4, 1943.

BLOSSOM TIME (47)
> Revival of standard adaptation of 1921-22. Produced by the Messrs. Shubert. Ambassador Theatre, Sept. 4, 1943.

JACOBOWSKY and the COLONEL (417)
> Adapted by S. N. Behrman from *Jacobowsky und der Oberst* by Franz Werfel. Produced by the Theatre Guild in association with John H. Skirball. Martin Beck Theatre, Mar. 14, 1944. Staged by Elia Kazan.

HELEN GOES to TROY (97)
> Operetta adapted by Gottfried Reinhardt, John Meehan, Jr. and Herbert Baker from Max Reinhardt's version of Jacques Offenbach's *La Belle Helene*. Music arranged by Erich Korngold. Produced by Yolanda Mero-Irion for the New Opera Co. Alvin Theatre, Apr. 24, 1944. Settings were by Robert Edmond Jones.

°GAS (?)
> Uncredited adaptation of *Gas* (the entire trilogy) by Georg Kaiser. Produced by Erwin Piscator's Dramatic Workshop. New School for Social Research. The group was giving a series of plays. Date of first performance of *Gas* unknown.

1944-45

THE MERRY WIDOW (32)
> Same adaptation as the previous season's new version. Produced by Yolanda Mero-Irion and the New Opera Co. City Center, Oct. 7, 1944.

EMBEZZLED HEAVEN (52)
> Adapted by L. Bush-Fekete and Mary Helen Fay from Franz Werfel's novel, *Der Veruntreute Himmel*. Produced by the Theatre Guild. National Theatre, Oct. 31, 1944. Designed as a vehicle for Ethel Barrymore.

°THE PRIVATE LIFE of the MASTER RACE (6)
> Adapted by Eric Bentley from *Furcht und Elend des Dritten Reiches* by Bertolt Brecht. Music by Hanns Eisler. Produced by the Theatre of all Nations. Pauline Edwards Theatre of the City College of New York, June 12, 1945.

°MAEDCHEN in UNIFORM (?—although most ELT productions ran one week) Barbara Burnham's adaptation of Christa Winsloe's *Gestern und Heute* revived by Equity Library Theatre as one of its productions for this season.

1945-46

MR. STRAUSS GOES to BOSTON (12)
> Musical adapted by Leonard L. Levenson, with lyrics by Robert Sour, from a story by Alfred Grünwald and Geza Herczeg. Music by Robert Stolz. Produced by Felix Brentano. Century Theatre, Sept. 6, 1945.

THE SONG of BERNADETTE (3)
Adapted by Jean and Walter Kerr from Franz Werfel's novel, *Das Lied von Bernadette*. Produced by Victor Payne-Jennings and Frank McCoy. Belasco Theatre, Mar. 26, 1946.

°THE AFFAIRS of ANATOL (one week)
Adapted by Harley Granville-Barker from *Anatol* by Arthur Schnitzler. Produced by Equity Library Theatre. George Bruce Branch of the New York Public Library, first week of June, 1946.

1946-47

YOURS IS MY HEART (36)
Adapted by Harry Graham and Ira Cobb from *Das Land des Lächelns* by Karl Farkas. Music by Franz Lehár, adapted by Felix Guenther. Produced by Arthur Spitz. Shubert Theatre, Sept. 5, 1946.

THE CHOCOLATE SOLDIER (70)
Revision of standard 1909-10 adaptation by Guy Bolton and Bernard Hanighen. Produced by J. H. Del Bondia and Hans Bartsch for the Delvan Co. Century Theatre, Mar. 12, 1947.

°CROWN COLONY (?)
Uncredited adaptation from *Das Heilige Experiment* by Fritz Hochwälder. Produced by Fordham University. Penthouse Theatre.

°HANNELE (?)
Unlisted adaptation of *Hanneles Himmelfahrt* by Gerhart Hauptmann. Produced by the Dramatic Workshop of the New School for Social Research.

1947-48

°GAS (?)
Uncredited adaptation of *Gas* (the entire trilogy) by Georg Kaiser. Produced by On Stage. Cherry Lane Theatre, Aug. 18, 1947, through Aug. 30, 1947.

°GALILEO (6)
Translated by Charles Laughton, with lyrics by Albert Brush, from *Leben des Galilei* by Bertolt Brecht. Music by Hanns Eisler. Produced by Experimental Theatre. Maxine Elliott's Theatre, Dec. 7, 1947. Mr. Laughton also starred.

°CHAFF (10)
Adapted by A. Zatz from an undesignated play by Ferdinand Bruckner (Theodor Taggers). Produced by the Dramatic Workshop of the New School for Social Research. President Theatre, Mar. 17, 1948.

1948-49

°FROM MORN till MIDNIGHT (?, probably one week)
Adapted by Ashley Dukes from *Von Morgens bis Mitternachts* by Georg
Kaiser. Produced by Equity Library Theatre. Dec., 1948.

°OUTSIDE the DOOR (?)
Translated by Erwin Piscator and Zoe Lund-Schiller from *Draussen vor der
Tür* by Wolfgang Borchert. Produced by the Dramatic Workshop of the
New School for Social Research. March 1, 1949. Directed by Erwin
Piscator.

1949-50

°THE SCAPEGOAT (?)
By John F. Mathews, based on the novel *Der Prozess* by Franz Kafka.
Produced and Directed by Erwin Piscator and the Dramatic Workshop.
President Theatre, Apr. 19, 1950.

°EARTH SPIRIT (?)
Uncredited adaptation from *Erdgeist* by Frank Wedekind. Produced by
Studio 7. Provincetown Playhouse, June 6, 1950.

1950-51

°THE CIRCLE of CHALK (?)
Translated by James Laver from *Der Kreidekreis*, a play based on a Chinese
fantasy. The German was by Klabund (Alfred Henschke). Produced by the
Studio Theatre of the New School for Social Research, Dec. 1, 1950, at the
President Theatre.

°A HOUSE in BERLIN (?)
Adapted by Vernon Brooks and William Kennedy from *Als der Krieg zu
Ende War* by Max Frisch. Produced by the Dramatic Workshop of the New
School for Social Research, at the school, Dec. 26, 1950.

DARKNESS at NOON (186)
Play by Sidney Kingsley based on Daphne Hardy's popular translation of
the novel of the same name by Arthur Koestler. (The novel first appeared
in the United States, thus its title was in English from the beginning,
although the manuscript was written in German.) Play was produced by the
Playwrights' Co., Alvin Theatre, Jan. 13, 1951.

1951-52

None

1952-53

None

1953-54

THE STRONG ARE LONELY (7)
Adapted by Eva Le Gallienne from *Das Heilige Experiment* by Fritz Hochwälder. Produced by Walter P. Chrysler, Jr. Broadhurst Theatre, Sept. 29, 1953.

°THE THREE-PENNY OPERA (95)
Adapted by Marc Blitzstein from *Die Dreigroschenoper* by Bertolt Brecht. Music by Kurt Weill. Produced by Carmen Capalbo and Stanley Chase. Theatre de Lys, Mar. 10, 1954. It re-opened on Sept. 20, 1955, for a record-breaking run.

FLEDERMAUS (15)
Adapted by Ruth and Thomas Martin from the Haffner-Genée *Die Fledermaus*. Music by Johann Strauss. Produced by the New York City Light Opera Co. City Center, May 19, 1954.

°GOAT SONG (?, probably one week)
Translated by Ruth Langner from *Bocksgesang* by Franz Werfel. Produced by Equity Library Theatre.

°JACOBOWSKY and the COLONEL (?, probably one week)
Adapted by S. N. Behrman from *Jacobowsky und der Oberst* by Franz Werfel. Produced by Equity Library Theatre.

1954-55

None

1955-56

°THE TRIAL (131)
Adapted by Aaron Fine and Bert Greene from *Der Prozess*, the novel by Franz Kafka. Produced by Theatre 12. Provincetown Playhouse, June 14, 1955.

°LA RONDE (132)
Translated by Eric Bentley from *Reigen* by Arthur Schnitzler. Produced by Leigh Connell, Theodore Mann and José Quintero. Circle in the Square, June 27, 1955.

°THE THREE-PENNY OPERA (2,611)
Same adaptation as production of 1953-54 with the same director and largely the same cast. Produced by Carmen Capalbo and Stanley Chase in association with Lucille Lortel. Theatre de Lys, Sept. 20, 1955.

°SPRING'S AWAKENING (15)
Adapted by Bert Greene from *Frühlings Erwachen* by Frank Wedekind.
Produced by Theatre 12. Provincetown Playhouse, Oct. 9, 1955.

THE MATCHMAKER (486)
By Thornton Wilder, from his own *The Merchant of Yonkers* (1938), based
on *Einen Jux Will Er Sich Machen* by Johann Nestroy, which in turn was
based on *A Day Well Spent* by John Oxenford. Produced by the Theatre
Guild. Royale Theatre, Dec. 5, 1955.

°THE PRIVATE LIFE of the MASTER RACE (?)
Adapted by Eric Bentley from *Furcht und Elend des Dritten Reiches* by
Bertolt Brecht. Produced by the Open Stage. Open Stage Theatre, Jan. 30,
1956.

°THE BEAVER COAT (?)
Translated by Ludwig Lewisohn from *Der Biberpelz* by Gerhart Hauptmann. Greenwich Mews Theatre, Mar. 28, 1956.

°THE GALLANT CASSIAN (?)
Translated by Adam Gowans from *Der Tapfere Cassian*, an adult puppet
play by Arthur Schnitzler. Puppets designed by Shirley O'Donnol. Produced
by Lester Hackett and George Ortman as a curtain-raiser for Jean Genet's
The Maids. Tempo Playhouse, May 18, 1956.

1956-57

°THE GOOD WOMAN of SETZUAN (24)
Adapted by Eric Bentley, assisted by Maja Apelman, from *Der Gute Mensch
von Setzuan* by Bertolt Brecht. Produced by the Phoenix Theatre, Dec. 18,
1956. Incidental music by Paul Dessau. Mr. Bentley directed.

°VOLPONE (130)
Translated by Ruth Langner from Stefan Zweig's adaptation of Ben Jonson's
play. Produced by Sidney Bernstein and Gene Frankel in association with
Ronnie Lee. Rooftop Theatre, Jan. 7, 1957.

°METAMORPHOSIS (1 special performance)
An experiment integrating acting and movement, from the story, *Die Ver-
wandlung*, by Franz Kafka. Produced by the Greater New York Chapter of
ANTA. Theatre de Lys, Feb. 19, 1957. Music by Kenyon Hopkins and Betty
Walberg.

THE MERRY WIDOW (15)
Revival of the 1943-44 adaptation. Produced by the New York City Center
Light Opera Co. City Center, April 10, 1957.

1957-58

°THE TRANSPOSED HEADS (2 special performances)
Opera by Peggy Glanville-Hicks, based on a story, *Die Vertauschte Köpfe*,

by Thomas Mann. Produced by T. Edward Hambleton and Norris Houghton (for the Phoenix Theatre) presenting Chandler Cowles's production under the auspices of the Contemporary Music Society. Phoenix Theatre, Feb. 10, 1958.

°FOOLS ARE PASSING THROUGH (24)
Adapted by Maximilian Slater from *Die Ehe des Herrn Mississippi* by Friedrich Dürrenmatt. Produced by William Grimes and Nahum Yablonovitz. Jan Hus Auditorium, Apr. 2, 1958. Directed by Mr. Slater.

THE VISIT (189)
Adapted by Maurice Valency from *Der Besuch der Alten Dame* by Friedrich Dürrenmatt. Produced by the Producers' Theatre. Lunt-Fontanne Theatre, May 5, 1958. Played for 16 additional performances after returning from the road in 1959-60.

1958-59

°LULU (16)
Translated by Stephen Spender and Frances Fawcett from *Erdgeist* by Frank Wedekind. Produced by David Ross and staged by him. 4th Street Theatre, Sept. 29, 1958.

°ROYAL GAMBIT (87)
Translated and adapted by George White from *Heinrich VIII und seine Frauen* by Hermann Gressieker. Produced by David Ellis. Sullivan Street Playhouse, Mar. 4, 1959.

THE SEVEN DEADLY SINS (?)
Translated by W. H. Auden and Chester Kallmann from the ballet-cantata *Die Sieben Todsünden der Kleinbürger,* text by Bertolt Brecht and music by Kurt Weill. New York City Center of Music and Drama.

1959-60

THE DEADLY GAME (39)
Play by James Yaffe based on the novella, *Trapps,* by Friedrich Dürrenmatt. Produced by Alton Wilkes and Joe Manchester in association with Emil Coleman. Longacre Theatre, Feb. 2, 1960.

THE VISIT (16)
Return from the road of the production of 1957-58. Produced by the City Center by Arrangement with the American Theatre Society and the Producers' Theatre. City Center, Mar. 8, 1960.

°THE JACKASS (2)
Adapted by George White from a radio script, *Der Prozess um des Esels Schatten* by Friedrich Dürrenmatt. Produced by Quartet Productions in association with John Eyre. Barbizon Plaza Theatre, Mar. 23, 1960.

°LA RONDE (?)
A new translation by Hans Weigert and Patricia Newhall of *Reigen* by
Arthur Schnitzler. Produced by Patricia Newhall and Hans Weigert in
association with Frank Rohrbach. Theatre Marquee, May 9, 1960. Directed
by Miss Newhall.

1960-61

°THE SIGN of JONAH (53)
Adapted by George White from *Das Zeichen des Jona* by Guenter Rutenborn. Produced by Donald H. Goldman. Players' Theatre, Sept. 8, 1960.

°IN the JUNGLE of CITIES (69)
Translated by Gerhard Nellhaus from *Im Dickicht der Städte* by Bertolt
Brecht. Produced by Living Theatre Productions, Inc. (Judith Malina and
Julian Beck) as part of the Living Theatre Repertory Program. Living
Theatre, Dec. 20, 1960.

°THE MAGNIFICENT HUGO (5)
Adapted by Louis S. Bardoly from *Ein Besserer Herr* by Walter Hasen-
clever. Produced by Cornelius Productions, Inc. in association with Albert
Penn. Comedy Theatre, April 7, 1961.

1961-62

DO YOU KNOW the MILKY WAY? (16)
Unlisted translation of *Kennen Sie die Milchstrasse?* by Karl Wittlinger.
Produced by Ninon Tallon, Paul Feigay, and Dick Button by arrangement
with the Vancouver International Festival. Billy Rose Theatre, October 16,
1961. Staged by Herbert Berghof.

THE GAY LIFE (113)
Musical comedy suggested by Arthur Schnitzler's *Anatol*. Book by Fay and
Michael Kanin. Music and lyrics by Arthur Schwartz and Howard Dietz.
Produced by Kermit Bloomgarden. Sam S. Shubert Theatre, Nov. 18, 1961.
Staged by Gerald Freedman. Starred Walter Chiari, Barbara Cook, and
Jules Munshin.

°BRECHT on BRECHT (424)
Selected readings of work by Bertolt Brecht. Translated by numerous peo-
ple, Eric Bentley among them. Some translations by George Tabori who
arranged the readings. Produced by the Greater New York Chapter of
ANTA and Cheryl Crawford. Theatre de Lys, Jan. 3, 1962. Directed by
Gene Frankel. With Lotte Lenya, George Voskovec, and Viveca Lindfors.

ROMULUS (69)
Adapted by Gore Vidal from *Romulus der Grosse* by Friedrich Dürrenmatt.
Produced by Roger L. Stevens, in association with Henry Guettel. Music
Box Theatre, January 10, 1962. Staged by Joseph Anthony. With Cyril
Ritchard and Howard DaSilva.

°AN EVENING of BRECHT (1)
Special performance at Brooklyn College's George Gershwin Theatre, Feb. 10, 1962. Eric Bentley played, sang, and recited poems and songs by Bertolt Brecht. A performance of *The Exception and the Rule*, Bentley's translation of *Die Ausnahme und die Regel*, followed.

1962-63

°MAN IS MAN (175)
Translated by Gerhard Nellhaus from *Mann ist Mann* by Bertolt Brecht. Produced by The Living Theatre at The Living Theatre, Sept. 18, 1962. Directed by Julian Beck.

°A MAN'S a MAN (175)
Adapted by Eric Bentley from *Mann ist Mann* by Bertolt Brecht. Produced by the New Repertory Theatre Company. Masque Theatre, Sept. 19, 1962. Directed by John Hancock.

°THE ELEPHANT CALF (3)
Adapted by Eric Bentley from *Das Elephantenkalb* by Bertolt Brecht. Produced by the Theatre of Ideas, Inc. Shirley Broughton Studio, Jan. 6 and 13, 1963. Additional special performance at Masque Theatre, Jan. 22, 1963.

°ROYAL GAMBIT (9)
Revival of 1958-59 translation by George White of Hermann Gressieker's play. Master Theatre, Jan. 25, 1963.

ANDORRA (9)
Adapted by George Tabori from play of the same name by Max Frisch. Produced by Cheryl Crawford and Roger L. Stevens. Biltmore Theatre, Feb. 9, 1963. Staged by Michael Langham. With Horst Buchholtz and Hugh Griffith.

°THE FIREBUGS (8)
Adapted by Mordecai Gorelik from *Biedermann und die Brandstifter* by Max Frisch. Produced by Sidney Bernstein, in association with Beverly Landau, Stanley Swerdlow, and Omar K. Lerman. Maidman Playhouse, Feb. 11, 1963. Directed by Gene Frankel and Mordecai Gorelik.

°THE GOOD WOMAN of SETZUAN (12)
Limited engagement of Eric Bentley's translation of *Der Gute Mensch von Setzuan* by Bertolt Brecht. Produced by the Institute for Advanced Study in the Theatre Arts (IASTA), at the Institute, Mar. 10, 1963.

°DO YOU KNOW the MILKY WAY? (94)
Revival of previous season's Broadway failure. Produced by Nimara Productions. Gramercy Arts Theatre, Mar. 14, 1963. Staged by Michael Howard.

MOTHER COURAGE and HER CHILDREN (52, after 19 previews)
Adapted by Eric Bentley from *Mutter Courage und Ihre Kinder* by Bertolt Brecht. Music by Paul Dessau. Produced by Cheryl Crawford and Jerome

Robbins. Martin Beck Theatre, Mar. 28, 1963. Directed by Jerome Robbins. Starred Anne Bancroft.

°THE GOOD SOLDIER SCHWEIK (8)
Adapted by Robert Kalfin from the novel by Jaroslav Hasek, which had inspired a number of adaptations in the past. Produced by the Gate Theatre, Apr. 8, 1963. Directed by Robert Kalfin. Starred night-club comedian Irwin Corey.

°THE EMPEROR (24)
Adapted by George White from a play about Nero by Hermann Gressieker. Produced by Jeff Britton, in association with Ted Marshall and Minette Hirsch. Maidman Playhouse, Apr. 16, 1963.

°THE WORLD of KURT WEILL in SONG (245)
An evening of songs performed in both English and German by Will Holt and Martha Schlamme. Most translations of German lyrics by Marc Blitzstein; some by Will Holt, who also arranged and directed the program. Selections included songs which Weill had written with American lyricists. Produced by Tanya Chasman and E. H. Gilbert. One Sheridan Square, June 6, 1963. This was a limited engagement which re-opened on May 12, 1964, and ran long enough to reach 245 performances.

1963-64

°SAINT JOAN of the STOCKYARDS (8)
Limited engagement at Barnard-Columbia University Summer Theatre Workshop. Translated by Frank Jones from *Die Heilige Johanna der Schlachthöfe* by Bertolt Brecht. Music by Robert Rogers. Minor Latham Playhouse, July 3, 1963.

°BRECHT on BRECHT (55)
Revival by ANTA of success of previous two seasons. Sheridan Square Playhouse, July 9, 1963.

°WALK in DARKNESS (24)
By William Hairston, based on a novel by Hans Habe. Produced by Greenwich Players, Inc. and Stella Holt-Roscius. Greenwich Mews Theatre, Oct. 28, 1963.

ARTURO UI (8)
Adapted by George Tabori from *Der Aufhaltsame Aufstieg des Arturo Ui* by Bertolt Brecht. Produced by David Merrick with Neil Hartley. Music by Jule Styne. Lunt-Fontanne Theatre, Nov. 11, 1963. Directed by Tony Richardson. Starred Christopher Plummer.

HELLO DOLLY! (989 and still running at end of 1965-66 season)
Musical comedy based on Thornton Wilder's *The Matchmaker*. See 1955-56 for full history of adaptation. Book by Michael Stewart. Music and lyrics by Jerry Herman. Produced by David Merrick. St. James Theatre, Jan. 16, 1964. Directed by Gower Champion. Starred Carol Channing.

THE DEPUTY (316)
> Adapted by Jerome Rothenberg from *Der Stellvertreter* by Rolf Hochhuth. Produced by Herman Shumlin with Alfred Crown and Zvi Kolitz. Brooks Atkinson Theatre, Feb. 26, 1964. Directed by Herman Shumlin. Performers included Jeremy Brett and Emlyn Williams.

°HELL is OTHER PEOPLE (1)
> One special performance at Carnegie Hall of scenes from Brecht and Sartre. Produced by Richard Fulton, May 9, 1964. Directed by George Tabori.

°THE AWAKENING of SPRING (8)
> Translated by Mascha Beyo and adapted by Arthur A. Seidelman and Donald Levin from *Frühlings Erwachen* by Frank Wedekind. Produced by Theatre Vanguard and John Savoca. Pocket Theatre, May 12, 1964. Directed by Arthur A. Seidelman. Characters and locale Americanized.

1964-65

THE MERRY WIDOW (40)
> Revival of the Lehár operetta. Book revised by Milton Lazarus. New lyrics by Forman Brown. Produced by Music Theater of Lincoln Center. New York State Theater (Lincoln Center), Aug. 17, 1964. National tour followed New York run.

THE PHYSICISTS (55)
> Adapted by James Kirkup from *Die Physiker* by Friedrich Dürrenmatt. Produced by Allen-Hodgdon, Inc., and Stevens Productions, Inc. Martin Beck Theatre, Oct. 13, 1964. Directed by Peter Brook. Cast included Hume Cronyn, Jessica Tandy, George Voskovec, and Robert Shaw.

°WAR and PEACE (102)
> Adapted by Robert David MacDonald from a dramatization based on Tolstoi's novel by Erwin Piscator, Alfred Neumann, and Guntram Prufer. German play first produced at Schiller Theater in Berlin, 1955. Produced by the Association of Producing Artists (APA) as part of their repertory. Phoenix Theatre, Jan. 11, 1965.

°BAAL (59)
> Adapted by Eric Bentley and Martin Esslin from play of same name by Bertolt Brecht. Produced by the Circle-in-the-Square. Martinique Theatre. May 6, 1965. Directed by Gladys Vaughan.

°THE EXCEPTION and the RULE (141)
> Adapted by Eric Bentley from *Die Ausnahme und die Regel* by Bertolt Brecht. Greenwich Mews Theatre, May 20, 1965. Directed by Isaiah Sheffer.

Bibliography

I. BOOKS

Bab, Julius. *Die Chronik des deutschen Dramas*. 5 vols. Berlin: Oesterheld
& Co. Verlag, 1922-26.

——. *Neue Wege zum Drama*. Berlin: Oesterheld & Co. Verlag, 1911.

——. *Das Theater der Gegenwart: Geschichte der dramatischen Bühne
seit 1870*. Leipzig: Verlagsbuchhandlung von J. J. Weber, 1928.

Bänzinger, Hans. *Frisch und Dürrenmatt*. Bern & Munich: Francke Verlag,
1960.

Bentley, Eric. *In Search of Theatre*. New York: Alfred A. Knopf, 1953.

——. *The Playwright as Thinker*. New York: Reynal & Hitchcock, 1946.

——, ed. *The Storm over the Deputy*. New York: Grove Press, 1964.

——, ed. *Seven Plays by Bertolt Brecht*. New York: Grove Press, 1961.

Block, Haskell M., and Robert G. Shedd, eds. *Masters of Modern Drama*.
New York: Random House, 1962.

Blum, Daniel, ed. *Theatre World: Season 1944-45* [and each season there-
after]. New York: Guide Printing Co.—The Kalkhoff Press, 1945-46;
Stuyvesant Press Corp., 1947; Daniel Blum, 1948-49; Greenberg,
1950-57; Philadelphia: Chilton Co., 1958-65.

Brown, John Mason. *The Modern Theatre in Revolt*. New York: W. W.
Norton & Co., 1929.

Brown, T. Allston. *A History of the New York Stage, 1732-1901*. 3 vols. New
York: Dodd, Mead & Co., 1903.

Carter, Huntley. *The Theatre of Max Reinhardt*. London: Frank and Cecil
Palmer, 1914.

Chandler, Frank W. *Modern Continental Playwrights*. New York: Harper &
Bros., 1931.

Chapman, John. *Broadway's Best, 1956-57* [and each season thereafter].
Garden City, N.Y.: Doubleday & Co., 1957-61.

——, ed. *The Burns Mantle Best Plays of 1947-48; and The Year Book of
the Drama in America*. New York: Dodd, Mead & Co., 1948. [Pub-
lished for each season thereafter until 1951-52. The name of Burns
Mantle was deleted from the title beginning in 1951.]

Chapman, John, and Garrison P. Sherwood, eds. *The Best Plays of 1894-
1899; and The Year Book of the Drama in America*. New York: Dodd,
Mead & Co., 1955.

Cheney, Sheldon. *The Art Theatre*. New York: Alfred A. Knopf, 1925.
———. *The New Movement in the Theatre*. New York: Mitchell Kennerley, 1914.
Clurman, Harold. *Lies Like Truth*. New York: Macmillan, 1958.
Cole, Toby, ed. *Playwrights on Playwriting: The Meaning and Making of Modern Drama from Ibsen to Ionesco*. New York: Hill & Wang, 1960.
Cordell, Richard A., and Lowell Matson, eds. *The Off-Broadway Theatre*. New York: Random House, 1959.
Deutsch, Helen, and Stella Hanau. *The Provincetown: A Story of the Theatre*. New York: Farrar & Rinehart, 1931.
Downer, Alan S. *Fifty Years of American Drama, 1900-1950*. Chicago: Henry Regnery Co., 1951.
Dukes, Ashley. *Modern Dramatists*. Chicago: Charles H. Sergel & Co., 1911.
———. *The Youngest Drama: Studies of Fifty Dramatists*. Chicago: Charles H. Sergel & Co., 1924.
Eaton, Walter Pritchard. *The Theatre Guild: The First Ten Years*. New York: Brentano's, 1929.
Esslin, Martin. *Brecht: The Man and His Work*. Garden City, N.Y.: Doubleday Anchor, 1961.
———. *The Theatre of the Absurd*. Garden City, N.Y.: Doubleday Anchor, 1961.
Faust, Albert B. *Das Deutschtum in den Vereinigten Staaten: in seiner Bedeutung für die Amerikanische Kultur*. Leipzig: B. G. Teubner, 1912.
Fechter, Paul. *Das Europäische Drama: Geist und Kultur im Spiegel des Theaters*. 3 vols. Mannheim: Bibliographisches Institut AG, 1958.
Felheim, Marvin. *The Theatre of Augustin Daly*. Cambridge: Harvard University Press, 1956.
Fergusson, Francis. *The Human Image in Dramatic Literature*. Garden City, N.Y.: Doubleday Anchor, 1957.
Flanagan, Hallie. *Arena: The Story of the Federal Theatre*. New York: Duell, Sloan & Pearce, 1940. [Miss Flanagan is sometimes listed as Hallie Flanagan Davis.]
Gagey, Edmond M. *Revolution in American Drama*. New York: Columbia University Press, 1947.
Garten, H. F. *Modern German Drama*. Fair Lawn, N.J.: Essential Books (imprint of Oxford University Press, Inc.), 1959.
Gassner, John. *Form and Idea in Modern Theatre*. New York: Dryden Press, 1956.
———. *Masters of the Drama*. 3rd ed. New York: Dover Publications, 1954.
———. *Theatre at the Crossroads*. New York: Holt, Rinehart & Winston, 1960.
———. *The Theatre in Our Times*. New York: Crown Publishers, 1954.
———, ed. "Introduction," *Twenty Best European Plays on the American Stage*. New York: Crown Publishers, 1957.
Geissler, Rolf, ed. *Zur Interpretation des Modernen Dramas: Brecht— Dürrenmatt—Frisch*. Special sections by Therese Poser and Wilhelm

Ziskoven. Frankfurt, Berlin, and Bonn: Verlag Moritz Diesterweg, 1960.

Goodman, Randolph. *Drama on Stage*. New York: Holt, Rinehart & Winston, 1961.

Gorelik, Mordecai. *New Theatres for Old*. New York: Samuel French, 1940.

Gregor, Joseph. *Der Schauspiel Führer*. 6 vols. Stuttgart: Hiersemann Verlag, 1953.

Hapgood, Norman. *The Stage in America, 1897-1900*. New York: Macmillan, 1901.

Heuser, Frederick W. J. *Gerhart Hauptmann: Zu seinem Leben und Schaffen*. Tübingen: Max Niemeyer Verlag, 1961.

Hewitt, Barnard. *Theatre U.S.A., 1668-1957*. New York: McGraw-Hill Book Co., 1959.

Huneker, James G. *Iconoclasts: A Book of Dramatists*. 2nd ed. New York: Charles Scribner's Sons, 1909.

Jones, Robert Edmond. *The Dramatic Imagination*. New York: Duell, Sloan & Pearce, 1941.

Klarmann, Adolf D., ed. [Franz Werfel] *Gesammelte Werke: Die Dramen*. 2 vols. (successively paginated). Frankfurt: S. Fischer Verlag, 1959.

Kracauer, Siegfried. *From Caligari to Hitler: A Psychological Study of the German Film*. Princeton: Princeton University Press, 1947 (Noonday Press reprint, 1959).

Kronenberger, Louis, ed. *The Best Plays of 1952-53: The Burns Mantle Yearbook*. [Published for each season thereafter.] New York: Dodd, Mead & Co., 1953-1961.

Krutch, Joseph Wood. *The American Drama Since 1918*. Rev. ed. New York: George Braziller, 1957.

——. *"Modernism" in Modern Drama*. Ithaca: Cornell University Press, 1953.

Leuchs, Frederick [Fritz] A. H. *Early German Theatre in New York, 1840-1872*. New York: Columbia University Press, 1928.

Macgowan, Kenneth, and Robert Edmond Jones. *The Theatre of Tomorrow*. New York: Boni & Liveright, 1921.

Macgowan, Kenneth, and William Melnitz. *Golden Ages of the Theater*. Englewood Cliffs, N.J.: Prentice-Hall Spectrum Books, 1959.

Mann, Erika, and Klaus Mann. *Escape to Life*. Boston: Houghton Mifflin Co., 1939.

Mantle, Burns, ed. *The Best Plays of 1919-20; and The Year Book of the Drama in America*. [Published for each season thereafter until 1946-47.] Boston: Small, Maynard & Co., 1920-25; New York: Dodd, Mead & Co., 1926-47.

—— and Garrison P. Sherwood, eds. *The Best Plays of 1899-1909; and The Year Book of the Drama in America*. Philadelphia: Blakiston Co., 1944.

——. *The Best Plays of 1909-1919; and The Year Book of the Drama in America*. New York: Dodd, Mead & Co., 1933.

Moderwell, Hiram K. *The Theatre of Today.* 3rd ed. New York: Dodd, Mead & Co., 1927.

Morgan, Bayard Quincy. *A Critical Bibliography of German Literature in English Translation, 1481-1927; and Supplement, 1928-1935.* 2nd ed. Stanford: Stanford University Press, 1938.

Nathan, George Jean. *Theatre Book of the Year* [Published annually, 1943-51.] New York: Alfred A. Knopf, 1943-51.

Odell, George C. D. *Annals of the New York Stage.* Vol. XV. New York: Columbia University Press, 1949.

Piscator, Erwin. *Das Politische Theater.* Berlin: Adalbert Schultz Verlag, 1929.

Pochmann, Henry A. *German Culture in America, 1600-1900.* Madison: University of Wisconsin Press, 1957.

Quinn, Arthur Hobson. *A History of the American Drama from the Civil War to the Present Day.* 2nd ed. New York: F. S. Crofts & Co., 1937.

Samuel, Richard, and R. Hinton Thomas. *Expressionism in German Life, Literature and the Theatre (1910-1924).* Cambridge, England: W. Heffer & Sons, Ltd., 1939.

Sayler, Oliver M., ed. *Max Reinhardt and His Theatre.* New York: Brentano's, 1924.

———. *Our American Theater.* New York: Brentano's, 1923.

Schlossmacher, Stephan. *Das Deutsche Drama im Amerikanischen College und Universitäts-Theater.* Emsdetten: H. & J. Lechte Verlag, 1938.

Schmidt, Dolores Barracano, and Earl Robert Schmidt, eds. *The Deputy Reader: Studies in Moral Responsibility.* Chicago: Scott, Foresman & Co., 1965.

Scholz, K. W. H. *The Art of Translation, With Special Reference to English Renditions of the Prose Dramas of Gerhart Hauptmann and Hermann Sudermann.* Philadelphia: Americana Germanica Press, 1918.

Shipley, Joseph T. *Guide to Great Plays.* Washington, D.C.: Public Affairs Press, 1956.

Shirer, William L. *The Rise and Fall of the Third Reich.* New York: Simon & Schuster, 1960.

Sokel, Walter H. *The Writer in Extremis: Expressionism in Twentieth-Century German Literature.* Stanford: Stanford University Press, 1959.

Thomas, J. Wesley. *Amerikanische Dichter und die deutsche Literatur.* Goslar: Volksbücherei Verlag, 1950.

Tynan, Kenneth. *Curtains.* New York: Atheneum, 1961.

Ulanov, Barry. *Makers of the Modern Theater.* New York: McGraw-Hill Book Co., 1961.

Weisstein, Ulrich. *The Reception of Twentieth Century German Literature in the United States. Proceedings* of the Second Congress of the International Comparative Literature Association, II (1959), 548-57.

Willet, John. *The Theatre of Bertolt Brecht.* New York: New Directions Books, 1959.

II.   ARTICLES

Adler, Henry. "Brecht and After," *Drama,* Vol. LXIII (Winter, 1961), 29-31.

Altman, John. "Mephisto's Emissary," *Theatre Arts,* Vol. XXXV (March, 1951), 28-31.

Anshutz, Grace. "Expressionistic Drama in the American Theatre," *Drama,* Vol. XVI (April, 1926), 245-46, 278-80.

Ayer, Charles C. "Foreign Drama on the English and American Stage: II. German Drama," *University of Colorado Studies,* Vol. VII, No. 1 (December, 1909), 63-71.

Becker, William. "Broadway: Classics and Imports," *Hudson Review,* Vol. VII (Summer, 1954), 258-71.

Bentley, Eric. "German Writers in Exile, 1933-43," *Books Abroad,* Vol. XVII (Autumn, 1943), 313-17.

"Bertolt Brecht: An Iconoclast in the Theatre," *Times Literary Supplement,* March 9, 1956, 141-42.

Blackburn, Clara. "Continental Influences on Eugene O'Neill's Expressionistic Dramas," *American Literature,* Vol. XIII (May, 1941), 109-33.

Blake, Warren B. "Our Un-American Stage," *Independent,* Vol. LXXII (March 7, 1912), 503-508.

Blankenagel, John C. "Early Reception of Hauptmann's *Die Weber* in the United States," *Modern Language Notes,* Vol. LXVIII (May, 1953), 334-40.

Borneman, Ernst. "Two Brechtians," *Kenyon Review,* Vol. XXII (Summer, 1960), 465-92.

Clark, Barrett H. "Experiments and Fantasies," *Drama,* Vol. XVI (April, 1926), 250, 278.

——. "Native and Foreign Drama on Broadway," *Drama,* Vol. XV (December, 1924), 52-53.

Clurman, Harold. "The Achievement of Bertolt Brecht," *Partisan Review,* Vol. XXVI (Fall, 1959), 624-28.

Crémieux, Benjamin. "Presenting Max Reinhardt," *Living Age,* Vol. CCCXLV (January, 1935), 410-13.

Dürrenmatt, Friedrich. "Problems of the Theatre," trans. from the German by Gerhard Nellhaus, *Tulane Drama Review,* Vol. III (October, 1958), 3-26.

Dummer, E. H. "Hermann Sudermann, A Contributor to American Culture," *American-German Review,* Vol. XIII (February, 1947), 26-29.

Emerson, Helen. "A Criticism of Meltzer's Translations of *Hanneles Himmelfahrt* and *Die Versunkene Glocke,*" *German Quarterly,* Vol. XXI (1948), 163-74.

"Essential Difference Between an American Play and a European Play," *Current Opinion,* Vol. LVIII (February, 1915), 97-99.

Francke, Kuno. "German Literature and the American Temper," *Atlantic Monthly,* Vol. CXIV (November, 1914), 655-64.

Freedley, George. "The Equity Library Theatre: Its Aim and Achievement," *Theatre Annual, 1947,* 37-42.

Frenz, Horst. "Georg Kaiser," *Poet-Lore,* Vol. LII (Winter, 1946), 363-69.

"Freud's *Doppelgänger,*" *Time,* Vol. LXIX (January 14, 1957), 51-52.

Frey, John R. "America and Franz Werfel," *German Quarterly,* Vol. XIX (March, 1946), 121-28.

Fulton, A. R. "Expressionism—Twenty Years After," *Sewanee Review,* Vol. LII (July, 1944), 398-413.

Gassner, John. "Forms of Modern Drama," *Comparative Literature,* Vol. VII (1955), 129-43.

———. "New Critics Are Old Hat," *Theatre Arts,* Vol. XXXVII (May, 1953), 23-25, 89-90.

Hamilton, Clayton. "European Dramatists on the American Stage," *Bookman,* Vol. XXXI (June, 1910), 410-21.

Hecht, Werner. "The Development of Brecht's Theory of the Epic Theatre, 1918-1933," Trans. from the German by Bayard Quincy Morgan, *Tulane Drama Review,* Vol. VI (September, 1961), 40-97.

Heller, Peter. "Die deutsche Literatur aus Amerikanischer Sicht," *Welt und Wort,* Vol. XI (April, 1956), 105-107.

Hersh, Burton. "The Man in the Ironic Mask," *Horizon,* Vol. IV (May, 1962), 36-41.

Hill, Claude. "The Stature of Arthur Schnitzler," *Modern Drama,* Vol. IV (May, 1961), 80-91.

———. "Wedekind in Retrospect," *Modern Drama,* Vol. III (May, 1960), 82-92.

Hoffman, T. "American Theatre Is Un-American," *Theatre Arts,* Vol. XXXVII (March, 1955), 70-73, 94-96.

Kern, Edith. "Brecht's Popular Theater and Its American Popularity," *Modern Drama,* Vol. I (December, 1958), 157-65.

Klarmann, Adolf D. "Friedrich Dürrenmatt and the Tragic Sense of Comedy," *Tulane Drama Review,* Vol. IV (May, 1960), 77-104.

Langner, Lawrence. "The Magic Curtain," *Theatre Arts,* Vol. XXXIX (October, 1955), 17-29, 81-89.

Lenya, Lotte. "That Was a Time!" *Theatre Arts,* Vol. XL (May, 1956), 78-80, 92-93.

Loram, Ian C. "Carl Zuckmayer: German Playwright in America," *Educational Theatre Journal,* Vol. IX (1957), 177-83.

Maren, Roger. "Kurt Weill and His Public," *Reporter,* Vol. XIX (October 2, 1958), 41-44.

"Max Reinhardt, 1873-1943," *Theatre Arts,* Vol. XXVIII (January, 1944), 46-52.

"Max Reinhardt, the Maker of a New Mimic World," *Current Literature* (later known as *Current Opinion*), Vol. LI (September, 1911), 311-15.

Müller, Wilhelm. "Deutsche Stücke auf der amerikanischen Bühne," *Deutsch-Amerikanische Geschichtsblätter,* Vol. IV (October, 1904), 21-25.

Muller, Siegfried H. "Gerhart Hauptmann's Relation to American Literature and His Concept of America," *Monatshefte für deutschen Unterricht*, Vol. XLIV (1952), 333-39.

New York Theatre Critics' Reviews, 1940 to date (known as *Critics' Theatre Reviews*, 1940-42).

Paetel, Karl O. "Deutsches Theater in Amerika," *Deutsche Rundschau*, Vol. LXXXI (March, 1955), 271-75.

Parker, Robert Allerton. "Foreign Invasion of Broadway," *Arts and Decoration*, Vol. XVII (August, 1922), 262, 284-86.

Puknat, Siegfried B. "Mencken and the Sudermann Case," *Monatshefte für deutschen Unterricht*, Vol. LI (1959), 183-89.

Rogoff, Gordon. "Mr. Dürrenmatt Buys New Shoes," *Tulane Drama Review*, Vol. III (October, 1958), 27-34.

Sayler, Oliver M. "Translation and the Theatre," *North American Review*, Vol. CCXV (January, 1922), 109-16.

——. "Year Ahead, With Europe as Preceptor," *Theatre Arts*, Vol. VI (October, 1922), 267-75.

Schevill, James. "Bertolt Brecht in New York," *Tulane Drama Review*, Vol. VI (September, 1961), 98-107.

Schultz, H. Stefan. "German Expressionism: 1905-1925," *Chicago Review*, Vol. XIII (Winter/Spring, 1959), 8-24.

Seidlin, O. "Frank Wedekind's German-American Parents," *American-German Review*, Vol. XII, No. 6 (1946), 24-26.

Sherwin, Judith J. "The World Is Mean and Man Uncouth," *Virginia Quarterly Review*, Vol. XXXV (Spring, 1959), 258-70.

Travis, Steve. "The Rise and Fall of the Theatrical Syndicate," *Educational Theatre Journal*, Vol. X (March, 1958), 35-40.

Turner, Darwin T. "Dreams and Hallucinations in Drama of the Twenties," *College Language Association Journal*, Vol. III (March, 1960), 166-72.

Wellwarth, George E. "Friedrich Dürrenmatt and Max Frisch: Two Views of the Drama," *Tulane Drama Review*, Vol. VI (Spring, 1962), 14-42.

Zeydel, Edwin H. "The German Theatre in New York City," *Jahrbuch der deutsch-amerikanischen Historischen Gesellschaft von Illinois*, Vol. XV (1915), 255-309.

III.   UNPUBLISHED SOURCES

Cappel, Edith. "The Reception of Gerhart Hauptmann in the United States." Ph.D. dissertation, Columbia University, 1953.

Index

All plays are listed under their most familiar title in English, followed by their German title in parentheses. Only untranslated plays or those most often performed under their German titles are listed in German. For listings of specific plays, see title rather than playwright.

DATE DUE

FEB 9 1977		
FEB 2 8 1978		
GAYLORD		PRINTED IN U.S.A.